Progressions

Progressions

WITH READINGS

Fifth Edition

BARBARA FINE CLOUSE

Longman

New York San Francisco Boston
London Toronto Sydney Tokyo Singapore Madrid
Mexico City Munich Paris Cape Town Hong Kong Montreal

Vice President and Editor-in-Chief: Joseph Opielo
Senior Acquisitions Editor: Steven Rigolosi
Marketing Manager: Melanie Craig
Supplements Editor: Donna Campion
Production Manager: Ellen MacElree
Project Coordination, Text Design, and Electronic Page Makeup: Electronic Publishing Services Inc., NYC
Cover Designer/Manager: John Callahan
Photo Researcher: PhotoSearch, Inc.
Manufacturing Buyer: Roy Pickering
Printer and Binder: R.R. Donelley & Sons Company
Cover Printer: Phoenix Color Corp.

For permission to use copyrighted material, grateful acknowledgment is made to the copyright holders listed throughout this book, which is hereby made part of this copyright page.

Library of Congress Cataloging-in-Publication Data
Clouse, Barbara Fine.
    Progressions : with readings / Barbara Fine Clouse.—5th ed.
      p.   cm.
    Includes index.
    ISBN 0-205-33375-3
    1. English language—Rhetoric. 2. English language—Grammar. 3. College readers. 4.
    Report writing.   I. Title.
    PE1408.C5355   2002
   808'.042—dc21   00-065490

Please visit our website at http://www.ablongman.com/clouse

ISBN 0-205-33375-3

1 2 3 4 5 6 7 8 9 10 DOH 04 03 02 01

For Betty Fine Shepherd and Lee Fine

Brief Contents

Detailed Contents

PART THREE   The Essay

PART FOUR   Effective Sentences

PART SIX   From Reading to Writing

Thinking, Learning, and Writing in College

These boxed elements help students apply chapter contents to critical thinking strategies, study skills, and writing in other disciplines.

Checklists and Tips

Preface

Progressions focuses on both product and process. In addition to treating sentence-level concerns, paragraph structure, and essay structure, it presents a range of procedures students can follow as they move from idea generation to drafting to revising to editing and on to proofreading. In short, students learn both the characteristics of effective writing and procedures for generating such writing.

To support the student working toward proficiency, *Progressions* includes the following features:

- **Accessible prose** Clear, concise, jargon-free explanations are at just at the right level. They are neither overwhelming nor condescending.

- **Abundant examples** Each consideration—whether at the sentence, paragraph, or essay level—is illustrated, usually more than one time.

- **Student models** Because illustrations are taken predominantly from student papers, they represent attainable goals.

- **Abundant, varied exercises** To provide ample opportunity to practice, a generous number of exercises appear after each concept explained. These exercises are of many kinds, including whole discourse.

- **Detailed coverage of the writing process** *Progressions* describes a number of procedures for handling each stage of the writing process. Students can sample procedures until they discover techniques that work well for them.

- **Emphasis on revision** To help students appreciate the recursive nature of writing, the need for revision, and the stages writers work through, Chapter 1 presents a student essay as it developed from idea generation through successive drafts to finished copy. Annotations explain the changes in each stage of the essay and what prompted them. Revision is emphasized throughout the text, with a range of revision strategies, including reader response and revision checklists, presented.

- **Helpful procedures, checklists, and tips** All writing assignments are accompanied by procedures students can easily follow. These procedures are an important support system for the student. Also, checklists appear as an aid to students as they revise, and tips are given for specific strategies.

- **Collaborative activities** Collaborative learning activities appear in sections labeled "Working Together."

- **Complete coverage of the paragraph** Students can hone rhetorical and editing skills at this level and then move on to longer essays.

- **Emphasis on editing** Considerable emphasis is given to sentence-level concerns. Particularly helpful are specific strategies for finding and correcting errors with fragments, comma splices, run-ons, agreement, and pronoun reference.

- **Pretests and post tests** Accompanying each discussion of a grammar or usage point are a pretest and post test to help students assess their strengths and weaknesses and how much they have learned.

- **Comprehension aids** To aid comprehension and to provide easier access, main points are highlighted in the margins or grouped in short lists. Also, chapter goals are given as a form of prereading.

- **Instruction in reading and writing in response to reading** A chapter on reading and writing in response to reading (including writing summaries and taking essay examinations) is provided because these are vital academic survival skills and because of the strong reading–writing link. This chapter includes 11 previously published essays, many of which are followed by questions and writing assignments (at both the paragraph and the essay level). Earlier sections of the text treating methods of development are cross-referenced to the essays so students can study professional pieces in addition to student models.

- **Interesting, varied writing assignments** A generous variety and number of writing assignments range in difficulty, so students can progress as they are ready. The assignments include both experiential and analytic topics, as well as topics based on readings and photographs.

- **Problem-Solving Guide** Appendix I, which offers suggestions for working through writing problems, is a ready reference for students who get stuck along the way.

- **Ten Tips for ESL Students** Appendix II offers helpful hints to students who speak English as a second language.

- **Answers to Pretests** Appendix III provides answers to the pretests, so students can determine their level of competence with each point of grammar discussed.

FEATURES NEW TO THIS EDITION

The fifth edition of *Progressions* includes important new features, providing increased support for the developing writer.

- In every chapter, "Thinking, Learning, and Writing in College" features apply chapter concepts to critical thinking, study skills, or writing in other disciplines. These help students see the importance and applications of what they are learning.

- Each pattern of paragraph development is now presented in a separate chapter. In some cases, particularly for persuasion, the discussion has been expanded.

- Chapters 1 and 2 have been combined for a more seamless discussion of the writing process.

- Exercises and examples have been refreshed.

- More whole and continuous discourse exercises have been included.

- At the suggestion of reviewers, some grammar discussions have been expanded and others have been streamlined.

THE TEACHING AND LEARNING PACKAGE

A complete **Instructor's Manual** (0-321-09451-4) is available to accompany *Progressions*. In addition, the following supplements are available either free or at greatly reduced prices.

A Website with additional activities and exercises is also provided free with this book. Visit us at **http://www.ablongman.com/clouse**.

For Additional Reading and Reference

The Dictionary Deal. Two dictionaries can be shrinkwrapped with any Longman Developmental English title at a nominal fee. *The New American Webster Handy College Dictionary* is a paperback reference text with more than 100,000 entries. *Merriam Webster's Collegiate Dictionary*, tenth edition, is a hardback reference with a citation file of more than 14.5 million examples of English words drawn from actual use. For more information on how to shrinkwrap a dictionary with your text, please contact your Longman sales representative.

Penguin Quality Paperback Titles. A series of Penguin paperbacks is available at a significant discount when shrinkwrapped with any Longman Developmental English title. Some titles available are Toni Morrison's *Beloved*, Julia Alvarez's *How the Garcia Girls Lost Their Accents*, Mark Twain's *Huckleberry Finn, Narrative of the Life of Frederick Douglass*, Harriet Beecher Stowe's *Uncle Tom's Cabin*, Dr. Martin Luther King Jr.'s *Why We Can't Wait*, and plays by Shakespeare, Miller, and Albee. For a complete list of titles or more information, please contact your Longman sales consultant.

The Pocket Reader, First Edition. This inexpensive volume contains 80 brief readings (1-3 pages each) on a variety of themes: writers on writing, nature, women and men, customs and habits, politics, rights and obligations, and coming of age. Also included is an alternate rhetorical table of contents. 0-321-07668-0

100 Things to Write About. This 100-page book contains 100 individual assignments for writing on a variety of topics and in a wide range of formats, from expressive to analytical. Ask your Longman sales representative for a sample copy. 0-673-98239-4

Newsweek Alliance. Instructors may choose to shrinkwrap a 12-week subscription to *Newsweek* with any Longman text. The price of the subscription is 57 cents per issue (a total of $6.84 for the subscription). Available with the subscription is a free "Interactive Guide to *Newsweek*"—a workbook for students who are using the text. In addition, *Newsweek* provides a wide variety of instructor supplements free to teachers, including maps, Skills Builders, and weekly quizzes. For more information on the Newsweek program, please contact your Longman sales representative.

Electronic and Online Offerings

The Longman English Pages Web Site. Both students and instructors can visit our free content-rich Web site for additional reading selections and writing exercises. From the Longman English pages, visitors can conduct a simulated Web search, learn how to write a resume and cover letter, or try their hand at poetry writing. Stop by and visit us at **http://www.ablongman. com/englishpages**.

The Longman Electronic Newsletter—Twice a month during the spring and fall, instructors who have subscribed receive a free copy of the Longman Developmental English Newsletter in their e-mailbox. Written by experienced classroom instructors, the newsletter offers teaching tips, classroom activities, book reviews, and more. To subscribe, visit the Longman Developmental English Web site at **http://www.ablongman.com/basicskills**, or send an e-mail to **Basic Skills@ablongman.com**.

The Writer's ToolKit Plus. This CD-ROM offers a wealth of tutorial, exercise, and reference material for writers. It is compatible with either a PC or Macintosh platform, and is flexible enough to be used either occasionally for practice or regularly in class lab sessions. For information on how to bundle this CD-ROM FREE with your text, please contact your Longman sales representative.

Daedalus Online. Longman and The Daedalus Group are proud to offer the next generation of the award-winning Daedalus Integrated Writing Environment. Daedalus Online is an Internet-based collaborative writing environment for students. The program offers prewriting strategies and prompts, computer-mediated conferencing, peer collaboration and review, comprehensive writing support, and secure, 24-hour availability.

For educators, Daedalus Online offers a comprehensive suite of online course management tools for managing an online class, dynamically linking assignments, and facilitating a heuristic approach to writing instruction. For more information, visit **http://daedalus.pearsoned.com**, or contact your Longman sales representative.

For Instructors

Electronic Test Bank for Writing.
This electronic test bank features more than 5,000 questions in all areas of writing, from grammar to paragraphing, through essay writing, research, and documentation. With this easy-to-use CD-ROM, instructors simply choose questions from the electronic test bank, then print out the completed test for distribution: 0-321-08117-X. Print version is also available.

Competency Profile Test Bank, Second Edition.
This series of 60 objective tests covers ten general areas of English competency, including fragments, comma splices and run-ons, pronouns, commas, and capitalization. Each test is available in remedial, standard, and advanced versions. Available as reproducible sheets or in computerized versions. Free to instructors. Paper version: 0-321-02224-6. Computerized IBM: 0-321-02633-0. Computerized Mac: 0-321-02632-2.

Diagnostic and Editing Tests, Third Edition.
This collection of diagnostic tests helps instructors assess students' competence in standard written English for purpose of placement or to gauge progress. Available as reproducible sheets or in computerized versions, and free to instructors. Paper: 0-321-08382-2. Computerized IBM: 0-321-08782-8. Computerized Mac: 0-321-08784-4.

ESL Worksheets, Third Edition.
These reproducible worksheets provide ESL students with extra practice in areas they find the most troublesome. A diagnostic test and post-test are provided, along with answer keys and suggested topics for writing. Free to adopters: 0-321-07765-2.

80 Practices.
A collection of reproducible, ten-item exercises that provide additional practices for specific grammatical usage problems, such as comma splices, capitalization, and pronouns. Includes an answer key. Free to adopters: 0-673-53422-7.

CLAST Test Package, Fourth Edition.
These two 40-item objective tests evaluate students' readiness for the CLAST exams. Strategies for teaching CLAST preparedness are included. Free with any Longman English title.

Reproducible sheets: 0-321-01950-4. Computerized IBM version: 0-321-01982-2. Computerized Mac version: 0-321-01983-0.

TASP Test Package, Third Edition. These 12 practice pre-tests and post-tests assess the same reading and writing skills covered in the TASP examination. Free with any Longman English title. Reproducible sheets: 0-321-01959-8. Computerized IBM version: 0-321-01985-7. Computerized Mac version: 0-321-01984-9.

Teaching Online: Internet Research, Conversation, and Composition, Second Edition. Ideal for instructors who have never surfed the Net, this easy-to-follow guide offers basic definitions, numerous examples, and step-by-step information about finding and using Internet sources. Free to adopters. 0-321-01957-1.

Teaching Writing to the Non-Native Speaker. This booklet examines the issues that arise when non-native speakers enter the developmental classroom. Free to instructors, it includes profiles of international and permanent ESL students, factors influencing second-language acquisition, and tips on managing a multicultural classroom: 0-673-97452-9.

For Students

Researching Online, Fifth Edition. A perfect companion for a new age, this indispensable new supplement helps students navigate the Internet. Adapted from *Teaching Online*, the instructor's Internet guide, *Researching Online* speaks directly to students, giving them detailed, step-by-step instructions for performing electronic searches. Available free when shrinkwrapped with any Longman Developmental English text. 0-321-09277-5

Learning Together: An Introduction to Collaborative Theory. This brief guide to the fundamentals of collaborative learning teaches students how to work effectively in groups, how to revise with peer response, and how to co-author a paper or report. Shrinkwrapped free with any Longman Developmental English text. 0-673-46848-8

A Guide for Peer Response, Second Edition. This guide offers students forms for peer critiques, including general guidelines and specific forms for different stages in the writing process. Also appropriate for freshman-level course. Free to adopters. 0-321-01948-2

Thinking Through the Test, by D.J. Henry. This special workbook, prepared specially for students in Florida, offers ample skill and practice exercises to help student prep for the Florida State Exit Exam. To shrinkwrap this workbook free with your textbook, please contact your Longman sales representative. Also available: Two laminated grids (one for reading, one for writing) that can serve as handy references for students preparing for the Florida State Exit Exam.

ACKNOWLEDGMENTS

For their help revising the fourth edition, I gratefully acknowledge the following reviewers: Michael J. Hricik–Westmoreland County Community College, Julia Ruengert–Ozark Technical Community College; Judy Brandon–Clovis Community College; Mary Multer Greene–Tidewater Community College.

And to Denny, Greg, and Jeff: Thank you for your unstinting understanding and support. You are the best.

Barbara Fine Clouse

Progressions

Chapter 1

The Writing Process: Planning—Writing—Rewriting

What do successful writers do? Let me tell you first what they don't do—they don't work fast or produce a finished piece in one sitting. Instead, they work through a series of three stages. Stage one is planning, when writers consider the ideas they want to express and the order they want to write them in. Stage two is **writing**, when writers first put their ideas down in composition form. Stage three is **rewriting**, when writers reconsider the draft to shape and refine it.

The stages of writing are
1. planning
2. writing
3. rewriting

You too should learn to work through several stages. Do not expect your writing to roll off your pen or pop off the keys in perfect form. Instead, expect to work and rework a piece, gradually shaping it to a satisfying finished product.

You should also realize that different people favor different writing processes. Some people need to plan more extensively than others; some like to get feedback and some prefer to work alone; some outline extensively and some informally. There are many ways to approach writing.

The rest of this chapter will discuss the planning, writing, and rewriting stages writers work through. You will learn:

1. how to use five techniques (listing, brainstorming, clustering, freewriting, and journal writing) to discover ideas to include in your writing

2. how to order your ideas

3. how to use linking words and phrases (called **transitions**) so your reader can follow your order of ideas

4. how to write a first draft

5. how to refine your draft into a finished piece of writing

◆ ◆ ◆

PLANNING YOUR WRITING: GENERATING IDEAS

Occasionally, a writer gets lucky and all the right ideas spill onto the page in a burst of inspiration. However, that is extremely rare, so do not spend too much time staring at a blank page. Go after the ideas you need by listing, brainstorming, clustering, freewriting, and journal writing. **Listing, brainstorming, clustering, freewriting,** and **journal writing** are techniques described in this chapter for discovering writing topics and ideas in the absence of inspiration.

All writers get stuck sometimes. When they do, listing, brainstorming, clustering, freewriting, and journal writing can help.

Listing

Listing can supply writing topics and ideas to develop those topics. To list, spill out every idea that occurs to you, without evaluating how good the ideas are. Just record everything you think of. One idea will lead to another until you have a list of useful and not-so-useful thoughts. You may need to pause at times to think of ideas, but if you let yourself write everything that comes to mind without restraining yourself, you will develop a helpful list.

When listing, do not evaluate how good your ideas are; write everything that occurs to you.

Here is a list developed by a student who wanted to write about athletics:

football	*player salaries*
baseball	*player strikes*
basketball	*what sports mean to boys*
coaching	*betting*
training	*athletic scholarships*
college	*opportunities for women*
professional	*recruiting violations*
when I was cut from	*preventing injuries*
the basketball team	*Little League*
great athletes	
(Michael Jordan, etc.)	

Study your list to find a writing topic.

When you run out of ideas, review your list and decide on a topic. The student who wrote the above list decided to write about the time he was cut from the basketball team.

Next, list again—this time to discover ideas for writing about your topic. Here is the student's second list. Notice that he crossed out the ideas he decided not to include, the ones not closely enough related to his topic.

went to every practice—played well

really wanted it bad

was sure I made the team

~~*my father wanted it bad too*~~

after school, checked list—didn't see my name

~~*it was like the time I struck out in Little League*~~

cried all the way home

was embarrassed—all my friends made the team

Luis didn't talk to me anymore

~~*Jerrold also didn't make the team*~~

felt like a failure

lost friends because they were always at practice, etc.

felt sorry for myself and stupid

After crossing out ideas, some writers determine a suitable order for their ideas and number them to reflect this order. The result is a **scratch outline**, a guide that tells the writer what ideas will appear in the first draft and what order they will appear in. Here is the student writer's list turned into a scratch outline.

An idea—generation list can be turned into a scratch outline.

②*went to every practice—played well*

①*really wanted it bad*

③*was sure I made the team*

~~*my father wanted it bad too*~~

④*after school, checked list—didn't see my name*

~~*it was like the time I struck out in Little League*~~

⑤*cried all the way home*

⑧*was embarrassed—all my friends made the team*

⑩ *Luis didn't talk to me anymore*

~~*Jerrold also didn't make the team*~~

⑥*felt like a failure*

⑨*lost friends because they were always at practice, etc.*

⑦*felt sorry for myself and stupid*

PRACTICE 1.1

Assume you will write about a person you admire. The subject can be a famous person, a friend, a relative, a teacher, a coach, or anyone you regard highly. To decide whom you will write about, use the space below to list the names of everyone you can think of that you admire for any reason at all, no matter how small. (Try to list at least five people.)

Study your list and select the person you wish to write about. Using a separate sheet of paper, spend about ten minutes listing to discover the reasons you admire this person. Write three of these reasons in the spaces provided. Number your ideas to show which will appear first, second, and third.

_____

_____

_____

Brainstorming

To brainstorm, ask questions about your topic.

Brainstorming is asking questions about your topic. The answers can supply ideas to include in your writing.

Some of the following questions will be suited to your topic, and some of them will not be. Each time you brainstorm, select the appropriate questions and disregard the rest. (You will probably think of additional questions suited to your particular topic.)

Who was involved?	Why is it important?
What happened?	What can be learned?
When did it happen?	What is it like (or different from)?
Why did it happen?	What does it mean?
Where did it happen?	What is (was) the cause?
How did it happen?	What is (was) the effect?
How is it done?	How is it made?

Here is a list of brainstorming questions and answers a student used when she wrote about getting married right out of high school. Notice that the writer used some of the questions in the preceding list but not others; also notice that she added questions she thought of that were especially suited to her particular topic.

What happened?

I got married right after high school graduation.

Why did it happen?

I was pregnant. I felt I had to get married.

What was it like?

At first very exciting because I felt mature and more sophisticated than my friends. I was glad to be away from my parents.

Then what happened?

My husband joined the service. I was alone most of the time and missed out on what my friends were doing. It was lonely and scary.

What was the effect?

The marriage lasted seven years and then we divorced. I felt cheated out of some very good years. Now I must raise my son alone. It's hard.

What can be learned?

Teen marriages are difficult. They are no solution to an unplanned pregnancy. I was stupid to get married. If you're pregnant, think about all your choices.

After brainstorming, study your answers to find a specific writing topic. When the student writer studied her brainstorming, she decided to write about why teen marriages are a problem, using her own experience as an example. Select your topic on the basis of which answers interest you or on the basis of what you have the most information on.

Study your brainstorming to find a specific topic.

PRACTICE 1.2

Assume you will write about a difficult decision you made. If you cannot think of a decision you want to write about, try listing on another sheet of paper. After settling on the decision, on a separate page, brainstorm for about fifteen minutes to develop ideas that might appear in the writing. When your brainstorming is complete, study your answers and decide on a specific writing topic. Write it here:

_____

Now, in the spaces provided, record five ideas that could appear in your writing about a difficult decision.

1. _____

   _____

2. _____

   _____

3. _____

   _____

4. _____

   _____

5. _____

   _____

Clustering

Clustering helps you see how your ideas relate to each other.

Clustering is an excellent idea-generation technique because it helps you see how your ideas connect to each other. To cluster, write one general idea down in the center of a large sheet of paper and circle it:

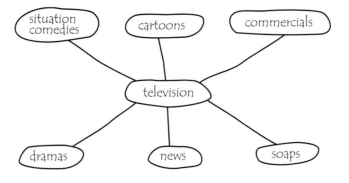

Next, around the circled general idea, write related ideas and connect them to the central circle.

As you think of more ideas, write them down, circle them, and connect them to the ideas they are the most closely related to:

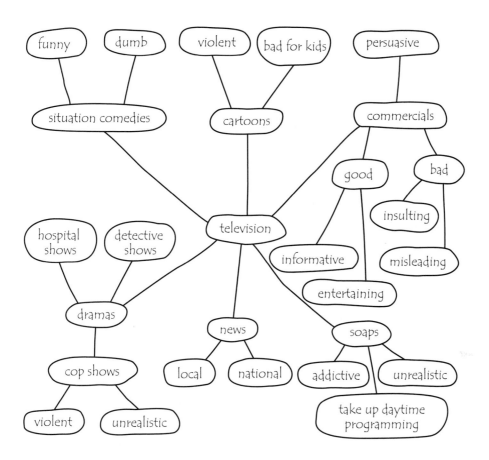

Continue writing, circling, and connecting ideas until you can think of nothing more. Do not censor yourself or evaluate the worth of your ideas—just write down everything you think of.

Sometimes one clustering gives you enough to get underway. If not, study what you have and settle on a topic for your writing. For example, the writer of the preceding clustering decided to write about television commercials. Once you have settled on a topic, do a second clustering with your topic circled in the middle.

A second clustering can be done to discover ideas for developing a topic.

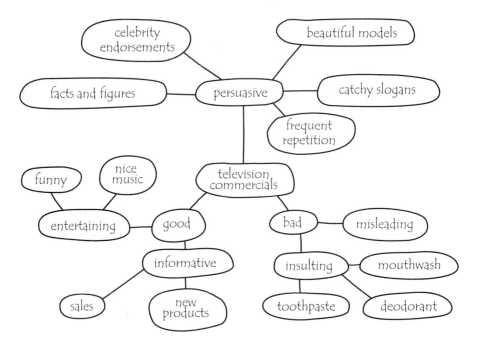

The student writer of this second clustering decided to write about the techniques used in television commercials to persuade people to buy products. She used the ideas clustering around the "persuasive" circle in her writing.

PRACTICE 1.3

Assume you have been asked to write about education reform. On a separate sheet, develop a clustering with "education reform" circled in the center. When you discover a topic, write that topic here.

_____

Now, on a separate sheet, develop a second clustering. Place your topic in the center. When you can think of nothing more to add to the clustering, record four of the ideas you thought of here.

1. _____

2. _____

3. _____

4. _____

Freewriting

Freewriting is nonstop writing that works like this: for ten to fifteen minutes, write anything and everything that comes to mind. Do not decide whether your ideas are good or bad. Just record everything, even the silly ideas. Also, do not worry about grammar, spelling, or neatness. If you cannot think of anything to write, then write anything, even "I don't know what to write," the alphabet, the names of your family members, or your feelings at the moment. Eventually, more ideas will occur to you, and you can record them. Continue this way, without lifting your pen from the page.

When time is up, read your freewriting. Most people find they have discovered at least one good idea. Many people find more than one good idea. These ideas will require shaping, but they can get you started.

The following freewriting was done by a student searching for ideas about college life. Notice that the writer was not concerned about grammar, spelling, and correctness. Also, notice the free flow of thought; the author did not eliminate silly or irrelevant ideas but used them as a springboard to more serious and relevant ones.

> When freewriting, do not stop, do not censor yourself, and do not worry about grammar, spelling, or neatness.

How has college affected me, that's a loaded question. I'm 42 so coming here was really scarry. I didn't think I could keep up with the kids, I thought I was too rusty and out of practice. I was so insecure that I overdid it, studying ridiculous amounts of time for even little quizzes. Well when I started getting grades on things I realized that I was doing better than the people younger than me and that really boosted my confidence. The first time I had to write a paper I was a basket case, I didn't do so good, but now I'm getting better thanks to the writing center. It's lonely sometimes cause its hard to talk to eighteen year olds about my divorce or the kids or money problems, but their sweet and they see me as a mother so I help them alot. The best effect is that for the first time in years since Dan walked out I feel like I have a future. I know I'll get my degree and go on to make a living and support myself and the kids. Its an awful lot of work. Did I say that already? I think I'm running out of things to say. Running. I do alot of that. With school, the job, the kids stuff, all I do is run, run, run. No wonder I'm exhausted all the time. I'll bet none of these kids here could keep up with me. I guess I feel pretty proud of myself. What else can I say? I can't think I can't think Oh am I tired now I can't think because I'm tired. One other effect is that my kids think its cool that moms in school, sometimes we even study together. I think I feel older being around so many young people, but I do feel like I can do anything they do and that's a good feeling.

In her freewriting, the student discovered several ideas she could write about: the insecurity she felt when she returned to college, how the Writing Center helped her become a better writer, acting like a mother to younger students, feeling as if she has a future, her exhaustion, her pride in herself, and what it is like to be around younger people in school. The student decided that she wanted to write about her exhaustion, so she made that idea her writing topic.

A second freewriting focusing on an idea discovered in the first freewriting can be helpful.

Often, one freewriting gets the writer started. Other times, a second freewriting is needed, which focuses on the idea or ideas that surfaced in the first freewriting. Here is the student's second freewriting, which focuses on her exhaustion:

> I don't know if I can even explain the exhaustion I feel. No matter how hard I work there's always more to do. I get up at 5:00, make lunch and throw in a load of laundry, and straighten the house. But that's a joke because the house always looks like a disaster area no matter how much straightening I do. I cant ever get to the real cleaning. You should see the inside of my refrigerator, its disgusting. I get the kids off to school by 8 and then I leave to be at my job by 9. I work as a bookkeeper all day and then race home at five, throw supper on the table and leave for class. Class goes until 9 and then I come home to the kids and all their homework and problems. I can't even start my homework until they are in bed at 11 so sometimes I'm up way past midnight and then it all starts over. That pretty much sums it up, no there's more. The exhaustion is mental more than physical. All the planning and worrying. Dance lesson, soccer practice, doctor appointments, teacher conferences its so hard to fit it all in. Now what do I say. I guess there's the exhaustion that comes from being on my own and not having anyone to help or count on. I guess I can count on Jeannie, but she has her own problems and I hate to bother her too much. My biggest worry is that I'm not spending time with the kids. And I worry about all the bills. The worrying exhausts me too.

After a second freewriting, read your work and underline useful ideas the way the student writer did. Remember, do not expect polished thoughts; just find raw material to shape. Perhaps the second freewriting will provide enough ideas to get you started. If not, try brainstorming, clustering, or listing. Idea-generation techniques are often used in combination.

PRACTICE 1.4

Assume you plan to write about ways you have changed in the past three to five years. On a separate paper, freewrite for ten or fifteen minutes to discover ideas for this writing. Remember, do not stop writing for any reason, do not reject any ideas, and do not worry about grammar, spelling, or neatness. If necessary, freewrite a second time until you have at least four ideas. Record these ideas below.

1. _____

   _____

2. _____

   _____

3. _____

   _____

4. _____

   _____

Keeping a Journal

A journal is not a diary, which is a place to record what happened during the day. In a journal, writers explore their ideas and feelings. Journal writing helps writers solve problems, get in touch with their feelings, vent anger, and discover what they think about issues. Furthermore, a journal can be an excellent source of ideas for writing.

By keeping a journal, writers can explore how they think and feel. They can also develop a storehouse of ideas to use in their writing.

To keep a journal, buy a notebook, and write in it every day, at the same time every day if you can manage it. Date each entry before you write and then take off—write anything that you are moved to write. Do not get hung up on spelling, handwriting, or grammar. This writing is for you.

Journal entries can be about anything, but here are some possibilities:

1. Write about something that happened during the day that angered you, surprised you, cheered you, or moved your emotions in some way.
2. Write about a person you admire, love, hate, respect, or do not understand.
3. Write about how school or work is going.
4. Write about your goals.
5. Write about your family relationships.
6. Write about possible solutions to a problem you are having.
7. Write about changes you would like to make.
8. Write about your childhood.
9. Write about your classmates.

10. Freewrite about the first thing that comes to your mind.

11. Write about something you recently read or watched on TV.

12. Describe what you would like your life to be like in five years.

13. Write about what makes you happy or sad.

14. Write about how you feel about your writing.

15. Write about what is important to you.

Make regular entries in your journal, and you will soon have a considerable body of material. When you need ideas for writing, paging through your journal may turn up what you need to get started or keep going. The following sample journal entry shows how keeping a journal can help you think things through and discover topics.

> 6-8-00 I heard a very disturbing news report today. A high school teacher in New York was tortured and killed by a former student who was after the man's PIN number so he could withdraw money from his ATM account. It is not unusual to hear about murder and robbery, but this report has me very upset. The teacher was hugely popular at a tough inner city school. He was known as a kind man who really cared about kids. I heard some of his students interviewed. One student said that every student in the school was robbed as a result of this. Then I watched a film clip of the teacher dancing at the June prom with one of his students.
>
> I've never believed in the death penalty, and I guess I still don't, but my belief is much less strong. The nineteen-year-old who has been arrested is legally an adult. If he is found guilty, I don't think I'd be upset if he were put to death. Loss of this caring teacher, who worked in a school many others wouldn't go near, is terribly sad. Loss of the murderer and torturer and robber doesn't strike me as so bad.
>
> It's scary to find my views shaken like this. I used to know how I felt about capital punishment. Now I'm not so sure. The truth is, I want vengeance, and I don't even know the teacher who was killed. Is vengeance justice?

Working Together: Generating Ideas

Other people can help us discover ideas because they often think of things we overlook, or they say something that triggers our thinking.

Other people can help a writer who needs ideas.

Working with others can be as simple as asking people what they think about a particular subject. Just say, "I have to write a paper on _____; do you have any ideas?" The response may get you started. Working together can also involve sitting down with one or more people and working in a more formal way. Listing, brainstorming, and clustering, in particular, lend themselves to this approach.

To list with one or more people, assign a person to write down what everyone says. Then group members begin saying any and all ideas that occur to them while the recorder gets them down in list form. Listing with others is helpful because one person usually says something that prompts someone else to get an idea.

Brainstorming can also be done with more than one person. Take turns asking questions while the person who needs the ideas answers the questions and records those answers.

To use clustering in a group, assign one group member to do the writing. All group members speak their ideas as they occur to them, and the group decides where on the clustering to connect each idea. Clustering in a group has the same advantage as listing in a group: one person's ideas stimulate the thinking of other people.

 ## *Tips for Generating Ideas*

1. Do not wait for inspiration. If ideas do not occur to you right away, use the idea-generation techniques.

2. Write about what you know. Even the idea-generation techniques cannot help you come up with ideas on a subject you do not know very much about.

3. Try each idea-generation technique to learn what works best for you. Even if you think a technique will not work for you, give it a try. You may be surprised to discover what it can do.

4. Use more than one technique. Sometimes combining techniques yields more ideas than using one technique by itself.

5. Keep your writing topic in mind as you go about your activities. Ideas can occur while you are walking across campus, washing the car, eating lunch, or engaging in other routines.

6. Give yourself enough time. If you wait until the last minute, you will not allow time for ideas to surface.

7. Accept rough ideas. Idea generation is the earliest stage of writing, so things will be rough. Do not reject ideas just because they are not polished; you can polish during revision.

8. Force yourself to write. Writing stimulates thinking, so sit down and fill a page with whatever occurs to you, and you may hit upon a brainstorm.

Thinking, Learning, and Writing in College   **Learning Strategies**

Many idea generation techniques are also excellent learning strategies.

1. <u>Listing</u> can help you learn lecture and textbook material. After studying a portion of your lecture notes or class text, stop, look away from the material, and list all the important points that you can think of. Then look back at the material to determine whether you omitted anything. If so, add it to the list in a contrasting color and study the list. Writing this way helps "set" the learning.

2. <u>Clustering</u> can also help you learn material and see the relationships among the points you learn. Write and circle a major point you are studying and then add all the points you can think of that are related to the circled point. Check your text and lecture notes for omissions and add them in a contrasting color.

3. <u>Brainstorming</u> is an excellent way to prepare for a test with a study partner. Each of you should draft questions about the material. Then trade questions and answer them. Discuss your answers and pay special attention to areas of sketchy or incorrect information.

4. A special kind of journal called a **learning log** is a powerful strategy for improving comprehension and retention. Keep a separate notebook for each subject and in each one record your reactions to reading assignments and lectures. Note how you can use the material, how it relates to your experience and learning in other classes, areas of agreement and disagreement, and any questions you have.

PLANNING YOUR WRITING: ESTABLISHING AUDIENCE AND PURPOSE

Typically, writers write for any one or more of these purposes:

to share something with the reader

to inform the reader of something

to persuade the reader to think or act a particular way

to entertain the reader

Your purpose is important because why you are writing influences the nature of your writing. For example, say you are writing about Thanksgiving. To <u>share</u> with your reader, you might tell about your family celebrations at your grandparents' house. To <u>inform</u> your reader, you might compare modern Thanksgiving celebrations with those of the nineteenth century. To <u>persuade</u> a reader of something, you might argue that Thanksgiving should be a day of mourning because of our treatment of Native Americans. Finally, to <u>entertain</u>, you could tell an amusing story about the time you made a fool of yourself at your first Thanksgiving dinner at your in-laws' house.

Like purpose, your audience (the reader) will affect the nature of a piece. Aspects like your reader's age, sex, socioeconomic standing, political views, religion, and family background can influence the detail you include. In addition, how much your reader knows about your topic and how much your reader cares about your topic will affect what you do. Say, for example, that you are writing to convince your reader to pass a school levy. If your audience has children, you can discuss improving education. However, if your reader has no children, you may want to mention the improved property values that result from better schools.

You may be thinking that all this talk about audience is unnecessary because your audience is your writing teacher. However, to prepare you for writing outside the classroom, your writing teacher can assume the identity of any reader you have in mind.

To appreciate how audience and purpose affect writing, consider the options for writing about VCRs. Possibilities include:

1. explaining how to program a VCR (a manufacturer might write this in the owner's manual for the purchaser)

2. convincing someone to purchase a particular brand of VCR (a store owner might write this in an advertising brochure for a potential customer)

3. writing an entertaining article on the problems of owning a VCR (a newspaper columnist might write this for the readers of a daily newspaper)

4. explaining how the VCR has affected family life (a psychologist might write this for the readers of Family Circle magazine)

5. explaining how the VCR affects the movie industry (a studio executive might write this for the readers of an industry trade magazine)

Each of these pieces will be different because the audience and purpose will be different. The differences will be in the kinds of details, the vocabulary, and the approach. Let's look at each of these elements.

Kinds of Details   Purpose affects the details a writer uses. The piece about how to program a VCR will include all the steps, but the piece convincing a reader to buy a particular brand will only mention that programming is uncomplicated. Similarly, audience affects the details chosen. If the reader of the piece about how to program the VCR is knowledgeable about electronics, then it may not be necessary to explain where buttons are located,

A writer's audience and purpose affect the kinds of details, the vocabulary, and the approach.

but this information would be needed for a reader who knows nothing about the equipment.

Vocabulary   Your audience will determine the level of vocabulary. For example, say that you are writing about the effects of the VCR on family life. For an audience of psychologists you can use the term *projection*, but for the average parent you may need to say "attributing your own faults to someone else."

Approach   Audience and purpose also affect the approach you take. For example, humor would be appropriate in the piece on the problems of using a VCR that is meant to entertain the readers of a newspaper. However, humor would be misplaced in the owner's manual that explains how to program the device.

Tips For Identifying Audience and Purpose

Part of your planning should involve identifying your audience and purpose. Asking the following questions can help with this:

1. Do I want to entertain my reader?
2. Do I want to inform my reader? If so, of what?
3. Do I want to convince my reader to think or act in a certain way? If so, in what way?
4. Do I want to share something with my reader? If so, what?
5. Who will my reader be? (Your instructor can assume the identity of any reader you want.)
6. What does my reader already know about my topic?
7. What strong feelings does my reader hold about my topic?
8. How interested will my reader be?
9. Will my reader's age, sex, race, economic level, political beliefs, or religion influence the response to my topic?

PRACTICE 1.5: WORKING TOGETHER

Each group member should find a piece of writing: a newspaper article, a recipe, a magazine article, a business letter, an advertisement, an editorial, an owner's manual, a book or movie review, a textbook chapter, and so on. As a group, analyze each piece and determine the intended audience and purpose and the effect of these factors on the kind of detail, the amount of detail, the vocabulary, and the approach.

PLANNING YOUR WRITING: ORDERING IDEAS

Writers arrange their ideas in a way that helps explain or prove the central idea. Often an effective arrangement is a movement from **general–to–specific**. In this arrangement, a sentence presents the central idea, which is a general point. The detail that follows provides specific ideas that explain or prove the central idea. Although other effective arrangements are possible, for now we will concern ourselves with general-to-specific order.

Three common general-to-specific arrangements are **chronological order, spatial order,** and **emphatic order**.

Part of a writer's planning is finding a suitable order for ideas. Often a general-to-specific order is effective.

Chronological Order

Chronological order is time order: events are arranged in the order they occurred. Chronological order is used most frequently when a story is told and the writer arranges details according to what happened first, second, and so forth. In the paragraph that follows, details are arranged chronologically:

In chronological order, events are arranged in the order they occurred.

> The seven ten-year-olds arrived within minutes of each other. I explained that Gregory would be back in a half hour, so they all raced through the downstairs looking for the best hiding places. Julio and Emil hid behind the couch, while Heath and Tod crouched between the end table and wall. Jordan crawled under the dining room table, and Josh scrambled in behind him. Jeffrey found a perfect spot behind the front door. Soon we heard the slam of a car door, and we knew Greg was home. After he walked in the front door, the boys jumped out from their hiding places and yelled, "Surprise!"

Spatial Order

With a **spatial order**, details are arranged according to their location in a particular area. Spatial order is especially useful when you are describing some location. Spatial order involves moving through space in some sequence: top to bottom, front to back, near to far, left to right, and so forth. Details in this paragraph are arranged in a spatial order:

With a spatial order, details are arranged according to their location.

> When I entered the living room, I was appalled by what I saw. Empty potato chip and pretzel bags littered the coffee table and couch; their contents formed a layer of crumbs on the carpet. The antique, crystal lamp on the table next to the couch was resting on its side, and the table itself held at least ten beer cans, all of them squashed in the middle. Beneath the table, the once-beige carpet was stained with a dark splotch that I knew would be permanent. Worst of all was the sight of my teenage son, who had been left in charge. There he was, sprawled across the couch asleep or unconscious—I wasn't sure which.

Emphatic Order

To arrange detail in an emphatic order, begin with your least important point and move to your most important. Also, you can begin with your second most important point and end with your most important.

With **emphatic order**, a writer begins with the least important detail and moves to the most important detail. Think of emphatic order as saving the best for last to provide a big finish.

A variation on emphatic order is to begin with the second most important point and end with your most important, sandwiching other points in between. This gives the strongest possible opening and closing. The following paragraph arranges details in an emphatic order:

> For several reasons, voters should pass the school levy when it is placed on the ballot during the August special election. First, the additional funds will allow the senior class to take a trip to Washington. More important, passage of the levy means the elementary schools can add computer instruction to the curriculum. Without this instruction, our students will lag behind others in the country. Finally, if the levy passes, our school system can pay its debts and avoid a state loan that will jeopardize its financial well-being for years to come.

Combining Orders

A writer can use any combination of chronological, spatial, and emphatic orders.

A writer can use any combination of chronological, spatial, and emphatic orders in the same piece. For example, look back at the paragraph that illustrates chronological order on p. 17. Notice that for the most part the ideas are arranged according to what happened first, second, third, and so forth. However, notice that a spatial order is also used when the paragraph explains where the children hid (between the end table and the wall, behind the front door, and so forth).

Now look again at the paragraph illustrating spatial order on p. 17. For the most part, ideas are arranged according to their location, but some emphatic order is also apparent. You can tell this because the second to the last sentence begins, "Worst of all." This phrase suggests that the most important detail is at the end.

Deciding on an Effective Order

Many times your instinct will suggest the best order for your ideas. For example, when you are telling a story, you will sense that a time order is called for; when you are describing a scene, you will feel the need for a spatial order; when you are arguing a point, you will realize an emphatic order is effective.

When a writer's instincts do not suggest an effective order, drawing up more than one outline can help the writer decide on the best arrangement.

When you do not sense the best order for your ideas, outlining can help. Try outlining your ideas, using different arrangements, and then study your outlines to determine which seems best. You already learned about the scratch outline in this chapter. Later you will learn about another outlining technique (see p. 157).

TIPS FOR ORDERING IDEAS

1. Do not resist outlining. It can save you time in the long run by making the draft go more smoothly. Try a scratch outline (p. 3) or outline map (p. 157) to order your ideas.

2. Outline more than once. If you are having trouble ordering your ideas, try two or more different arrangements to see what works best.

3. Try different kinds of outlines to see what works best for you.

4. Decide whether spatial, chronological, or emphatic order will work the best before you begin ordering your ideas.

Thinking, Learning, and Writing in College   Writing in Other Classes

You will have many occasions to use chronological, spatial, and emphatic orders in other classes.

1. In response to an exam question in an American history course, you might need to explain why the United States entered World War I. To do so, you could give the events leading to the U.S. entry in the order they occurred, that is, in <u>chronological order</u>.

2. To complete a biology lab report, you might need to detail what you see under the microscope by describing the aspects of the slide from top to bottom, that is, in <u>spatial order</u>.

3. A position paper in an education course might require you to argue for or against the pass/fail grading system. You likely would present the reasons for your view in order of their importance, that is, in <u>emphatic order</u>.

PRACTICE 1.6

1. For each of the following paragraphs, indicate whether the order of ideas is chronological, spatial, or emphatic. In one paragraph, a combination of orders is used.

   A. The exasperated mother explained to her son for the fourth time why he could not get a puppy. First, she said, paper training the animal would be too much trouble, especially since no one was home during the day. Then there was the fact that puppies are expensive and their budget was too tight to allow for dog food purchases and veterinarian bills. Most important, she said that they live in an apartment and their lease expressly prohibits all pets except birds.

The ideas are arranged in _____ order.

B. Paper recycling is an interesting process. First, the paper is put into a vat of water with chemicals that remove the ink and turn the paper into soft pulp. This vat is called a pulper. From the pulper, the pulp goes to a machine that removes staples, clips, and anything else that is not paper. Next, the pulp is cleaned and mixed with water to form a thick paste that is spread on a metal sheet where it is heated, dried, and smoothed. When the paste dries, it is crisp, new paper.

The ideas are arranged in _____ order.

C. When I walked into the sixty-dollar-a-night hotel room, I was outraged by what I saw. Directly in front of me was an unmade bed, its sheets a dingy gray. The wall behind the bed was stained with a brown splotch that looked alarmingly like dried blood. There were no drapes on the window; instead, a tattered blind partially blocked the sun. I turned to check the bathroom to my right. There the situation was just as bad: dirty towels were on the floor; the sink was rust-stained, and the mirror above it was opaque with dust and lint. Furious, I stormed out of the room to find the manager and get a full refund.

The ideas are arranged in _____ order.

2. Assume that each of the following sentences is the first sentence of a paragraph, the sentence that presents the writer's central idea. In the space provided, indicate whether the order of ideas is likely to be spatial, chronological, emphatic, or some combination of these.

A. It would be a serious mistake to zone Fifth Avenue to allow the construction of a shopping plaza.

The order of ideas is likely to be _____.

B. The kitchen of the model home is the most efficient one I have seen.

The order of ideas is likely to be _____.

C. The military should not be responsible for the development of experimental spacecraft.

The order of ideas is likely to be _____.

D. My first day of college did not go well.

   The order of ideas is likely to be _____.

E. Anyone can learn to change the oil in a car.

   The order of ideas is likely to be _____.

3. For each of the following writing topics, use the idea-generation technique of your choice to develop at least four ideas. Do this on a separate sheet. Then, in the space provided, write the ideas in the order they are likely to appear in the writing.

   A. Topic: Changes I'd Most Like to Make in Myself

   First idea _____

   Second idea _____

   Third idea _____

   Fourth idea _____

   The order of my ideas is _____.

   The idea-generation technique I used is _____.

   B. Topic: A Time When Something Did Not Go as Expected

   First idea _____

   Second idea _____

   Third idea _____

   Fourth idea _____

   The order of my ideas is _____.

   The idea-generation technique I used is _____.

   C. Topic: Why the Internet should (or should not) be censored.

   First idea _____

   Second idea _____

   Third idea _____

Fourth idea _____

The order of my ideas is _____.

The idea-generation technique I used is _____.

USING TRANSITIONS

Transitions are words and phrases that help a reader follow the order of ideas. Some transitions are a clue that chronological order has been used, some transitions are a clue that spatial order has been used, and some transitions are a clue that emphatic order has been used.

Take another look at the paragraph illustrating chronological order on p. 17. Notice that the transitions soon and after suggest a time sequence. Now look at the paragraph illustrating spatial order on p. 17. Notice that transitions like next to, beneath, and across indicate that ideas are arranged according to location. Finally, reread the paragraph illustrating emphatic order on p. 18. In this case, the transition more important provides the clue that emphatic order has been used.

Transitions are discussed now because they help writers clarify the order of ideas for the reader. However, checking for effective use of transitions is part of revising, not the early planning stages of writing.

The chart that follows notes some common transitions used to signal chronological, spatial, and emphatic orders. (A more complete discussion of transitions begins on p. 235.)

Transitions are words and phrases that help the reader understand the order of ideas.

Transition Chart

Transitions That Signal Chronological Order	first, second, third…, next, then, after, before, in the meantime, finally, at the same time, during, meanwhile, at first, when, as soon as
	Before the shortstop could make the play at second, the runner slid into the bag.
Transitions That Signal Spatial Order	nearby, near to, beside, over, far from, next to, under, around, through, in front of, behind, surrounding, alongside, away from, on top of, toward, at
	Behind the sofa I found the black leather glove I lost last January.

Transitions That Signal Emphatic Order	more important, most important, most of all, best of all, of greatest significance, least of all, even better

The tax proposal will burden the poor. More important, it will cause industry to relocate to other areas.

PRACTICE 1.7

1. Read the following paragraph and circle every transition that signals chronological, spatial, or emphatic order. (You will circle five transitions in all.)

   All children who swim should be taught a number of important safety rules. First, they should be taught to swim only where there is supervision. Next, they should be cautioned to dive only in designated areas. Even better, they should be told not to dive at all, since each year hundreds of people suffer permanent, crippling injuries as a result of diving. If caught in a strong current, a child should know to swim across that current or parallel to shore. Once free of the current, the child should head for shore at once. Most important, all children should be taught never, ever to swim alone.

2. In the following sentences, fill in the blanks with transitions according to the directions given. If you need help selecting a transition, refer to the chart beginning on p. 22.

   A. Use transitions that signal chronological order:

   Paula and Ivan began a new financial program.

   _____ they refinanced their home mortgage, and

   _____ they began a regular savings program.

   B. Use a transition that signals emphatic order:

   Contrary to popular belief, regular exercise decreases a person's

   appetite. _____ exercise helps prevent bone loss, which is vital in preventing osteoporosis.

C. Use transitions that signal spatial order:

Lee spent weeks redecorating Rosa's room to make it more suitable

for a five-year-old. _____ the bed she stenciled nursery

rhyme characters on the wall, and _____ the closet she

built shelves to hold toys. _____ the windows she hung
yellow curtains.

3. Working Together: With two or three of your classmates, write sentences according to the directions. Use a separate sheet.

A. Write two sentences that describe the location of some of the things in your writing classroom. Begin the second sentence with a transition that signals a spatial order.

B. Write two sentences about what you did this morning. Begin the second sentence with a transition that signals chronological order.

C. Write two sentences that tell why foreign languages should (or should not) be taught in high school. Begin the second sentence with a transition that signals emphatic order.

WRITING YOUR FIRST DRAFT

A first draft is the first version of a piece of writing. It is also known as a rough draft because it is likely to have problems the writer will solve later, when the draft is refined.

After generating ideas and deciding on a suitable order, writers consider most of their planning complete. They are ready to put their plan in action by writing a **first draft**, which is the earliest version of a piece of writing.

You should understand what a first draft is and what it is not. A first draft is not a finished piece of writing; it is not something the writer is completely satisfied with; it is not something that can be copied over and handed to a reader. Instead, a first draft is a first effort. It has problems, mistakes, and areas the writer is unsure about. Thus, a first draft is often called a **rough draft**.

 Tips For Writing the First Draft

1. Write your draft from beginning to end in one sitting. The sooner you get your draft down, the sooner you will know what raw material you have to work with.

2. Forget perfection. You can improve the draft later. For now, just get your ideas down the best way you can.

3. If you get stuck, skip the troublesome part and push on. Later you can work out the problem.

4. Do not spend much time making changes as you go. Save most of your changes for later, when you revise the draft.

5. As you draft, refer often to your list of generated ideas so that you do not lose sight of the plan you have for your writing.

6. If you have trouble getting started, write your draft as if you were speaking to a close friend.

7. Above all, remember that a first draft is supposed to be rough. Do not feel frustrated if your draft is nowhere near as strong as you want your final version to be.

PRACTICE 1.8

When you completed number 3A for Practice 1.6, you generated and ordered ideas for a composition about things you would like to change about yourself. Using those ordered ideas as a guide, write a first draft for a paragraph. The first sentence of your draft should be one of these:

The change I'd most like to make in myself is _____.
(You fill in the blank.)

or

The changes I'd most like to make in myself are _____

and _____. (You fill in the blanks.)

Develop your paragraph by explaining why you want to make the change or changes.

Follow the suggestions described in "Tips for Writing the First Draft," and remember that the draft is supposed to be rough. (Save your draft because you will use it in a later activity.)

REWRITING: REVISING YOUR FIRST DRAFT

Once the first draft is complete, a writer makes changes to improve the writing and make it suitable for a reader. The process of making changes is **revision**. Revision is an important aspect of any writing project, and frequently the most time-consuming.

When writers revise, they make changes in their first draft to improve it. This revision process is very important and often time-consuming.

Revision Concerns

When writers shape their drafts during revision, they try to see their work from a reader's viewpoint. They are concerned with several things, noted for you here:

1. adding detail where necessary to prove or explain a point
2. deleting detail that is not clearly related to the central idea
3. making sure detail is arranged in a logical order
4. making changes necessary for clarity
5. eliminating problems with word choice
6. adding transitions where needed
7. improving the flow of sentences, if necessary
8. making sure everything is suited to the audience and purpose

During revision, a writer is concerned with detail and sentence effectiveness, not with grammar and usage.

You may have noticed from the list that during revision the writer does not attend to matters of correctness such as spelling, punctuation, and subject-verb agreement. Does this surprise you? If so, you are not alone, for many people think that revising means "fixing up" a piece of writing by correcting the mistakes. However, this is not the case. Mistakes in grammar, spelling, punctuation, and such are attended to after revising—during editing. During revision, the writer works to improve detail and sentence effectiveness.

✳ *TIPS FOR REVISING*

1. Before revising, leave your work for a day. This time-out lets you rest and clear your head so you can view your draft objectively and find problems.

2. Before revising, type or word-process your first draft. You will be amazed at the number of problems you notice when your work is no longer in your own handwriting.

3. At least once, read your draft out loud very slowly. Sometimes writers hear problems they fail to see. (Be careful to read what is actually on the page—not what you meant to write.)

4. Revise in stages so you do not attempt too much at once. For example, the first time through, check to be sure everything is related to the point you are making. The second time, be sure you have enough detail. The third time, study word choice and clarity (word choice is discussed on p. 264). The fourth time, check for flow and transitions (flow is discussed on p. 217).

5. Many changes can be made directly on the draft. Do not be afraid to scratch out, draw arrows, and write in margins. Revision is often a "messy" process.

6. Periodically, leave your work for a few hours to refresh yourself. You will be more productive when you return.

Working Together: Reader Response

Successful writers know that they can get valuable revision advice from others. For this reason, successful writers are always handing a draft to someone and saying, "Read this and tell me what you think." When we let others read our work in progress, we can get a clearer sense of its strengths and weaknesses so we can make effective revisions. The Reader Response Sheet on p. 28 can be copied and given to people who will evaluate your drafts. First, review the following suggestions.

If You Are the Writer Seeking Information

1. Give your readers a legible draft; recopy or retype if necessary.

2. If you want information not covered by the questions on the response sheet, write out additional questions.

3. Get the opinions of at least two readers. (Make copies of your draft so each reader is evaluating an unmarked writing.)

4. Do not automatically accept the responses. Instead, weigh them out carefully and make thoughtful decisions about which responses to accept and which to reject.

5. If your readers disagree or if you are unsure if a response is reliable, ask your instructor for advice.

6. After you study the completed response sheets, talk to your readers to learn why they responded as they did. Ask them any questions you have and make notes about their responses.

If You Are the Reader Evaluating a Draft

1. Read the entire draft before writing any comments.

2. Explain why you react as you do. Rather than say, "Paragraph 2 is unclear," say, "Paragraph 2 is unclear because I don't understand why you believe more men should become elementary education majors."

3. Give specific suggestions for revision. Rather than say, "Add more detail," say, "Add more detail about why you were so angry when you did not make the team so I understand what caused the emotion." In other words, suggest a revision strategy.

READER RESPONSE SHEET

Writer's Name _____

Reader's Name _____

1. In a sentence, state the writer's main point.

2. What do you like best about the draft? Be specific.

3. Do all the details clearly relate to the main point? Place parentheses around unrelated details.

4. Underline any unclear points. What can be done to clarify?

5. Place brackets around any points that need more explanation. What detail should be added?

6. Are ideas arranged in an easy-to-follow order? If not, what changes should be made?

7. Place an ! next to any particularly effective word choice; circle any ineffective word choice.

8. Does the draft hold your interest? Explain why or why not.

PRACTICE 1.9

Reread the list of revision concerns on p. 26 and then proceed with this Practice exercise.

1. Reread the draft you wrote for Practice 1.8. As you do, place a check mark beside anything you wish to revise. (Remember, do not be concerned with grammar and usage at this point.)

    A. Did you notice problems with the draft that you did not notice

    when you wrote it? _____

    If you did, you have seen how leaving your work can help you become more objective.

    B. How many check marks did you place?_____

2. Take a few moments and type or word-process your draft; then reread it. On the typed copy place a square beside anything you would like to change. (Do not be concerned with grammar and usage at this point.)

    A. Did you notice problems on the typed copy that you did not notice

    before?_____

    If you did, you have seen how typing or word-processing a draft can help a writer.

    B. How many squares did you place? _____

3. Read your draft out loud very slowly. Each time you hear a problem you did not notice before, place an X by the problem.

    A. Did you hear any problems that you did not notice before?

    _____

    If you did, you have seen how reading a draft aloud can help a writer.

    B. Did reading your draft out loud give you a fresh slant on your work?

    _____

4. Go over your draft again and answer these questions:

    A. Do you need to eliminate points that are not related to the main

    point you want to make?_____

B. Do you need to add details so your point is well established?

_____

C. Do you need to make changes to improve word choice?

_____

D. Do you need to make changes to increase clarity? _____

E. Do you need to add transitions? _____

F. Do you need to improve the flow of your writing because it sounds

choppy? _____

(Save your draft because you will need it for a later activity.)

5. Working Together: Photocopy the Reader Response Sheet on p. 28 and trade drafts with a classmate. Each of you should fill out a response sheet and then answer the following question:

What did you learn about your draft as a result of getting reader response?

_____

_____

REWRITING: EDITING YOUR DRAFT

While revising, you may work through several drafts before you are satisfied with the detail, organization, and wording. Once you are satisfied, you can turn your attention to grammar and usage. The process of finding and correcting errors in grammar and usage is **editing**. Careful editing is important because mistakes distract readers and lead them to question your ability.

Writers edit to find and correct errors in grammar and usage that detract from the effectiveness of their writing.

Editing Concerns

During editing, a writer has much to consider. Here is a list of many of these editing concerns, which are explained on the pages in parentheses.

eliminating sentence fragments (p. 240)

eliminating run-on sentences and comma splices (p. 255)

using correct verb forms (p. 307)

avoiding inappropriate tense shifts (p. 342)

achieving agreement between subjects and verbs (p. 330)

achieving agreement between pronouns and antecedents (p. 347) eliminating faulty pronoun reference (p. 358)

avoiding person shifts (p. 372)

eliminating misplaced and dangling modifiers (p. 387 and p. 388)

using comparative and superlative forms correctly (p. 383)

capitalizing correctly (p. 391)

punctuating correctly (p. 396)

spelling correctly (p. 296)

 ## TIPS FOR EDITING

1. Look for the mistakes you often make. For example, if you frequently write sentence fragments, look especially for fragments.

2. Edit in stages. The first time through, look for one kind of mistake you are in the habit of making. The second time, look for another kind of mistake you often make. Continue this way and then edit one more time for all other errors.

3. Read your draft out loud to hear errors that you overlooked visually. (Be careful to read exactly what is on the page.)

4. Edit very slowly, using a pen to point to each word and punctuation mark as you go. Make sure you read what the pen is pointing to. If you are reading ahead of your pen, you are going too fast to do an effective job. Also, be sure to read exactly what is on the page—not what you meant to write.

5. Place a ruler under the line you are editing. This will help you focus and prevent you from building up too much speed. EDITING CANNOT BE DONE QUICKLY.

6. When in doubt, ask your instructor or another reliable person, or check chapters of this book. Do not guess about a grammar rule.

7. Trust your instincts. If they tell you there is a problem, the chances are good there really is a problem. Even if you cannot name the problem, pause and deal with the troublesome section of your writing.

8. Learn the grammar and usage rules. Also, pay careful attention to the errors your instructor notes on your papers. Be sure you understand the nature of each error and how to correct it. If you do not, ask your teacher for help.

9. Spend time away from your work before you begin to edit—to clear your head and improve your chances of finding mistakes.

PRACTICE 1.10

1. Review the list of editing concerns on pp. 30–31. Which of these
   concerns have you had trouble with in the past? _____
   _____

2. What pages of this text cover the concerns you noted in your answer
   to number 1? _____
   _____

3. Look again at the list of editing concerns. Is there anything in that list
   that you have never heard of before? Anything that you do not know
   the meaning of? If so, what?_____
   _____

4. What pages of this text cover the concerns you noted in your answer
   to number 3? _____
   _____

5. When you completed Practice 1.9, exercise number 2, you typed a
   copy of a draft. Using a pen to point to each word and punctuation
   mark in that draft, edit very slowly, looking for errors in grammar and
   usage. Be sure to read what you actually wrote—not what you meant
   to write. Make corrections directly on the page, referring to later chapters as necessary. How many errors did you find? _____
   _____

6. Check the draft one separate time for each kind of mistake you have a
   habit of making. Place a ruler under each line as you go. If you are
   unsure how to correct any errors that you find, consult later chapters.
   How many errors did you find? _____
   _____

7. What pages of later chapters do you think you should study first?
   _____ What pages do you think you should study
   second?_____

REWRITING: PROOFREADING YOUR FINAL COPY

After careful editing, copy or type your writing into its final form, the one you will give your reader. You will then be tempted to consider your work complete and go off to reward yourself with a movie or chocolate shake. STOP. Your writing is not complete until you have run a final check for errors you may have made while copying or typing. This final check is **proofreading**. Proofreading is important because all of us make copying or typing errors.

Writers proofread their final copy to check for careless errors made while recopying or typing.

TIPS FOR PROOFREADING

1. Before proofreading, leave your work for a few hours to refresh yourself and increase your chances of finding errors.

2. Proofread very slowly. Go too quickly and you will overlook errors because you will see what you wanted to write instead of what you actually did write. Point to each word and linger over it for a second to be sure you are not letting mistakes get by you.

3. Place a ruler under each line to keep the pace slow.

4. Ink in minor corrections neatly if your instructor permits. A page with many corrections should be retyped or recopied in the interest of neatness. (Neatness does impress a reader.)

WRITING WITH A COMPUTER

Most writers find that computers make composing more efficient. If you do not own your own computer, your school is likely to have a computer lab open to students; stop in.

Whether you already write with a computer or are new to the process, consider the following tips.

1. Learn your word-processing program thoroughly. If you must learn your school's program, ask a lab assistant for help. Write some practice pieces to get comfortable with all the commands and so you can concentrate on your writing without worrying about how the machine functions.

2. Work through the entire writing process at the computer, if you like. The planning, writing, and rewriting techniques you customarily use on paper can often be done at the machine.

3. To generate ideas, try freewriting with the screen dark. You are likely to make more keystroke errors, but you will be less likely to censor yourself, so ideas may flow more readily.

4. When you outline and revise, use your select and move functions to rearrange things.

5. Revise and edit both on the screen and on print copy. Looking at a screen gives you a different perspective from looking at print copy. If you consider both, you will do a thorough job.

6. When you edit, make full use of spelling and grammar checks that accompany your program, but remember, these are not foolproof or complete. You must still edit carefully on your own.

7. Do not be fooled by appearance—revise and edit carefully. Because the machine copy looks so good, you may think a draft is in better shape than it really is.

8. Back up your work frequently in case a power failure or other "catastrophic" event causes your work to disappear. For extra insurance, at the end of every session, print out everything you have written.

OBSERVING A STUDENT WRITER AT WORK

Now you will again consider the writing process, but this time you will do so by observing the various stages of a student writer's work in progress. You will follow the work of Will, who wrote about the effects of moving frequently when he was a child. As you see how Will moved from idea generation to finished essay, you will notice the following:

1. A writer often works through several drafts.
2. Effective writing has a central point.
3. Effective writing does not move away from its central point.
4. Effective writing has details in a logical order.
5. Effective writing is free of grammar and usage errors.

Planning: Generating Ideas

You have learned that writers cannot sit around waiting for inspiration. Instead, they must go after the ideas they need by using one or more idea-generation techniques.

Here is the clustering and brainstorming Will did when he worked to generate ideas. When Will was asked to write about an event or a circumstance that had a significant impact on him, he decided to write about being the son of a career soldier in the army, about being what he calls being an "army brat." To come up with a more specific topic, Will wrote the following clustering.

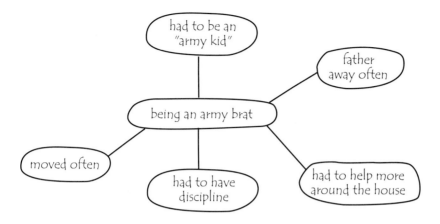

After considering his clustering, Will decided to write about the effects of moving frequently when he was a child. To come up with ideas to develop his topic, he wrote the following brainstorming list.

changed schools a lot
always behind or ahead in class
became self-reliant
lost friends
never felt I belonged
saw a lot of the country
learned to love change (?)
~~started to hate my father but outgrew it~~

Notice that when he reviewed his list, Will crossed out the last item because he decided he did not want to discuss it. Remember, during idea generation, you can add and delete ideas at any point. Also notice that Will placed a question mark next to a point he was not sure he wanted to discuss.

Planning: Establishing Audience and Purpose

To establish the audience and purpose for his writing, Will answered many of the questions on page 16. He decided that his audience would be his best friend, Tony. He characterized Tony as someone who knew that Will's father was in the army, but he did not realize how seriously Will was affected by the frequent moving around. He considered Tony to be a reader who would be interested in what he had to say.

Answering the questions on page 16 also helped Will establish his purpose as informing Tony about an important part of his life so that his friend would understand him better.

Planning: Ordering Ideas

To develop a scratch outline that would guide his drafting, Will numbered the ideas in his brainstorming list in the order he would write them up. Notice that in the process of doing this, he thought of another idea, which he added to the list (tell about Mike).

(1) changed schools a lot

(2) always behind or ahead in class

(3) never felt I belonged

(4) lost friends (tell about Mike)

(5) became self-reliant

(6) learned to love change (?)

(7) saw a lot of the country

Writing the First Draft

You learned that a first draft is usually rough because it is only a first effort. The following is Will's first, rough draft. Notice that to some extent Will departed from his idea-generation material and scratch outline. This is not unusual. Writers often go in new directions as ideas surface during the writing process.

One fact of my life rises above all others. My father is in the army. I spent my childhood moving from place to place. I lived from one end of the country to the other, I lived in New England, Alaska, and about seven states in between. This lifestyle has had a definite impact on me.

While travelling all over the country might sound exciting to you, it does have drawbacks. For one thing, I had to change schools every couple of years, which was really hard for me because I never knew how I would compare to the rest of the students academically. I also worried about fitting in and whether I would be treated like an outsider.

While the first few weeks in a new place were hard, the last ones were even worse because I had to say goodbye to friends who I know I would probably never see them again. This was the case when I had to leave my best friend, Mike. I met him my very first day of school in a brand new town. Mike was the only one who instantly made contact with me. We became inseperable from that moment on. Mike was like a brother to me, leaving him left a hole that no one has been able to fill. I'm not really sure why Mike and I somehow lost touch with each other, but I sure wish

I knew where he was now because I would write him and try to renew our friendship.

Although there have been these disadvantages, my life as an Army brat has had its good points too. I know much more about the United States and its people than the average person, I have seen more different kinds of people than anyone else I know except my father. I have become more self-reliant, I also learned how to cope with the loss of friends and how to make new friends fast. You can't move as many times as I have and be shy.

Long ago I decided I would never force my kids to move as often as I did, however, I notice that if I live in a place more than a few years I get restless. There is so much out there to see, I feel like I have only just begun to see it.

Reader Response to Will's First Draft.   Will's writing teacher read his first draft and gave him the following written response to consider when he revised. As you read it, consider whether you reacted similarly to the draft.

Will,

Your topic interests me because I have always wondered how people are affected by frequent moves in childhood. However, I need some more details to better understand the impact on you. In paragraph 2, tell me more about fitting in academically and socially. I would also like to know more about your friendship with Mike. I can tell he was important to you. Perhaps you could say more about how you met and the nature of your friendship. This information could replace the detail about losing touch with Mike, since that strays a bit from your focus. I like that you give the advantages as well as the disadvantages of moving often, but I could use more detail to better appreciate the positive aspects. Your last paragraph makes an excellent conclusion. It really helps me appreciate the restlessness you feel.

1. Are any of the instructor's reactions to Will's draft the same as your reactions? Which ones?

   _____

   _____

   _____

2. Do you disagree with any of the instructor's reactions? Which ones? Why do you disagree?

   _____

   _____

3. Do you have any reactions to Will's draft that are not noted in the instructor's comments? What are they?

_____

_____

_____

Rewriting: Revising the First Draft

Using his teacher's responses and his own ideas as a guide, Will revised to produce the following second draft. The changes are noted in the margin. Notice that Will focused on his detail when he revised this time.

One fact of my life rises above all others. My father is in the army. I spent my childhood moving from place to place. I lived from one end of the country to the other, I lived in New England, Alaska, and about seven states in between. This lifestyle has had a definite impact on me.

While travelling all over the country might sound exciting to you, it does have drawbacks. For one thing, I had to change schools every couple of years, which was really hard for me because I never knew how I would compare to the rest of the students academically.(A) Sometimes I was ahead of the class and sometimes I needed tutoring to catch up. I also worried about fitting in and whether I would be treated like an outsider(B) because my clothes were not right or I had an accent or I did not know the local slang.

Ⓐ Sentence added to explain not fitting in academically.

Ⓑ Words added to explain not fitting in socially.

While the first few weeks in a new place were hard, the last ones were even worse because I had to say goodbye to friends who I know I would probably never see them again. This was the case when I had to leave my best friend, Mike.(C) I met him my very first day of school in a brand new town. I walked into biology class in front of twenty-five strangers,

Ⓒ Detail added on relationship with Mike.

feeling that familiar fear and awkwardness as I made my way over to my new lab partner. Mike looked up from his frog and immediately made a wisecrack that made me laugh. As soon as school was over, we would meet in the woods behind his house and go exploring. We spent Saturdays biking around town, then we spent evenings at each other's houses. Mike was like a brother to me, leaving him left a hole that no one has been able to fill. Ⓓ

⒟ Irrelevant material omitted.

Although there have been disadvantages, my life as an Army brat has its good points too. I know much more about the United States and its people than the average person, I have seen more different kinds of people than anyone else I know except my father. ⒺI have fished alongside New England fishermen, and watched loggers in Washington and shrimpers in South Carolina. I have lived in an old farmhouse in the Midwest and in an old mill town in Ohio. I have played with kids whos houses line the shore of the Mississippi and kids who live in high rise apartments. ⒻMost importantly, I have become more self-reliant, I also learned to cope with the loss of friends and how to make new friends fast. You can't move as many times as I have and be shy.

ⒺThree sentences added to tell about people he met.

ⒻTransition added.

Long ago I decided I would never force my kids to move as often as I did, however, I notice that if I live in a place more than a few years I get restless, ⒼMy almost as if I am ready to move on. There is so much out there to see, I feel like I have only just begun to see it.

ⒼExplanatory words added.

To understand better the kinds of changes made during revision, answer these questions.

1. What do you think of the details Will added?

_____

_____

2. Do you think Will needs to add any additional details? Explain.

_____

_____

_____

3. What does revision G contribute to the essay?

_____

_____

4. Did Will solve the problem of irrelevant detail? Explain.

_____

_____

_____

5. Did Will make any ineffective revisions? Explain.

_____

_____

_____

Reader Response to Will's Second Draft

Will,

You did an excellent job of adding explanatory detail; your new material about meeting different people is particularly helpful and well written. I would still like to know more about your relationship with Mike and your efforts to fit in socially. Those points seem important. When you revise, read your introduction out loud to hear the choppiness. You should be able to smooth that out. When you edit, look for comma splices.

Revising and Editing the Draft

On the basis of his instructor's reactions to his second draft, Will did additional revising. Then he edited to eliminate errors in grammar and usage. The result was Will's final draft, which appears here.

(A) On the Move

(A) Title added.

(B) Because my father is in the army, I have spent most of my life moving from place to place. I have lived from one end of the country to the other, from New England to Alaska and about seven states in between. This lifestyle has had a definite impact on me.

(B) Intro revised to eliminate choppiness.

(C) While traveling all over the country might sound exciting to you, it does have drawbacks. For one thing, I had to change schools every couple of years, which was really hard for me because I never knew how I would compare to the rest of the students academically. Sometimes I was ahead of the class and sometimes I needed tutoring to catch up. I also worried about fitting in and whether I would be treated like an outsider because my clothes were not right or I had an accent or I did not know the local slang. (D) If I spoke too much, I could unintentionally say the wrong thing because I did not know the local customs. If I said too little for fear of offending, I was considered shy or conceited. As a result, I could never relax and feel like one of the gang.

(C) Spelling corrected.

(D) Detail added to further explain problems fitting in.

While the first few weeks in a new place were hard, the last ones were even worse because I had to say goodbye to friends (E) I knew I would never see again. This was the case when I had to leave my best friend, Mike. I met him my very first day of school in a brand new town. I walked into biology class in front of twenty-five strangers, feeling that familiar fear and awkwardness as I made my way over to my new lab partner. (F) Mike looked up from the frog he was dissecting and in a corny accent said, "Velcome, Igor—care for some

(E) Sentence structure revised and tense corrected.

(F) Mike's wisecrack given.

Ⓖ Spelling corrected.

Ⓗ Comma splice eliminated.

Ⓘ Comma splice eliminated.

Ⓙ Tenses corrected.

Ⓚ Comma splice eliminated.

Ⓛ Spelling corrected.

Ⓜ Comma splice eliminated.

Ⓝ–Ⓞ Comma splices eliminated.

lunch?" as he dangled the mutilated frog in front of my face. We were inseparable from that moment on. As soon as school was over, we would meet in the woods behind his house and go exploring. We spent Saturdays biking around town. Then we spent evenings at each other's houses. Mike was like a brother to me, and leaving him left a hole that no one has been able to fill.

Although there were these disadvantages, my life as an army brat had its good points too. I know much more about the United States and its people than the average person. I have seen more different kinds of people than anyone else I know except my father. I have fished alongside New England fishermen, and watched loggers in Washington and shrimpers in South Carolina. I have lived in an old farmhouse in the Midwest and in an old mill town in Ohio. I have played with kids whose houses line the shore of the Mississippi and kids who live in high rise apartments. Most importantly, I have become more self-reliant. I also learned to cope with the loss of friends and how to make new friends fast. You can't move as many times as I have and be shy.

Long ago I decided I would never force my kids to move as often as I did. However, I notice that if I live in a place more than a few years I get restless, almost as if I am ready to move on. There is so much out there to see, and I feel like I have only just begun to see it.

Thinking, Learning, and Writing in College   **Your Writing Process**

Students often think that the procedures they learn and use in writing class are suitable for that class only. In fact, you should use the successful procedures you discover in your writing class for all your writing tasks in all your classes.

WRITING ASSIGNMENT

You now understand that writers do not sit around waiting for inspiration. Instead, they work for their ideas using idea-generation techniques. Also, you know that writers expect to write and rewrite drafts until the composition is ready for a reader.

In addition to understanding how writers operate, you have also learned about some of the qualities of effective writing:

1. Effective writing has a central point.
2. Effective writing does not move away from its central point.
3. Effective writing has enough detail.
4. Effective writing has details in a logical order.
5. Effective writing is free of grammar and usage errors.

Now it is time to put your knowledge into practice by writing a paragraph. To develop a central point for this paragraph, fill in the blanks in this sentence:

The best way to _____ is _____.

You may fill in the blanks any way you wish. Here are some examples:

The best way to make friends on campus is to join the ski club.
The best way to shop is through a catalog.
The best way to impress a date is to plan the perfect picnic.
The best way to stay fit is to take up bicycling.

If you are unsure how to proceed, some or all of the following procedures may help.

PLANNING

1. Freewrite for 10–15 minutes and then list three reasons to support your view. (For other ways to generate ideas, see p. 2.)
2. Review your idea-generation material and make a list of the ideas you want to include.
3. Study your list of ideas. Do they lend themselves to a chronological (time) order, spatial (across space) order, or emphatic (from least important point to most important point) arrangement? Number the ideas in your list to correspond to the order you would like to have in your paragraph. Now you have a scratch outline.

WRITING

4. Using your scratch outline as a guide, write through your first draft in one sitting. Allow this draft to be rough. If you get stuck, skip the troublesome part and push on. To ensure a clear statement of your central point, begin your draft with the sentence with the filled-in blanks.

5. Take a break for at least several hours (a day would be even better) to clear your head so you can do a better job of revising.

REWRITING

6. Check each sentence in your draft against the first one. Be sure each sentence is directly related to your central point. If the relevance of a sentence is unclear, strike it or find a way to establish the relationship to your central idea.

7. Give your draft to someone whose judgment you trust. Ask that person to mark where more detail is needed. However, you have the final say. Do not add detail unless you decide the reader is correct in calling for more.

8. Leave your work for at least a few hours to clear your head. Then type or word-process your draft and reread it to see if problems you overlooked in your own handwriting are apparent in typed copy. Check especially to make sure the meaning of all your sentences is clear. Note: Reader response can be very helpful during revision. Refer now to p. 27.

9. What kinds of grammar and usage mistakes do you make? Edit one separate time for each kind of error. Then leave your work for at least a few hours. When you return, read your draft aloud to listen for errors. Place a ruler under each line as you go so you do not build speed.

10. Check spellings of any words that look misspelled.

11. Copy or type your paragraph into its final form. If you are tired after this, take a break before you proofread.

12. Proofread by pointing to each word and reading what you are pointing to. To ensure that you read exactly what is on the page, force yourself to linger over each word momentarily.

Chapter 2

Paragraph Basics

A **paragraph** is a group of sentences developing one central point. Most paragraphs have two parts: the sentence that presents the central point of the paragraph (the **topic sentence**) and the sentences that develop that central point (the **supporting details**). In addition, some paragraphs will have a **closing**, a sentence or two to tie things off neatly.

The two main parts of a paragraph are the topic sentence and the supporting details. A closing may also appear.

This chapter will help you learn how to write an effective paragraph. You will learn about

1. the structure of a paragraph
2. the need for adequate detail
3. the need for specific detail
4. the need for relevant detail

◆　◆　◆

A SAMPLE PARAGRAPH

As you read the following sample paragraph, decide which sentence presents the central point. That is the **topic sentence**. Also decide which sentences develop the central point. Those sentences are the **supporting details**.

A Lounge for Women over Thirty

Because so many women in their thirties, forties, and fifties are returning to school, our university should set up

The topic sentence presents the central point of the paragraph, and the supporting details develop the central point.

a special lounge area for these students. Women in this age group are often uncomfortable in the student union because they are surrounded by students no older than twenty-two or so. They are not interested in the upcoming rock concert or fraternity party, so often they find they have little to discuss with their younger counterparts. A special lounge would provide a meeting place for the older women. It would be a place they could go knowing they would find others who share the same interests and concerns. Also, this lounge would be a place these students could come together to help each other with their unique problems, the ones they face as a result of returning to school after a long absence. It would also provide a place for group study. Finally, because many returning to school after an absence need some brushing up, the lounge could be a place for tutoring activities. If the university provided this facility, this important group of students would feel more comfortable as they pursued their degrees.

1. Which sentence presents the central point of the paragraph? That is, which sentence is the topic sentence?

   _____

2. Most of the sentences after the topic sentence are the

   _____.

3. The last sentence is the _____.

If you identified the first sentence of the paragraph as the topic sentence, you were correct. This sentence provides the central point of the paragraph (the university should provide a lounge for female students over thirty). The remaining sentences (except the last) are the supporting details (they develop the central point). The last sentence is the closing (it ties the paragraph off neatly).

PRACTICE 2.1

Each group of sentences could be part of a paragraph. One sentence could be a topic sentence, and the others could be part of the supporting details. Write *TS* if the sentence could be a topic sentence, and *SD* if it could be part of the supporting details. Number 1 is done as an example.

1. _SD_ He humiliates players by yelling at them in front of fans.

_TS_ My nephew's baseball coach should be fired.

_SD_ The coach allows pitchers to give up too many runs before he pulls them out.

2. _____ Delays in arrivals and departures are at an all-time high.

_____ Baggage is routinely lost.

_____ Deregulation of the airlines has created several problems.

_____ Overbooking of flights is commonplace.

3. _____ Giant toads may weigh three pounds and grow to twelve inches.

_____ Giant toads have glands that secrete a poison strong enough to kill a dog.

_____ The number of giant toads in Florida is increasing.

_____ If you go to Florida, watch out for the giant toads.

4. _____ People can learn to manage their stress.

_____ Regular exercise helps control stress.

_____ Focusing on successes rather than defeats keeps stress in check.

_____ Talking things out with a sympathetic friend relieves stressful feelings.

5. _____ The eleven-month school year saves school districts money.

_____ The eleven-month school year will be commonplace in twenty years.

_____ The eleven-month school year keeps students from forgetting important concepts over a long summer recess.

_____ The eleven-month school year makes efficient use of staff and facilities.

6. _____ Saline is injected into the blood vessel.

_____ The procedure is quick, taking only a few moments.

_____ Sclerotherapy eliminates spider veins in the legs.

_____ Sclerotherapy involves only minor discomfort in most cases.

THE TOPIC SENTENCE

The **topic sentence** presents the central point of the paragraph. An effective topic sentence usually has two parts: a part that presents the writer's topic and a part that presents the writer's view of that topic. Here are some examples (the topic is underlined once, and the writer's view is underlined twice):

A topic sentence includes the writer's topic and the writer's view of the topic.

1. Property taxes are an ineffective way to finance public education.

2. Many people do not know how to relax.

3. I greatly admire my Aunt Hattie.

4. Changing my major from engineering to computer science proved to be a smart move.

5. Warrick Inn's best feature is its country charm.

PRACTICE 2.2

For each topic sentence, underline once the words that present the topic and underline twice the words that present the view of the topic. Number 1 is done as an example.

1. If you plan to purchase a new car, proceed cautiously.

2. Considering its size and location, the house is overpriced.

3. The aging shopping mall is exceptionally dreary.

4. The new state law requiring high school proficiency testing was not carefully thought out.

5. A stress management course should be taught on all college campuses.

6. If you ask me, nurses are the most underappreciated healthcare providers.

7. The auto workers' strike will have serious consequences throughout the economy.

8. Psychologists are coming to understand that birth order significantly affects personality.

9. Carlos Morales is the most qualified candidate for student government.

10. After the party, the living room looked like a war zone.

11. The effects of depression can be devastating.

Writing Effective Topic Sentences

You have learned that your topic sentences should include both a topic and your view of that topic. In addition, there are other points to remember.

Avoid topic sentences that are statements of fact or too broad. Also, avoid the formal announcement, vague language, and reference to the title.

1. **Avoid Statements of Fact.** A topic sentence that states a fact leaves you with nothing to say in the supporting detail. Consider these factual statements:

> I wake up every morning at 6:30.

> Education is very important.

> Soap operas are on in the daytime.

These are narrow statements of fact that offer no room for the writer's views. What can you say after noting that you wake up at 6:30? Who does not agree that education is important? How can you develop a whole paragraph about the fact that daytime TV includes soap operas?

Statements of fact can be rewritten to be more effective by including the writer's view:

I highly recommend waking up early each day.

To attract better teachers, we must pay higher salaries.

The number of daytime soap operas should be reduced.

2. **Avoid Very Broad Statements.** They are impossible to treat adequately in a single paragraph. Consider these statements:

The Vietnam War affected our country profoundly.

Our educational system must be revamped.

These topic sentences could not be managed in one paragraph. Broader statements like these require treatment in essays made up of several paragraphs.

3. **Avoid Vague Words.** Words such as *nice, interesting, great, good,* and *bad,* do not give your reader a clear sense of your view.

| vague: | Being a camp counselor last summer was great. |
| clearer: | Being a camp counselor last summer helped me decide to become a teacher. |

| vague: | Playing in piano recitals was awful. |
| clearer: | Playing in piano recitals made me feel self-conscious. |

4. **Avoid Formal Announcements.** Topic sentences like these are generally considered poor style:

This paragraph will discuss how to interview for a job.

I plan to explain why this university should offer a major in hotel management.

The following sentences will describe my first day of college.

Topic sentences like these are far more appealing:

Remember two points when you interview for a job.

A major in hotel management is needed at this university.

My first day of college was hectic.

5. **Avoid Using a Pronoun to Refer to Something in the Title.** If your title is "The Need for Campaign Finance Reform," avoid a topic sentence like this: "It is needed for a variety of reasons." Instead, write this: "Campaign finance reform is needed for a variety of reasons."

6. Place the Topic Sentence First. The topic sentence can actually appear anywhere in the paragraph. However, placing it first is convenient. You can try other placements as you become more experienced.

Thinking, Learning, and Writing in College

Highlighting Topic Sentences

If you like to study by highlighting or underlining portions of your textbooks, pay special attention to topic sentences. Because they convey a paragraph's central point, you will probably want to highlight or underline them.

PRACTICE 2.3

If the topic sentence is acceptable, write *OK* on the blank; if it is too broad, write *broad* on the blank; if it is a statement of fact, write *fact* on the blank; if the language is vague, write *vague* on the blank; if the sentence is a formal announcement, write *announcement* on the blank.

1. _____ The time I spent working as a hospital orderly was great.

2. _____ Computers are a fact of life.

3. _____ Living in a dorm is miserable.

4. _____ The most pressing problems facing us today are world hunger and overpopulation.

5. _____ I will explain here why I believe grading on the curve is unfair.

6. _____ Children need lots of attention.

7. _____ Professor Wu's group dynamics class is interesting.

8. _____ My paragraph will describe the campus commons at sundown.

9. _____ Two tricks will help a dieter maintain willpower.

10. _____ The Cameron triplets are very different: Jud is an optimist; Jake is a pessimist; Judy is apathetic.

PRACTICE 2.4: WORKING TOGETHER

With the members of your group, pick three of the unacceptable topic sentences from *Practice 2.3* and rewrite them to make them acceptable. Use a separate sheet.

PRACTICE 2.5

If the statement includes both the topic and view, write *OK* on the blank; if the topic is missing, write *topic;* if the view is missing, write *view.*

1. _view_____ It was so unexpected I was not sure what to do.

OK 2. ~~topic~~__ In my senior year, a championship basketball game taught me the true meaning of sportsmanship.

3. ___OK____ Job-sharing has benefits for an employer.

4. _topic___ I began my student teaching in a seventh grade study hall.

5. _view____ It was very depressing to be there.

topic 6. __OK___ The governor's tax bill will be voted on in November.

PRACTICE 2.6: WORKING TOGETHER

With the members of your group, select two of the unacceptable topic sentences in *Practice 2.5* and rewrite them on a separate sheet to make them acceptable.

PRACTICE 2.7

For each subject given, write an acceptable topic sentence. Remember to include both a topic and view. Also, avoid broad statements, statements of fact, vague language, and formal announcements. The first one is done as an example. (If you are stuck for ideas, try listing, brainstorming, clustering, or freewriting.)

1. pets _My calico cat, Cali, has an annoying habit._____

2. your favorite holiday _____

3. a childhood memory _____

4. a favorite teacher _____

5. your first day of college _____

6. television _____

PRACTICE 2.8

For each list of supporting details, write an acceptable topic sentence. Avoid broad statements, statements of fact, vague language, and formal announcements.

1. topic sentence _____

   _____

   A. Check local fashions and be sure your child dresses to conform to them.

   B. Ask the new teacher to assign a friendly classmate as a lunch or gym partner.

   C. Instruct your child to strike up conversations and not just wait for others to introduce themselves first.

   D. After a week, have your child invite one of his or her new classmates over after school.

2. topic sentence _____

   _____

   A. I wanted to study criminal justice.

   B. I was offered a scholarship to play football.

   C. I wanted to move away from home.

   D. My girlfriend was attending college.

3. topic sentence _____

   _____

   A. walls covered with grease stains

   B. pieces of cereal, cat food, and dried food all over the floor

   C. dried jelly and other, unidentified matter caked on the refrigerator door

   D. the smell of rotting garbage

4. topic sentence _____

   _____

   A. Running improves cardiovascular fitness.

   B. It helps manage stress.

   C. It helps maintain desired weight.

D. It can be competitive or noncompetitive, as the runner prefers.

5. topic sentence _____

_____

A. Professor Rios involves students in class discussions.

B. She gives extra help to those who need it.

C. She never criticizes anyone who makes an error.

D. She gives fascinating lectures.

THE SUPPORTING DETAILS

The **supporting details** develop the topic sentence. They are all the ideas (facts and opinions) you present to show why you have your particular view of your topic. Turn back to p. 45 and reread "A Lounge for Women over Thirty." Notice that the first sentence presents the writer's topic and view: the university should set up a lounge for female students over thirty. The sentences after the topic sentence are the supporting details, which explain why the university should set up the lounge.

Supporting details develop the topic sentence by explaining why the writer has the particular view of the topic. Supporting details should be adequate, specific, and relevant.

To be effective, supporting details should be *adequate, specific,* and *relevant.* These characteristics are discussed next.

Adequate Detail

To be effective, a paragraph must have enough supporting details so that the reader understands why the writer has his or her view of the topic. Thus, *adequate detail* means enough supporting details (facts and opinions) to develop the writer's topic sentence.

Read and think about this paragraph:

My high school biology teacher changed my life. He saw I was heading for trouble and straightened me out. He also helped me improve my grades so I could play basketball. In fact, he even helped me get into college. I will always be grateful to Mr. Friedman for being there when I needed help the most.

The paragraph begins with a fine topic sentence that includes both topic and view: the topic is the biology teacher, and the view is that he changed the writer's life. However, the supporting details are not adequate. Too few points are made to demonstrate that the topic sentence idea is true. The reader still needs information. How did the teacher straighten the writer out? How did he help the writer improve his grades? How did he help the writer get into college?

Supporting details must be adequate; the writer must supply enough information so that the reader understands why the writer has his or her view.

Now read and think about this revised paragraph:

9

My high school biology teacher changed my life. He saw I was heading for trouble and called me in after school one day. He explained that he cared what happened to me and wanted to help if he could. When I told him how depressed I was, he arranged counseling at the local mental health center. He also helped me improve my grades by showing me how to take notes and study efficiently. As a result, I regained my basketball eligibility. In fact, Mr. Friedman even helped me get into college by talking to admissions counselors on my behalf. I will always be grateful to Mr. Friedman for being there when I needed help the most.

You probably feel more satisfied after reading the revised version because necessary details have been added. The supporting details in the paragraph are now *adequate.*

PRACTICE 2.9

One of the following paragraphs has adequate detail. The others lack necessary information, so the reader will likely feel unsatisfied at the end. If the paragraph has adequate detail, write *OK* on the blank; if it does not have adequate detail, write *X* on the blank.

Darlene, the Practical Joker

_____ 1. My sister, Darlene, is a practical joker. She drives everybody crazy with her jokes. Once she played this amazing joke on my father. She spent months planning it so everything would work just right. Even though the joke only lasted a moment, Darlene felt it was worth the effort. However, I'm not sure Dad saw it that way. Another time Darlene almost lost her best friend because of a joke she played on her. The problem was that she embarrassed her friend in the school cafeteria. Last April Fool's Day Darlene hired a male stripper to crash my grandmother's seventy-fifth birthday party. What a scene that was! I sure wish someone would play a practical joke on Darlene so she could get a taste of her own medicine.

What a Bargain!

_____ 2. When I bought the '75 Mustang for $1800 I was sure I got a bargain until everything started going wrong. First, I had to pay a lot of money to have the engine repaired, and then I noticed how much body work was needed. Last week the suspension system was diagnosed as terminal, so there's more money I'll have to fork over for this four-wheeled "bargain." I'll never buy another used car again.

Adjusting to College

_____ 3. A new college student can expect to make several adjustments before the freshman year is over. First, the student must learn to cope with more freedom. Mom and Dad are not around to set a curfew or limit activities. This means the student has only a conscience to guide behavior. With this freedom comes more responsibility to adjust to. Mom and Dad may not be limiting activities, but they are also not around to wash clothes, remind the student of appointments, and force the student to study. This means the student better learn to take care of things or things just won't be taken care of. Finally, the student must learn to adjust to pressure. Exams, crazy roommates, registration hassles, and book lines are just some of what can cause tension. The student must learn to take the pressure of college life or forget that degree. Fortunately, most students make the necessary adjustments before the sophomore year begins.

PRACTICE 2.10: WORKING TOGETHER

Two of the paragraphs in *Practice 2.9* lack adequate detail. With some classmates, list details that could be added to help make the supporting details adequate.

1. Darlene, the Practical Joker

_____

_____

_____

_____

_____

2. What a Bargain!

_____

_____

_____

_____

_____

Specific Detail

Adequate supporting details are specific. Specific detail helps a reader form a clear, detailed understanding of the writer's meaning. The opposite of specific detail is general statement, which gives the reader only a vague sense of the writer's meaning. The following examples show the difference between general and specific.

general statement: The car went down the street.

specific detail: The 1962 Impala sedan rattled down Oak Street, dragging its tailpipe.

You probably formed a clearer picture in your mind when you read the sentence with specific detail. Also, you probably found the specific detail more satisfying than the general statement. Because specific detail is more satisfying and helps the reader form a clearer mental picture, strive for specific supporting details.

Use Specific Words

One way to provide specific detail is to use specific words. **Specific words** are more exact than general words, so they help the reader form a clear mental picture. Study the following lists of specific and general words to appreciate the difference between the two.

General Words	Specific Words
dog	collie
song	"Home on the Range"
book	*Tuesdays With Morrie*
music	jazz
run	sprint
said	shouted
take	grab

Now consider these two sentences to appreciate the difference specific words can make.

A. The young child was on the floor.

B. Ten-year-old Miro was sprawled across the living room floor.

Sentence B is more interesting because it gives the reader a clearer mental picture. This clearer mental picture comes from replacing the general words *young, child,* and *was on* with the more specific *ten-year-old, Miro,* and *sprawled across.* Also, the words *living room* are added to identify where Miro was.

To be sure your words are specific, choose specific nouns and verbs; also, use modifiers.

Specific Nouns:	Nouns are words for people, places, ideas, emotions, and things. Instead of general nouns like *movie, car,* and *restaurant,* choose specific nouns like *The Sixth Sense, Camaro,* and *IHOP*.
Specific Verbs:	Verbs are words that show action. Instead of general verbs like *went, spoke,* and *looked,* choose specific verbs like *raced, shouted,* and *glanced*.
Specific Modifiers:	Modifiers are words that describe nouns and verbs. Often you can use modifiers to make your detail more specific. Add the modifier *pounding* to describe the noun *rain,* and you get the specific *pounding rain.* Add the modifier *carefully* to the verb *stepped,* and you get the specific *stepped carefully.* When you use modifiers, be sure they are specific ones. Rather than the general "sang *badly,*" choose the more specific "sang *off-key*"; rather than the general "*nice* house," choose the more specific "*roomy* house".

PRACTICE 2.11

Next to each general noun or verb, write a more specific alternative. The first two are done as examples.

1. shoes ***penny loafers***

2. walk ***stroll***

3. drink _____

4. hit _____

5. college course _____

6. looking _____

7. house _____

8. said _____

9. flower _____

10. took _____

PRACTICE 2.12

Use one or more specific modifiers with each noun and verb. The first two are done as examples.

1. the sweater *the pink angora sweater*

2. study *study dilgently*

3. the commercial _____

4. drive _____

5. the rose _____

6. barking _____

7. the kitten _____

8. sang _____

9. the apartment _____

10. sleep _____

PRACTICE 2.13

Rewrite each sentence by using a more specific alternative for each underlined word and by following the directions in parentheses. The first one is done as an example.

1. The <u>dog</u> <u>went</u> down the <u>street</u>. (Add a specific modifier after the sub-

   stitute for *went*.) *The German shepherd dashed excitedly*

   down Laurel Ave.

2. The <u>man</u> <u>left</u> his <u>tools</u> on the <u>floor</u>. (Add a specific modifier before

   floor.) _____

   _____

   _____

3. Several <u>items</u> <u>of</u> <u>clothing</u> were scattered across the floor in Ralph's bedroom. (Add a specific modifier before *bedroom*.)

   _____

   _____

4. <u>A</u> <u>number</u> <u>of</u> <u>things</u> were good bargains at the garage sale. (Add a spe-

   cific modifier before *garage sale*.) _____

   _____

   _____

5. Jan decided to buy the car that Stavros was selling, even though it had
   <u>so</u> <u>much</u> <u>wrong</u> <u>with</u> <u>it</u>. (Add a specific modifier either before or after

   decided.) _____

   _____

   _____

6. The scouts <u>went</u> <u>away</u> from the campsite because it smelled <u>bad</u>. (Add

   a specific modifier before *scouts*.) _____

   _____

   _____

PRACTICE 2.14

Rewrite the sentences to make them more specific. Change general
nouns, verbs, and modifiers to specific ones, and add specific modifiers
where you wish. The first one is done as an example.

1. A variety of people were at the convention. *Executives, laborers,*

   students, and parents attended the third annual ham radio

   convention in Morgantown.

2. Rhoda and I worked hard in the yard. ~~The~~ *My daughter*
   Rhoda and I worked hard on
   mowing and raking the yard.

3. The dish I ordered at the restaurant tasted terrible. *The sirloin steak I ordered at TGI Fridays tasted terrible.*

4. The baby cried in the middle of the night. *The baby cried at 4:00am after being startled by lightning.*

5. The smell in Jim's apartment was awful. *Because of Jim's negligence to wash dishes, his apartment smelled awful.*

6. The view from the window was very nice. *The view of NYC through the penthouse window was wonderful.*

7. The heat made me miserable. *The one hundred and three degree weather was towrcher to my skin.*

8. The teacher helped the girl feel good. *By giving Jane some test taking advice, Mrs. Mein gave her confidence.*

9. The dog made so much noise that he kept me awake all night. *The barking Saint Bernard was so noisy he kept me up until three in the morning.*

10. The desk was in terrible condition. *After being used for twenty years the desk was in terrible condition.*

Follow General Statements with Specific Statements

Another way to make your supporting details specific is to follow general statements with specific ones. Here is a paragraph with general statements that are *not* followed by specific ones.

Myrtle Beach, South Carolina, is the perfect summertime family vacation spot. First, there is something for everyone to do. Also, there is a range of excellent accommodations, all reasonably priced. For those who like to take side trips, there are a number of places a person can see in just a day.

The detail in this paragraph is not adequate—there is not enough of it, so you probably come away feeling unsatisfied. To make the detail adequate, follow each general statement with one or more specific ones, as in the following revision. (The specific statements are underlined to make studying the paragraph easier.)

Myrtle Beach, South Carolina, is the perfect summertime family vacation spot. First, there is something for everyone to do. In addition to miles of beautiful beach and warm ocean to swim in, over three dozen fine golf courses are available. Fishing is possible from rental boats, off piers, and from the shore. For the kids, water slides, grand prix car and boat rides, dozens of beautiful miniature golf courses, and an amusement park provide hours of fun. For the confirmed shopper, an outlet park with 98 stores, three shopping malls, several plazas, and numerous specialty shops provide more than ample shopping. Also, there is a range of excellent accommodations, all reasonably priced. Hotel rooms are available and so are efficiency apartments. One-, two-, and three-bedroom condominiums are plentiful. In fact, you can stay in a beautiful three-bedroom condominium right on the beach for as little as $120.00 a night. For those who like to take side trips, there are a number of places a person can see in just a day. Picturesque Conway, beautiful Brookgreen Gardens, quaint Pawley's Island and Murrells Inlet, and historic Georgetown all make comfortable day trips.

Thinking, Learning, and Writing in College   **Identifying General and Specific Points**

Textbook discussions are often arranged with general statements followed by specific ones. If you like to underline or highlight as a study aid,, pay special attention to the general statements. They are prime candidates for marking because they usually convey major points.

PRACTICE 2.15

Follow each general statement with a specific statement. The first one is done as an example.

1. Six-year-old Leo and five-year-old Juanita were not getting along.

   They refused to share their toys and spent the afternoon arguing

   about everything from the best cartoon show to what game to play.

2. Suddenly the weather turned threatening. _____

   _____

   _____

3. Some television commercials insult the viewer's intelligence.

   _____

   _____

4. The cost of textbooks is outrageous. _____

   _____

   _____

5. Dr. Stone is a dedicated teacher. _____

   _____

   _____

6. The service at Harry's New York Deli is excellent. _____

   _____

   _____

PRACTICE 2.16: WORKING TOGETHER

With the members of your group, write three specific points that could be made after each of the following general statements. The first one is done as an example.

1. The students in third period history class were out of control.

   The students in the back were talking loudly among themselves.

   Two boys were roaming around the room.

   When the teacher called for order, the students talked back to him.

2. Dave treats people badly.

   _____

   _____

   _____

3. Driving with Chuyen is a frightening experience.

   _____

   _____

   _____

4. To succeed in college, students need effective study habits.

   _____

   _____

   _____

   _____

5. Baby-sitting for the Carlson twins aged me ten years.

   _____

   _____

   _____

6. The gale force winds caused extensive damage to the coastal town.

   _____

   _____

   _____

The following paragraphs lack specific details because general statements are not followed by specific ones. On a separate sheet, revise these paragraphs with some classmates by following general statements with specific ones.

1. Don't Eat at Joe's

     Joe's Eatery on Third Avenue is the worst restaurant in town. When I was there last Tuesday, I was appalled by the condition of the dining room. Also, the service could not have been worse. When my food finally arrived, I had to send it back because it was poorly prepared. Things at Joe's are so bad that I would not be surprised if the place went out of business soon.

2. How to Protect Your Health in College

     College students should be conscious of how to take care of their health. First, they should choose carefully what they eat in the dining hall. Also, they should schedule a regular exercise session. Equally important is building in some recreation time because too much work will lead to stress. Finally, students should know what to do in the event they do become ill on campus.

Relevant Detail

Relevant detail means that the supporting details are directly related to the topic and view presented in the topic sentence. Details that stray from the topic and view create a **relevance problem** (sometimes called a problem with **unity**.)

Supporting details must be relevant. This means they must be clearly related to the topic and view presented in the topic sentence.

The following paragraph has two relevance problems. As you read it, look for the supporting details that are not directly related to the topic sentence.

The Left-Handed Advantage

Left-handed people have the advantage in baseball and tennis. For one thing, left-handed batters are in a better position to run to first base. Left-handed first basemen also have an edge. At first base players often field balls hit to the right side of the infield. Of course, left-handed basemen wear their gloves on their right hands, so they can catch balls without moving around, the way right-handed players have to. Unfortunately, the left-handed third baseman does not enjoy the same advantage. In tennis, too, a left-handed player is fortunate. A right-handed player generally has little experience playing a lefty, but a lefty has considerable experience playing a righty. Thus, right-handed players will be more confused playing left-handed players than left-handed players will be playing right-handed players. This fact alone helps explain the large number of left-handed tennis champions. Outside of sports, lefties still face problems with door handles and radio knobs meant to be used with the right hand, with right-handed scissors, and with writing from left to right. Still, in sports, the left-handed athlete has an advantage.

You probably noticed two relevance problems in the paragraph. First, the sentence that says the third baseman does not have an advantage is not relevant because it does not relate to the point presented in the topic sentence: that left-handed people *do* have an advantage. Second, the sentence that discusses the problems lefties have outside of tennis and baseball with knobs, doors, scissors, and writing is not relevant because it does not discuss the advantage in tennis and baseball.

You should eliminate supporting details that are not relevant to your topic sentence, or alter the details to make them relevant.

PRACTICE 2.18

In the following paragraphs, draw a line through the details that are not relevant.

1. Not Necessarily

People say that the squeaky wheel gets the grease, but my experience proved otherwise. I had been working at Gas City for three years. I began ten hours a week as a regular gas jockey, but soon I was working thirty hours a week. Each of those hours was at minimum wage. I liked this job much better than the one I used to have making fries at Hot Dog House. Mr. Stanko, the boss, said I was one of the best kids who has ever worked for him. He said he trusted me, and he said I was a hard worker. About six months ago, he started asking me to open and close the station on occasion. I knew this was a real vote of confidence and decided the time was right to ask for a raise. I worked up my courage and politely made my request—which was not so politely refused. Then I decided to be a squeaky wheel. I asked once a week for a fifty-cent-an-hour raise. After my fourth request, Mr. Stanko said it was obvious I was very unhappy, so he was going to let me go. I was too proud to ask him not to, so I was out of work. I was an unemployed squeaky wheel, and there was no grease in sight.

2. Hank

    My friend Hank is a remarkable person. Although he was abused by his parents until he was sixteen and placed in a foster home, Hank is a kind, gentle guy. Studies show that abused children often become abusive adults, but Hank is different. He is a Big Brother to a fatherless child and treats this boy with love and compassion. He also works summers as a swim instructor at a local day camp, where he is a favorite among all the campers. He plans to major in math. Hank underwent three years of therapy to work through the problems that his parents caused. Clearly he has beaten the odds because he shows no signs of becoming abusive the way his parents were.

THE CLOSING

    Many times a final sentence is needed to bring the paragraph to a satisfying finish. This sentence is the **closing**.

    Often an appropriate closing suggests itself. However, if you are unsure how to handle your closing, write a sentence that refers to the topic and/or view presented in your topic sentence. For example, look at the closing of "The Left-Handed Advantage" on p. 65. Notice that this final sentence mentions the left-handed athlete; this refers to the topic noted in the topic sentence (left-handed people). Also notice that the closing mentions that left-handed people have an advantage in sports; this refers to the view in the topic sentence (having an advantage in baseball and tennis).

    Another way to handle the closing is to answer the question "So what?" about your topic sentence. The final sentence of "A Lounge for Women Over Thirty" on p. 46 takes this approach.

> A separate closing may be needed to give a paragraph a satisfying finish. This closing sentence can refer to the topic or the view presented in the topic sentence. It can also answer the question "So what?"

PRACTICE 2.19: WORKING TOGETHER

    The following paragraph lacks a closing. Work with some classmates to add a closing sentence that provides a satisfying finish. Use any approach you like, including the ones that have been described.

    Wildlife habitat destruction occurs in many ways. First, habitats are ruined when large areas are taken over for agricultural, residential, and industrial purposes. Some animals, like the mountain lion, have had their environments destroyed with the clearing of forests. Another factor leading to habitat destruction is pollution. Chemicals are released into the air and water, spoiling streams, rivers, and land environments. Finally, habitats are destroyed when people bring non-native plants and animals into an area. The non-native plant or animal may interfere with the careful balance of the native ecosystem.

_____

_____

_____

 A Paragraph Checklist

Before submitting your paragraph to a reader, be sure you can answer yes to the questions in the following list:

1. Do you have a topic sentence with your topic and view?

2. Is your detail adequate? Check each general noun, verb, and modifier. Are these appropriate, or should you find more specific alternatives? Do you have enough specific details?

3. Is all your detail relevant? Compare each sentence, one at a time, to your topic sentence and ask yourself if each is directly related to the topic and view.

4. Does your paragraph end in a satisfying way?

5. Have you edited carefully, more than once? Follow the editing procedures on p. 31. Leave nothing to chance—if you are unsure about a spelling, grammar, or usage point, consult Chapters 13–21 or your instructor.

6. Did you leave your work whenever you needed to rest and clear your head?

7. Did you proofread slowly and carefully, one word and punctuation mark at a time?

WRITING ASSIGNMENT

Write a paragraph that explains *one* influence a person has had on you. Before you begin this assignment, read the sample student paragraph and the tips that follow.

Megen

Because of a nine-year-old named Megen, I decided to major in physical therapy. I met Megen last quarter, when I worked as an orderly at St. Joseph's Hospital. She was only nine, but she had experienced more pain in those nine years than most people experience in a full lifetime. Megen was paralyzed, but she never used that as an excuse to stop trying. Each day I would wheel Megen down for her grueling physical therapy sessions. I would watch and encourage her as she worked through exercises that brought beads of sweat to her forehead and upper lip. Sometimes the pain was so great she cried, but she never stopped working as long as there was the slightest chance it would help. More than anything, Megen wanted to go to school and play with the other nine-year-olds, and she was willing to work as hard as she could for her dream. But it wasn't to be, for Megen died October 19th. I will never forget Megen's courage, for it showed me what I wanted to do with the rest of my life. It showed me that I wanted to be a physical therapist and help others strive for their dreams.

Like this sample paragraph, your paragraph will explain who influenced you, what that influence was, and how the influence occurred. Also, your topic sentence should name the person who influenced you (this will be your topic) and note what the influence is or was (this will be your view of the topic).

Before beginning your paragraph, read the following tips. One or more of them may prove helpful to you.

 TIPS FOR WRITING YOUR PARAGRAPH

Planning

1. To select a person and influence, think about your teachers, parents, coaches, clergy, friends, relatives, teammates, and neighbors. Do not limit yourself to the recent past, but think all the way back to your childhood. Consider your fears, wishes, ambitions, successes, failures, talents, and career plans. Did someone influence one of them? If you need help discovering ideas, try listing, brainstorming, clustering, journal writing, or freewriting. Once you have decided on the person and influence, fill in the blanks in the following sentence:

   Because of_____, I_____.

   Put the person's name in the first blank and the influence in the second blank to get something like this:

   Because of Uncle Harry, I am no longer afraid of high places.

   The sentence will remind you of your topic and view.

2. Answering these questions should prove helpful:

What happened?	Why is it important?
Who was involved?	How did it happen?
When did it happen?	What was the effect?

Why did it happen?   Will the effect continue?
Where did it happen?   Are you happy about the effect?

See p. 2 for additional idea-generation techniques.

3. Review the ideas you generated and make a list of the ones you would like to use. Check every point on your list against the sentence you developed when you filled in the blanks. Is each of your ideas relevant?

4. Study your list of ideas and decide on an appropriate order. Number the ideas in your list to reflect this order.

Writing

1. Begin with a topic sentence that names the person and the influence he or she has or had on you. This topic sentence can be a version of the planning sentence you developed when you filled in the blanks.

2. Using your list of numbered ideas as a guide, write through your first draft in one sitting. Do not worry about word choice, spelling, grammar, and punctuation. When you revise and edit, you can attend to these. If you get stuck, skip the difficult parts for now and go on.

3. After drafting, take a break for a day so you can be more objective when you revise.

Rewriting

1. Check your topic sentence to be sure it includes your topic (the person who influenced you) and your view of the topic (how that person influenced you).

2. Circle every general noun, verb, and modifier. If the circled words are too vague, find more specific alternatives.

3. Underline each general statement. Put parentheses around the specific statements that follow the general ones. Decide whether you have enough specific statements.

4. This might be a good time to take a break. When you return, check each sentence against the topic sentence to be sure all of your supporting details are relevant.

5. Give your draft to someone with good judgment about writing. Ask that person to mark where more detail is needed, where relevance is unclear, or where meaning is unclear. (See p. 26 for additional revision procedures, and p. 27 for more on using reader response.)

6. Take a break if you need one. When you return, type or word-process your draft. Problems you overlooked in your own handwriting may be apparent in type.

7. Edit one separate time for each kind of error you habitually make.

8. Read your draft out loud to listen for errors. Be sure you read *exactly* what is on the page, not what you *meant* to write. To avoid building too much speed, point with a pen to each word as you read and do not let your eyes move ahead of what you are pointing to.

9. Check the spelling of any word that might be misspelled. (See p. 31 for additional editing procedures.)

10. Copy or type your paragraph into its final form, and take a break before proofreading.

11. Proofread by pointing to each word on the page and reading what you are pointing to. Do not let your eyes move ahead and be very careful to read exactly what is on the page.

Note: Before submitting your paragraph, be sure you can answer yes to all the questions in the paragraph checklist on p. 67.

Visit the Clouse Website!

For additional exercises, quizzes,
and Internet activities, visit our Website at:

http://www.ablongman.com/clouse

For even more activities, visit the Longman English pages at:

http://www.ablongman.com/englishpages

Chapter 3

Narration

Narration is story-telling.

Narration is story-telling. You tell, hear, and read stories often. When you explain to your roommate what happened on your date last night, you tell a story. When your friend writes to you about the minor car accident she was in, you read a story. When you listen to a classmate tell what happened during the third quarter of the football game, you hear a story. (For examples of narration in essays, see "A Deadly Afternoon" on p. 161 and "On Being 17, Bright, and Unable to Read" on p. 447.)

◆　◆　◆

A SAMPLE NARRATIVE PARAGRAPH

The following narrative paragraph, written by a student, will be used to illustrate several points about narration:

Able-bodied but Addle-brained

I became very angry the day I saw an able-bodied woman get out of a car she had just parked in a handicapped space. Last Thursday I had just gotten out of my car in Kmart's parking lot when a woman in a beat-up Ford Fairlane swerved into a spot clearly marked for handicapped parking. She emerged with three children, all under six, and headed for the entrance. If she had a handicap, I saw no sign of it. I caught up with her and said, "Excuse me, but you parked in a handicapped spot." She just looked at me as if I had beamed down from Mars, and then she said that she was handicapped because she had three kids.

That made me furious. I yelled at her that if she considered her children handicaps, she should be investigated. Then I told her that I would report her to store security and ask that her car be towed. When I told the security police officer what happened, he said there was nothing he could do because she had not broken a law. I was so angry at the insensitive woman that I stormed out of the store without doing my shopping. If you ask me, any able-bodied person who parks in a handicapped space should have to spend a week in a wheelchair. I guarantee the person would be more careful about parking after that.

THE TOPIC SENTENCE

The topic sentence of a narrative paragraph includes the event to be narrated and how the writer feels about the event.

A topic sentence includes the writer's topic and the writer's view of the topic. In the topic sentence of a narrative paragraph, the topic is the event to be narrated. The view is how the writer feels about the event. Let's look again at the topic sentence of "Able-bodied but Addle-brained":

I became very angry the day I saw an able-bodied woman get out of a car she had just parked in a handicapped space.

Here the topic (the event to be narrated) is the day the able-bodied woman parked in a handicapped space. The view of the topic is that it made the writer angry.

One approach to expressing a view in a topic sentence for a narrative paragraph is to note why the story is important, as in this example:

An apartment fire last week that caused the death of three children underscores the need for family fire drills.

Here the topic (the event to be narrated) is an apartment fire causing the death of three children. The view of the topic explains why it is important to tell the story: it shows the need for family fire drills.

PRACTICE 3.1

The sentences that follow could be topic sentences for narrative paragraphs. Underline the topic (the event to be narrated) once and the writer's view of the topic (how the writer feels about the event or why the event is important) twice. The first one is done as an example.

1. The day my dog was killed I learned the importance of leash laws.
2. My most frightening experience occurred on a Boy Scout hike.
3. My family witnessed a surprising act of courage when our town flooded after Hurricane Floyd.

4. The need for gun education was made apparent by the recent accidental shooting of a three-year-old.

5. Mayor Fuentes's block watch program had an unexpected effect on
   one neighborhood.

6. When my little sister choked on a piece of steak, my mother sprang
   into action.

7. One of my happiest moments occurred when Dad taught me how to
   fish.

8. I felt like a hero when the Rayen Tigers won the City Series basketball
   championship.

9. My first day as a college student was hectic.

10. Getting my ham radio license was the high point of my year.

PRACTICE 3.2: WORKING TOGETHER

Working with some classmates, write a topic sentence for a narrative
paragraph about each of the subjects given. Remember to include the event
narrated and your view of the event or the importance of the event. The
first one is done as an example.

1. a first experience *My first baby-sitting job was a nightmare.*

2. a childhood memory _____

   _____

3. a school experience _____

   _____

4. a time spent with a friend _____

   _____

5. a holiday celebration _____

   _____

6. a time when you were disappointed (or pleasantly surprised)

   _____

   _____

SUPPORTING DETAILS

To develop supporting details for a narrative paragraph, you can answer these questions:

Supporting details for a narrative paragraph answer most or all of the questions, who? what? when? where? why? how?

Who was involved?	Where did it happen?
What happened?	Why did it happen?
When did it happen?	How did it happen?

Notice that the answers to most of these questions make up the supporting details for "Able-bodied but Addle-brained."

1. Who was involved?

   the writer and a woman

2. What happened?

   The writer became angry and had a confrontation with a woman who parked in a handicapped space.

3. When did it happen?

   last Thursday

4. Where did it happen?

   Kmart's parking lot

5. Why did it happen?

   The woman was insensitive.

6. How did it happen?

   This question is not answered. (A narrative paragraph sometimes answers most, but not all, of the questions.)

Supporting details in a narrative paragraph are arranged in a **chronological** (time) **order**. This means the details are arranged in the order that they occurred, so what happened first is written first, what happened second is written second, and so forth. (Chronological order is also discussed on p. 17.) Reread "Able-bodied but Addle-brained" and notice the chronological order.

PRACTICE 3.3

We have all had our embarrassing moments. Pick one of yours, and assume you will write a paragraph narrating what happened. To develop supporting details, on a separate sheet answer the who? what? when? where? why? and how? questions.

PRACTICE 3.4

To practice arranging details in chronological order, list on a separate sheet the first ten things you did today. Be sure to list the activities in the order they occurred.

Supporting details for a narrative paragraph are arranged in chronological order.

TRANSITIONS THAT SIGNAL CHRONOLOGICAL ORDER

Transitions are words that help the reader identify the order of ideas. Because you use chronological order when you write narration, now is a good time to review the transitions that signal this order in the chart on pp. 22–23.

PRACTICE 3.5

Read the following narrative paragraph written by a student and answer the questions after it:

A Deadly Afternoon

It was a rainy and miserable afternoon of my senior year, on May 19 to be exact, when a dramatic incident showed me what I wanted to do with my life. I was walking to my seventh period class when I noticed a disturbance in the hallway. Tom's girlfriend had broken up with him, and he was threatening to beat her up. He had pinned her against the wall, causing her to tremble violently. "Let her go!" I shouted as I grabbed for his arm. He squinted at me like he was having trouble focusing, and then he stormed away, muttering, "I'll make you sorry, both of you." At that point, the principal showed up, so I walked away. Before going to class, I stepped into the bathroom. Tom was there. At first I was scared, but then I noticed the blood spreading across his shirt and the knife on the floor. At that instant, Tom sagged to the floor. His skin had a blue cast, and the blood covered his chest. I ran to the door and screamed for help, but I was too late. Tom didn't make it. He was pronounced dead at the hospital. When I learned of his death, I realized how troubled people can be. I decided at that point to major in psychology and become a school counselor to help troubled kids like Tom.

On a separate sheet, answer the following questions about "A Deadly Afternoon":

1. What is the topic sentence? The writer's topic? The view?

2. Which of the who? what? when? where? why? how? questions are answered? What are the answers?

3. Are the supporting details adequate? Explain.

4. The writer chooses specific words. For example, instead of saying "afternoon," he says "seventh period." Cite four other examples of specific words.

5. Are all the supporting details relevant to the topic sentence? Explain.

6. Cite three examples of transitions to signal chronological order.

7. Does the author bring the paragraph to a satisfying close? What approach does the author use for the closing sentence?

Thinking, Learning, and Writing in College   Using Narration

You will have many occasions to use narration in other college classes. For example, on a history midterm, you may be asked to narrate the events that led to the Confederate defeat at Gettysburg. If you are an education major, you may be asked to observe in a classroom and record what goes on in chronological order. For a social work internship, you may be asked to write a case study that is a narrative account of the interaction you have with a client.

 Checklist for a Narrative Paragraph

Before submitting your narrative paragraph, be sure you can answer yes to all the questions in the following checklist:

1. Do you have a topic sentence that presents the event to be narrated and your view of the event?

2. Have you answered who? what? when? where? why? how? If one or more of these questions is unanswered, is it appropriate not to answer?

3. Have you used specific nouns, verbs, and modifiers?

4. Does every sentence advance the story?

5. If spoken words (conversation) are important to the story, have you included them and checked pp. 422–424 for correct punctuation?

6. Are your supporting details in chronological order?

7. Have you used transitions to signal chronological order?

8. Does your paragraph have a satisfying closing?

 ### *Tips for Planning Your Narrative Paragraph*

1. Brainstorm for ideas for your supporting details by answering the who? what? when? where? why? how? questions. See p. 2 for other idea-generation techniques.

2. Make a chronological list of everything that happened.

3. Decide how you feel about the event you are narrating or its importance. That will be your view. Now use that information to compose a topic sentence.

WRITING ASSIGNMENT

For your narrative paragraph, you have a choice of topics. If you choose one of the first seven topics, one of the topic sentences you drafted when you completed *Practice 3.2* may help. If you choose the eighth topic, the supporting details you developed when you completed *Practice 3.3* may help.

1. Tell a story about a first experience.

2. Narrate a childhood memory.

3. Narrate a school experience.

4. Tell a story about a time when you were angry.

5. Narrate an event that changed your thinking.

6. Tell a story about a time when you were disappointed.

7. Tell a story about a time when you were pleasantly surprised.

8. Tell the story of an embarrassing moment.

9. See p. 447 for narrative paragraph assignments based on the published essay "On Being 17, Bright, and Unable to Read." See p. 458 for an assignment based on "Money for Morality."

10. ***Respond to a photograph*** Assume you are a newspaper reporter and write a one-paragraph nnews article that narrates an account of the accident described in the photograph. Be sure to provide all the facts by answering the who? what? when? where? why? and how? questions. Also, write your news story in a way that will keep the reader's interest.

Bob Daemmrich/Stock, Boston

Visit the Clouse Website!

For additional exercises, quizzes, and Internet activities, visit our Website at:

http://www.ablongman.com/clouse

For even more activities, visit the Longman English pages at:

http://www.ablongman.com/englishpages

Chapter 4

Description

Description uses words to create a mental picture of a person, object, or scene. Thus, writers of description choose words and details that will most clearly paint that mental picture for the reader.

Description can be a part of many kinds of writing encountered every day. For example, your college catalog may describe the beauty of your campus, your biology text may describe the appearance of a cell, and a mail order catalog may describe the features of the clothing it is selling. (For an example of description in an essay, see "My Place of Solitude" on p. 162.)

A descriptive paragraph gives the reader a mental picture of a person, object, or scene.

◆　◈　◆

A SAMPLE DESCRIPTIVE PARAGRAPH

The descriptive paragraph that follows was written by a student. As you read it, notice how carefully words and details were chosen to paint a clear mental picture.

The Plant

The plant I work in five days of every week is extremely depressing. Everywhere I look, there are strips of peeling green paint, revealing the dingy gray underneath. The gloom is highlighted by bright gold sparks welders throw as they fuse cold steel. To the right of my work area, three men (more like robots) hang parts like garments on moving clothesline conveyors. They don't smile, and they don't talk. They just work. Behind the robot-men, hoses swell like arteries as they pump the foul-smelling lacquer paint to sprayers that change dingy gray metal to various colors. To my left, gray metal desks roll down a conveyor toward more robot-men, who wrap them in plastic. As the desks roll by, air tools scream as they drive screws to fasten parts, and giant presses pound, pound, pound as they gobble up steel to transform into useful shapes. Each day I remind myself that I will one day earn my degree, so I do not have to work in this depressing factory.

THE TOPIC SENTENCE

The topic sentence for a descriptive paragraph will include your topic and your view of the topic. The topic is what you describe; the view is your dominant impression of what you are describing. A **dominant impression** is your main reaction to what you are describing. Take another look at the topic sentence of "The Plant":

> The plant I work in five days of every week is extremely depressing.

The writer's topic (what is described) is *the plant where the writer works.* The writer's dominant impression of (main reaction to) the plant is that it is *extremely depressing.*

When you shape your topic sentence, keep your topic narrow enough for treatment in one paragraph. It would be difficult, for example, to describe your whole house in one paragraph, but you could describe your bedroom.

Also be sure to express your dominant impression in specific language. Avoid words like *nice, bad, great,* and *awful,* and use more specific alternatives like *peaceful, hectic, exciting,* and *run-down.*

The topic sentence for a descriptive paragraph mentions what you are describing and your dominant impression.

The topic should be narrow enough to be treated in one paragraph. The dominant impression should be expressed in specific language.

PRACTICE 4.1

Write a topic sentence for each of the subjects given. Include what you are describing and your dominant impression. Also, be sure your topic is narrow enough, and be sure your dominant impression is expressed in specific language. The first one is done as an example. (If you have trouble thinking of ideas, try listing or freewriting.)

1. a campus cafeteria at noon *At noon, the cafeteria in*

   Beeman Hall is a hectic place.

2. your bedroom _____

3. a particular outdoor area on campus _____

_____

4. a kitchen after a five-year-old has made breakfast _____

_____

5. a favorite restaurant _____

_____

6. your writing classroom_____

_____

SUPPORTING DETAILS

The supporting details for a descriptive paragraph are sensory details. **Sensory details** appeal to one of the five senses (sight, sound, smell, taste, and touch). Most of the details in "The Plant" appeal to sight, but some details appeal to sound ("air tools scream" and "presses pound"), one detail appeals to smell ("foul-smelling lacquer"), and one appeals to touch ("cold steel").

In a descriptive paragraph, words must be specific. The writer of "The Plant" chose specific nouns, verbs, and modifiers like these:

Descriptive details are sensory details.

In a descriptive paragraph, nouns, verbs, and modifiers are specific.

strips of peeling green paint   air tools scream
hoses swell like arteries   gobble up steel
giant presses pound   dingy gray

Now is a good time to review the discussion of specific word choice on p. 56.

PRACTICE 4.2: WORKING TOGETHER

With some classmates, write one description that could be used as supporting detail for each topic sentence. Be sure your words are specific. Also, try to appeal to a different sense in each sentence. The first one is done as an example.

1. Dan's old car is ready for the junk yard. *The tail pipe, eaten away by rust, hangs so low it almost scrapes the ground.*

2. The children's playroom is a disaster area. _____

3. The mall on Christmas Eve was hectic. _____

4. Eleni's backyard is beautifully landscaped. _____

5. The atmosphere of the Paris Cafe is romantic. _____

6. My grandmother's attic is spooky. _____

TRANSITIONS THAT SIGNAL SPATIAL ORDER

Descriptive paragraphs often have transitions that signal spatial order.

A spatial arrangement often works well for descriptive details. With a spatial arrangement, you move from front to back, from top to bottom, from inside to outside, from left to right, or in some other ordered way across space. To help your reader identify the spatial arrangement, use transitions that signal spatial order. These appear in the chart on pp. 22–23.

The writer of "The Plant" used transitions to signal spatial order. Some of these are listed here:

<u>To the right of</u> my work area

<u>Behind</u> the robot-men

<u>To my left</u>, gray metal desks

PRACTICE 4.3

The following descriptive paragraph was written by a student. Notice the specific words and the details that appeal to the senses. Answer the questions after the paragraph to check your understanding.

A View of Winter

The view from the window over my kitchen sink revealed the harsh winter we were enduring. Acres of yellowed field grass lay matted on the frozen ground. Trees that once stood majestically in the field were now stripped of their colorful foliage. Their naked limbs were straining under the pressure of the winter wind. Row after row of dried corn stubs stood erect, in silent testimony to the tall, productive plants they had once been. To the right, a gray, weather-beaten doghouse lay on its side, unable to protect its Irish setter any longer. Behind the useless doghouse, a child's swing, tossed by the wind, creaked a lonely tune. Overhead, gray, heavy clouds hovered close to the Earth like a shroud covering the lifeless scene. Then suddenly, a gust of wind parted a cloud, and the sun's warmth caressed my face to remind me to take hope. Spring would eventually arrive.

On a separate sheet, answer the following questions about "A View of Winter":

1. What is the topic sentence? According to the topic sentence, what will be described, and what is the dominant impression?
2. What senses are appealed to? Give an example of a description that appeals to each of these senses.
3. Give five examples of specific word choice.
4. Give three examples of transitions to signal spatial order.
5. Are all the supporting details relevant? Explain.
6. Does the paragraph come to a satisfying finish? Explain.

Thinking, Learning, and Writing in College   **Using Description**

Description is a frequent part of college writing. For example, in a music appreciation class, you may be asked to describe the melodies of various musical compositions. In an advertising class, you may need to describe magazine advertisements to point out their persuasive techniques. In a cultural anthropology class, you may be required to describe the ritual dress of a group of people. A sociology course may require you to describe living conditions of the homeless, and a biology lab may require you to describe a slide viewed under a microscope.

 Checklist for a Descriptive Paragraph

Before submitting your descriptive paragraph, be sure you can answer yes to the following questions:

1. Does your topic sentence mention what will be described and your dominant impression?
2. Is your topic narrow enough for one paragraph? Is your dominant impression expressed in specific language?
3. Have you used sensory details that appeal to as many senses as possible?
4. Have you used specific nouns, verbs, and modifiers?
5. Have you included enough descriptions to show why you formed your dominant impression?
6. Have you used transitions, especially spatial ones, where needed?
7. Are all your details relevant to both your topic and your dominant impression?

 Tips for Planning Your Descriptive Paragraph

1. Write an early version of your topic sentence that includes what you are describing and your dominant impression.
2. If you have trouble deciding on your dominant impression, complete this sentence:

   The place I am describing makes me feel _____.

   Fill in the blank with an emotion or mood (cheerful, depressed, nervous, excited, angry, scared, peaceful, etc.).

3. Make a list of the details to include. Try to include some descriptive words, but don't worry about getting the descriptions down in perfect form. For example, your list might include something like "smelled bad." Later you can revise that to a more specific "smelled like stale cigar smoke."

4. Number the ideas in your list in the order in which they will appear in your draft.

5. See p. 2 for additional idea-generation techniques.

WRITING ASSIGNMENT

Pick one of the following topics for your descriptive paragraph:

1. Use one of the topic sentences from *Practice 4.1*.

2. Describe a place you go when you want to be alone.

3. Describe your favorite nightspot.

4. Describe your study area or the library reference room.

5. ***Respond to a photograph.*** Assume you work for a travel agency and are preparing a travel brochure. Write a paragraph describing the outdoor scene in the accompanying photo. Your goal is to describe the place in a way that will make the readers of the brochure want to visit it. Also remember to include a topic sentence that conveys a dominant impression of the place you are describing.

Adam Woolfitt/Woodfin Camp & Associates

Chapter 5

Illustration

Writers and speakers use examples to make their points clear. Consider this conversation between Bob and Julio:

Bob: The food in this cafeteria stinks.
Julio: What do you mean?
Bob: The meat is always rubbery, the mashed potatoes are cold, and the Jell-O is hot.

To explain what he meant, Bob gave examples: rubbery meat, cold potatoes, and hot Jell-O. Another name for an example is an **illustration**. A paragraph with supporting details made up of examples is an **illustration paragraph**.

An illustration paragraph has examples for supporting details.

Because examples clarify points and make the general more specific, illustration is a frequent component of all writing, whether it is developed with description, narration, comparison, or some other approach. (For examples of illustration in essays, see "One Step Forward and Two Steps Back" on p. xxx and "Black Men and Public Space" on p. xxx.)

A SAMPLE ILLUSTRATION PARAGRAPH

The following illustration paragraph, written by a student, will be used to explain several points about illustration:

With My Head in the Clouds

As someone who is 6 feet 9 inches tall, I speak with authority when I say that the world is not set up for tall people. For example, everything that is supposed to be high is too low. Not long ago I was home for dinner with my parents. As I stood up from the table to go into the kitchen,

I slammed my head into the chandelier, causing the lights to sway wildly and my head to throb annoyingly for hours. Each time I enter a room, I must duck to avoid hitting my head on a door frame. Beds are also not made with the very tall in mind. I do not fit in a standard size bed, so I have to sleep diagonally across a double bed to keep my feet from dangling off the end. Cars are an even bigger problem. I have to recline my seat and push it back to keep my head from scraping the ceiling. Because this is so uncomfortable and a little bit dangerous, I often drive with the sunroof open so I can keep the seat in a proper position. Of course, there is still the problem of getting into the car. I will smash my head if I forget to fold myself over like an envelope. Most people think that height has its advantages, but on most days, I do not see them.

THE TOPIC SENTENCE

The topic sentence of an illustration paragraph includes the general statement that will be explained or clarified with examples. Like most sentences, it includes both a topic and the view of the topic. Consider this topic sentence from "With My Head in the Clouds":

> As someone who is 6 feet 9 inches tall, I speak with authority when I say that the world is not set up for tall people.

The writer's topic is tall people. The writer's view of that topic is that the world is not set up for them. The examples in the rest of the paragraph will show how the world is not geared for tall people.

PRACTICE 5.1

Write a topic sentence that could be developed with examples for each of the subjects given. Be sure to include a topic and view. The first one is done as an example. (If you have trouble thinking of ideas, try listing or freewriting.)

1. surprise parties *Surprise parties rarely go as planned.*

   _____

2. taking tests in school _____

   _____

3. first impressions _____

4. waiting in a doctor's office _____

_____

5. daytime television _____

_____

6. fast food restaurants _____

_____

SUPPORTING DETAILS

The supporting details for an illustration paragraph are examples that develop the topic sentence. Look again at "With My Head in the Clouds." The topic sentence presents this idea as the central point of the paragraph:

… the world is not set up for tall people.

To support this point, the author uses several examples:

Everything that is supposed to be high is too low. (the chandelier; door frames)

Beds are too small.

Cars are too small. (adjusting the seat; driving with the sunroof open; getting into the car)

To have adequate detail, use enough examples. To have specific details, use specific words and follow general statements with specific ones.

To have adequate detail, use enough examples to support your topic sentence. In one paragraph, three examples are usually enough. If they are highly detailed, two examples may be enough. In addition, use specific nouns, verbs, and modifiers to make your examples specific, and follow general statements with specific ones.

Sometimes examples can be effectively arranged in an emphatic or chronological order.

It is often effective to place your examples in emphatic order, saving your strongest example for last. (See p. 18 on emphatic order.) The examples in "With My Head in the Clouds" are in emphatic order. The clue to this is that the last set of examples is introduced with the words "an even bigger problem." If your examples occurred in a particular time order, you can arrange them in chronological order (discussed on p. 17).

PRACTICE 5.2: WORKING TOGETHER

Complete this practice with some classmates. Under each topic sentence, list three examples that can be used for supporting details. The first one is done as an example.

1. Ms. Lyons did more work than the average fifth-grade teacher.

   She took her class camping to collect leaf specimens.

   She visited a sick student at home to tutor her.

   She skips lunch to grade papers.

2. Tension is a part of a college student's life.

   _____

   _____

   _____

3. Cars can be more trouble than they are worth.

   _____

   _____

   _____

4. Television advertisements often mislead the public.

   _____

   _____

   _____

5. Parents sometimes take children where they do not belong.

   _____

   _____

   _____

6. Advertisements cause people to want products they do not need.

   _____

   _____

   _____

TRANSITIONS THAT SIGNAL ILLUSTRATION, ADDITION, AND EMPHATIC ORDER

In Chapter 1 you learned that **transitions** help the reader identify the order of ideas. When you write your illustration paragraph, three kinds of transitions may be helpful: transitions that signal illustration, transitions that signal addition, and transitions that signal emphatic order. These appear in the following chart:

Transition Chart

Transitions That Signal Addition	also, and, and then, in addition, too, furthermore, further, moreover, equally important, another, first, second, third …

The children hid from the babysitter at bedtime. *Another example* of their bad behavior occurred when they hid her car keys.

Transitions That Signal Illustration	for example, for instance, an illustration of this, to illustrate

Juan's math teacher is too easy. *For instance*, she has not assigned homework for at least a month.

Transitions That Signal Emphatic Order	more important, most important, most of all, best of all, of greatest importance, least of all, even better, the best (worst) case (example, instance, time)

Louise is often thoughtless. *One of the worst cases* of her thoughtlessness occurred when she did not pick up her six-year-old sister at school because she wanted to finish watching her soap opera.

PRACTICE 5.3

Reread "With My Head in the Clouds" on p. 86. Notice that most of the examples are introduced with a transition. On a separate sheet, list the transitions that introduce examples, and tell what each signals.

PRACTICE 5.4

The illustration paragraph that follows is a revision of a piece written by a student. Read it and answer the questions to test your understanding.

One Step Forward and Two Steps Back

Americans are proud of their technological advancements, but technology often comes with a price. Consider the cordless phone, for example. Yes, it gives us freedom to move around. However, more often than not, these phones cross frequencies with other phones so that we hear other people's conversations, and they hear ours. What we gain in mobility we lose in privacy. We also lose clear conversations, for these phones snap, crackle, and pop more than most breakfast cereals. The Internet is another example. It offers computer users almost limitless access to a staggering amount of information. However, users are so glued to their computer screens day and night that they no longer have a life away from their PCs. Once on the information highway, people become so obsessed that they do not take the exit ramp. Another example, one that I read about, concerns the computer-designed magnesium wheels General Motors put on its cars not too long ago. Thanks to a computer error, the tire seals did not fit properly. As a result, thousands of car owners woke up to discover that their brand new cars had flat tires. Certainly, technological advances make life easier, but they are not without their problems.

On a separate sheet, answer the following questions:

1. What is the topic sentence of "One Step Forward and Two Steps Back"? What is the writer's topic? The view of the topic?
2. How many examples does the writer use?
3. Are the supporting details adequate? Explain.
4. Are all the supporting details relevant? Explain.
5. List the transitions that introduce examples and tell what they signal.
6. Does the paragraph have a satisfying closing? Explain.

Note: For the essay version of "One Step Forward and Two Steps Back," see p. 163.

Thinking, Learning, and Writing in College   Using Illustration

Because examples are so important for clarifying points, you will use illustration frequently in your college writing. For example, in a political science course, you could use examples of campaign funding abuse in a research paper about how our presidential races are financed. In a paper for an education class about alternative schools, you could cite examples of successful and unsuccessful charter schools. A midterm exam in a business class might ask you to explain and illustrate three kinds of management techniques, and an examination in a literature class might ask you to define and illustrate *irony*.

Checklist for an Illustration Paragraph

Before submitting your illustration paragraph, be sure you can answer yes to all the questions in this checklist:

1. Do you have a topic sentence that presents your topic and view?
2. Do you have enough examples to support your topic sentence?
3. Have you used specific nouns, verbs, and modifiers?
4. Have you followed general statements with specific ones?
5. Have you used transitions to move from example to example?
6. Does your paragraph have a satisfying finish?

 Tips for Planning Your Illustration Paragraph

1. If you need help discovering ideas, freewrite for 10–15 minutes (see p. 9).
2. Place each example at the top of a column. Under each example, list the details you will include to develop the example.
3. Write an early version of your topic sentence. Be sure it includes your topic and your view of the topic.
4. Number the examples in the order in which they will appear in your first draft. Consider whether a chronological or emphatic order is desirable.
5. See p. 2 for additional idea-generation techniques.

WRITING ASSIGNMENT

You have a choice of topics for your illustration paragraph:

1. Write an illustration paragraph with one of the topic sentences from *Practice 5.1* or *5.2.* You may be able to use some or all of the examples you generated when you completed *5.2.*
2. Write a paragraph illustrating one of the personality traits of someone you know. First, pick a person (your best friend, a boss, your cousin,

a neighbor, a teacher, etc.). Then decide on a personality trait (greedy, generous, optimistic, lazy, ambitious, sloppy, neat, stubborn, fair, cooperative, loving, etc.). Your supporting details will be examples of the person showing the trait.

3. Use examples to illustrate the following:

High school did (or did not) prepare me for college.

4. Use examples to illustrate the following:

Things are not always what they seem.

5. See p. 468 for an illustration paragraph assignment based on "Time to Look and Listen." See p. 453 for an assignment based on the published essay "My Way."

6. ***Respond to a photograph.*** Use the accompanying photograph as a starting point, and think about the fact that the shopping malll has become more than a place to purchase items; it has become a place to have fun. Then write a paragraph that illustrates that the shopping mall is a source of entertainment.

Barbara Peacock/FPG International

Chapter 6

Process Analysis

A process analysis explains how something is made or done, or how something works.

A **process analysis** explains how something is made or done, or how something works. For example, a biology textbook uses process analysis to explain how plants turn carbon dioxide into oxygen. A recipe uses process analysis to explain how to make a dish; instructions packaged with a toy tell how to put the toy together; and magazine articles explain how to save money on home mortgages or how to improve a marriage. (For examples of process analysis in essays, see "Making Money with a Garage Sale" on p. 165 and "Green Frog Skin" on p. 459.)

◆　◆　◆

A SAMPLE PROCESS ANALYSIS

The following process analysis, a revision of a piece written by a student, will be used to illustrate several points.

Making Money with a Garage Sale

If you plan it right, you can make a great deal of money from a garage sale. First, you must gather all the saleable items collecting dust in your basement and attic. Do not include anything badly broken, but keep everything else. The items you think are the most worthless are likely to be the first to sell. Toys and tools are hot sellers, but clothes (unless they are children's) probably will not sell very well. Next—and this is very important—clean this junk up. Dirty items will not sell, but you will be surprised at the weird stuff that goes if it is clean. Once your items are clean, it is important to display them properly, so get lots of tables, even if you have to rent them. Arrange everything attractively, trying to keep housewares together, toys together, and so forth. Now for the most important part, pricing. I have just three words of advice: cheap! cheap! cheap! Remember, this trash has been in your basement collecting spider eggs for the past five years, so do not get greedy. Price it to move because the last thing you want to do is drag this stuff back in the house because it did not sell. If you really want a great sale, advertise. Put signs up and place an ad in the classifieds. Finally, pamper your customers by providing grocery bags for carrying those marvelous purchases home in, and by serving coffee—for twenty-five cents a cup, of course. Believe me, follow this advice, and you can turn your unwanted items into extra cash.

THE TOPIC SENTENCE

The topic sentence for a process analysis includes the topic and view of the topic. The topic is the process. The view of the topic can explain why you think the reader should understand the process. Look again at the topic sentence of "Making Money with a Garage Sale":

> If you plan it right, you can make a great deal of money from a garage sale.

In this case the topic (process to be explained) is having a garage sale. The view of the topic (why the reader should understand the process) is that, with the right planning, there is money to be made.

The topic sentence of a process analysis mentions the process that will be explained and why the reader should understand the process.

PRACTICE 6.1

For each topic sentence, tell the process to be explained and why the reader should understand the process. The first is done as an example.

1. If you want to keep your sanity, register the way I do.

    Process *registration (registering the way the author does)*

    Reason to understand process *to keep sanity*

2. To get the best value for your money, shop carefully for a used car.

   Process _____

   Reason to understand process _____

3. In order to survive, every baby-sitter should know how to handle children who act like monsters.

   Process _____

   Reason to understand process _____

4. To move up the corporate ladder, you must learn how to network.

   Process _____

   Reason to understand process _____

5. College students must learn how to relax so the pressures of studying do not overwhelm them.

   Process _____

   Reason to understand process _____

6. To have a successful garden, you must plan carefully.

   Process _____

   Reason to understand process _____

SUPPORTING DETAILS

Supporting details for a process analysis are the steps performed. Sometimes the writer must also explain what is *not* done or how to perform a step.

The supporting details for a process analysis are the steps in the process. Look back at "Making Money with a Garage Sale," and you will see that the supporting details are all the things a person must do—all the steps that must be performed—in order to have a profitable garage sale. A brief description of items needed to perform the process is sometimes included as well.

Sometimes it is necessary to include something that should *not* be done, as a warning to the reader. For example, in "Making Money with a Garage Sale," the reader is cautioned not to include badly broken items.

If the proper way to perform a step is not clear, you should explain. Notice in "Making Money with a Garage Sale" that the writer explains how to display items properly—use lots of tables, arrange things attractively, and keep like things together.

Finally, the supporting details for a process analysis are most often arranged in a chronological (time) order. This means the steps are given in the order they are performed.

The supporting details are usually arranged in chronological order.

PRACTICE 6.2: WORKING TOGETHER

With some classmates, pick three of the following processes. On a separate sheet, list the steps performed in each of these processes.

1. checking a book out of your campus library
2. picking an advisor
3. registering with a minimum of trouble
4. buying a used car
5. planning a party
6. failing an exam (be humorous)
7. Christmas shopping at the last minute
8. editing
9. interviewing for a job
10. using a search engine

TRANSITIONS THAT SIGNAL CHRONOLOGICAL ORDER

If the supporting details in your process analysis are arranged in chronological order, you should signal that order with transitions (see p. 22). Notice that in "Making Money with a Garage Sale," the writer uses several transitions to signal chronological order:

First, you must gather ...
Next—and this is very important ...
Now for the most important part ...
Finally, pamper your customers.

PRACTICE 6.3

The following process analysis was written by a student. Study it and then answer the questions that follow.

Taming Final Examinations

To succeed in college, students must know how to study for final examinations. First, you should set up a review schedule about two weeks before exam week begins. To do this, divide your work up among all the available study days; decide what you will study each day and for how long. This way, nothing will be left to chance. Next, develop a new approach to your studies so the material does not seem stale. For example, pretend you are an instructor and study the material so you can teach it. Outlining the course is also a good idea. However, do not make your outline too long, or all your time will go into writing it. Instead, keep it to about three pages. The thought you put into the outline will serve as review. Study the textbook, class notes, quizzes, previous tests, and class handouts regularly, each day of the two weeks if possible. The night before the test, review everything. However, do not stay up too late, or you will be too tired to do well. On the day of the final exam, you can feel confident that you have prepared well, and nothing beats exam jitters better than confidence.

On a separate sheet, answer the following questions about "Taming Final Examinations":

1. What is the topic sentence? What process will be analyzed? Why is it important to understand the process?
2. Where does the writer explain how to perform a step?
3. Where does the writer say what not to do?
4. In what order are the supporting details arranged?
5. The writer uses two transitions to signal chronological order. What are they?
6. Are all the steps in the process clearly explained?
7. Are all the supporting details relevant to the topic sentence?
8. Does the essay come to a satisfying close? Explain.

Thinking, Learning, and Writing in College   Using Process Analysis

You will have many opportunities to use process analysis in your college writing. For example, in an economics class you might have to explain how a market economy works. A biology midterm could require you to explain how positive and negative reinforcement work, and a linguistics course could require you to explain how words change meaning.

Checklist for a Process Analysis

Before submitting your process analysis, be sure you can answer yes to the following questions:

1. Do you have a topic sentence that mentions the process and why the reader should understand the process?
2. Have you included every step in the process?
3. Where necessary, have you explained how steps are performed?
4. If it is important, have you explained what *not* to do?
5. Have you used specific nouns, verbs, and modifiers?
6. Are supporting details in a chronological or other suitable order? Have you signaled the order with transitions?
7. Are all of your details clearly relevant to the topic sentence?
8. Does your paragraph have a satisfying closing?

 Tips for Planning Your Process Analysis

1. Write an early version of your topic sentence that mentions the process and why the reader should understand the process.
2. List every step performed in the process—do not leave anything out.
3. Is there anything the reader should be careful not to do? If so, add that to your list.
4. Number the steps in your list in the order they are performed.

WRITING ASSIGNMENT

For your process analysis paragraph, you have your choice of topics:

1. Use one of the processes in *Practice 6.2*. For three of these, you have already listed the steps performed.
2. Use one of the topic sentences in *Practice 6.1*.
3. Pick something you do better than many people and describe that process.
4. Explain how to deal with jealousy.

5. ***Respond to a photograph***. The college student in the accompanying photograph shows signs of stress. Decide why the student is stressed and then write a paragraph explaining a process for dealing with that stress.

Akos Szilvasi/Stock Boston

Visit the Clouse Website!

For additional exercises, quizzes, and Internet activities, visit our Website at:

http://www.ablongman.com/clouse

For even more activities, visit the Longman English pages at:

http://www.ablongman.com/englishpages

Chapter 7

Definition

A **definition** explains the meaning of something. Most often when we think of definitions, dictionary meanings come to mind. However, here we are considering definitions that do more than the typical dictionary entries. We are considering the longer, more detailed piece that explains the meaning of complex terms or ideas. For example, to help explain the United States's political system, a political science text can define *electoral college* in one or more paragraphs.

Sometimes a writer wants to express his or her personal meaning for a term. For example, stress can mean different things to different people. To express *your* meaning, you can define stress from a college student's point of view.

For examples of definition in essays, see "Runner's High" on p. 166, "On Being 17, Bright, and Unable to Read" on p. 447, and "My Way!" on p. 451.

◆   ◆   ◆

A SAMPLE DEFINITION PARAGRAPH

The following definition, written by a student, will be used to illustrate several points about writing definition. As you read, notice that the paragraph presents the writer's personal meaning.

A definition paragraph explains a complex term or the writer's personal meaning of a word.

The Crazed Coupon Clipper

The crazed coupon clipper is a fanatic. Fired up at the prospect of saving a few quarters, this species accumulates hundreds, even thousands, of cents-off coupons. Strangely though, it does not even matter if the clipper can use the products the coupons are good for. My father has been a crazed clipper for years. His coupon envelope marked "pets" is so fat with coupons for dog biscuits, cat food, and flea collars you would think we had dozens of cats and dogs running around. The funny thing is, we have not owned a dog, cat, or any other four-legged animal since I was born. While the clipper may appear to be organized (having coupons arranged alphabetically in labeled envelopes), do not be fooled—every crazed clipper has grocery bags, shoe boxes, and crates hidden at the back of the closet with unfiled, largely expired coupons jammed in. The clipper is harmless for the most part; however, the species can be dangerous when turned loose in a market that offers double-coupon savings. Stay out of these places, for dozens of crazed clippers will be there with glazed eyes and fistsful of coupons. So ecstatic are they at the prospect of doubling their savings that they race their carts frantically about, snatching products in a savings frenzy. More than once, normal shoppers have been run over by clippers crazed by the thought of saving twice as much. So beware! If ever you open your newspaper only to find rectangular holes where the news used to be, you no doubt have a crazed coupon clipper under your roof.

THE TOPIC SENTENCE

The topic sentence of a definition paragraph includes the term being defined and a main characteristic of the term.

The topic sentence for a definition paragraph includes the term being defined (this is your topic) and a main characteristic of what is being defined (this is your view of the topic). Take another look at the topic sentence of "The Crazed Coupon Clipper":

The crazed coupon clipper is a fanatic.

The writer's topic is the *coupon clipper;* this is the term to be defined. The main characteristic of the coupon clipper is that he or she is a *fanatic;* this is the writer's view of the topic.

PRACTICE 7.1

Write topic sentences for paragraphs defining each of the terms given. Be sure to mention a main characteristic of what you are defining. The first one is done as an example.

1. optimism *Optimism is the ability to think postively even*

    when things look the worst.

2. the exercise fanatic _____

    _____

3. exam anxiety _____

    _____

4. courage_____

    _____

5. an intellectual _____

    _____

6. the Monday blues _____

    _____

SUPPORTING DETAILS

The supporting details for a definition paragraph develop the characteristic of the term being defined. One way to do this is to use description. "The Crazed Coupon Clipper" relies on description to show what the clipper is like in a store that offers double-coupon savings.

> The supporting details for a definition paragraph develop the characteristic of the term being defined.

Examples can also be part of your supporting details. In "The Crazed Coupon Clipper," the writer's father is an example that shows the clipper clips coupons for products that are not used.

> The supporting details may include description and examples.

If your audience has a misconception about what you are defining, you may explain what something is *not*. For example, when defining *patriotism*, you may explain that patriotism is *not* a blind love of every aspect of a country. After this explanation, you can go on to explain what patriotism *is:* loving a country while disliking its faults and trying to correct them. In "The Crazed Coupon Clipper," the writer explains that the clipper is not really as organized as he or she appears.

> The supporting details may mention what something is *not*.

Try not to write a definition that sounds as if it really came from a dictionary. For example, if you are defining *freedom,* avoid saying "Freedom is the state of being at liberty or free of confinement." The definition should be in your personal writing style. Also, avoid stating the obvious. For example, if you are defining *situation comedy,* do not say that it is a kind of tele-

> Do not write a definition that sounds like it came from a dictionary, and do not state the obvious or use a term in its own definition.

vision program. Finally, do not use a term in its own definition. If you are defining a *floppy disk,* do not say, "A floppy disk is a disk that. . ."

PRACTICE 7.2: WORKING TOGETHER

Complete this practice with some classmates. Assume you are writing a definition paragraph with this topic sentence:
Writer's block is the curse of the writing student.

1. List three ideas that could be used for supporting details. (If you are stuck for ideas to complete numbers 1–4, try one or more of the idea-generation techniques.)

   _____

   _____

   _____

2. List an example that could be used to develop one of the ideas you wrote for number 1. _____

   _____

3. List three details that could be included in a description of a student with writer's block._____

   _____

   _____

4. Mention one thing that writer's block is not._____

   _____

PRACTICE 7.3

The following definition paragraph was written by a student. Read it and answer the questions that follow.

Christmas Spirit

Christmas spirit is a joyous feeling that results from the anticipation of a wondrous celebration. It is a feeling of excitement as you walk through the mall and realize Christmas carols are filtering through the speaker system. It is the tingle you get when your eyes catch the snow and tinsel shimmering in store windows draped in red and green. When you step outside and feel the brisk, cold wind brush your face, Christmas spirit is the hope for a white December 25, the hope for the beauty of quarter-sized snowflakes floating down to blanket a frozen earth. Christmas spirit is the joy of helping people. It is Mr. Jones shoveling the walk of an elderly neighbor or Mrs. Smith distributing loaves of her Christmas bread to shelters and halfway houses or children collecting toys for the poor. No, Christmas spirit has not been commercialized as some say. It is the special excitement people feel as they look forward to the one day of the year devoted exclusively to peace and love.

On a separate sheet, answer the following questions about "Christmas Spirit":

1. What is the topic sentence of "Christmas Spirit"? According to the topic sentence, what term will be defined, and what is the main characteristic of the term?
2. Which two sentences provide description?
3. Which sentence provides examples?
4. Give three examples of specific word choice.
5. Where does the writer explain what Christmas spirit is *not?*
6. Has the writer avoided obvious statements? Has the writer avoided a dictionary style?
7. Are the supporting details adequate? Explain.
8. Are all the details relevant? Explain.
9. Does the paragraph come to a satisfying close? Explain.

Thinking, Learning, and Writing in College   Using Definition

Every course you take has the potential to require writing definition. In a criminal justice class, you might have to define *reasonable force* or *civil disobedience;* in a literature class, you might have to define *symbolism* or *stream-of-consciousness*; in a labor studies class, you might have to define *mutual gains bargaining*. For a media course, you might write a paper defining *pornography*, for a women's studies class, you might write a paper defining *sexual harassment*, and for a philosophy course, you might write a paper defining *morality.*

Checklist for a Definition Paragraph

Before submitting your definition, be sure you can answer yes to every question in the following list:

1. Do you have a topic sentence that mentions the term to be defined and a main characteristic of the term?

2. Have you provided enough supporting details to convince your reader that the main characteristic is what you say it is?

3. Have you used description and examples where these would be helpful?

4. If necessary, have you explained what the term is *not*?

5. Have you avoided stating the obvious? Have you avoided a dictionary style?

6. Have you used specific nouns, verbs, and modifiers?

7. Are all your details relevant to your term and its main characteristic?

8. Does your paragraph have a satisfying closing?

 Tips for Planning Your Definition Paragraph

1. Brainstorming answers to these questions may be helpful:

   What are three characteristics of what I am defining?

   What, if anything, can I describe?

   What examples can I provide?

   What is my topic *not*?

   What is my topic similar to?

   What is my topic different from?

   What does it look like? Sound like? Feel like?

   Why is it valuable?

   What can it be used for?

2. Write an early version of your topic sentence. Be sure it mentions what will be defined and a main characteristic.

3. Make a list of ideas you will include and number them in the order they will appear in your draft.

4. See p. 2 for additional idea-generation techniques.

WRITING ASSIGNMENT

Here is a choice of topics for your definition paragraph:

1. Define one of the terms in *Practice 7.1*. If you choose one of these, you already have a draft of a topic sentence.

2. Define writer's block. If you choose this, you may be able to use some of the ideas you developed for *Practice 7.2*.

3. Define a college student.   7. Define jock.

4. Define pressure.   8. Define freshman.

5. Define blind date.   9. Define friendship.

6. Define working mother.   10. Define tacky.

11. See p. 457 for a definition paragraph assignment based on "Money for Morality" and p. 464 "The Company Man."

12. ***Respond to a photograph***. Using the accompanying photograph for one source of ideas, define *glamour* or define *style*.

William Strode/Woodfin Camp & Associates

Chapter 8

Comparison and Contrast

A comparison shows similarities; a contrast shows differences; a comparison and contrast shows both similarities and differences.

A paragraph that **compares** shows how two things are similar, a paragraph that **contrasts** shows how two things are different, and a paragraph that **compares and contrasts** shows both similarities and differences. Comparison and contrast are important because they often help us decide which of two people or things is better. For example, by comparing and contrasting two political candidates, we can decide who to vote for. By comparing and contrasting two cars, we can decide which to buy. Comparison and contrast also help us better understand the items compared and contrasted. For example, by comparing and contrasting the workings of the human brain and a computer, we can better understand the operation of both.

For examples of comparison and contrast in essays, see "Identical but Different" on p. 167, and "If You Had to Kill Your Own Hog" on p. 472.

◆　◆　◆

SAMPLE COMPARISON AND CONTRAST PARAGRAPHS

The following paragraphs were written by students. They will be used to illustrate several points about comparison and contrast.

Shake the Image of the Sheik

The Arab sheik is nothing like his media image. As a result of media portrayal, the sheik is commonly considered to have a protruding paunch, bulging eyes, and a hawklike nose. He sports a bushy mustache and headdress. The sheik is typically thought to be self-indulgent and cruel to others. He is thought to live a life of luxury and lust amid oil wells and harems of beautiful women. His days are said to be spent in idleness and his nights in reckless passion. In reality, the sheik is very different. Physically, his looks and dress vary. He can be dressed in western clothes. He can be thin, with small eyes and flat stomach. He is a dedicated man, who often sacrifices much to his people. He is a Muslim religious leader, scholar, or head of an Arab family, clan, tribe, or village, respected for his leadership abilities and wisdom. In the ancient Middle East, the sheik was the one people went to for advice. He was the head of the institutions that controlled law, religion, and education. He was not and is not the arrogant womanizer who struts around the desert, leading a life of leisure and comfort. That image was created by Hollywood directors and is unfair and untrue.

Identical but Different

My twin sister, Loretta, and I look very much alike, but we have very different personalities. Because we look so much alike, Loretta and I are frequently mistaken for each other by teachers and those who do not know us well. We both wear our curly, auburn hair to the shoulder. We both are just over five feet, and weigh about the same. Our facial features mimic each other, although I think Loretta is prettier, and she thinks that I am, so I guess it is a toss-up. From our earliest days, we became accustomed to responding to "Hey Twin" because people cannot tell us apart. On the other hand, our personalities have always been different. As children, Loretta liked beautiful Barbie Dolls in sophisticated, feminine outfits, and I preferred rugged G. I. Joes in full battle gear. Loretta would always want my G. I. Joes to be boyfriends for her Barbie Dolls. Of course, I would never consent to such a thing. Another difference was apparent in school, where Loretta was the more serious student. When we had class together, she would be listening attentively to the teacher. However, I was busy passing notes and planning the night to come. Predictably, Loretta's grades were always excellent, and mine were rather ho-hum. As adults, my twin is quiet and conservative and always seems to do the right thing. In contrast, I am outgoing and adventurous--and always in trouble. Thus, while Loretta and I may look identical, inwardly we are very different people.

THE TOPIC SENTENCE

The topic sentence for comparison and contrast includes the writer's topic and view. It can also indicate whether the paragraph will compare, contrast, or both.

The topic sentence for comparison and contrast includes the writer's topic and view of the topic. The topic is the items to be compared and/or contrasted. The view can be how the writer feels about the items. Take another look at the topic sentence of "Shake the Image of the Sheik":

The Arab sheik is nothing like his media image.

The writer's topic is the Arab sheik. The writer's view is that there is a difference between the media image of the sheik and the real sheik.

Now look at the topic sentence of "Identical but Different":

My twin sister, Loretta, and I look very much alike, but we have very different personalities.

The topic is the author and her twin sister. The writer's view is that they look alike but have different personalities.

Notice that both topic sentences indicate whether the paragraph will compare, contrast, or both. The first topic sentence makes clear that the writer will contrast, and the second topic sentence makes clear that the writer will compare and contrast.

PRACTICE 8.1: WORKING TOGETHER

With some classmates, write a topic sentence for each subject, being sure to give topic and view. Indicate whether the paragraph will compare, contrast, or both. The first one is done as an example.

1. two friends *My friend Jeremy is always optimistic, but Phyllis constantly expects the worst.*

2. two teachers _____

_____

3. two television comedies _____

_____

4. two ways of studying _____

_____

5. two birthday celebrations _____

_____

6. high school and college _____

_____

SUPPORTING DETAILS

When you compare, your supporting details explain the ways the items are alike; when you contrast, your supporting details explain the ways the items are different; when you compare and contrast, your supporting details explain the points of similarity and the points of difference. Be careful, however, to avoid statements of the obvious. For example, if you contrast your history and science teachers, it would be silly to note that they teach different subjects.

Avoid statements of the obvious.

ORDERING SUPPORTING DETAILS

Your supporting details can be ordered two ways: subject-by-subject or point-by-point. In a **subject-by-subject pattern**, you say everything about your first subject and then you go on to say everything about your second subject. "Shake the Image of the Sheik" follows this pattern. First the writer explains the popular image, and then she explains what the sheik actually *is* like. An outline of this paragraph using the subject-by-subject pattern looks like this:

A subject-by-subject pattern discusses first one subject and then the other. The same points should be discussed for both subjects.

I. Popular image

   A. Appearance

   B. Personality

   C. Lifestyle

II. Reality

   A. Appearance

   B. Personality

   C. Lifestyle

Notice that the writer discusses the same points (appearance, personality, lifestyle) for both subjects. You too should discuss the same points for both subjects.

The point-by-point pattern alternates between subjects. The points discussed for one subject should also be discussed for the other.

The ideas in the contrast part of "Identical but Different" are ordered in a **point-by-point pattern**. A point is made about one subject and then it is made about the second subject. Another point is made about the first subject and then it is made about the second, and so on. Here is an outline of the contrast portion of that paragraph:

I. As children
   A. Loretta
   B. Author

II. In school
   A. Loretta
   B. Author

III. As adults
   A. Loretta
   B. Author

Notice that with the point-by-point pattern, too, the writer must treat the same points about both subjects.

If you want to discuss both similarities and differences, you can do what the writer of "Identical but Different" does. You can briefly mention the similarities and then go on to explain the differences using a point-by-point pattern.

To compare and contrast, first mention the similarities and then explain the differences using a point-by-point pattern.

PRACTICE 8.2

1. Read "Let's Hear It for Tradition" on p. 114. The supporting details are arranged in a point-by-point pattern. To understand this pattern better, complete the following outline of the paragraph.

I. Number of people
   A. In the past
   B. Now

II. Food preparation
   A.
   B.

III. Opening gifts
   A.
   B.

IV.

    A.

    B.

2. Read "College Is Not What I Expected" on p. 114. The supporting details are arranged in a subject-by-subject pattern. To understand this pattern better, complete the following outline.

  I. What college was expected to be

    A. Fun

    B. Meeting people

    C.

  II. What college really is

    A.

    B.

    C.

TRANSITIONS THAT SIGNAL COMPARISON AND CONTRAST

The transitions in the following chart signal comparison and contrast.

Transition Chart

Transitions That Signal Comparison	similarly, in like manner, likewise, in the same way
	The college football coach must have years of experience before he becomes a head coach. *Similarly,* a professional football coach is an assistant coach for a long time before taking on the top spot.
Transitions That Signal Contrast	in contrast, however, on the other hand, on the contrary, conversely, but
	I thought motherhood would be nothing but bliss. *However*, I soon learned it is a trying time.

PRACTICE 8.3

There are three transitions of contrast in "Identical but Different" (p. 109). On a separate sheet, write the sentences that contain these transitions; underline each transition.

PRACTICE 8.4

The following paragraphs were written by students. Read them and answer the questions that follow.

College Is Not What I Expected

Now that I have been a college student for half a year, I can say that college is not what I thought it would be. After being accepted at YSU, I thought about all the fun I would have living away from home. I figured I would meet a lot of new people and do a lot of new things. I never had much trouble with my high school classes, so I did not think college work would be too tough. After being here a short time, I know I was wrong. I have not had much fun yet. Most of the nightlife centers around bars, and I am not much of a drinker. I have been to a few parties, but everyone seems to know everyone else, and no one knows me. I usually stand around with my roommate, and usually we go home early without meeting anyone. Most of the time I cannot go out anyway because I have to study so much. The homework keeps me up late at night, and still it is a struggle to get Cs. Everyone tells me I need more time to adjust to college life, so maybe things will look up for me soon, and college will be more like I expected it to be.

Let's Hear It for Tradition

The Christmas gatherings we used to have at my grandparents' house were much better than the celebrations I now have at my house. It used to be that all the aunts, uncles, and cousins gathered for a festive reunion. Now the gathering is just my husband, my children, and me. In the past, every family brought a tasty dish, so no one had too much work to do. Now I spend days knocking myself out making turkey with all the trimmings. My aunts used to bake scrumptious cobblers and pies to go with all the traditional holiday cookies. Somehow my children's iced trees and stars do not compare, although they are special in their own right. At my grandparents' there was a ritual for opening gifts that took the whole afternoon. Everyone took turns opening one gift at a time. This stretched out the excitement and allowed everyone a chance to ooh and aah. In contrast, my children rip into their gifts in record time without savoring anything. There was conversation and laughter at my grandparents'. Everyone tried to catch up on what had happened since the last gathering. Now, however, we talk about what we talk about any other day. I miss the old gatherings. However, Grandma and Grandpa and most of the aunts and uncles are gone, and the rest of us are too scattered around the country to have many gatherings.

1. What is the topic sentence for each paragraph? What does each topic sentence mention as the topic and the view of the topic? Do the topic sentences indicate the writer will compare, contrast, or do both?

2. For each paragraph indicate whether the detail is arranged in a subject-by-subject pattern or point-by-point pattern.

3. In each paragraph, are the points discussed for one subject also discussed for the other?

4. Does either paragraph include statements of the obvious?

5. In "Let's Hear It for Tradition," what transitions signal contrast?

6. Does either paragraph have a problem with adequate or relevant detail? Explain.

7. Do the paragraphs come to a satisfying close? Explain.

Thinking, Learning, and Writing in College

Using Comparison and Contrast

By comparing and contrasting, writers can evaluate subjects. For this reason, it is a frequent component of college writing. For example, an exam in an art appreciation class may require you to compare and contrast the styles of two Renaissance painters, and an exam in an exercise physiology class could require you to compare and contrast two methods of strength training. A research paper in economics might involve comparing and contrasting socialism and capitalism, while a report in a history class could require you to compare and contrast the foreign policies of two presidents, and one in an education class could involve comparing and contrasting two methods of reading instruction.

 Checklist for Comparison and Contrast

Before submitting your paragraph, be sure you can answer yes to every question on the following list:

1. Does your topic sentence mention your topic (what will be compared and/or contrasted) and your view of the topic?

2. Have you avoided obvious comparisons and contrasts?

3. Have you ordered your details with either a point-by-point or subject-by-subject pattern?

4. Have you discussed the same points for both subjects?

5. Have you used transitions, especially of comparison and contrast, where these are needed?

6. Have you used specific nouns, verbs, and modifiers?

7. Are all supporting details relevant to the topic sentence?

8. Does your paragraph have a satisfying closing?

 ### Tips for Planning Your Comparison and Contrast

1. List every comparison and/or contrast you can think of without evaluating the worth of your ideas. Then go back and circle the ones you want to use. Remember, you cannot mention everything, so stick with the key points. (If you have trouble thinking of ideas, try some of the idea-generation techniques.)

2. Write an early version of your topic sentence that mentions what will be compared and/or contrasted and your view.

3. Outline your ideas. Use the point-by-point pattern or the subject-by-subject pattern, modeled on pp. 111-112. If you are mentioning many points, a point-by-point pattern may be easier for your reader to follow. As an alternative, place each of your points on a separate index card. Arrange the cards in either a point-by-point or a subject-by-subject pattern and write your draft from the cards.

WRITING ASSIGNMENT

To keep your paragraph manageable, explain just the differences between two subjects. If you want to treat similarities or both similarities and differences, speak to your instructor first. Also, be sure to keep your focus narrow. You probably cannot discuss all the differences in a single paragraph, so limit yourself to a few key ones.

Here is a choice of topics:

1. Use one of the topic sentences you wrote for *Practice 8.1.*

2. Contrast any of the following:

> two ways of dieting
>
> two ways to ask for a date
>
> two ways to study
>
> two automobiles

two situation comedy characters

two soap opera characters

the techniques of two athletes who play the same sport

3. Contrast the way something is (or was) with the way you thought it would be.

4. ***Respond to a photograph.*** The accompanying photograph shows a family from the 1950s. Using that photograph for ideas if you like, contrast some aspect of family life today with that aspect of family life during an earlier time. For example, you can contrast the role of the mother today and during the 1950s, your family vacations today and when you were a child, styles of disciplining children today and in the 1960s, and so forth.

Lambert/Archive Photos

Visit the Clouse Website!

For additional exercises, quizzes,
and Internet activities, visit our Website at:

http://www.ablongman.com/clouse

For even more activities, visit the Longman English pages at:

http://www.ablongman.com/englishpages

Chapter 9

Cause-and-Effect Analysis

A **cause-and-effect analysis** explains why something happens (causes) or the results of an event (effects). Because people need to understand why events occur and the effects of those events so they can better understand their world, cause-and-effect analysis occurs frequently. For example, to analyze cause, a biology textbook can explain why leaves turn color in autumn, or a magazine article may explain why women live longer than men. To analyze effects, a newspaper editorial may predict the results of passing a tax bill, or a medical journal may explain the results of using a particular medication.

For examples of cause-and-effect analysis in essays, see "What Happened When I Quit Smoking" on p. 168, "On Being 17, Bright, and Unable to Read" on p. 447, "Students in Shock" on p. 443, "The Company Man" on p. 462, "Time to Look and Listen" on p. 465, and "Black Men and Public Space" on p. 482.

◆　◆　◆

SAMPLE CAUSE-AND-EFFECT ANALYSES

Each of the following cause-and-effect analyses was written by a student. The first paragraph explains causes, and the second explains effects. These paragraphs will be used to illustrate points about cause-and-effect analysis.

Fitness and the Media

The media are causing people to feel dissatisfied with their bodies. At any time of the day or night, a half dozen aerobics or weight training programs are on television. The people on these shows do not have normal bodies—they have super bodies. Normal channel surfing folks see these people and instantly feel inadequate. Commercials are no better. They are loaded with bodies beautiful selling Nordic Tracks, exercise videos, and health spa memberships. One look at these people and a perfectly healthy, reasonably fit person feels hopelessly out of shape. Leafing through a magazine does not bring any relief, either. The pages are filled with ads for Slimfast and articles about how to cut fat. Of course, all are illustrated by bodies with 0% body fat, so the reader, no matter how fit and trim, feels like a whale. It is time the media bombardment stopped because it is causing people with perfectly fine bodies to feel dissatisfied with themselves.

What Happened When I Quit Smoking

When I quit smoking two years ago, I was miserable. First of all, I gained fifteen pounds. As a result, I looked terrible, and I was like a sausage in a casing when I wore my clothes. Even worse, I was so irritable no one could stand to be near me. I snapped at people and picked fights with my best friend. Once I screamed at my girlfriend and called her a nag when she reminded me to go buy my mother a birthday present. I did not mean it, but she spent the rest of the night in tears. For the first month, I was actually hallucinating. I would turn suddenly, thinking I heard a sound, or jump up startled, feeling like something clammy had touched me. At night I would wake up in a cold sweat after dreaming about smoking a Winston. It has been two years since I have had a cigarette, and I am in much better shape now, but I still have some weight to lose and in social situations I still get a little jumpy.

THE TOPIC SENTENCE

The topic sentence for a cause-and-effect analysis can mention your topic and whether you are treating causes or effects. For example, look again at the topic sentence of "Fitness and the Media":

The media are causing people to feel dissatisfied with their bodies.

The writer's topic is the media. The topic sentence indicates that causes will be explained since it is stated that the media are *causing* people to feel dissatisfied with their bodies.

Now look at the topic sentence of "What Happened When I Quit Smoking":

When I quit smoking two years ago, I was miserable.

Here the topic is the time the writer quit smoking. The words *I was miserable* present an effect that will be explained.

PRACTICE 9.1

The topic sentence mentions the topic and suggests whether causes or effects will be explained.

For each of the following subjects, write a topic sentence for a cause-and-effect analysis. Then indicate whether the paragraph will explain *causes* or *effects*. The first one is done as an example. (If you cannot think of ideas, try one or more of the idea-generation techniques.)

1. homelessness *Both economic and social factors can*

   lead to homelessness.—causes

2. losing a job _____

   _____

3. exam anxiety _____

   _____

4. moving to a new city _____

   _____

5. working while attending school _____

   _____

6. teenage pregnancy _____

   _____

SUPPORTING DETAILS

The statement of cause or effect is a general statement that should be followed by one or more specific statements. The specific statements can be explanation, examples, description, or narration.

Each time you mention a cause or an effect, think of that sentence as a general statement that must be followed by one or more specific statements (see p. xx for a discussion of following general statements with specific ones). The specific statements can be explanation, illustration, description, or narration. For example, look again at "Fitness and the Media." The first cause is given in the general statement, "At any time of the day or night, a half dozen aerobics or weight training programs are on television." This is followed by specific explanation that the people on these shows make others feel inadequate.

Now look again at "What Happened When I Quit Smoking." The general statement of the first effect is gaining fifteen pounds. This is followed by the specific description of looking like a sausage in a casing. Sometimes a general statement of cause or effect is followed by a brief narration. This is the case when the writer follows the general statement of being irritable with the story of making his girlfriend cry. Examples, too, can follow a general statement of cause or effect. Notice that after the general statement of hallucinations as an effect, the writer gives a specific example of a hallucination.

Do not assume that an earlier event is the cause of a later event. For example, if a university builds new residence halls and then experiences an enrollment increase, you may be tempted to assume that the residence halls *caused* the increase. However, other factors may be the cause: a new recruitment campaign, a tuition decrease, or an increased unemployment rate.

> Do not assume that an earlier event caused a later event, and remember that an event may have more than one cause or effect.

Finally, remember that most events have more than one cause or effect. You need to consider all possibilities. The enrollment increase may actually be the result of the new residence halls, the recruitment campaign, the tuition decrease, *and* the unemployment rate.

PRACTICE 9.2: WORKING TOGETHER

Complete this practice with some classmates. After each topic sentence, write one cause or one effect (whichever is appropriate) in a general statement. Then note a specific point that could be made after the general statement. The first one is done as an example. (If you need help discovering ideas, try the idea-generation techniques.)

1. Our football team is doing poorly for three reasons.

   general statement: *Many of our starters are inexperienced freshmen.*

   specific point: *Nichols, the quarterback; Sanders, the end; Zanders and Michaelson in the backfield are all first-year players.*

2. Jan is failing history, and no one is surprised.

   general statement: _____

   _____

   specific point: _____

   _____

3. The rate of teenage drinking has increased for a number of reasons.

   general statement: _____

_____

specific point: _____

_____

4. Owning a pet can be beneficial.

general statement: _____

_____

specific point: _____

_____

5. Several benefits will come from raising teacher salaries.

general statement: _____

_____

specific point: _____

_____

6. If the school levy does not pass, the result will be disastrous.

general statement: _____

_____

specific point: _____

_____

TRANSITIONS THAT SIGNAL EFFECT

These transitions signal that one thing is the result of another:

as a result	hence	because
consequently	therefore	then
thus	for this reason	

Look again at these sentences from "What Happened When I Quit Smoking": "First of all, I gained fifteen pounds. *As a result,* I looked terrible." The italicized transition signals that what comes after it is a result of what comes before it. If your paragraph explains effects, you will probably use some of the transitions in the preceding list.

PRACTICE 9.3

Here are two cause-and-effect analyses written by students. Read them and answer the questions that follow.

Why Children Grow Up Too Fast

The reasons children become sexually active at an early age are clear. For one thing, there is a great deal of peer pressure for sexual experimentation. I know one fourteen-year-old who ran around with sixteen- and seventeen-year-olds. The older kids made it clear that to be accepted, the fourteen-year-old would have to demonstrate her maturity by sleeping with a particular seventeen-year-old. Parents are also a contributing factor. Parents are now more open with their sexual displays and speech. They tell dirty jokes in front of children and tease about sex in front of them. Parents are also more lenient. They are letting their children wear makeup, date, and wear mature fashions at a younger age, all of which lead to growing up faster. Finally, the greater sexual explicitness of rock lyrics has caused children to mature faster. These lyrics teach kids that sex is expected and virginity is outdated. Thus, it is no surprise that today's youth are engaging in sex at an early age.

Raising the Driving Age

Recently, there has been some discussion about raising the driving age from sixteen to seventeen, and perhaps even eighteen; however, I believe that raising the driving age would have negative consequences. First of all, many teenagers hold jobs that require them to drive distances to get to work. If sixteen-year-olds cannot drive, they cannot work, and if they cannot work, then they cannot bring extra income into the family. This could create a financial hardship in some cases. Furthermore, teens who do not work are more likely to get into trouble because they have too much time on their hands. You might think that parents, particularly mothers, could drive their teenagers to work, but both mothers and fathers are working these days and unavailable to drive their children around. Also, because both parents work now, teenage drivers are a real help. The working mother, in particular, appreciates having a sixteen-year-old around to help with errands. Take away the sixteen-year-old's license and the already overworked working mother has an even harder time. Finally, if the sixteen-year-old cannot drive, then dating becomes difficult. Teenagers are supposed to date. It is a part of the maturation process. Yet modern dating requires a car to get to malls, theatres, restaurants, and parties. Without a license, the sixteen-year-old would be denied this important part of growing up. Yes, teenage drivers have accidents, but they are often because of lack of experience, not age. A new seventeen-year-old driver is just as likely to have an accident as a sixteen-year-old. So, let's not take away the sixteen-year-old's ability to drive. Both the sixteen-year-old and the family would suffer.

On a separate sheet, answer the following questions about "Why Children Grow Up Too Fast" and "Raising the Driving Age":

1. Which paragraph explains causes and which explains effects?
2. What is the topic sentence for each paragraph? Which words mention the topic? Which words mention whether causes or effects will be explained?
3. In "Why Children Grow Up Too Fast," which sentences present general statements of cause? In "Raising the Driving Age," which sentences present general statements of effect?
4. Are the general statements followed by specific ones?
5. In "Why Children Grow Up Too Fast," one general statement is followed by an example. What is that example?
6. Cite two examples of transitions that signal effect.
7. Are there any problems with adequate or relevant detail? Explain.
8. Do the paragraphs come to a satisfying close? Explain.

Thinking, Learning, and Writing in College   Using Cause-and-Effect Analysis

You will use cause-and-effect analysis often in your college writing. In a history class, for example, you may have to write about the causes or effects of the Industrial Revolution. In an exercise physiology class, you may need to write about the causes of stress fractures or the effects of repetitive motion. In an educational psychology class, you may need to write about the causes of violence in schools or the effects of second language learning. In environmental science, you may write about the causes or effects of global warming, and in a business class, you may write about the causes or effects of the growth of Internet commerce.

Checklist for Cause-and-Effect Analysis

Before submitting your cause-and-effect analysis, be sure you can answer yes to these questions:

1. Do you have a topic sentence that mentions your topic and whether you will explain causes or effects?

2. Are all your general statements of cause or effect followed by specific explanation, example, narration, or description?

3. Did you avoid assuming that an event was necessarily caused by an earlier event?

4. Did you consider that an event likely has multiple causes or effects?

5. Where needed, have you used transitions to signal effect and transitions to signal addition?

6. Have you used specific nouns, verbs, and modifiers?

7. Are all your supporting details relevant to your topic sentence?

8. Does your paragraph have a satisfying closing?

 Tips for Planning Your Cause-and-Effect Analysis

1. Write an early version of your topic sentence that mentions your topic and whether you will explain causes or effects. If you are unsure what to write about, try listing or freewriting.

2. If you are explaining causes, list every cause you can think of; if you are explaining effects, list every effect you can think of.

3. Study your list and cross out ideas you do not wish to include. Then number the remaining ideas in the order they will appear in your first draft.

WRITING ASSIGNMENT

Here are possible topics for your cause-and-effect analysis. Remember to settle on causes or effects; do not try to explain both.

1. Use one of the topic sentences you wrote for *Practice 9.1.*

2. Explain what would happen if _____ (you fill in the blank). For example, you can explain what would happen if tuition were lowered, if there were no required courses, if smoking were illegal, if public schools were in session eleven months, and so forth.

3. Explain how attending college has affected you.

4. Explain what causes people to drop out of high school.

5. See p. 450 for an assignment based on "On Being 17, Bright, and Unable to Read" and p. 468 for an assignment based on "Time to Look and Listen."

6. ***Respond to a photograph.*** As the accompanying photograph shows, Americans rely heavily on their cars. Explain either the causes or the effects of this dependence on the automobile.

Robert Fox/Impact Visuals

Visit the Clouse Website!

For additional exercises, quizzes, and Internet activities, visit our Website at:

http://www.ablongman.com/clouse

For even more activities, visit the Longman English pages at:

http://www.ablongman.com/englishpages

Chapter 10

Classification

A **classification** places items in groups according to some principle. For example, colleges can be classified or grouped according to their location, according to their size, according to their course offerings, or according to how expensive they are. To classify cars, you might identify these groups: high-performance cars, luxury cars, and family cars. Items are placed in a group because they share characteristics. Thus, all cars in the high-performance group have similar features (such as engine size and the ability to travel fast); all cars in the luxury group have similar features (such as leather seats and electronic dashboards); all cars in the family car group have similar features (such as seating for six or more and good gas mileage).

> A classification paragraph places items in groups according to some principle.

Classification is important because it helps us sort and group things. To appreciate its importance, think of how hard it would be to find a book in the library without a classification system. (For an example of classification in an essay, see "Different Kinds of Shoppers," on p. 169.)

◆ ◆ ◆

A SAMPLE CLASSIFICATION PARAGRAPH

The following classification paragraph, written by a student, will be used to illustrate several points about classification.

Different Kinds of Shoppers

After working at Kmart for over a year, I have come to know well the four different kinds of shoppers. The first shopper is the browser. Browsers have endless amounts of time to waste. Nonchalantly, they wander around my department picking up every item that catches the eye. Unfortunately, browsers never put things back in the right place, so I have to straighten stock when they leave. The browsers are also a pain because they want to look at every item locked in the showcase. Of course, after all this, the browsers leave without buying a thing. The dependent shoppers are also annoying. They have to be shown where everything is, including the items in front of their noses. Dependent shoppers never bother to look for anything. They walk through the front door, find a clerk, and ask him or her to get a dozen items. The hit-and-run shoppers are much easier to deal with. They are always frantic and rushed. They will buy anything, regardless of price, if they can get it fast. Price does not matter. One recent hit-and-runner raced in, asked breathlessly if he could pay for a stereo by check, picked out the first one he saw, and bought two of them. He wrote a check for over four hundred dollars as if it were $1.98 and raced out. Independent shoppers are the easiest to deal with. They want no part of sales clerks except for ringing up the sales. Independent shoppers find what they want on their own, put things back in the right places, and never ask questions. As far as I am concerned, this world needs more independent shoppers.

THE TOPIC SENTENCE

The topic sentence mentions the topic and indicates that things will be placed in groups.

The topic sentence for a classification paragraph presents the topic and includes words to let the reader know the paragraph will place things in groups. Look again at the topic sentence of "Different Kinds of Shoppers":

After working at Kmart for over a year, I have come to know well the four different kinds of shoppers.

This topic sentence indicates that the writer's topic is shoppers. The words "the four different kinds of shoppers" indicate that the paragraph will place things into groups (classify them).

PRACTICE 10.1

The sentences below could be topic sentences for classification paragraphs. Underline the topic once and underline twice the words that indicate items will be placed in groups. The first one is done as an example.

1. <u>Three chief types</u> of <u>baby-sitters</u> can be identified by most mothers of small children.

2. All automobiles fall into one of three groups.

3. An athlete soon learns of the several kinds of coaches.

4. Four categories of employers exist in the workplace.

5. Most horror movies are one of three types.

6. Four ways to study for an exam are practiced by college students.

SUPPORTING DETAILS

Place things in groups according to *only one* principle. For example, you may group shoppers according to how hard they are to deal with (like the writer of "Different Kinds of Shoppers") or according to age or according to how carefully they shop. However, you cannot mix the groupings. You cannot discuss the careful shopper, the careless shopper, and the teenage shopper, for you would be using two principles of classification.

> Place items in groups according to a single principle of classification.

When you develop your supporting details, think of each sentence that presents a particular group as a general statement that must be followed by specific statements. For example, look again at "Different Kinds of Shoppers." Each of the following sentences presents a group:

> The sentence that mentions a particular group is a general statement that must be followed by specific statements that describe the group.

The first shopper is the browser.

The dependent shoppers are also annoying.

The hit-and-run shoppers are much easier to deal with.

Independent shoppers are the easiest to deal with.

After each general statement that presents a group, specific statements explain what the members of the group are like.

PRACTICE 10.2: WORKING TOGETHER

This exercise, which you can complete with classmates, will let you practice grouping according to a principle of classification. On a separate sheet, list things included in the broad category given. Then study your list and write down one principle of classification. Next state the groups that fit in the classification, and give items in the groups. More than one principle of classification will be possible, and you may not use every point in your list when you give the groups and items in the groups. The first one is done as an example.

1. kinds of examinations (list)

open book	*multiple choice*	*midterms*
take home	*true/false*	*finals*
in-class	*fill-in-the-blanks*	*fair*
essay	*hard*	*unfair*
objective	*opinion*	*evaluation*
definition	*easy*	*matching*

principle of classification *degree of difficulty* _____

group 1 *easy* _____

group 2 *moderately hard* _____

group 3 *hard* _____

items in group 1 *true/false, matching* _____

items in group 2 *multiple choice* _____

items in group 3 *essay, fill-in-the-blanks* _____

2. kinds of teachers (list on separate sheet)

principle of classification _____

group 1 _____

group 2 _____

group 3 _____

people in group 1 _____

people in group 2 _____

people in group 3 _____

3. kinds of restaurants (list on separate sheet)

   principle of classification _____

   group 1 _____

   group 2 _____

   group 3 _____

   items in group 1 _____

   items in group 2 _____

   items in group 3 _____

4. kinds of friends (list on separate sheet)

   principle of classification _____

   group 1 _____

   group 2 _____

   group 3 _____

   people in group 1 _____

   people in group 2 _____

   people in group 3 _____

PRACTICE 10.3

After each topic sentence, list three classification groups. Then state the principle of classification. The first one is done as an example.

1. I have attended three kinds of dinner parties.

group 1 *formal* _____

group 2 *semiformal* _____

group 3 *casual* _____

principle of classification **_degree of formality_** _____

2. Bosses fall into one of three groups.

group 1 _____

group 2 _____

group 3 _____

principle of classification _____

3. It is possible to identify three kinds of birthday celebrations.

group 1 _____

group 2 _____

group 3 _____

principle of classification _____

4. A salesclerk is usually one of three types.

group 1 _____

group 2 _____

group 3 _____

principle of classification _____

5. Radio stations can be classified according to the audience they appeal to.

group 1 _____

group 2 _____

group 3 _____

principle of classification _____

6. A person can have one of three kinds of neighbors.

group 1 _____

group 2 _____

group 3 _____

principle of classification _____

PRACTICE 10.4

Study this classification paragraph written by a student and answer the questions that follow.

Three Kinds of Students

College students fall into three categories: the grinds, the goof-offs, and the well-adjusted. The grinds are easily recognized. They live for school, so they spend all their waking hours in pursuit of an education. You know them: they answer every question, they do every assignment, and they linger after class to discuss the lecture with the teacher. When not in class, they are in the library, and when not in the library, they are in the bookstore buying a 300-page book for extra-credit reading. The grinds always throw off the curve because they study so hard. The next group is the goof-offs. They are the ones in school to party hearty. You won't see them in class or in the library—they're too busy shooting pool in the student union or drinking suds in a local bar. As for the bookstore, well, the goof-offs haven't found it yet because they haven't bought their books. The goof-offs are important to academic life because they help balance out the curve the grinds keep throwing off. Between the grinds and the goof-offs are the well-adjusted. They study and pull passing grades, but they know how to party, too. They might skip a good time to cram for finals, but they are known to party instead of study for a test that only counts 25 percent. The well-adjusted know life is short, so they take college seriously but know the importance of fun as well. Fortunately, on our campus the well-adjusted outnumber the grinds and goof-offs.

On a separate sheet, answer the following questions about "Three Kinds of Students":

1. What is the topic sentence? What is the topic? Which words mention that items will be placed in groups?
2. What is the principle of classification?
3. What general statements mention the particular groups?
4. Are there enough specific statements after the general statements?
5. Does the paragraph come to a satisfying close? Explain.

Thinking, Learning, and Writing in College   Using Classification

Classification is common in college writing. In a computer science class, you might be asked to classify kinds of programming language or search engines. In an advertising class, you might be asked to classify kinds of radio advertisements, and in a communications class, you might need to classify kinds of hate speech. An assignment in a sociology class might require you to classify kinds of nuclear families, and one in a political science class might require you to classify ways to organize city governments.

Checklist for a Classification Paragraph

Before submitting your classification, be sure you can answer yes to these questions:

1. Do you have a topic sentence that presents the topic and mentions that items will be placed in groups?
2. Have you classified according to a single principle?

3. Do you have general statements that mention each group?

4. Are your general statements followed by specific details?

5. Does your paragraph have a satisfying closing?

 ## *Tips for Planning Your Classification Paragraph*

1. To decide on a principle of classification, list every way you can classify your subject. For example, if your subject is restaurants, you could list these ways to classify:

food	decor and atmosphere
service	price
patrons	location

   Study your list and decide on your principle of classification.

2. Make columns on a sheet for each of the groups in your classification. For example, if you were classifying restaurants according to their food, you might have one column for fast food, one for home-style cooking, and one for gourmet food. In each column list every characteristic you can think of, without pausing to decide if your ideas are good or not.

3. Study your columns and cross out the ideas you do not want to include. Decide which group you want to handle first, second, and third, and number the columns accordingly.

4. Write an early version of your topic sentence that includes your topic and words that mention what you will classify.

WRITING ASSIGNMENT

For your classification paragraph, you have a choice of topics:

1. Use one of the topics and principles of classification in *Practice 10.2*.

2. Use one of the topic sentences in *Practice 10.3*. You may want to use the groups and principle of classification you developed when you completed this exercise.

3. Classify types of scary movies.

4. Classify types of sports fans.

5. Classify methods of studying.

6. Classify all kinds of lies.

7. ***Respond to a photograph.*** Using the accompanying photograph for ideas if you like, classify different kinds of sports fans. If you wish, you may limit yourself to football fans, basketball fans, college fans, or some other similar kind.

Catherine Karnow/Woodfin Camp & Associates

Chapter 11

Persuasion

Persuasion, which aims to convince a reader to think or act a particular way, is a big part of our lives. Advertisements try to persuade us to buy certain products, classmates try to persuade us to lend them our biology notes, friends try to persuade us to vote for their favorite candidates. Similarly, we try to persuade teachers to postpone exams, friends to lend us their cars, and parents to send us more money.

For examples of persuasion in essays, see "No Degree Required" on p. 171, "Green Frog Skin" on p. 459, and "If You Had to Kill Your Own Hog" on p. 472.

A persuasive paragraph aims to convince a reader to think or act a certain way.

◆　◆　◆

A SAMPLE PERSUASIVE PARAGRAPH

The following persuasive paragraph, written by a student, will be used to illustrate several points about persuasion.

Wear a Helmet

Every state should pass a law requiring motorcyclists to wear helmets. First of all, helmets provide increased visibility. Motorcycles are sometimes hard to see, but the glare from a helmet can help solve this problem. Many times I have seen the flash of a helmet before I have seen the motorcycle itself. Because automobile drivers are not conditioned to look for motorcyclists, anything that increases the cyclist's visibility will improve safety. The main reason for requiring helmets is decreasing the number of deaths. As proof of this, I offer a friend of mine who swerved to miss a car that pulled out in front of him. As a result, my friend hit a ditch at sixty miles per hour. He had several broken bones and some horrendous bruises, but because he was wearing a helmet, he did not sustain a head injury that could have killed him. Another friend of mine was married only three months when a car pulled out in front of his '58 Harley. Wearing no helmet, he hit the car at thirty miles per hour. He flew off the bike and hit his head on the curb. After a week in a coma, he died. If he had worn a helmet, he might have lived. Because helmets increase visibility and provide protection, all motorcyclists should be required by law to wear them.

THE TOPIC SENTENCE

The topic sentence should include a debatable issue and the writer's stand on the issue.

The topic sentence for a persuasive paragraph includes the writer's topic and view. The topic must be a debatable issue, and the view should indicate the writer's stand on that debatable issue. Look again at the topic sentence of "Wear a Helmet":

> Every state should pass a law requiring motorcyclists to wear helmets.

The topic is state laws requiring motorcyclists to wear helmets, an issue that is debatable because people disagree about whether such laws are a good idea. The view gives the writer's stand on the issue: all states should pass the laws.

PRACTICE 11.1

1. On a separate sheet, give the debatable topic and writer's stand for each topic sentence.

    example: Jan Mineo is the best candidate for governor.
    debatable topic: who is the best candidate for governor
    stand: Mineo is the best candidate.

    A. The federal government should not subsidize galleries that display pornographic art.

    B. State property taxes are a poor way to finance public education.

    C. Students should have a say in the hiring and firing of teachers.

    D. Laws should be passed requiring the recycling of aluminum cans.

    E. Deregulation of the airline industry has caused more problems than it has solved.

2. For each of the following subjects, write a topic sentence for a persuasive paragraph. The first one is done as an example.

A. placing warnings on compact discs with sexually explicit lyrics.

It serves no useful purpose to put warnings on CDs with

sexually explicit lyrics

B. 55 m.p.h. speed limit

_____

_____

C. having to pass an exam to get a high school diploma

_____

_____

D. sending women into combat

_____

_____

E. the sale of handguns

_____

_____

F. required courses in college

_____

_____

SUPPORTING DETAILS

The supporting details are the reasons for your stand. Since your goal is to persuade, you will include the reasons most likely to convince your reader to think or act the way you want. To be as convincing as possible, remember these points about supporting details.

The supporting details are the reasons for the writer's stand.

Each reason is presented in a general statement that must be followed by specific statements.

1. Each time you present a reason, you are providing a general statement that must be followed by specific statements. In "Wear a Helmet," the reasons for the writer's view are presented in these general statements:

> First of all, helmets provide increased visibility.
>
> The main reason for requiring helmets is decreasing the number of deaths.

Each of the general statements is followed by specific statements. The first general statement is followed by the explanation that the helmets produce glare and by an example of the writer seeing this glare. The second general statement is followed by two examples of what happened to the writer's friends.

Avoid name-calling and expressions like "most people believe."

2. Avoid name-calling. Saying things like, "Only the uninformed believe" or "As any fool knows" will alienate a reader. You can attack ideas, but do not attack people.

3. Avoid expressions like "most people believe" unless you are sure they are true.

You can mention reasons against your view and go on to make those reasons less compelling. You can also note what would happen if your stand were or were not adopted.

4. You can mention one or more of the most compelling reasons against your view and then say something to make the objections less powerful, like this:

> Some people say that helmet laws infringe on personal freedom. In fact, they are no more a threat to freedom than seatbelt laws.

5. You can consider the consequences of adopting or not adopting your stand, like this:

> if stand is adopted: If states require motorcyclists to wear helmets,fewer motorcyclists will die or sustain brain damage.
>
> if stand is not adopted: Without mandatory helmet laws, we are risking the lives of motorcyclists unnecessarily.

Details are often arranged in an emphatic order.

Transitions that signal emphatic order are often used.

Typically the supporting details are arranged in an emphatic order (see p. 18). That is, they gradually build up to the most convincing reason, which appears last. Writers often use transitions that signal this emphatic order. These transitions are discussed in Chapter 1, and now is a good time to review that material (see p. 22).

PRACTICE 11.2: WORKING TOGETHER

With some classmates, list three reasons to support each topic sentence. The first one is done as an example. If you have trouble thinking of reasons, try listing, brainstorming, or freewriting.

1. Little League baseball places too much pressure on young children.

   A. *pressure to win*

   B. *pressure not to let teammates down*

   C. *pressure not to let parents down*

2. Beer and wine commercials should (or should not) be banned.

   A. _____

   B. _____

   C. _____

3. Places with over seventy-five employees should (or should not) have a day-care center.

   A. _____

   B. _____

   C. _____

4. Parents should (or should not) help select the textbooks used in public schools.

   A. _____

   B. _____

   C. _____

5. Alcohol should (or should not) be banned on college campuses.

   A. _____

   B. _____

C. _____

6. An eleven-month school year is (or is not) a good idea.

A. _____

B. _____

C. _____

PRACTICE 11.3

Complete the following on a separate sheet:

1. Select one of the topic sentences from *Practice 11.2* and write a sentence or two that mentions a reason against your stand and says something to make that objection less powerful.

2. Select one of the topic sentences from *Practice 11.2* and write a sentence or two that mentions what would happen if your stand were adopted. Then write a sentence or two that mentions what would happen if your stand were *not* adopted.

3. Arrange the reasons you developed for one of the topic sentences in *Practice 11.2* in an emphatic order.

PRACTICE 11.4

Here is a persuasive paragraph written by a student. Read it and answer the questions that follow.

No Degree Required

We should discontinue the requirement that people must earn teaching degrees before they can teach in elementary, middle, or high school. The requirement that a person have a teaching degree from a four year college means that talented, knowledgeable people, people who would be terrific teachers, cannot give what they have to offer—just because they have not taken a handful of teaching courses. Consider an accountant who loves children and has a way of inspiring them. He or she cannot teach arithmetic without earning a teaching degree even though that person already has the knowledge and talent to be a fine teacher. Or what about a former U.S. Senator who loves children and knows the government inside out? That person cannot teach social studies without going back to school to earn a teaching degree. In both cases and countless more like them, people who could educate and inspire young people are prevented from doing so. This fact is particularly disturbing when you consider that the accountant and Senator probably know more about math and government than some people with teaching degrees who are currently teaching math and social studies. Of course, we can't let just anyone with knowledge of a subject into the classroom. We must be sure the person has the other qualities necessary to teach. We should set up training programs to teach prospective teachers about classroom management, and we should have tests to judge the knowledge and talent of people who want to teach. Then we should require a year of probation to weed out those who are not suitable. Beyond that, anyone with the knowledge, desire, and talent should be able to teach. Deans of colleges of education all over the country are likely to cry out that only accredited schools can train teachers, but that point of view is self-serving. After all, our current method of requiring teaching degrees has done little to assure quality education.

On a separate sheet, answer the following questions:

1. What is the topic sentence of "No Degree Required"? What is the writer's debatable topic? What is the writer's stand on the topic?

2. Write the general statements that present the reasons for the writer's stand.

3. The first general statement that presents a reason is followed by: (pick one)

   A. explanation

   B. example

   C. explanation and example

4. The second general statement that presents a reason is followed by: (pick one)

   A. explanation

   B. example

   C. explanation and example

5. The third general statement that presents a reason is followed by: (pick one)

    A. explanation

    B. example

    C. explanation and example

6. What reason against the writer's stand is given? How does the writer attempt to make that reason less powerful? Does the writer succeed in making the reason less powerful? Explain.

7. Does the paragraph have a satisfying closing? Explain.

    Note: For the essay version of "No Degree Required," see p. 171.

Thinking, Learning, and Writing in College   **Using Persuasion**

Persuasion is an important part of college writing because it requires you to do more than recall information—it requires you to analyze, evaluate, and draw conclusions. In other words, persuasion is a real test of your understanding of material and how carefully you have reflected on it. Thus, in an education class, you might be asked to argue for or against proficiency examinations. In a labor studies class, you may be asked to argue for or against unions for public employees. In a literature class, you might need to give and then defend your interpretation of a poem. In an architecture class, you might have to explain and defend how to design a particular space. In an ethics class, you might need to argue for or against the medical use of fetal tissue.

 Checklist for a Persuasive Paragraph

Before submitting your persuasive paragraph, be sure you can answer yes to the following questions:

1. Do you have a topic sentence that presents a debatable topic and your stand on the topic?

2. Have you presented each reason for your stand in its own general statement?

3. Have you followed each general statement with specific statements?

4. If appropriate, have you mentioned important reasons against your stand and made them less compelling?

5. If appropriate, have you noted what would happen if your stand were or were not adopted?

6. Have you avoided name-calling and expressions like "most people believe"?

7. Are your supporting details arranged in an emphatic or other logical order?

8. If needed, have you used transitions to signal emphatic order?

9. Does your paragraph have a satisfying closing?

 ## Tips for Planning Your Persuasive Paragraph

1. Write an early version of your topic sentence that includes your debatable topic and your stand on the topic.

2. List every reason you can think of to support your stand. Do not evaluate how good your ideas are; just write everything that occurs to you.

3. Study your list and cross out the reasons that are not very persuasive. Try to discover three good reasons for your view (or two reasons that you can develop well).

4. If possible, number your ideas in an emphatic order, saving your most persuasive reason for last.

5. After each general statement that presents a reason for your stand, ask yourself whether you can explain the reason, give an example, or tell a story.

6. List the reasons you can think of against your stand. Is there one you should mention and make less powerful?

7. Note what would happen if your stand were and were not adopted. Should you mention one of these?

WRITING ASSIGNMENT

Here is a choice of topics for your persuasive paragraph:

1. Use one of the topic sentences you developed in response to number 2 of *Practice 11.1*.

2. Use one of the topic sentences from *Practice 11.2*. You may also use some or all of the reasons you developed when you completed this exercise.

3. Write a paragraph to persuade someone who graduated from your high school to attend your college.

4. Write a paragraph to convince your reader that a specific change is needed at your college (a change in registration, course requirements, dorm rules, parking facilities, etc.).

5. Write a paragraph to convince your reader that giving final examinations is a good (or bad) practice.

6. Write a paragraph to convince your reader that Internet chat rooms are a harmful (or helpful) phenomenon.

7. See p. 458 for a paragraph assignment based on "Money for Morality" and p. 468 for an assignment on "Time to Look and Listen."

8. ***Respond to a photograph.*** Do you think students who look like the ones in the accompanying photograph are dressed appropriately for school? Express your view by writing a paragraph arguing either for or against dress codes in public schools.

Elizabeth Crews/Stock Boston

Chapter 12

Writing an Essay

In college, you will often write **essays**, which are compositions made of several paragraphs. Because the essay has several paragraphs, it allows you to develop a topic in more detail than you can in a single paragraph. When you write research papers, book reviews, reports, summaries, and other papers in your classes, you will use the essay form so you can treat your topic in the appropriate depth. To help you write essays, in this chapter you will learn:

1. how to structure an essay

2. how to plan an essay

3. how other students have developed essays

An essay is a composition made of several paragraphs.

◆ ◆ ◆

THE PARTS OF AN ESSAY

An essay has three parts:

the introduction
the supporting paragraphs
the conclusion

Each part serves an important purpose. The **introduction** presents the writer's central point and stimulates the reader's interest in that point. The **supporting paragraphs** provide details to prove or develop the central point. The **conclusion** brings the essay to a satisfying finish.

The parts of an essay are the introduction, supporting paragraphs, and conclusion.

147

Essay Part	Function
introduction	presents the writer's central point and stimulates interest in that point
supporting paragraphs (at least 2)	provide details to develop the central point
conclusion	brings essay to a satisfying close

You may have noticed the similarities between essay and paragraph parts. These similarities are shown in this chart:

Paragraph Part		Function		Essay Part
topic sentence	➔	presents writer's central point	⬅	introduction
supporting details	➔	develop writer's central point	⬅	supporting paragraphs
closing	➔	brings writing to satisfying close	⬅	conclusion

A Sample Essay

The following essay, written by a student, illustrates the three essay parts. As a study aid, these parts are labeled in the margin.

Let's Pay College Athletes

Introduction: The first three sentences create interest and the last presents the central point, which is that colleges should pay their athletes.

College athletics is big business. A great deal of money is at stake, so colleges are under pressure to recruit the best players. To do so, they offer full and partial scholarships, hoping to lure players to their schools. However, rather than offer scholarships, colleges should pay the players a salary.

Supporting paragraph: Sentence 1 presents the first point to support the central point (athletes on scholarships have a difficult time). The rest of the paragraph develops the point.

Athletes attending school on scholarships have a difficult time. To keep their scholarships, they must carry full-time loads. Because their sport demands so much of their time, they often find that they do not have enough time to study. As a result, their grades suffer. However, if athletes were paid, they could attend part-time and perform better academically without being stretched so thin.

Supporting paragraph: Sentence 1 presents the second point to support the central point (without athletic scholarships, people could still afford to attend school). The rest of the paragraph develops the point.

Some people say that without athletic scholarships many students could not afford to attend school, but this is not true. Paid athletes would simply use their salary to pay for tuition and books. Some athletes may even decide to save their salary and wait to attend school until they are finished playing ball. They could thus attend during the offseason or when their athletic careers are over, when they can really focus on their studies.

Paying college athletes would also eliminate the people who are in college but who will never graduate. Some scholarship athletes were recruited to play ball, but they really are not college material. Paid athletes would not have to take classes, and we would be left with qualified students in the classroom, not athletes who are marking time for four years or trying to get a shot at the pros. Furthermore, the seats these athletes now occupy could go to academically qualified students who <u>do</u> want to graduate.

Supporting paragraph: Sentence 1 presents the third point to support the central point (eliminating athletes who will never graduate). The rest of the paragraph develops this point.

If we paid athletes, colleges would benefit financially. Attendance would be up at games because the level of play would be high. Also, tuition could be collected from the students who take the athletes' places in classrooms.

Supporting paragraph: Sentence 1 presents the fourth point to support the central point (colleges would benefit financially). The rest of the paragraph develops this point.

Awarding athletic scholarships is an old tradition. However, not all traditions stand the test of time. Now we should reconsider how we recruit athletes. Why not just pay them and let them decide if they want to use the money to attend college? Everyone would benefit.

Conclusion: This paragraph brings the essay to a satisfying finish.

The Introduction

The introduction has two purposes: it stimulates interest in the essay, and it mentions what the central point will be. The portion of the introduction that stimulates interest is the **lead-in**. The portion that presents the central point is the **thesis**.

The lead-in creates interest in the essay, and the thesis indicates what the central point is.

The Lead-in   To stimulate interest in the essay, a writer can approach a lead-in several ways.

1. **Give Background Information.** Tell your reader something he or she should know to understand the importance of your thesis or some of the detail in your essay.

On the first day of classes, students who applied for guaranteed student loans were inconvenienced by a lack of funds. Clearly, the loans should be distributed in advance.

The writer's central point is that guaranteed student loan funds should be distributed in advance. The first sentence is the lead-in, which provides the background fact that students did not have their loans on the first day of school.

2. **Tell a Story.** A brief story can create interest in your essay and help prove the truth of the thesis.

> When I was nine, I woke up in the middle of the night to the sounds of yelling. Terrified, I went to the top of the stairs and discovered my parents were screaming at each other. I sat there, confused, shaken, and unable to move. Then the horrible thing happened. I watched my father throw a vase at my mother. It missed her and shattered against the wall. However, from that moment on, I knew that married people should not stay married "for the sake of the children."

The thesis is that people should not stay married because they think divorce will hurt the children. To create interest in this point and help prove its truth, the writer tells a story from her childhood.

3. **Ask a Question That Relates to Your Thesis**.

> Do you change from a nice, polite, helpful, caring individual into a monster when you park in one of the campus parking decks? If so, you are not alone, because parking in these structures brings out the worst in everybody.

The question in the lead-in relates to the writer's thesis: parking in the campus decks brings out the worst in people.

4. **Describe a Person or a Scene.**

> My legs were shaky and weak. My whole body trembled, and my heart pounded violently in my throat. My palms were wet. The smell of chlorine sickened my stomach as the screams of children having fun and the hum of gossiping adults surrounded me. I knew I had to jump if I was ever going to overcome my fear of water.

The writer's thesis is his effort to overcome his fear of water by jumping in. The lead-in creates interest by describing how the writer felt just before the jump.

5. **Use an Interesting Quotation.** However, be sure that the quotation is not an overused expression such as "Don't count your chickens before they hatch."

> In "School Is Bad for Children," John Holt says that "any kid in class who, for whatever reason, would rather not be there not only doesn't learn anything himself but makes it

a great deal tougher for anyone else." Because Holt is right, I believe we should abolish compulsory school attendance.

The writer's thesis is that we should abolish compulsory attendance. The quotation in the lead-in is not an overused saying likely to bore a reader.

The Thesis The **thesis** is the sentence or two in the introduction that indicates what the central point of the essay is. The thesis should indicate the writer's topic and the writer's view of the topic. Look again at the thesis of "Let's Pay College Athletes":

> However, rather than offer scholarships, colleges should pay the players a salary.

In this case, the writer's topic is paying players. The view of the topic is that colleges should do so.

Sometimes you can shape an effective thesis by mentioning your topic, view, and the main points you will make in your supporting paragraphs. Here is such a thesis:

> I love my brothers, but living with them is difficult because they eat all the food, they expect me to be their maid, and they treat me like a child.

This thesis lets the reader know the topic (living with the writer's brothers), the writer's view (it is difficult), and the ideas that will be developed in the supporting paragraphs (the brothers eat all the food, they want the writer to be their maid, and they treat the writer like a child).

In addition to noting the topic and view, an effective thesis is like the topic sentence of a one-paragraph composition in other ways. These are listed for you here:

1. The thesis should not be a statement of fact.
2. The thesis should not be too broad.
3. The thesis should not include vague words.
4. The thesis should not be a formal announcement.
5. The thesis should not mention the title.

Turn now to pp. 48–53 and review these qualities.

> The thesis includes the writer's topic and the writer's view of the topic.

> To be effective, the thesis should have all the qualities of a topic sentence of a one-paragraph composition.

PRACTICE 12.1

On a separate sheet, write the thesis for each of the sample introductions on pp. 149–151. For each thesis, underline the topic once, and underline the view of the topic twice.

PRACTICE 12.2: WORKING TOGETHER

For each topic given, work with some classmates to write a thesis for an essay. Include a topic and your view of the topic. Also, be sure to meet the five requirements for an effective thesis. The first one is done as an example.

1. an annoying relative *My cousin Lee is very stubborn.* _____

   _____

2. the best way to relax (Mention two or three points that will be devel-

   oped in supporting paragraphs.) _____

   _____

3. the rewards of college life _____

   _____

4. the frustrations of college life _____

   _____

5. television advertisements _____

   _____

6. exam anxiety _____

   _____

Supporting Paragraphs

Supporting paragraphs prove that the thesis idea is true. They develop the thesis.

Supporting paragraphs provide detail to prove the truth of the idea in the thesis. Thus, in "Let's Pay College Athletes," the supporting paragraphs (paragraphs 2, 3, 4, and 5) provide details to prove that paying college athletes is a good idea.

A supporting paragraph has a topic sentence and supporting details.

Supporting paragraphs have two parts: the topic sentence and the supporting details. The **topic sentence** presents the focus of the **supporting paragraph**, and the **supporting details** develop that focus.

The topic sentence presents the focus of the supporting paragraph; this will be the aspect of the thesis to be discussed. The topic sentence must be relevant to the thesis.

The Topic Sentence The topic sentence presents the focus of the supporting paragraph. Here are the topic sentences for the supporting paragraphs of "Let's Pay College Athletes":

Athletes attending school on scholarships have a difficult time.

Some people say that without athletic scholarships many students could not afford to attend school, but this is not true.

Paying college athletes would also eliminate the people who are in college but who will never graduate.

If we paid athletes, colleges would benefit financially.

Notice that each topic sentence presents some aspect of the thesis. That is what a topic sentence does: it indicates which aspect of the thesis will be discussed in the supporting paragraph. Also notice that each topic sentence is relevant to the thesis. This is an important point to remember: all your topic sentences must be related to the thesis.

Supporting Details   **Supporting details** develop the point in the topic sentence. Look back at the supporting paragraphs of "Let's Pay College Athletes" to see how the supporting details develop the topic sentences.

> Supporting details develop or support the idea in the topic sentence.

    When you studied the one-paragraph composition, you learned the characteristics of effective supporting details. These characteristics also apply to the essay. They are listed for you here:

1. Supporting details must be adequate.
2. Supporting details must be relevant.
3. Supporting details must be specific.
4. Specific words should be used where appropriate.
5. General statements should be followed by specific ones.
6. Supporting details may be arranged in spatial, chronological, or emphatic order.

    Review the characteristics of effective supporting details on pp. 53-56 .

PRACTICE 12.3

    Pick two thesis statements you wrote when you completed *Practice 12.2*. For each of these thesis statements, write two topic sentences that could be in supporting paragraphs. Be sure the topic sentences are relevant to the thesis. (If you need help thinking of ideas, try listing, clustering, brainstorming, or freewriting.)

Example

    Thesis: <u>*My cousin Lee is very stubborn.*</u>

Topic sentence: *Once Lee refused to go to the prom because he wasn't chosen for the prom committee.*

Topic sentence: *Lee will never apologize to anyone for anything, even when he knows he is wrong.*

1. Thesis: _____

_____

Topic sentence: _____

_____

Topic sentence: _____

_____

2. Thesis: _____

_____

Topic sentence: _____

_____

Topic sentence: _____

_____

PRACTICE 12.4: WORKING TOGETHER

The following are thesis statements and topic sentences for three essays. With some classmates, write three relevant supporting details on a separate sheet to develop each topic sentence. The first one is done as an example. (If you need help with ideas, try the idea-generation techniques.)

1. Thesis: Baby-sitting is not an easy way to make money.

   Topic sentence: The children can be difficult to care for.

   Supporting detail: *Marco refused to eat supper.*

   Supporting detail: *Carlotta wasn't toilet-trained.*

Supporting detail: *Ed hit his brother.*

Topic sentence: The parents can be just as hard to deal with.

Supporting detail: *The Calloways returned at 3 a.m.*

Supporting detail: *The Chus did not pay.*

Supporting detail: *The Kellys didn't tell me where they were going.*

2. Thesis: People often change when they get behind the wheel of a car.

   Topic sentence: Normally calm people become enraged.

   Topic sentence: Also, normally cautious people become reckless.

3. Thesis: Two kinds of salesclerks work in the mall.

   Topic sentence: The first kind of clerk ignores me.

   Topic sentence: The second kind of clerk smothers me with attention.

4. Thesis: In my study skills class I learned an excellent way to study.

   Topic sentence: Preparations before sitting down to study are important.

   Topic sentence: Students should follow a specific procedure once they sit down to study.

The Conclusion

The **conclusion** brings the essay to a satisfying finish. Some approaches to the conclusion are illustrated here.

> The conclusion brings the essay to a satisfying finish.

1. **Refer to the Topic or View Presented in the Thesis.**   Here is an example for an essay with this thesis: Student loans should be distributed before the term begins.

   > Students count on their loan money to pay for tuition, books, and other college related expenses. Therefore, to avoid problems for students, the loans should be given out before classes begin.

2. **Summarize the Main Points of the Essay.**   Here is an example for an essay with this thesis: We should abolish compulsory school attendance.

   > Compulsory attendance serves no purpose because when students are required to attend against their will, they disrupt the classroom and distract the teacher's attention. Students who do not want to be in school will not learn anyway, so we should let them leave and enter the

workforce or the military, where they can contribute to society and earn their way in the world.

3. **Introduce an Idea Closely Related to the Thesis or Main Points of the Essay.**   Here is an example for an essay with this thesis: I knew I had to jump in the pool if I was ever going to overcome my fear of water.

> Now that I have overcome my fear of water, I feel better about myself. I realize that I can face whatever obstacles are in my path by using the same courage I used to jump in the pool.

4. **Combine Approaches.**   Here is an example for an essay with this thesis: People should not stay married "for the sake of the children." The conclusion combines a restatement of the thesis and a summary of main points.

> More often than not, staying married for the sake of the children is a mistake. The spouses' resentment and anger grow until the children are affected by the tension. Ultimately, the children are better off living with one parent in an atmosphere of harmony than with two parents in an atmosphere of discord.

PRACTICE 12.5

The following student essay lacks a conclusion. On a separate sheet, write a suitable conclusion and indicate the approach or combination of approaches you used.

Braces at Twenty-One

I was seventeen and without a care in the world when my mother woke me at 9:00 a.m. for my dental appointment. After the dentist finished checking my teeth, he informed me that I had no cavities, but I needed braces. The news came as a total shock because I thought only children got braces. I have had them for four years now, and I can truly say that having braces at the age of twenty-one creates serious problems.

Because the braces make me look younger than I really am, people never believe I am twenty-one and in college. Once when I met a friend's father, he wanted to know what high school I went to. When I go to the local bars, the person carding twists my ID every possible way, sure that it is a fake and I am too young to drink. When I am out with friends, people always think I am the kid brother who is tagging along. All of this makes me feel very self-conscious.

The braces also affect my social life. I am afraid girls do not want to go out with someone who wears braces, so I hesitate to ask for dates. If I do manage to get a date, I am in the embarrassing situation of excusing myself after I eat so I can go get the food out of my braces. Kissing is not the fun it should be, either, because when my lips are pressed against the metal, they get sore.

Worst of all, the braces are painful. By the age of seventeen, a person has adult teeth that are pretty well set. When the dentist tightens my braces, all the teeth in my mouth hurt because they are difficult to move. I am unable to eat anything harder than Jell-O for a week. The tightening of my braces also gives me headaches from my upper jaw to the top of my skull. The insides of my lips become raw, and it is difficult to talk. It seems that as soon as the pain passes, it is time to go back to the dentist to get my braces tightened again.

PLANNING THE ESSAY WITH AN OUTLINE MAP

Many writers find that outlining an essay before writing the first draft helps ensure solid organization, adequate detail, and relevance. After generating ideas and before drafting, try writing an outline map. To do this, fill in a mapping form like the one that follows:

Approach to lead-in: _____

_____

Early version of thesis: _____

_____

Paragraph 2 Topic Sentence Idea	Paragraph 3 Topic Sentence Idea	Paragraph 4 Topic Sentence Idea
Supporting Detail ↓	Supporting Detail ↓	Supporting Detail ↓

continued

Supporting Detail Supporting Detail	Supporting Detail Supporting Detail	Supporting Detail Supporting Detail
Approach to conclusion: _____ _____		

To illustrate how the outline map can help you plan an essay, here is a completed map for the essay "Let's Pay College Athletes" on p. 148:

Approach to lead-in: Reasons for scholarships—to get good players.

Early version of thesis: Instead of getting scholarships, college ball players should be paid a salary.

Paragraph 2 Topic Sentence Idea	Paragraph 3 Topic Sentence Idea	Paragraph 4 Topic Sentence Idea	Paragraph 5 Topic Sentence Idea
Being a scholarship athlete is hard.	Athletes without money could still go to school.	Would eliminate students who do not want to be in school.	Would make more money.
Must be full-time student. Sport is time-consuming. Without scholarship, could attend part-time.	Use salary for expenses. Attend while playing or later.	Fewer unqualified students in classes. Places available for more qualified students	Better games—bigger attendance. More tuition from students who take athletes' places.
Approach to conclusion: The fact that we've always had athletic scholarships doesn't mean we should continue to have them.			

The outline map allows you to check the relevance of your topic sentences and supporting details. You can compare each topic sentence idea against the early version of your thesis to be sure each one is relevant to the thesis. Similarly, you can check the details in each column against the topic sentence idea at the top of the column to be sure each is relevant to the topic sentence.

The outline map can also help you decide if your detail is adequate. If you have few details in a column, you may need to generate additional ideas.

The number of columns (supporting paragraphs) in a map will vary from essay to essay. However, you should have at least two.

If you do not have enough ideas to fill in the map, return to idea generation and then finish the map.

PRACTICE 12.6

The following essay was written by a student. Read it and answer the questions that follow to test your understanding.

Insecure Hospital Employment

At one time, working in a hospital meant secure employment. Even when our economy was at its worst, hospital employees could count on regular paychecks. They never worried about standing in long unemployment lines. Unfortunately, this is no longer true. The effects of our declining economy have reached hospitals at last, and problems have resulted for everyone, employees and patients alike.

Although it took awhile, the effects of unemployment in the general workforce finally reached hospitals. Eventually unemployment benefits and union health care benefits ran out for the jobless, and suddenly many people could no longer afford even a brief hospital stay. Elective surgery was put off indefinitely and even required procedures were neglected because of lack of money. Fewer patients are in hospitals as a result, and one must wonder about the state of our health. Obviously with fewer patients, hospitals must cut their staffs.

Another reason for hospital layoffs is the increased number of ambulatory care facilities. These units are treating patients who once were treated in hospital emergency rooms. For some, it makes sense to use an ambulatory care facility because this can be less expensive and more convenient. For others, insurance companies dictate use of ambulatory care units. Either way, the effect on hospitals is to cause more layoffs.

With fewer patients being cared for by hospital personnel, the need for such personnel is decreased and layoffs occur. This has many effects, including low hospital morale. The workers who remain on the payroll feel threatened and insecure. They become worried about whether they will be the next to be axed, and this affects their performance. Certainly, worried, depressed employees do not make good employees.

Another detrimental effect of layoffs is understaffing. When the number of workers on a shift is reduced, there are fewer employees to do the required work. For example, under normal working conditions a registered nurse on a general, medical floor has approximately nine patients to be responsible for. However, once the staff is diminished, the patient load increases, and the nurse no longer has time for needed breaks. The nurse is overworked and unable to perform at peak efficiency. The morale of the overworked nurse declines even more, and more seriously, patient care suffers.

Understaffing is aggravated by the high absenteeism that occurs after layoffs. Employees not laid off experience a great deal of stress because they are overworked and worried about losing their own jobs. This stress leads to fatigue and illness, which leads to absenteeism. To make matters worse, when employees call in, they are often not replaced with substitutes. As a result, the remaining employees become more overworked and depressed.

All of this has an adverse effect on patients. People who require the best that medicine can offer are treated by overworked personnel who are more likely to make mistakes. Not only is patient welfare jeopardized, but so is patient comfort. Layoffs mean poor kitchen and laundry service, irritable orderlies, and slower response to requests.

Finally, the layoff of hospital personnel worsens the hospital's unemployment situation. Unemployed hospital workers have their medical benefits interrupted. Thus, if the unemployed worker should require hospital care, he or she is likely to postpone it. This reduces the hospital census more and leads to additional layoffs.

A vicious cycle exists. The high unemployment rate in general means fewer admissions, and this creates unemployment among hospital workers. This leads to a higher general unemployment, which causes even more hospital layoffs. And through it all, everyone, including the patient, suffers.

On a separate sheet, answer the following questions:

1. What is the thesis of "Insecure Hospital Employment"? What is the writer's topic? What is the writer's view of the topic?

2. What approach is used for the lead-in?

3. What is the topic sentence of each supporting paragraph? What does each topic sentence present as the focus?

4. Is each topic sentence relevant to the thesis?

5. Are the supporting details adequate? Explain.

6. Are the supporting details relevant? Explain.

7. What approach is used for the conclusion?

STUDENT ESSAYS TO STUDY

The student essays that follow illustrate the types of writing explained in Part Two: narration, description, illustration, process analysis, cause-and-effect analysis, definition, comparison and contrast, classification, and persuasion.

Narration

The following narrative essay is an expansion of the paragraph on p. 75. Before studying this essay, review the discussion of narration beginning on p. 71. (For an example of narration in a published essay, see "On Being 17, Bright, and Unable to Read" on p. 447.)

A Deadly Afternoon

Many of my friends are anxious because they have no idea what they want to do with their lives. They have tried a number of majors, but, so far, they have not discovered anything they feel passionate about, and they worry that they will never find something they can get excited about doing. I am fortunate that I do not have their concern because I discovered what I wanted to do even before I came to college. On a rainy and miserable afternoon of my senior year, on May 19 to be exact, a dramatic incident showed me what I wanted to do with my life.

I was walking to my seventh period class when I noticed a disturbance in the hallway. I could see that Tom had Collette pinned against the wall, causing her to tremble violently. Collette had broken up with Tom just a few days earlier, and everyone was waiting for trouble because Tom had a history of violence and most sensible people were afraid of him. If I had stopped to think, I probably would have run for help, but instead I acted reflexively. I grabbed Tom's arm and shouted, "Let her go!" He squinted at me like he was having trouble focusing, and at that moment I became afraid. Then, suddenly he stormed away muttering, "I'll make you sorry, both of you." At that point, the principal showed up, so I told her what I knew and walked away.

I was shaken up, so before going to class, I stepped into the bathroom to splash water on my face. I was startled to see that Tom was there. At first I was scared. Tom had a short fuse and liked to use his fists. I fully expected him to lash out at me for my interference in the hallway. Then I noticed the blood spreading across his shirt and the knife on the floor. At that instant, Tom sagged to the floor. His skin had a blue cast, and the blood covered his chest. I ran to the door and screamed for help. Instantly, the principal and three teachers arrived. They frantically tried to stop Tom's wound from bleeding. After what seemed like hours, the paramedics arrived. They did what they could, but Tom did not make it. He was pronounced dead at the hospital. Everyone knew Tom was violent, but no one expected him to turn that violence on himself.

Eventually, it came out that Tom was an abused child who equated love and violence. His life had been an extremely difficult one of poverty and deprivation, as well as abuse. There were some pretty good reasons for his antisocial behavior, and if any of us had bothered to look more closely, we would have seen them.

Tom's death made me realize how troubled people can be. I decided at that point to major in psychology and become a school counselor to help troubled kids like Tom.

Description

The next essay is a description. Before studying it, review the discussion of description beginning on p. 79.

My Place of Solitude

Whenever I need to be alone, I go to Cherry Flat, a little-known area in the mountains of Sequoia National Forest. It is a peaceful, isolated, rustic place.

To get to Cherry Flat, I have to ascend Sugarloaf Mountain. The road resembles a snake. The turns are so sharp I cannot resist the temptation to take a quick peek back to make sure the rear end of my car made it around with me. A little-used turnoff at the summit leads down a deeply rutted, muddy lane to Cherry Flat.

Cherry Flat is a primitive campground. There is only a small, unpainted, rough wood hut with a half moon cut into the door. The only place to pitch a tent is on one of the four flat spots carved out of the sloping hillside.

Any hardship I encounter because of the lack of conveniences is made up by the spectacular scenery. Majestic mountains surround the camp. Redwood Mountain stands to the north; Burnt Point is to the east, and Big Baldy, its granite dome glistening, to the west. The Kaweak River at the bottom of the gorge resembles a silvery ribbon. My eyes are slowly pulled upward following the march of tall pines to the crest of Redwood Mountain where the azure sky begins.

After setting up camp, I hike down the mountain and explore along the river. The trail is a mile long and drops one thousand feet in elevation on its way to the bottom. Halfway, I stop for a sip of clear, cool spring water that is trickling down the face of a rock ledge. Down a steep section and around a bend, the path leads past Disappearing Creek. In a small pool are brilliantly colored rainbow trout. The fish, when they sense my presence, dart away to hide. Lying on a smooth, warm boulder beside the swift running river, I like to watch the billowy clouds float by. The trail ends by a small waterfall. Water spills over the edge and falls twenty feet into a deep pool below. Ripples radiate outward and lap gently on the shore.

As the light grows dim and the clouds glow orange and pink, the sun inches its way behind a mountaintop. I relax and enjoy a cold drink back at camp—a fitting end to a peaceful day.

Illustration

The following illustration essay is an expansion of the paragraph on p. 90. Before studying the essay, review the discussion of illustration beginning on p. 86. (For an example of illustration in a published essay, see "Black Men and Public Space" on p. 482.)

One Step Forward and Two Steps Back

Americans love technology. Every time some new time-saving or labor-saving device hits the market, we rush out to buy it. Price is no object. If it is new and more advanced, we want it. Americans are proud of our technological advancements, but technology often comes with a price.

Consider the cordless phone, for example. Yes, it gives us freedom to move around. However, more often than not, these phones cross frequencies with other phones so that we hear other people's conversations, and they hear ours. What we gain in mobility, we lose in privacy. We also lose clear conversations, for these phones snap, crackle, and pop more than most breakfast cereals. If you use your phone for business, that can be a real problem. Then, there is the matter of finding the phone in the first place. Since the user tends to leave the phone wherever the last conversation ended, hunting the phone up for the next call can be a frustrating challenge. If you were the last user, chances are good that you will find it after painstakingly recalling the events of the previous five hours, but if someone else in your household has used it—forget finding the thing. It can be anywhere from the tool chest in the basement to the potted plant on the back porch. Of course, since no one replaces the phone in its cradle for recharging, the chances are good that your conversation will be cut off mid-sentence as your batteries sputter to the end of their lives.

The Internet is another example. It offers computer users almost limitless access to a staggering amount of information. However, users are so glued to their computer screens day and night that they no longer have a life away from their PCs. Almost weekly, some new service, bulletin board, or information source is added to the Internet, so users can never feel on top of things. They must spend ever increasing amounts of time "staying informed." Thus, once on the information highway, people become so obsessed that they do not take the exit ramp.

Another example that I read about concerns the computer-designed magnesium wheels General Motors put on its cars not too long ago. Thanks to a computer error, the tire seals did not fit properly. As a result, thousands of car owners woke up to discover that their brand new cars had flat tires. By the time GM figured out what went wrong, recalled the cars, and fixed them, it had lost a tremendous amount of money. The people who bought the cars were frustrated and unhappy, so it is unlikely they will buy GM products again soon.

It is commonly believed that everything has its price, and technological devices are no different. They may make life easier, but they are not without their problems.

Process Analysis

The next essay, an example of process analysis, is an expansion of the paragraph on p. 94. Before studying the essay, review the discussion of process analysis beginning on p. 94. (For an example of process analysis in a published essay, see "Green Frog Skin" on p. 459.)

Making Money with a Garage Sale

Have you noticed how many garage sales there are every spring, summer, and fall? Do you assume people must be crazy to flock to these things just to buy other people's junk? Maybe they are crazy, but people do love to buy other people's used stuff, and if you plan it right, you too can make a great deal of money from a garage sale.

First, you must gather all the saleable items collecting dust in your basement and attic. Do not include anything badly broken, but keep everything else. The items you think are the most worthless are likely to be the first to sell. Remember that Buddha statue with the clock in the belly that you would not be caught dead having in your living room? That will sell. So will the velvet painting of Elvis, the pink lawn flamingoes, and all those trashy trip souvenirs. Toys and tools are hot sellers, but clothes (unless they are children's) probably will not sell very well.

Next—and this is very important—clean this junk up. Dirty items will not sell, but you will be surprised at the weird stuff that goes if it is clean. Two days before the sale, take an afternoon, a bottle of Fantastik spray cleaner, and some paper towels and get the years of dust and grime wiped away. Be careful, though. Once this stuff is clean, you may be tempted to keep it. This would be a big mistake. Not only will you not make a profit, but you will be stuck with your own junk again.

Once your items are clean, display them properly. Get lots of tables, even if you have to rent them. Arrange everything attractively, trying to keep housewares together, toys together, and so forth. Do not crowd the items, and put large objects to the rear of the table so you do not hide the smaller things from the discriminating eyes of eager bargain hunters.

The most important part is pricing. I have just three words of advice: cheap! cheap! cheap! Also, be prepared to bargain. Shoppers will often ask if you will take less than you are asking, and your answer should always be yes. Remember, this trash has been in your basement collecting spider eggs for the past five years, so do not get greedy. Price it to move because the last thing you want to do is drag this stuff back in the house because it did not sell.

Also, write the price of each item on a white sticker placed on the object.

If you really want a great sale, advertise. Put signs up on telephone poles and trees, directing people to the sale, and place an ad in the classifieds.

Finally, pamper your customers. Provide grocery bags for carrying those marvelous purchases home in, and serve coffee—for twenty-five cents a cup of course. If the day is hot, lemonade or iced tea at a reasonable price is always a hit.

Follow these steps, and you can pocket a significant amount of money. I once made two hundred dollars with a garage sale and got my basement cleaned out for good measure.

Definition

The next essay is an example of definition. Before studying it, review the characteristics of definition on p. 101. (For an example of definition in a published essay, see "On Being 17, Bright, and Unable to Read" on p. 447 and "My Way!" on p. 451.)

Runner's High

Some people run religiously (five or six times a week); some run periodically (five or six times a month); and some run whenever they feel an urge to be physically fit (once a year). What makes these people run? What inner drive makes them go out onto the lonely road, with their Walkmans by their sides and their large sticks to beat off attacking dogs? Do they like the feel of Ben Gay rubbed all over their tired, aching bodies? No, these people run to experience that special feeling known as runner's high.

Some runners feel this high when they begin running, while others feel the rush as soon as they are finished. The most common time to feel the high, though, is about halfway into the run when the adrenalin is pumping.

The high is difficult to explain to nonrunners, but put simply it feels like getting an A on a final exam you were sure you failed. The high takes you by surprise. Just when you feel you are about to see your dinner come out through your nose, the high picks you up and gives you incentive to keep going. The high is similar to a painkiller in the way it suppresses the pain in your joints. It also relaxes your tense muscles. In some instances, it even replenishes your energy, which makes you go farther and faster.

The high can even be the deciding factor in a race. If a runner peaks too early and experiences the high, then the runner will more than likely "hit the invisible wall" sooner and therefore lose the race.

If the high lasted longer than its normal few seconds (or even minutes in distance races), then the track world would have an incredible number of outstanding runners. However, all good things end, and a runner's high disappears just as suddenly as it comes.

Many people wonder why runners make themselves suffer so much just to achieve a few moments of bliss. Unfortunately, there is no way to explain this to someone who has never experienced runner's high.

Comparison and Contrast

The next essay is an example of contrast. Before studying it, review the characteristics of comparison and contrast on p. 108. (For an example of comparison and contrast in a published essay, see "If You Had to Kill Your Own Hog" on p. xxx.

Identical but Different

There are two kinds of twins, fraternal and identical. Fraternal, or dizygotic twins, are the product of two fertilized ova. Identical twins develop from a single fertilized ovum. I am an identical twin. My twin sister Loretta is older by six minutes. During our infancy, my twin and I were so identical that our baby bracelets were left on for quite a while after we were released from the hospital. Her bracelet identified her as Baby A; I was known as Baby B. Although physically we are still similar, my twin sister and I have very different personalities.

Loretta and I still look alike, so we are frequently mistaken for each other by teachers and those who do not know us well. We both wear our curly, auburn hair to the shoulder. We both are just over five feet, and I weigh only two pounds more than my twin. Our facial features mimic each other, although I have been told there is more of a sparkle in my eyes than in Loretta's. This, of course, angers my twin. I think Loretta is prettier, but she thinks I am, so I guess it is a toss-up. From our earliest days, we became accustomed to responding to "Hey Twin" because people cannot tell us apart.

When we were young, my twin and I realized that our interests were different. We would often play dolls together. Loretta had beautiful Barbie Dolls with sophisticated, feminine outfits. I had rugged G.I. Joes in full battle gear. Loretta would always want my G.I. Joes to be boyfriends for her Barbie Dolls. Of course, I would never consent to such a thing. Once Loretta was particularly persistent; she wanted Barbie and Joe to marry. I got angry and made one of my G.I. Joes drive through the little house we had constructed from old cardboard boxes and trample over her Barbies. Then I ran outside to play in the dirt pile behind our house, leaving Loretta crying in the midst of the destruction.

Another difference was apparent in school, where Loretta was the more serious student. When we had class together, she would be listening attentively to the teacher, while I was busy passing notes and planning the night to come. After dinner, Loretta would faithfully retreat to our bedroom to read and do her homework. I would race outside to throw a Frisbee, play basketball, or do anything that was not homework. Needless to say, Loretta's grades were excellent, and mine were rather ho-hum.

Even now, the difference in our personalities is obvious. My twin is quiet and conservative. She always does the right thing. I'm outgoing and adventurous--and always in trouble. A good example of this difference occurred during spring break in Florida. Loretta and I met some guys on the beach, and they invited us to a party. Loretta declined and begged me not to go. She said we hardly knew them and that they were rowdy. She was afraid we would get into trouble. I went anyway. Guess which twin was arrested two hours later for disorderly conduct?

Thus, Loretta and I may look identical, but inwardly we are very different people.

Cause-and-Effect Analysis

The following cause-and-effect analysis is an expansion of the paragraph on p. 119. Before studying the essay, review the characteristics of cause-and-effect analysis on p. 118. (For examples of cause-and-effect analysis in published essays, see "Students in Shock" on p. 443, "The Company Man" on p. 462, "Black Men and Public Space" on p. 482, and "Time to Look and Listen" on p. 465.)

What Happened When I Quit Smoking

People who have never smoked do not understand how difficult it is to kick the habit. They think quitting is a relatively simple matter of throwing the cigarettes away and never lighting up again. However, these people are wrong. When I quit smoking two years ago, I was miserable.

First of all, I gained fifteen pounds. As a result, I looked terrible, and I was like a sausage in a casing when I wore my clothes. Every morning it was a struggle to find something to put on that did not cut off my circulation. When I looked in the mirror, I was depressed by my appearance and self-conscious about how terrible I looked. I tried not to eat, but I had to do something if I was not going to smoke, and eating was the only alternative because it kept my hands and mouth busy.

Even worse, I was so irritable no one could stand to be near me. I snapped at people and picked fights with my best friend. I knew I was being unreasonable, but I could not help myself. Once I screamed at my girlfriend and called her a nag when she reminded me to go buy my mother a birthday present. I did not mean it, but she spent the rest of the night in tears.

For the first month, I was actually hallucinating. I would turn suddenly, thinking I heard a sound, or jump up startled, feeling like something clammy had touched me. Once in a movie theatre, I jumped a foot out of my seat because I thought I felt someone put a hand on my shoulder.

Even in my sleep there was no relief. I would wake up in a cold sweat several times a night after dreaming about smoking a Winston. Then I would lie in bed and shake, unable to get back to sleep because the craving was so bad. I would feel depressed because the pleasure I felt from smoking in my dream was not real.

It has been two years since I have had a cigarette, and I am in much better shape now, but I still have some weight to lose and in social situations I still get a little jumpy. Believe me, people who think it is easy to quit smoking have never been through what I have gone through.

Classification

The following classification essay is an expansion of the paragraph on p. 127. Before studying the essay, review the characteristics of classification on p. 127.

Different Kinds of Shoppers

Anyone who has been a salesclerk knows that shoppers fall into different categories. After working at Kmart for over a year, I have come to know well the four different kinds of shoppers.

The first shopper is the browser. Browsers do not have much to do with their lives, so they have endless amounts of time to waste. Nonchalantly, they wander around my department picking up every item that catches the eye. Unfortunately, browsers never put things back in the right place, so I have to straighten stock when they leave. I guess browsers think that salesclerks have as much time on their hands as they do. The browsers are also a pain because they want to look at every item locked in the showcase. Of course, after all this, the browsers leave without buying a thing.

The dependent shoppers are also annoying. They have to be shown where everything is, including the items in front of their noses. Dependent shoppers never bother to look for anything. They walk through the front door, find a clerk, and ask him or her to get a dozen items. Dependent shoppers can never make decisions for themselves. "Which color do you think is best?" they ask, and "Which watch do you think my niece will like better?" Half the time they just walk away without buying anything because they cannot decide what to get. Of course, they never leave empty-handed unless the salesclerk has spent at least fifteen minutes with them.

The hit-and-run shoppers are much easier to deal with. They are always frantic and rushed. They will buy anything, regardless of price, if they can get it fast. Price does not matter. One recent hit-and-runner raced in, asked breathlessly if he could pay for a stereo by check, picked out the first one he saw, and bought two of them. He wrote a check for over four hundred dollars as if it were $1.98 and raced out.

Independent shoppers are the easiest to deal with. They want no part of salesclerks except for ringing up the sales. They have done their homework. They know what they want, the particular brand, and the amount they are willing to pay. They find what they want on their own, put things back in the right places, and never ask questions. An independent shopper can walk into a store and five minutes later walk out again with the desired item.

Any salesclerk will tell you that dealing with the public is not easy. As far as I am concerned, this world needs more independent shoppers.

Persuasion

The following persuasive essay is an expansion of the paragraph on p. 142. Before studying the essay, review the characteristics of persuasion on p. 137. (For examples of persuasion in published essays, see "Green Frog Skin" on p. 459 and "If You Had to Kill Your Own Hog" on p. 472.)

No Degree Required

Education in the United States is in trouble. That statement won't surprise anyone because we hear it all the time. What <u>is</u> surprising is that we don't seem to be doing much about the problem. Well, one suggestion can improve the quality of education in the United States, and it won't even cost a lot of money. We should discontinue the requirement that people must earn teaching degrees before they can teach in elementary, middle, or high school.

The requirement that a person have a teaching degree from a four-year college means that talented, knowledgeable people, people who would be terrific teachers, cannot give what they have to offer—just because they have not taken a handful of teaching courses. Consider an accountant who loves children and has a way of inspiring them. He or she cannot teach arithmetic without earning a teaching degree, even though that person already has the knowledge and talent to be a fine teacher. Or what about a former U.S. Senator who loves children and knows the government inside out? That person cannot teach social studies without going back to school to earn a teaching degree. In both cases and countless more like them, people who could educate and inspire young people are prevented from doing so. This fact is particularly disturbing when you consider that the accountant and Senator probably know more about math and government than some people with teaching degrees who are currently teaching math and social studies.

Of course, we can't let just anyone with knowledge of a subject into the classroom. We must be sure the person has the other qualities necessary to teach. We should set up training programs to teach prospective teachers about classroom management, and we should have tests to judge the knowledge and talent of people who want to teach. Then we should require a year of probation to weed out those who are not suitable. Beyond that, anyone with the knowledge, desire, and talent should be able to teach. Deans of colleges of education all over the country are likely to cry out that only accredited schools can train teachers, but that point of view is self-serving. After all, our current method of requiring teaching degrees has done little to assure quality education.

An important benefit of this plan is that it taps an important source of potentially gifted teachers: retired people. These days, people are retiring younger, and they are looking for productive second careers. Teaching could be that career. Men and women with lifetimes of valuable experience and knowledge have much to share with young people. They should be able to teach without spending time and money to go back to school themselves to take courses that may not even make them better teachers. Furthermore, these people are, in many cases, financially secure because their children are grown and gone, their mortgages are paid off, and their expenses are fewer. Thus, they are likely to be more satisfied with the meager salaries that teachers often make. Hiring retirees to teach means we can spend less on teacher salaries, a real saving to financially troubled school districts.

With American education in trouble, we need creative solutions that do not cost more than school districts can afford. Hiring talented people without teaching degrees to educate our children can be one such solution.

Thinking, Learning, and Writing in College   Notetaking

Notetaking is an important part of college life. To be a successful notetaker,

- Carefully read the assigned material before class.
- Record only important points.
- Use abbreviations judiciously to maintain speed.

A key to successful notetaking actually occurs after class, when you should rewrite your notes as soon as possible to keep them organized and clear. In *some* cases, you may be able to do this with a variation of the outline map on p. 157, like this:

- At the top of the page, write out the subject of the lecture.
- At the top of the first column, write the first main point. Below that, write the important explanatory points and subpoints.
- At the top of the second column, write the second main point, and below it write the explanatory points and subpoints.
- Continue this way until you have rewritten and organized the day's notes.

 *Checklist for an Essay*

Before submitting your essay, be sure you can answer yes to these questions:

1. Does your introduction have a lead-in designed to create interest in your essay?
2. Does your introduction have a thesis that presents your topic and your view of the topic?
3. Is the thesis narrow enough? Did you avoid a statement of fact?
4. Does the thesis avoid a formal announcement?
5. Did you avoid inappropriate vague words in the thesis?
6. Does each supporting paragraph have a relevant topic sentence that presents the focus of the paragraph?
7. Are all the details in each supporting paragraph relevant to the topic sentence?
8. Are the details adequate and specific?
9. Are your details arranged in a logical order?
10. Have you used transitions where they are needed?
11. Does your conclusion bring the essay to a satisfying finish?
12. Have you edited carefully, more than once?
13. Did you proofread slowly and carefully, one word and punctuation mark at a time?

 Tips For Writing An Essay

Planning

1. Try one or more of the idea-generation techniques to find ideas for your essay. (See p. 2.)
2. Fill in an outline map like the one on p. 157.

Writing

1. Using your outline map as a guide, write your draft in one sitting, without worrying about grammar, usage, and such. Skip troublesome parts and push on to the finish.
2. To be more objective when you revise, leave your draft for a day.

Rewriting

1. To check your thesis, put one line under the topic and two lines under the view of the topic.

2. Give your introduction to two people to read. Ask them if this paragraph arouses their interest.

3. Put a wavy line under the topic sentence of each supporting paragraph. Check these topic sentences against the thesis to be sure they are relevant.

4. Check every sentence in each supporting paragraph for relevance to the topic sentence.

5. Circle each general noun, verb, and modifier. If some of these are too vague, find more specific alternatives.

6. Read your draft aloud. If you hear any abrupt shifts in direction, transitions may be needed.

7. Give your draft to someone whose judgment you trust. Ask that person to tell you whether anything is unclear and whether any point needs additional development. Also ask that person whether your conclusion brings the essay to a satisfying finish.

8. Check p. 31 for editing procedures.

9. Copy or type your draft into final form and consult p. 33 for proofreading procedures.

WRITING ASSIGNMENT

For your essay, you have a choice of topics.

1. Use one of the thesis sentences you developed for *Practice 12.2*. If you use one of these, check your responses to *Practice 12.3* for possible topic sentences.

2. Write an essay that tells about the disadvantages or problems you have experienced with something.

3. Write an essay to the seniors at a local high school explaining what they can expect if they attend your college.

4. Like the writer of "A Deadly Afternoon" on p. 161, tell the story of a time when you learned something important.

5. Use examples to illustrate the best or worst job you have had.

6. Like the writer of "My Place of Solitude" on p. 162, describe a place where you like to be alone.

7. Like the writer of "Making Money with a Garage Sale" on p. 165, describe how to do or make something that can earn a person some money.

8. Like the writer of "Runner's High" on p. 166, define a feeling or emotion.

9. Contrast the way something was and the way you expected it to be.

10. Like the writer of "What Happened When I Quit Smoking" on p. 168, explain the causes or effects of something you did.

11. Read "Different Kinds of Shoppers" on p. 169 and then classify the different kinds of salesclerks.

12. Read "No Degree Required" on p. 171 and write an essay arguing the opposite view.

13. For additional essay assignments, see p. 450, p. 453, p. 457, p. 461, pp. 464, and p. 467.

Visit the Clouse Website!

For additional exercises, quizzes, and Internet activities, visit our Website at:

http://www.ablongman.com/clouse

For even more activities, visit the Longman English pages at:

http://www.ablongman.com/englishpages

Chapter 13

Identifying Subjects and Verbs

In order to write effective sentences, writers must be able to identify subjects and verbs. To help you do so, this chapter will explain how to:

1. identify subjects in a variety of sentences

2. identify different kinds of verbs

◆ ◆ ◆

SUBJECTS AND VERBS

A sentence has both a subject and a verb. A **subject** is one or more words telling who or what the sentence is about. A **verb** is one or more words telling what the subject does or how the subject exists.

      s.   v.

Babies cry.

Babies: tells who the sentence is about, so this word is the subject.

cry: tells what the subject does, so this word is the verb.

PRETEST

To see how well you currently find subjects and verbs, underline each subject once and each verb twice. If you are unsure, do not guess; just move on. Check your answers in Appendix III.

1. Before work, Jeffrey's mother packed Jeffrey's school lunch.

2. Tuition at this school is the second lowest in the state.

3. Marcos has eaten peanut butter sandwiches for lunch every day this week.

4. Mother returned to school and studied business administration.

5. Many people in this city do not know about the proposed industrial park.

6. Joan and her brothers bought their parents a VCR for their anniversary.

7. The carton of Grandmother's clothes is in the attic.

8. Jacques has been studying for his law school entrance examination.

9. Are the keys still in the car?

10. There will be no excuse for tardiness.

11. Please answer me.

12. At last the holidays are over, and all of us can relax and recover.

13. The students in the reference room of the library are making too much noise.

14. There can be no accidents this time.

15. At the end of the summer, my parents and I will move to Texas and buy a small horse ranch.

IDENTIFYING VERBS

You may find the subject and verb of a sentence more easily if you first find the verb and then go on to find the subject. The verb will be the word or words that change form to show present, past, and future times (known as **tenses**).

I walk five miles every day.

In this sentence, the verb is *walk*. We know this because *walk* is the word that changes form to show present, past, and future time.

present tense:	Today I *walk*.
past tense:	Yesterday I *walked*.
future tense:	Tomorrow I *will walk*.

Because verbs indicate time, you can locate them with a simple test. Speak the words *today I, yesterday I,* and *tomorrow I* before a word or word group. If the result is sensible and if that word or word group changes form, it is a verb. Try the test with this sentence:

The wide receiver fumbled the football.

Can we say, "Today I *the*"? "Yesterday I *the*"? "Tomorrow I *the*"? No, we cannot, so *the* is not a verb. Can we say "Today I *wide*"? Can we say "Today I *receiver*"? "Today I *football*"? No, of course not, so *wide, receiver,* and *football* are not verbs. Notice, however, what happens if we apply the test to *fumbled:*

Today I *fumble.*

Yesterday I *fumbled.*

Tomorrow I *will fumble.*

Fumble changes form to indicate different tenses (times), so it is a verb.

> NOTE: a few verbs (like *cost*) do not change form to show time.

> CAUTION: Some words can be verbs in some sentences and sub-
> jects in others. Run is such a word.
>
> *run* as subject: My morning *run* was refreshing.
> *run* as verb: I *run* five miles before breakfast every day.
>
> A word that tells who or what a sentence is about is the subject of a
> sentence, even if it changes form to show time. (Subjects are dis-
> cussed on p. 184.)

Action Verbs, Linking Verbs, and Helping Verbs

Action Verbs   The most common kind of **verb** is the **action verb**, which
shows activity, movement, thought, or process. Here are some examples:

> Action verbs showing activity or movement: hit, yell, dance, kick,
> walk, run, eat, play (The trees *sway* in the breeze.)
>
> Action verbs showing thought: think, consider, wonder, remember,
> want, ponder (Pat *judges* people harshly.)
>
> Action verbs showing process: learn, try, read, enjoy (I can *explain*
> her anger.)

Linking Verbs   Another kind of verb is the **linking verb**, which links the
subject to something that renames or describes that subject. Here are two
examples:

> Roberto *is* the best skier in the group. [The verb *is* does not show
> action. Instead it links the subject *Roberto* with words that describe
> the subject—"the best skier in the group."]
>
> Yolanda *was* my best friend. [The verb *was* does not show action.
> Instead it links the subject *Yolanda* with words that rename the sub-
> ject—"my best friend."]

Review the following list of linking verbs so you will recognize them in your own sentences:

am	was	appear	taste
be	were	feel	smell
is	been	seem	look
are	being	sound	become

Helping Verbs   An action verb or linking verb can appear with another verb, called a **helping verb**. Here are some examples:

Grandma Ramirez *can speak* three languages. [The action verb is *speak;* the helping verb is *can.*]

The train *will be* late. [The linking verb is *be;* the helping verb is *will.*]

Review the following list of helping verbs so you will recognize them in your own sentences:

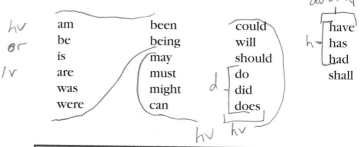

NOTES:

1. Some verbs are on both the linking and helping verb lists (*am, is, are, was, were,* for example). When these verbs appear alone, they are linking verbs. When they appear with other verbs, they are helping verbs.

   linking verb: The food *is* too spicy.

   helping verb: The tree *is* dropping its leaves.

2. A sentence can have more than one helping verb.

   two helping verbs: The plane *has been* delayed.

   three helping verbs: I *will have been* gone by then.

3. *Have, has, had* are usually helping verbs. However, the following examples show two times when they are action verbs:

   A cat *has* kittens. (*Has* means "gives birth to.")

   We *have* lunch at noon. (*Have* means "eat.")

PRACTICE 13.1

Identify each underlined verb as an action verb (av), helping verb (hv), linking verb (lv). The first is done as an example.

More than 260,000 people <u>are</u> <u>buried</u> at Arlington National Cemetery, which <u>conducts</u> approximately 5,400 burials each year. The average number of funerals held there <u>is</u> 20 a day. Of all the national cemeteries in the United States, Arlington <u>has</u> the second-largest number of people buried there. Calverton National Cemetery on Long Island <u>holds</u> the distinction of being the largest. At that cemetery, there <u>can</u> <u>be</u> as many as 7,000 burials a year.

The first graves in Arlington National Cemetery <u>were</u> <u>dug</u> by James Parks. Parks <u>was</u> a former Arlington Estate slave. He <u>was</u> <u>born</u> on the property and <u>can</u> <u>claim</u> to be the only person buried in the cemetery who <u>came</u> into this world on the property. He <u>is</u> <u>interred</u> in Section 15.

PRACTICE 13.2

Underline every verb in the following paragraph.

Almost everyone can recognize the opening of Ludwig van Beethoven's Fifth Symphony. The composer may have expected its popularity. However, he would have been surprised about one particular use of his composition. During World War II, the first four notes became a rallying cry for the Allies. The first three short notes and the one longer note sounded like the Morse code for the letter V—three dots and a dash. The Allies had adopted the "V" as the symbol for victory. Beethoven's first four notes from the Fifth Symphony were played every night between programs over the British Broadcasting Corporation and extensively in the United States as well. Clearly, the music had a stirring effect.

Sentences with More Than One Verb

A single sentence can have more than one verb, and each of these verbs can be composed of one or more words. Here is an example:

Paul *sat* at the window and *waited* for Maria.

This sentence has two one-word verbs: *sat* and *waited.* Now study this sentence:

My sister *arrived* at noon, but I *had gone.*

This sentence also has two verbs, but this time one is composed of one word, and the other is composed of two.

A sentence can contain any number of verbs, and each of these verbs may be composed of a different number of words. The next sentence illustrates this point. The verbs are underlined as a study aid.

As the storm <u>pounded</u> the small, coastal town, volunteers <u>evacuated</u> residents who <u>had ignored</u> earlier warnings that winds <u>could damage</u> property and life.

NOTE: Be careful of descriptive words such as *not, just, never, only, already,* and *always*. These words are not verbs, although they often appear with verbs.

Earl will not agree to such a scheme. (The verb is *will agree.*)

NOTE: A verb that follows *to* is known as an **infinitive**. The infinitive form will never be part of the complete verb functioning with the subject.

I hesitated to answer the question. (The complete verb is *hesitated,* not *answer,* which follows *to*).

PRACTICE 13.3

Underline each complete verb. Remember, a verb that follows *to* is not part of the complete verb, and descriptive words are not part of the verb. The first one is done as an example.

1. The tornado <u>had struck</u> before the warning siren <u>sounded.</u>
2. The class <u>asked</u> the instructor when the final examination <u>would be given.</u>
3. The fire alarm <u>sounded</u>, but many people <u>ignored</u> it because there <u>had been</u> so many false alarms in the past.
4. If I <u>were</u> you, I <u>would take</u> Professor Goldstein for history.
5. It <u>will be</u> years before we <u>know</u> the full effects of the new tax law.
6. If interest rates <u>rise</u>, many people <u>will</u> not <u>purchase</u> new homes.

PRACTICE 13.4

Underline each complete verb. Remember, verbs that follow *to* are not part of the complete verb, and descriptive words are not verbs. The first one is done as an example.

1. The versatile entertainer sang, danced, and told jokes.
2. Julio always asks the most perceptive questions in class.
3. Michael visited several car lots before he decided which used car to buy.
4. In his younger days, Sammy Davis, Jr., sang, danced, and played the drums in his Las Vegas act.
5. In my son's third-grade math class, students will learn how to multiply.
6. Jane has already left because she wants to arrive early.

REVIEW PRACTICE 13.5

Underline each complete verb.

Unlike hurricanes and winter storms, thunderstorms affect relatively small areas. The typical thunderstorm spans 15 miles in diameter and lasts an average of 30 minutes. Nearly 1,800 thunderstorms are occurring at any moment around the world—that is 16 million a year. Despite their small size, all thunderstorms are dangerous. They can produce lightning, which kills more people each year than tornadoes. Heavy rain from thunderstorms can lead to flash flooding. Furthermore, strong winds, hail, and tornadoes are also associated with some thunderstorms.

Thinking, Learning, and Writing in College

Understanding Texts and Exam Questions

Your reading comprehension and performance on tests can improve if you pay careful attention to verbs because verb choice affects meaning significantly. Consider, for example, how meaning is different in these sentences that might appear in a psychology textbook:

- Researchers believe that birth trauma can cause attention deficit disorder.
- Researchers suspect that birth trauma can cause attention deficit disorder.
- Researchers doubt that birth trauma can cause attention deficit disorder.

The choice of verbs will also affect how you answer examination questions, as the following examples show.

- Classify the effects of attention deficit disorder.
- Illustrate the effects of attention deficit disorder.
- Explain the effects of attention deficit disorder.

IDENTIFYING SUBJECTS

The **subject** of a sentence is who or what the sentence is about. You can locate the subject by asking "who or what?" before the verb. The answer will be the subject of the sentence. Consider this sentence:

Ivan earned the highest grade on the history midterm.

The verb in this sentence is *earned.* To find the subject, ask, "who or what earned?" The answer is "*Ivan* earned." Therefore, *Ivan* is the subject. Now look at this sentence.

Before Easter my cat was ill.

The verb is *was.* Ask "who or what was?" and the answer is *cat. Cat,* then, is the subject of the sentence.

PRACTICE 13.6

Underline the subject once and the verb twice. To find the verb, locate the word or words that change form to show time; to find the subject, ask "who or what?" before the verb.

1. Every child is familiar with Cracker Jack.
2. The snack was created by F. W. Rueckheim at the Chicago World's Fair in 1893.
3. The popular snack got its name from a popular expression of the day.
4. People used to say "crackerjack" to mean "great."
5. The toy prize was added to Cracker Jack boxes in 1912.
6. Cracker Jack's popularity has not declined over the years.

PRACTICE 13.7

Underline the subject once and the verb twice. To find the verb, locate the word or words that change form to show time; to find the subject, ask "who or what?" before the verb.

1. Champagne is often drunk at celebrations.
2. Surprisingly, this alcoholic beverage was invented by Dom Perignon, a Benedictine monk.
3. The cleric was put in charge of the vineyards at his monastery in 1668.
4. During his tenure there, Perignon developed sparkling wines.

5. These <u>wines</u> <u>were</u> <u>named</u> for the Champagne section of France.

6. Also, Dom Perignon <u>has come</u> to be the name of a very prestigious and expensive bottle of wine.

Sentences with Prepositional Phrases

A **preposition** shows how two things are positioned in time or space. Here are two examples.

The wallet was *behind* the couch. [*Behind* is a preposition; it shows how the wallet and couch are positioned in space: one is behind the other.]

We had dinner *before* the concert. [*Before* is a preposition; it shows how dinner and the concert are positioned in time: one was before the other.]

You can identify most (but not all) prepositions if you think of a box and a baseball. Any word that can describe the relationship of the baseball to the box is a preposition. The baseball can be *in* the box, *on* the box, *near* the box, and *under* the box; so *in, on, near,* and *under* are prepositions. Here is a list of some common prepositions:

about	before	in	through
above	between	into	to
across	by	like	towards
after	during	of	under
among	for	on	up
at	from	over	with

A **prepositional phrase** is a word group that begins with a preposition. Here are some examples of prepositional phrases. The prepositions are underlined as a study aid.

<u>about</u> this time	<u>among</u> my best friends	<u>at</u> noon
<u>by</u> tomorrow	<u>into</u> the lake	<u>to</u> me
<u>in</u> the back	<u>over</u> the rainbow	<u>on</u> the dog

The subject of a sentence will never be part of a prepositional phrase. Therefore, to find the subject of a sentence, cross out all prepositional phrases first. The subject will be among the remaining words.

The <u>leader</u> ~~of the scouts~~ is a wilderness expert. (The subject is <u>leader</u>.)

A <u>box</u> ~~of old clothes~~ is ~~on the kitchen table~~. (The subject is <u>box</u>.)

If you do not eliminate the first prepositional phrase in the preceding sentence, you might be fooled into thinking the subject is *clothes.* This sentence demonstrates the importance of crossing out prepositional phrases before identifying subjects.

PRACTICE 13.8

Cross out the prepositional phrases and then underline the subject. The first one is done as an example.

1. ~~In the middle of the night~~ heavy winds damaged the orchard.
2. The top of the dresser is covered with dust.
3. The flock of geese flew in formation across the horizon.
4. At the back of the lecture hall, one student slept with his head resting on a pile of books.
5. The last twenty minutes of the movie were fast-paced and cleverly directed.
6. With a little practice anyone can learn word-processing skills.

PRACTICE 13.9

Cross out the prepositional phrases and then underline the subject. The first one is done as an example.

1. The pile ~~of leaves~~ must be raked ~~into the street~~.
2. Six of us plan to visit New York during winter break.
3. The entire defensive line of the football team earned high grades last semester.
4. Some people with allergies find it difficult to live in this part of the country.
5. This stack of old encyclopedias can be taken to the used book sale.
6. In the corner, the mother cat stretched out for her nap.

Sentences with Inverted Order

The subject usually comes before the verb, as in this example:

        s.   v.

The children romped with the playful dog.

Sometimes the subject comes *after* the verb. Then the sentence has **inverted order**. A sentence that asks a question has inverted order.

v.   s.

Is the soup hot enough?

In this sentence the verb *is* comes first. When we ask "who or what is?" we get the answer *soup,* so *soup* is the subject. In this case, the subject comes after the verb.

A sentence that begins with *there is, there are, there was, there were, here is, here are, here was, here were* will also have inverted order.

v.   s.

There were twenty people on a waiting list for that apartment.

The verb is *were,* and the subject is *people. (Were* is the verb because it changes form to indicate different tenses, and *people* is the subject because it answers the question "who or what were?")

PRACTICE 13.10

For each sentence, underline the subject once and the verb twice. Remember, find the verb first and then find the subject by asking "who or what?" before the verb. The first one is done as an example.

1. Here are the folders.
2. Is the storm over yet?
3. There are twelve people in this elevator.
4. Was your week in Ft. Lauderdale relaxing?
5. In the kitchen drawer were three dirty knives.
6. Here are the missing files.

PRACTICE 13.11

For each sentence, underline the subject once and the verb twice. Remember, find the verb and then find the subject by asking "who or what?" before the verb. The first one is done as an example.

1. There are only three people here.
2. Is the exam next Tuesday or next Wednesday?
3. On the window sill sat the fat calico cat.
4. There is some confusion about the new graduation requirements.
5. Are you free for dinner Thursday night?
6. Beside the peaceful brook sat Rusty and his dog.

Sentences with More Than One Subject

A sentence can have more than one subject:

The *money* and the *credit cards* were stolen from my wallet.

The verb in this sentence is *were stolen.* When we ask "who or what were stolen?" we get the answer *money* and *credit cards.* Thus, *money* and *credit cards* are both subjects.

Now study this sentence:

Greg slid into home plate as the shortstop made a play at second base.

This sentence has two verbs: *slid* and *made.* When we ask "who or what slid?" we get *Greg* for an answer; when we ask "who or what made?" we get *shortstop* for an answer. Therefore, this sentence has two subjects: *Greg* and *shortstop.*

PRACTICE 13.12

Each sentence has more than one subject. Underline each of these subjects. If you have any trouble, begin by finding the verb or verbs (the word or words that change form to show tense) and then ask "who or what?" The first one is done as an example.

1. Both <u>Senator Polanski</u> and <u>Governor Perry</u> favor the proposed jobs bill.
2. The school board and the leaders of the teachers' union met behind closed doors for most of the afternoon.
3. Police work is rewarding, but police officers do not make much money.
4. Too many accidents have occurred at the junction of Routes 11 and 45, so a traffic light will be installed.
5. The singer and her accompanist performed an encore in response to the standing ovation.
6. The rain fell for hours, and soon the small streams began to flood low-lying areas.

PRACTICE 13.13

Each sentence has more than one subject. Underline each of these subjects. If you have trouble, find the verbs and then ask "who or what?" The first one is done as an example.

─1. Your <u>time</u> and your <u>energy</u> are needed on this project.

─2. The rabbit and her young fled in panic when the lawn mower ran over their burrow.

─3. Both the manager and the assistant manager apologized for the poor service.

+ 4. The fire alarm sounded, so the students filed out of the room in an orderly fashion.

+ 5. I planted a garden in my backyard, but the rabbits ate most of my crops.

─ 6. Two robins and three sparrows fed contentedly at the bird feeder outside the kitchen window.

REVIEW PRACTICE 13.14

Underline the subjects in the sentences in the following paragraph.

There are more than 2 billion quarts of ice cream eaten in the United States each year. With that figure, you would think ice cream originated in the United States, but the treat was first created in the Orient. Marco Polo encountered it there and brought the idea back to Italy. From Italy, recipes for the confection were carried to France. In France, ice cream became very popular with the nobility. An effort was made to keep the recipes for ice cream a secret from the common people. The first factory for the manufacture of ice cream was started in Baltimore in 1851, but the real development of ice cream did not occur until after 1900, with the advent of refrigeration. There is sugar in ice cream, but the treat is still a fairly nutritious food. One-third pint of vanilla ice cream has as much calcium as one-half cup of milk. Protein and vitamin B are also plentiful in vanilla ice cream.

POST TEST

Underline the subjects once and the verbs twice. You will have to draw on everything you have learned so far about subjects and verbs.

Part A

1. Six of us had decided to travel to Bowling Green for the big game.

2. For the past year, Juan, Lisa, and Maria have volunteered to work in the children's hospital for three hours every week.

3. The first American to orbit the earth was John Glenn.

4. Luis will never agree to your plan, but you may convince Margo.

5. As the price of cigarettes rises, more people will quit smoking.

6. The trees in Vermont have already changed color.

7. The quarterback faked a pass and then ran up the middle for a five-yard gain.

8. Why are you going alone on your vacation?

9. Behind the old barn there is a beautiful patch of clover in bloom.

10. You should take this book and return it to the library.

11. Here is the report, but I must have it back in a week.

12. On the top shelf of my closet are the clothes for the rummage sale.

13. More people must be told about organ donation programs, for such programs save lives.

14. Since Mario quit smoking, he has become irritable and generally unpleasant.

15. As more people become comfortable with computers, information will be processed faster than ever.

16. To me, cigarette smoking is offensive.

17. The pile of dirty clothes in the closet is beginning to smell.

18. You must add the eggs before you add the flour and salt.

19. Peter, Helen, and David decided that they would never campaign for Jeffrey in the student council election.

20. The question of fair play must be considered in this case.

Part B

People have dreams every night. The early dreams usually last only a few minutes, but the dream just before morning can be as long as an hour. This is the dream we are most likely to remember. There are conflicting explanations for dreams. Freud thought that dreams hide worrisome ideas. He said that troublesome thoughts would wake us if they were not disguised as something else. However, many scientists and dream researchers disagree. They have said that dreams are caused by the jumble of electrical impulses in the brain at night. Dreams occur when the brain tries to make sense of these confusing impulses. For example, if you dream that you cannot move, your brain may be trying to explain the paralysis of deep sleep.

Chapter 14

Writing Effective Sentences

T his chapter will help you learn to shape sentences to communicate your ideas clearly, effectively, and with the sophistication appropriate for a college student. You will learn how to

1. use coordination to show the relationship between ideas

2. use subordination to show the relationship between ideas

3. achieve sentence variety for a pleasing rhythm

4. use transitions to show the relationship between ideas and achieve a pleasing rhythm

5. achieve parallelism for balanced sentences

◆ ◆ ◆

IDENTIFYING CLAUSES

A **clause** is a group of words with both a subject and a verb (see Chapter 13 on how to identify subjects and verbs). The following word groups are clauses (the subjects are underlined once, and the verbs are underlined twice).

the snow fell softly

after the marathon runner crossed the finish line

Helen was not invited to the reception

before the storm warnings were issued

The following word groups are *not* clauses because they do not have both a subject *and* a verb. (Word groups that do not have both a subject *and* a verb are *phrases.*)

seeing the log in his path

in the pantry

behind the sofa in the den

frightened by the snarling dog

> NOTE: Take another look at the lists of clauses and phrases and notice that length has nothing to do with whether a word group is a clause or a phrase.

PRACTICE 14.1

Place an *X* next to each clause. Remember, a clause has both a subject and a verb. If you are unsure how to identify subjects and verbs, see Chapter 13.

1. _____ before Lorenzo could finish his sentence
2. _____ around the corner from my house
3. _____ against the wishes of her parents and friends
4. _____ she means well
5. _____ wishing I could help you more
6. _____ the lead singer was the best performer in the show
7. _____ federal funds were requested to repair the dam
8. _____ not wanting to intrude on Martha's privacy
9. _____ the construction foreman took full responsibility for the damage
10. _____ a hawk soared in the distance

Two Kinds of Clauses

There are two kinds of clauses: a clause that can stand as a sentence is a **main clause**; a clause that cannot stand as a sentence is a **subordinate clause**.

The following clauses are main clauses because they can be sentences. In fact, if you add capital letters and periods, you *do* have sentences.

main clause: the movie ended very late

sentence: The movie ended very late.

main clause: freedom of speech is our most valuable liberty

sentence: Freedom of speech is our most valuable liberty.

main clause: her advice was not very helpful

sentence: Her advice was not very helpful.

The following are subordinate clauses. They have subjects and verbs (all clauses do), but they cannot be sentences. To realize this, read the clauses out loud to hear that something more is needed.

subordinate clause: because the union went on strike

subordinate clause: as the doctor examined the patient's throat

subordinate clause: when the pitcher threw his best curveball

Subordinate clauses begin with words like those in the following list. Learning this list will help you recognize subordinate clauses more easily.

after	as soon as	if	until	whether
although	as though	in order to	when	while
as	because	since	whenever	
as if	before	so that	where	
as long as	even though	unless	wherever	

✳ *Tip For Identifying Clauses*

To decide whether a clause is main or subordinate, imagine yourself speaking the words to someone. If the listener would be left hanging on waiting for more, the clause is a subordinate clause. If the words would leave the listener with a sense of completeness, the clause is a main clause.

when the sun set behind the ridge

(Speak these words, and the listener is left hanging on, waiting for more. The clause is subordinate.)

the sun set behind the ridge

(Speak these words, and the listener is not left waiting for more. The clause is a main clause.)

PRACTICE 14.2

Write *SC* next to each subordinate clause and *MC* next to each main clause.

1. _____ after Tony checked the locks on the doors

2. _____ when he tried desperately not to show fear

3. _____ we asked the committee to reconsider its report

4. _____ the board of trustees raised tuition

5. _____ when the last vote was counted

6. _____ because the summer drought created a food shortage

7. _____ I left for the appointment ten minutes late

8. _____ before the movers lifted the chest of drawers in the attic

9. _____ the consumer price index points to a recession

10. _____ since Jan was awarded two scholarships

COORDINATION: METHOD I

Coordination is the proper joining of two main clauses in one sentence. (Remember, main clauses can stand as sentences.)

One way to join two main clauses in one sentence is to connect the main clauses with one of the following:

, and	, or	, so
, but	, for	, yet

Here are two main clauses:

The traffic light at Fifth and Elm is not working.

No major accidents have been reported.

Here are the main clauses properly joined in one sentence with a comma and the word *but:*

The traffic light at Fifth and Elm is not working, but no major accidents have been reported.

Here are two other main clauses:

Jake's frustration was building quickly.

He decided to get away for the weekend and relax.

These main clauses can be properly joined with a comma and *so:*

Jake's frustration was building quickly, so he decided to get away for the weekend and relax.

The words that can be used with a comma to join main clauses are called **coordinating conjunctions**. They appear in the chart that follows.

COORDINATING CONJUNCTIONS

1. , and (shows addition)

   Three of us wanted to visit the museum, and two of us wanted to see a play.

2. , but (shows contrast)
   , yet (shows contrast)

   Your plan is a good one, but we do not have the money to implement it.

   Your plan is a good one, yet we do not have the money to implement it.

3. , or (shows an alternative or choice)

   Professor Jennings explained that we could write a ten-page research paper, or we could take a final examination.

4. , for (means "because")

   The linoleum floor in the basement was buckling, for water had seeped in during the spring rains.

5. , so (means "as a result")

   The new model cars are in the showrooms, so now is the time to get a good deal on last year's models.

Coordination Rule: Method I

   Two main clauses can be joined as a single sentence with a comma and a coordinating conjunction.

Keep in mind that too much coordination in the same sentence creates an undesirable effect because the clauses seem carelessly strung together, like this:

I got in the car, and I started to back out of the garage, but I forgot that the garage door was closed, so I hit the door at about 20 mph, and I caused over a thousand dollars of damage to both the car and the garage.

To solve the problem of excessive coordination, reduce the number of main clauses in the same sentence.

When I got in the car and started to back out of the garage, I forgot that the garage door was closed. I hit the door at about 20 mph and caused over a thousand dollars of damage to both the car and garage.

The discussion of subordination beginning on p. 207 will show you how to use subordinate clauses to avoid excessive coordination.

PRACTICE 14.3

The following sentences are made up of two main clauses. To join the clauses properly, place a comma and write an appropriate coordinating conjunction on the blank.

1. Harry's throat was sore and raspy _____ his temperature was well above normal.

2. Scattered afternoon thunder showers are predicted _____ Enrico decided to begin painting the house anyway.

3. Mother enrolled in college _____ she has always regretted marrying before she earned her business degree.

4. The Cubs were behind by five runs in the fourth inning _____ the coach was forced to change pitchers.

5. Nicotine-flavored gum can help a person quit smoking _____ it is no substitute for willpower.

6. We could travel the turnpike and arrive quickly _____ we could take the back roads and enjoy the countryside.

7. In the lake behind the house, Gregory caught a three-foot catfish _____ Jorges caught a four-foot bass.

8. This afternoon while we are in Charleston, we can visit Ft. Sumter _____ we can go to an authentic plantation.

9. The highway department received a 30 percent increase in revenue _____ two-thirds of the roads remain in disrepair.

10. The board of education decided to cancel night football games

    _____ too much vandalism was occurring when the games were
    over.

Join the main clauses in one sentence, using a comma and coordinating conjunction. The first one is done as an example.

1. To earn tuition money, Josef dropped out of school for a semester.
   He took a job as a nurse's aid.

   To earn tuition money, Josef dropped out of school for a semester,

   and he took a job as a nurse's aid.

2. Maria and John are poor choices to head the committee.
   They are disorganized and unreliable.

   _____

   _____

3. The plot of the movie was boring and predictable.
   The actors were fresh and engaging.

   _____

   _____

4. You can borrow my laptop to type your term paper.
   You can pay someone to do it for you.

   _____

   _____

5. The National Weather Service issued a thunderstorm warning.
   The umpire postponed the Little League championship game.

   _____

   _____

6. Michael passed the ball to Jeff.

   Jeff kicked it into the net to score the winning goal.

   _____

   _____

7. Many people thought videocassette recorders would seriously hurt the movie industry.

   The opposite has proved to be true.

   _____

   _____

8. Currently, no cure exists for myasthenia gravis.

   Researchers are working hard to help those afflicted with this neuro-logical disorder.

   _____

   _____

9. Those in need of extra help can visit the Tutoring Center.

   They can go to the Student Services Office.

   _____

   _____

10. Self-hypnosis can help people suffering from stress.

    It is an effective relaxation technique.

    _____

    _____

11. Lorenzo began a rigorous exercise program.

    He had to lose ten pounds before winter practice drills began.

    _____

    _____

12. With the new state funds, the school board hired three teachers.
    They decided to remodel the high school library.

    _____

    _____

13. Thirty students were accepted into the medical program.
    Only two-thirds of them will eventually graduate.

    _____

    _____

14. Not everyone enjoyed the theatre department's production.
    Those who did raved about it.

    _____

    _____

15. Be sure to determine what you need before buying a computer.
    You could end up with a system that does not fill your needs.

    _____

    _____

16. Fifty percent of the student body was absent with the flu.
    The principal still did not cancel classes.

    _____

    _____

17. The luxury hotel boasts the ultimate in service.
    It claims to serve the best food in the state.

    _____

    _____

18. Wear brightly colored clothing when jogging in the street.
    Drivers might not see you until it is too late.

    _____

    _____

19. Colleges should begin offering more classes at night.
    Many potential students work during the day.

    _____

    _____

20. For this apartment to be livable, we must scrub all the walls.
    We must have the carpets cleaned.

    _____

    _____

PRACTICE 14.5

To create more coordination in the following paragraph, combine the following sentences by crossing out periods, adding commas and appropriate coordinating conjunctions, and eliminating capital letters: sentences 2 and 3, sentences 4 and 5, sentences 6 and 7, sentences 8 and 9, sentences 10 and 11, sentences 12 and 13.

example: Adolescence is a difficult time. ~~Teenagers~~ **, so teenagers** need their friends.

[1]When people become teenagers, they begin to need intimacy in their friendships. [2]Adolescents are eager to share their hopes and fears. [3]They enjoy trading secrets with others they trust. [4]Furthermore, teens have a stronger need for close friends than younger people. [5]They spend more time away from their parents. [6]Some parents fear the influence friends exert on their teenagers. [7]Contrary to popular belief, peer pressure is not necessarily stronger than family ties. [8]Still, friends are very important to teens. [9]They help them make key decisions about college and careers. [10]Also, friends help them sort out right decisions from wrong ones. [11]Friends provide "reality checks" for adolescents. [12]Some teen friendships are short lived. [13]Others last long into the teenagers' adulthood.

PRACTICE 14.6

On a separate sheet, write eight sentences. Each sentence should have two main clauses joined with a comma and a coordinating conjunction. Use each coordinating conjunction at least once.

COORDINATION: METHOD II

A second way to join main clauses in one sentence is to connect the clauses with one of the following:

; however,	; furthermore,	; consequently,
; nevertheless,	; therefore,	; moreover,
; nonetheless,	; thus,	

Here are two main clauses (word groups that can be sentences):

The editorial in Sunday's paper made a good point.
It will not change many people's minds.

Here are the main clauses properly joined in one sentence with a semi-colon and the word *however* and a comma:

The editorial in Sunday's paper made a good point; however, it will not change many people's minds.

Here are two other main clauses:

Next fall, tuition will increase by 10 percent.
The cost of living in a dorm will rise by 5 percent.

These main clauses can be properly joined with a semicolon and the word *furthermore* and a comma:

Next fall, tuition will increase by 10 percent; furthermore, the cost of living in a dorm will rise by 5 percent.

The words that can be used with a semicolon and a comma to join main clauses are **conjunctive adverbs**. A chart of the conjunctive adverbs follows.

CONJUNCTIVE ADVERBS

1. ; however, (means "but")
   ; nevertheless, (means "but")

continued

; nonetheless, (means "but")

The snow plows worked through the night to clear the roads; however, many streets were still impassable.

The snow plows worked through the night to clear the roads; nevertheless, many streets were still impassable.

The snow plows worked through the night to clear the roads; nonetheless, many streets were still impassable.

2. ; furthermore, (means "in addition")
   ; moreover, (means "in addition")

   To save money, the transit authority must raise fares; furthermore, it plans to reduce the number of buses in operation.

   To save money, the transit authority must raise fares; moreover, it plans to reduce the number of buses in operation.

3. ; therefore, (means "as a result")

   ; thus, (means "as a result")

   ; consequently, (means "as a result")

   I am hoping to earn a scholarship my sophomore year; therefore, I must maintain a B average.

   I am hoping to earn a scholarship my sophomore year; thus, I must maintain a B average.

   I am hoping to earn a scholarship my sophomore year; consequently, I must maintain a B average.

Coordination Rule: Method II

Two main clauses can be joined in a single sentence with a semicolon, a conjunctive adverb and a comma.

PRACTICE 14.7

The following sentences are made up of two main clauses. Join the clauses properly with a semicolon, an appropriate conjunctive adverb, and a comma. (The chart above will help you.)

1. The temperature only went up to 65 degrees __*; however,*__ most of us decided to go swimming anyway.

2. The mayor spoke to city council members for over an hour

   _____ he did not persuade them to pass the budget bill.

3. The examination has five essay questions and thirty true and false

   questions _____ I was able to complete it in less than the time allowed.

4. Julian is the top rebounder on the basketball team _____ he is a star defensive lineman on the football team.

5. Many researchers claim that children who watch violence on television become desensitized to violence in real life _____ too few parents control the amount of violence their children watch on the small screen.

6. Federal funding for public television has been cut _____ contributions from private businesses are being sought.

7. After the storm, power was not restored for twenty hours _____ much of the food in my refrigerator had to be thrown out.

8. Dr. Juarez explained that caffeine interferes with the body's absorption of iron _____ caffeine can contribute to the formation of cysts.

9. To write an effective persuasive essay, avoid personal attacks _____ acknowledge the point of view of those who disagree with you.

10. Some parents believe schools should pile on the homework _____ recent studies reveal that excessive amounts of homework are counterproductive.

PRACTICE 14.8

Join the main clauses in one sentence with a semicolon, a conjunctive adverb, and a comma. The first one is done as an example.

1. Emilio is a most charming child.
   He is a loyal, caring friend.

   Emilio is a most charming child; furthermore, he is a loyal,

   caring friend.

2. For years there were more teachers than teaching jobs.
   Now this trend is beginning to reverse itself.

   _____

   _____

3. To locate the escaped convict, the police set up roadblocks.
   They conducted a house-to-house search.

   _____

   _____

4. New signs have been put up on campus.
   It is easier to find most of the buildings.

   _____

   _____

5. Good writing skills are important for success in college.
   They are just as important on the job.

   _____

   _____

6. The school tax levy was defeated by voters.
   No new school texts can be purchased this year.

   _____

   _____

7. The new automobile assembly plant will be open by November.
   The unemployment rate in this area should drop.

   _____

   _____

8. Carlo was accepted into graduate school to study chemistry.
   He was awarded a scholarship for academic excellence.

   _____

   _____

9. Louise has been a hospital volunteer for three years.
   Now she has decided to apply for a paid position.

   _____

   _____

10. Writers who wait for inspiration may never get much done.
    Writers who freewrite for ideas will make more progress.

    _____

    _____

11. Gary was in top condition for the marathon.
    He still did not expect to place in the top ten.

    _____

    _____

12. Susan pretended she was not bothered by losing her job.
    Those close to her knew she was depressed.

    _____

    _____

13. The assembly-line workers ended their two-week strike.
    The plant would be back in operation by mid-afternoon.

    _____

    _____

14. Ivana earned a scholarship for her high math grades.
    She won a scholarship to play on the women's basketball team.

    _____

    _____

15. Some students become overly nervous when they take exams.
    They are too tense to perform well.

    _____

    _____

16. The firefighters were granted a 5-percent pay raise.
    They still make less than they deserve.

    _____

    _____

17. Phillip and Ricardo fought constantly.
    They remained close friends.

    _____

    _____

18. Most people avoid Sue Ellen because she is so stuck-up.
    She constantly brags about herself.

    _____

    _____

19. Route 11 is heavily congested at 5:00.
    I recommend taking the bypass.

    _____

    _____

20. Air fares have gone up dramatically in the past six months.
    Fewer people are booking flights.

    _____

    _____

REVIEW PRACTICE 14.9

On a separate sheet, rewrite the following paragraphs by joining some sentences with the coordination methods described earlier. Then read your revised version out loud to notice how much more smoothly it reads than the original. (More than one satisfactory revision is possible.)

A. A new amusement park ride is currently in the planning stages. Passengers will bounce off walls and posts. They will control giant flippers that knock their car back up a hill. The ride is called Mega Ball. It will make passengers feel like the silver ball in a pinball machine. They will be able to control their ride as they can in bumper cars. They will get the thrill of a scary ride. If they hit the flipper at the right time, they can have a longer ride. They do not even have to put in another quarter.

B. In 1920, Josephine Dickinson was newly married. She was a willing cook. She was somewhat clumsy and kept injuring herself in the kitchen. Her husband, Earl, a cotton buyer for the local Johnson and Johnson plant, found himself constantly tending to Josephine's little cuts and burns. One night, Earl tried to design a bandage that would stay in place. He unrolled a length of sterile gauze along the middle of the tape. Then he wrapped the whole assembly in crinoline. As needed, Josephine could cut an appropriate length from the roll. She could peel off the crinoline and apply the bandage. Earl told a company manager about his invention, which soon emerged as Johnson and Johnson's Band-Aid. At first, sales were slow. They soon gained momentum, thanks to a campaign giving Band-Aids to the Boy Scouts and butchers.

SUBORDINATION: METHOD I

A **main clause** has a subject and a verb and can stand as a sentence. A **subordinate clause** has a subject and a verb but cannot stand as a sentence.

main clause:	the doctor explained the symptoms
subordinate clause:	when the doctor explained the symptoms

In addition, you have learned that a subordinate clause is introduced by one of the **subordinating conjunctions**, words like the following:

after	as soon as	if	until	whether
although	as though	in order to	when	while
as	because	since	whenever	
as if	before	so that	where	
as long as	even though	unless	wherever	

A subordinate clause and a main clause can be joined in the same sentence. This joining is called **subordination**.

subordinate clause: since the polls do not close for another hour

main clause: we do not know the election results

Now here are the subordinate clause and main clause in one sentence:

Since the polls do not close for another hour, we do not know the election results.

In the preceding example, the subordinate clause comes before the main clause. You can also place the main clause first:

We do not know the election results since the polls do not close for another hour.

Here are another subordinate clause and main clause:

subordinate clause: when I graduated from high school
main clause: I expected to join the army.

Now here are the subordinate clause and main clause in one sentence:

When I graduated from high school, I expected to join the army.

or

I expected to join the army when I graduated from high school.

PUNCTUATION NOTE: When the subordinate clause comes before the main clause, place a comma after the subordinate clause.

PRACTICE 14.10

Each sentence has a main clause and a subordinate clause. Underline the subordinate clause once and the main clause twice. Draw a circle around the subordinating conjunction that introduces the subordinate clause. The first one is done as an example. (Notice the commas after the subordinate clauses at the beginning of sentences.)

1. (When) Paul saw the stranded motorist, he quickly pulled to the side of the road to help.

2. If it does not rain in the next day or two, most of the corn crop will be lost.

3. Because Scarsella's serves the best food in town, the restaurant is always crowded.

4. The woman was clearly embarrassed when a cake with candles was brought to her table in the center of the crowded restaurant.

5. Lizette decided to end her relationship with Howard since he had such a bad temper.

6. After the orchestra sounded its last note, the audience jumped to its feet.

7. Janice will leave for Florida when final exams are over.

8. Since I am working thirty hours a week in the record store, I can only attend school part-time.

9. The first-grade teacher was concerned about Tad because he seemed tired all the time.

10. While the insurance agent explained the difference between the two policies, I decided what to buy.

PRACTICE 14.11

Join the main clause and subordinate clause into a single sentence. Place the subordinate clause first or last according to the directions given. (Be sure to place a comma after a subordinate clause that comes before the main clause.) The first one is done as an example.

1. (Place the subordinate clause first.)

    while the teacher explained cell division

    the class took notes furiously

    While the teacher explained cell division, the class took notes

    furiously.

2. (Place the subordinate clause last.)

    because she had a frightening dream

    the child woke up crying

    _____

    _____

3. (Place the subordinate clause first.)

until you exercise regularly and quit smoking

you will be short of breath

_____

_____

4. (Place the subordinate clause last.)

since she was not sure what she wanted to do after high school

Tasha decided to enlist in the navy

_____

_____

5. (Place the subordinate clause first.)

although I loved the book

I hated the movie version of *Interview with the Vampire.*

_____

_____

6. (Place the subordinate clause last.)

before he auditioned for the lead in *West Side Story*

Juan took six weeks of voice lessons

_____

_____

PRACTICE 14.12

Change one of the main clauses to a subordinate clause by placing an appropriate subordinating conjunction in front of it (see the list on p. 207). Then join the new subordinate clause and the remaining main clause into a single sentence. Place some of the subordinate clauses first and some of them last. Also, place a comma after a subordinate clause that comes first. The first one is done as an example.

1. Diane and Mohammed moved to Virginia.
   Seth and Janet were afraid they would not see them again.

   Because Diane and Mohammed moved to Virginia, Seth and Janet

   were afraid they would not see them again.

2. Cass was unsure of what courses she should take next semester.
   She made an appointment with her academic advisor.

   _____

   _____

3. Kevin apologized for being inconsiderate.
   Miguel still could not forgive him.

   _____

   _____

4. The senator has no money to finance a reelection campaign.
   He decided not to seek a second term in office.

   _____

   _____

5. The employer improves working conditions.
   The union has vowed to remain on strike.

   _____

   _____

6. Many people believe anger is a destructive emotion.
   I find it to be a healthy, adaptive one.

   _____

   _____

PRACTICE 14.13

On a separate sheet, rewrite the following paragraph by joining some sentences with appropriate subordinating conjunctions to create subordination. Then read your revised version out loud to notice how much more smoothly it reads than the original. (More than one revision is possible.)

Las Vegas used to be an adults-only town. Now it attracts families with children. Casinos provide gambling for parents. Amusement facilities entertain the younger generation. At Circus Circus and Excalibur, for example, children can play games on midways. Parents gamble in the casino on the next floor. Outside the hotels, there is much for families to do. A huge Wet 'n Wild water park provides hours of fun. A theme park behind MGM Grand is a big draw for families. Once a playground for grownups, Las Vegas is now a family vacation site. There are some who say the old way was better.

PRACTICE 14.14

On a separate sheet, write five sentences that join one main clause and one subordinate clause. Three of the sentences should begin with the subordinate clause (remember to place a comma after the subordinate clause that comes at the beginning).

SUBORDINATION: METHOD II

One kind of subordinate clause begins with one of these words:

who, whose (to refer to people)

which (to refer to things and animals)

that (to refer to people or things)

These words are called **relative pronouns**, and the subordinate clauses they introduce are called **relative clauses**.

The second method of subordination involves joining a main clause and a relative clause, like this:

sentence:	The boy who won the award is my son.
main clause:	the boy is my son
relative clause:	who won the award.

Here are other examples:

sentence:	The class that I am taking is time-consuming.

main clause:	the class is time-consuming
relative clause:	that I am taking
sentence:	Jocelyn, whose art is displayed in the student gallery, will paint your portrait.
main clause:	Jocelyn will paint your portrait
relative clause:	whose art is displayed in the student gallery
sentence:	You may use my car, which needs gas.
main clause:	you may use my car
relative clause:	which needs gas

If a relative clause is needed to identify who or what is referred to, it is **restrictive**. If the relative clause is not needed to identify who or what is referred to, it is **nonrestrictive**.

restrictive:

The police officer *who saved the child from drowning* is my neighbor.

"Who saved the child from drowning" is needed for identifying the police officer. Without the clause, we cannot tell which police officer is referred to.

nonrestrictive:

Officer Manuel, *who saved the child from drowning,* is my neighbor.

"Who saved the child from drowning" is not needed for identifying who saved the child because the person's name is given.

PUNCTUATION NOTE: Set off nonrestrictive relative clauses with commas:

Bridgett, *who scored fifteen points*, was the most valuable player.
That man, *whose name I forget*, is suspicious looking.
That movie, *which appeals to me*, is playing at the Strand.

Do not set off restrictive clauses:

Any secretary *who works for me* must take dictation.

continued

The watch *that I found* looks valuable.

The child *whose balloon broke* began to cry.

NOTE: Whether a relative clause is restrictive can depend on the context the sentence appears in. Thus, if you earlier identified the child as Kim, the previous sentence will be punctuated like this:

The child, *whose balloon broke,* began to cry.

PRACTICE 14.15

Combine the sentences by turning the second sentence into a relative clause that begins with *who, whose, which,* or *that.* Place the relative clause after the subject of the first sentence. The first two are done as examples. Be prepared to explain your use of commas.

1. The mayor does not plan to run for reelection.
   The mayor does not get along with the city council.

   The mayor, who does not get along with the city council, does

   not plan to run for reelection.

2. The kitten is now a member of my family.
   I found the kitten last week.

   The kitten that I found last week is now a member of my family.

3. The large oak tree must be cut down.
   The tree was struck by lightning.

   _____

   _____

4. The book of Longfellow's poems is very old and valuable.
   I found the book in Grandfather's attic.

   _____

   _____

5. Frank Mussillo has decided to retire at the end of the summer.
   Frank Mussillo has been fire chief of our town for thirty years.

   _____

   _____

6. The Theatre Guild's production of *Porgy and Bess* has been held over
   for another week.
   The production is playing to packed houses every night.

   _____

   _____

7. The house needed more repairs than they realized.
   Pilar and David bought the house.

   _____

   _____

8. The woman offered to give me directions.
   The woman noticed my confusion.

   _____

   _____

9. Marty finally sold a short story to a literary magazine.
   Marty has been writing in his spare time for ten years.

   _____

   _____

10. Aunt Maria's arrival was a pleasant surprise to all of us.
    The arrival was unexpected.

    _____

    _____

11. The police officer questioned the witnesses.

The police officer was off duty.

_____

_____

12. The man offered to draw us a map.

The man noticed we were lost.

_____

_____

PRACTICE 14.16

On a separate sheet, write ten sentences of your own with relative clauses. Remember to use commas with clauses that are not needed for identification.

REVIEW PRACTICE 14.17: COORDINATION AND SUBORDINATION

The following paragraph can be improved with coordination and subordination. On a separate sheet, rewrite the paragraph according to the directions given at the end.

[1]A hotel in Florida, called Jules' Undersea Lodge, is located under the ocean. [2]The hotel is the size of a small house. [3]The hotel can accommodate six people. [4]You are ready to depart for the hotel. [5]A guide puts your belongings in a waterproof suitcase and secures it with screws to keep out water. [6]Then the guide takes you by boat to a platform from which you dive into the water. [7]Breathing fresh air pumped through a hose held in your mouth, you swim underwater to the lodge. [8]A guide carries your suitcase. [9]The guide swims with you. [10]The hotel itself has two bedrooms, a kitchen, and a living room. [11]The kitchen has a microwave and a fully-stocked refrigerator. [12]The living room has a VCR, stereo, and television. [13]You can relax in the lodge. [14]You can go diving outside. [15]You are ready to leave. [16]A guide swims with you back to the platform.

A. Join sentences 2 and 1 by making sentence 2 a relative clause.

B. Join sentences 4 and 5 by adding a subordinating conjunction to sentence 4 and making it a subordinate clause.

C. Join sentences 9 and 8 by making sentence 9 a relative clause.

D. Join sentences 11 and 12 by adding a comma and coordinating conjunction.

E. Join sentences 13 and 14 by adding a comma and coordinating conjunction.

F. Join sentences 15 and 16 by adding a subordinating conjunction to sentence 15 and making it a subordinate clause.

On a separate sheet, rewrite the passage to include coordination and subordination. Then read both the original and revision aloud to notice how much better the coordination and subordination make the revision sound. (Many revisions are possible.)

Meredith West and Andrew King studied cowbirds for many years. West and King are scientists in North Carolina. A male cowbird sings. The female cowbird lets him know what songs she likes without making a sound. She likes a song. She lifts her wing.

Cowbirds in different parts of the country sing different tunes. West and King put male cowbirds from North Carolina with female cowbirds from Texas. The males learned to sing Texas cowbird songs. The scientists were puzzled. The males learned these songs. The females did not make a peep. They videotaped the birds. They saw that the females would flash a wing when they liked a song. The males would repeat the song. The females liked it. Now, if the birds could just learn some Billy Joel tunes.

SENTENCE VARIETY

To improve the flow of your writing and to achieve a mature style, use a variety of sentence structures. This mix of sentence structures is known as **sentence variety**. You have already learned about subordination and coordination. When you use these, you are contributing to sentence variety. In addition, you can achieve sentence variety by using the sentence structures described on the following pages.

Begin with One or Two *-ly* Words

Words that end in *-ly* are descriptive words called **adverbs**.

Mother carefully eased the heavy cake pans out of the oven.

Carefully describes how Mother eased the pans out of the oven. An *-ly* word can be an excellent way to open a sentence:

Carefully, Mother eased the heavy cake pans out of the oven.

Hoarsely, the cheerleaders shouted for a touchdown.

Patiently, Dr. Vardova explained differential equations.

PUNCTUATION NOTE: When you open a sentence with an *-ly* word (adverb), place a comma after the word.

You can also begin a sentence with two *-ly* words:

Slowly and steadily, the workers slid the refrigerator into the narrow space next to the stove.

Quickly yet cautiously, Frank crossed the narrow bridge.

Loudly but politely, she explained her complaint to the manager.

Softly, sweetly, the nurse sang a lullaby to the infant.

As you can tell from the preceding examples, two *-ly* words can be separated with *and, but, yet,* or a comma.

PUNCTUATION NOTE: Two *-ly* words (adverbs) are separated with a comma when no word is between them. Also, when a pair of *-ly* words opens a sentence, place a comma after the second *-ly* word.

PRACTICE 14.18

Open the following sentences with *-ly* words (adverbs) of your choice. At least two sentences should begin with a pair of *-ly* words. The first one is done as an example.

1. The frustrated salesclerk explained for the third time why she could not give the customer a refund.

   Loudly, the frustrated salesclerk explained for the third time why

   she could not give the customer a refund.

2. Valerie arranged the roses and mums in the antique vase.

   _____

   _____

3. Ted maneuvered the car around the fallen rocks.

_____

_____

4. Dominic cradled his newborn daughter in his arms.

_____

_____

5. Jeffrey ran around the bases after hitting his third home run of the season.

_____

_____

6. The first-grade teacher showed the class how to write cursive letters.

_____

_____

7. Dr. Chun performed his duties as head of the art institute.

_____

_____

8. Jan entered the classroom ten minutes after the lecture had begun.

_____

_____

9. I shouted at the truck driver who changed lanes and cut me off.

_____

_____

PRACTICE 14.19

On a separate sheet, write two sentences of your own that begin with an *-ly* word (adverb) and two sentences that begin with a pair of *-ly* words. Remember to use commas correctly.

Begin with an *-ing* Verb or Phrase

The *-ing* form of a verb is the **present participle**. The present participle can be used as a descriptive word and an effective sentence opening.

Whistling, John walked past the cemetery.

Whistling is the *-ing* form of the verb *whistle*. In the preceding sentence, it describes John. Opening some of your sentences with present participles contributes to sentence variety. Here are more examples:

Crying, the child said that he fell off his bicycle.

Coughing, Maria left the classroom to get a drink of water.

Limping, I crossed the street.

You can also begin a sentence with an *-ing* verb phrase (**present participle phrase**). An *-ing* verb phrase is the present participle (*-ing* verb form) and one or more words that work with it. Here is a sentence that opens with a present participle phrase:

Whistling softly, John walked past the cemetery.

In this case, the present participle phrase is *whistling softly*, which describes John.

By opening some of your sentences with present participle phrases, you can achieve sentence variety. Here are more examples:

Crying pitifully, the child said that he fell off his bicycle.

Coughing into her handkerchief, Maria left the classroom to get a drink of water.

Limping more than usual, I crossed the street.

> CAUTION: Place the word the *-ing* word or phrase describes immediately after the *-ing* word or phrase, or the result will be rather silly. Here is an example:
>
> Dancing in the moonlight, the band played a romantic song.
>
> *Dancing in the moonlight* is a present participle phrase that is not followed by a word it can describe. As a result, the sentence says that

the band was dancing in the moonlight. (For more on this point, see **dangling modifiers** on pp. 387–388.)

PUNCTUATION NOTE: When you begin a sentence with a present participle or a present participle phrase, follow the participle or phrase with a comma.

PRACTICE 14.20

Open the following sentences with the *-ing* words (present participles) of your choice. At least two sentences should begin with *-ing* verb phrases. Remember to place commas correctly. The first one is done as an example.

1. Mother prepared Thanksgiving dinner for fourteen people.

   Working feverishly, Mother prepared Thanksgiving dinner for

   fourteen people.

2. Donna explained why tax reform would hurt the middle class.

   _____

   _____

3. Juanita accepted her award for scholastic achievement in mathematics.

   _____

   _____

4. Pete and Lorenzo tried to tell us what was so funny.

   _____

   _____

5. Jalil bench-pressed 250 pounds.

   _____

   _____

6. Diana planted tulip and daffodil bulbs in her spring garden.

_____

_____

7. The collie ran across the yard.

_____

_____

8. Dr. Dominic announced that everyone passed the exam.

_____

_____

9. The ten-year-old was bored by the pastor's sermon.

_____

_____

PRACTICE 14.21

On a separate sheet, write two sentences of your own that begin with an *-ing* verb (present participle) and two sentences that begin with an *-ing* verb phrase (present participle phrase). Be sure to follow the *-ing* verb or verb phrase with a word the participle can describe. Also, remember to use commas correctly.

Begin with an *-ed* Verb or Phrase

The *-ed* form of a verb is the **past participle**. The past participle can be used as a descriptive word and an effective sentence opening.

Frightened, the child crawled in bed with his parents.

Frightened is the *-ed* form of the verb *frighten*. In the preceding sentence, it describes the child. By opening some of your sentences with past participles, you can contribute to sentence variety in your writing. Here are more examples:

Tired, Dad fell asleep while watching the Raiders game.

Irritated, Mandy threw her books on the floor.

Excited, Leonid told his friends about his good fortune.

You can also begin a sentence with an *-ed* verb phrase (**past participle phrase**). An *-ed* verb phrase is the past participle (*-ed* verb form) and one or more words that work with it.

Frightened by the dark, the child crawled in bed with his parents.

In this case, the past participle phrase is *frightened by the dark,* which describes the child.

Opening some of your sentences with past participle phrases will help you achieve sentence variety. Here are more examples:

Tired after raking the leaves, Dad fell asleep watching the Raiders game.

Irritated by her low exam grade, Mandy threw her books on the floor.

Excited about being promoted to manager, Leonid told his friends about his good fortune.

CAUTION: Place the word the *-ed* verb or phrase describes immediately after the *-ed* verb or phrase, or the result will be a silly sentence, like this:

Delighted by the victory, a celebration was in order.

Delighted by the victory is a past participle phrase that is not followed by a word it can describe. As a result, the sentence says that a celebration was delighted by the victory. (For more on this point, see **dangling modifiers** on pp. 387–388.

PUNCTUATION NOTE: When you begin a sentence with an *-ed* verb (past participle) or an *-ed* verb phrase (past participle phrase), follow the *-ed* verb or verb phrase with a comma.

PRACTICE 14.22

Open the sentences with *-ed* verbs (past participles) of your choice. Begin at least two sentences with *-ed* verb phrases. Remember to place commas correctly. The first is done as an example.

1. The referee threw the coach out of the game.

   Angered, the referee threw the coach out of the game.

2. The kitten curled into a furry ball and fell asleep.

_____

_____

3. Three-year-old Bobby ran crying to his nursery school teacher.

_____

_____

4. Maria ran frantically after the man who stole her purse.

_____

_____

5. The tenants voiced their complaints to the apartment manager.

_____

_____

6. Lorenzo reached over and turned off the blaring alarm.

_____

_____

7. The steak was worth the twelve dollars I paid for it.

_____

_____

8. The police officer told Jeremy he was lucky to get off with just a warning.

_____

_____

9. The cookies were too brown to sell at the charity bazaar.

_____

_____

PRACTICE 14.23

On a separate sheet, write two sentences of your own that begin with *-ed* verbs (past participles) and two sentences that begin with *-ed* verb phrases (past participle phrases). Be sure to follow the *-ed* verb or verb phrase with a word the participle can describe. Also, remember to use commas correctly.

Begin with a Prepositional Phrase

A **preposition** shows how two things relate to each other in time or space. (See p. 185 for a more detailed explanation of prepositions.) Here is a list of common prepositions:

about	behind	inside	through
above	between	into	to
across	by	of	toward
along	during	off	under
among	for	on	with
around	from	out	within
before	in	over	without

A **prepositional phrase** is a preposition and the words that work with it. Here are examples of prepositional phrases:

in May	across the street	toward the end of the book
behind me	during the concert	inside the oven
on top	out of bounds	without a doubt

Beginning some of your sentences with prepositional phrases will help you achieve sentence variety. Here are examples of sentences that begin with prepositional phrases:

Under the kitchen table, Rags sat contentedly chewing on his bone.

In the spring, the senior class will travel to Washington.

From now on, everyone in this state must wear a seat belt.

PUNCTUATION NOTE: A prepositional phrase that begins a sentence is usually followed by a comma. However, you may omit the comma after a prepositional phrase made up of two words:

Between the oak trees, two squirrels were chasing each other.

By noon, all the sale items were sold.

or

By noon all the sale items were sold.

PRACTICE 14.24

Underline the prepositional phrases in the following sentences. (Several of the sentences contain more than one prepositional phrase.) The first one is done as an example.

1. The infant began crying <u>in the middle</u> <u>of the night</u>.
2. At ten o'clock, the church bells chimed in unison.
3. Charlie announced that there was a thief among us.
4. The truth of the matter is that no one cares.
5. With the help of everyone, the fund-raiser can be a huge success.
6. By daybreak, a foot of snow had fallen in our city.

PRACTICE 14.25

Combine the two sentences into one sentence that begins with the prepositional phrase or phrases in the second sentence. Remember to use commas correctly. The first one is done as an example.

1. The children woke up.

   They woke up in the middle of the night.

   In the middle of the night, the children woke up.

2. The fire alarm sounded.

   It sounded during our history examination.

   _____

   _____

3. The members of the committee decided to change the bylaws.

   They decided at their spring meeting.

   _____

   _____

4. The orchestra played a Gershwin medley.

   They played the medley after a fifteen-minute intermission.

   _____

   _____

5. A more efficient registration process will be tested.
   It will be tested at the beginning of the fall semester.

   _____

   _____

6. The flowering crab tree was severely damaged.
   It was damaged after the unexpected spring frost.

   _____

   _____

PRACTICE 14.26

On a separate sheet, write four sentences that begin with prepositional phrases. Remember to place a comma after each phrase, unless it is only two words; then, the comma is optional.

REVIEW PRACTICE 14.27: SENTENCE VARIETY

On a separate sheet, rewrite the paragraphs to add more sentence variety. Use a combination of the techniques you have learned: coordination, subordination, *-ly* openers, *-ed* verb openers, *-ing* verb openers, and prepositional phrase openers. You may add words and change word order.

A. Amelia Earhart and her navigator tried to fly around the world during the summer of 1937. They were supposed to stop at Howland Island to refuel. They never arrived. The pilot radioed compass readings hoping to be guided in. These, sadly, were the last words heard from Earhart. The plane was declared lost at sea after a long naval search. A number of theories have been advanced to explain Earhart's disappearance. Some say Earhart was spying for the United States. They say she was shot down over the Marshall Islands. The Marshall Islands were held by Japan. Others say a navigational error caused Earhart to miss Howland Island and crash at sea. Still others say the plane ran out of gas and crash-landed. The real cause of Earhart's disappearance will probably never be learned, although people will always admire the courage of the person who was the first woman to fly across the Atlantic Ocean.

B. Walter Gregg and his family should have taken a drive on the afternoon of March 11, 1958. They hung out at home instead. They were around to see their house demolished by an atomic bomb as a result. The accidental bombing occurred when the bomb bay doors of a U.S. Air Force jet accidentally opened. An atomic warhead fell out. The bomb crashed through the roof of the Greggs' house outside Florence, South Carolina. It obliterated the residence and gouged out a thirty-five-foot crater in the backyard. The explosion, luckily, was nonnuclear. What detonated was the TNT in the bomb's trigger device. The Greggs were slightly injured by flying debris. They accepted a $54,000 settlement from the government.

PARALLELISM: WORDS IN SERIES AND PAIRS

Parallelism refers to balance. For your sentences to have the necessary parallelism or balance, words that form pairs or series should all have the same form. Here is an example:

Ian enjoys skating and reading.

In this example, two words form a pair: *skating* and *reading.* Since both words take the same form (*-ing* verb forms), the sentence has the necessary parallelism or balance.

Here is another example of a sentence with parallelism. This time, there is balance among words that form a series:

Janet and Rico found the movie fresh, funny, and surprising.

In this example, three words form a series: *fresh, funny,* and *surprising.* Since each of these words takes the same form (each is an adjective that describes *movie*), the sentence has the necessary parallelism.

Now here is a sentence that lacks parallelism:

The doctor told the heart patient to avoid salt and that he should get more exercise.

In this example, two elements form a pair: *to avoid salt* and *that he should get more exercise.* The first element is a verb phrase, while the second is a clause. Because the elements in the pair take different forms, the sentence lacks parallelism. To achieve the necessary balance, the sentence needs two verb phrases or two clauses:

The doctor told the heart patient to avoid salt and to get more exercise. (two verb phrases)

or

The doctor told the heart patient that he should avoid salt and that he should get more exercise. (two clauses)

Here is another sentence that lacks parallelism:

This course demands patience, dedication, and a student must know how to research.

In this example, three elements form a series: *patience, dedication,* and *a student must know how to research.* The first two elements are nouns, but the third element is a clause. Because all the elements in the series do not have the same form, the sentence lacks parallelism. Here is the sentence revised to achieve parallelism:

This course demands patience, dedication, and research ability. (three nouns)

PRACTICE 14.28

The underlined element in the pair or series is not parallel. Rewrite the sentence to achieve parallelism. The first one is done as an example.

1. Joan's aptitude test revealed ability in math and <u>learning foreign languages</u>.

   Joan's aptitude test revealed ability in math and foreign languages.

2. The citizen's committee criticized the mayor's proposal because of its complexity and <u>it was expensive</u>.

   _____

   _____

3. To save money on his living expenses, Gustav got a roommate, ate out less often, <u>he fired his cleaning person</u>, and <u>he clipped coupons to use at the grocery store</u>.

   _____

   _____

4. Before agreeing to the surgery, Delores decided she would get a second opinion and <u>to see if she feels better in two weeks</u>.

   _____

   _____

5. The proposal for renovating the downtown business district suggests eliminating one-way streets, instituting on-street parking, and <u>we should reface some of the other buildings</u>.

_____

_____

6. My family decided we prefer a week at the ocean in a condominium to <u>spending a week in the mountains in a cabin</u>.

_____

_____

7. By three months, most infants will recognize their mother's voice, hold their heads up unassisted, and <u>three-month-old infants will grasp at objects placed within their reach</u>.

_____

_____

8. My piano teacher gave me a choice between playing one difficult piece or <u>I could play two less difficult ones</u>.

_____

_____

9. Geography 102 was canceled because the enrollment was low and <u>because of the illness of the instructor</u>.

_____

_____

10. The Emmy Awards broadcast was criticized for boring speeches, <u>because the production numbers were lackluster</u>, and for several tasteless jokes.

_____

_____

PRACTICE 14.29

Complete each sentence with a parallel element. The first one is done as an example.

1. Tony swaggered in, tipped his hat, and *smiled at everyone in the room.*

2. Most people expect Gregory to win the race for Student Government president because of his intelligence, integrity, and

   _____

3. I like spending a quiet Saturday evening alone better than

   _____

4. Marta approached the stage with her heart pounding, her palms sweating, and_____

   _____

5. To pass the course, Professor Lloyd explained that we would have to write a research paper, that we would have to pass a midterm examination, and that_____

   _____

6. Several committee members wanted to raise money with a rummage sale, but most wanted_____

   _____

7. Chez enjoyed the novel, but I found it predictable, sluggish, and

   _____

8. The new president of Little League is having trouble finding coaches, cleaning the fields, and _____

   _____

9. Lee has always liked small, informal weddings better than _____

_____

10. If you are not sure what courses to take next semester, you can

consult the college catalog or _____

_____

PRACTICE 14.30

Find and correct the faulty parallelism in the following paragraph.

Leonardo da Vinci, who lived from 1452 to 1519, was one of the world's great geniuses. No one before him or who has lived after has achieved so much in so many different fields. He was an outstanding painter, sculptor, and he was also an architect. He designed bridges, highways, weapons, costumes, and he invented scientific instruments. He also invented the diving bell and tank, and he designed flying machines, although they could not be built with the materials of the time. Da Vinci approached science and art in the same methodical manner: he made sketches to help him solve problems. He saw no difference between planning a machine and how he would plan a painting. Probably the most famous painting in the world, the Mona Lisa, was painted by Leonardo da Vinci in Florence.

PARALLELISM: PAIRS OF CONJUNCTIONS

Some conjunctions work in pairs. These conjunctions are:

either ... or	not only ... but [also]
neither ... nor	whether ... or
both ... and	if ... then

For parallelism, put the words that follow the second conjunction in the same form as the words that follow the first conjunction.

Either I will earn enough money to pay my tuition, or I will ask my parents for a loan.

The words that follow *either* take the same form as the words that follow *or* (both word groups are clauses). Thus, parallelism is achieved.

Here is another example:

Working full-time while going to school full-time is both tiring and foolish.

The word that follows *both* has the same form as the word that follows *and* (both words are modifiers). As a result, parallelism is achieved.

Now here is an example of a sentence that lacks parallelism:

This stretch of beach is not only beautiful, but it is private as well.

In this example, *not only* is followed by *beautiful* (a descriptive word), and *but* is followed by *it is private as well* (a clause). Because each conjunction is not followed by words in the same form, the sentence lacks parallelism. To achieve parallelism, follow each conjunction with words in the same form:

This stretch of beach is not only beautiful but private as well.

PRACTICE 14.31

Complete each of the following sentences with a parallel element. The first one is done as an example.

1. To pass Calculus II either I must get a tutor, or *I must go to the*

    math lab.

2. Luis will either trade his car in for a new model or_____

    _____

3. Either I will ask my parents for a loan to pay tuition, or_____

    _____

4. Professor Amin decided both to postpone the examination for a week

    and _____

    _____

5. Kwesi hopes not only to graduate a semester early but _____

    _____

6. The principal can neither enforce the dress code to the board of

   education's satisfaction nor _____

   _____

7. To improve economic conditions, the governor must not only attract

   new industry to our state but also _____

   _____

8. Jonathan is either helping those less fortunate than he or _____

   _____

9. Juanita is not only a good listener but_____

   _____

10. I disagree both with the mayor's decision to fire the police chief and

   _____

REVIEW PRACTICE 14.32: PARALLELISM

On a separate sheet, rewrite the following paragraph to eliminate problems with parallelism.

Friendships at work have their own set of guidelines. You should understand the difference between work friends and friends who are personal. Conversations with work friends focus mostly on office personalities, politics, and they center on work-related problems. You should neither confide personal information nor problems to work friends. To avoid complications, try to socialize mostly with coworkers who are at your level in the hierarchy. Unequal status can lead to envy, suspicion, or sometimes cause favoritism. Proceed carefully with office friendships with members of the opposite sex. Avoid any hint of romance, either during work hours or there should be no hint after work hours. If you follow these guidelines, you can enjoy friendships at work without unpleasant complications.

USING TRANSITIONS

Transitions help your reader understand the order of your ideas and their relationship to each other. In addition, transitions help your sentences flow smoothly. Here is an example:

> The health commissioner told the board of health that asbestos had to be removed from three schools. *Also,* he told the board that asbestos may be a problem in two libraries.

The transition *also* tells the reader that the idea in the second sentence functions in addition to the idea in the first sentence. The transition also helps the first sentence flow smoothly into the second. To appreciate this, read the sentences without the transition and notice the gap or abrupt shift:

> The health commissioner told the board of health that asbestos had to be removed from three schools. He told the board that asbestos may be a problem in two libraries.

Here is a chart that gives you many of the commonly used transitions:

Transition Chart

Transitions That Signal Addition	also, and, and then, in addition, too, furthermore, further, moreover, equally important, another, first, second, third ...
If the school levy does not pass, some teachers will be laid off. *Furthermore*, band and choir will be eliminated.	
Transitions That Signal Illustration	for example, for instance, an illustration of this is, to illustrate
Chuck became very irritable when he quit smoking. *For example*, when James asked to borrow his chemistry notes, Chuck yelled at him and called him irresponsible.	
Transitions That Signal Emphatic Order	more important, most important, most of all, best of all, of greatest importance, least of all, even better, the best [worst] case (example, instance, time, etc.)
Mayor DeSalvo has been working hard to bring new industry to our area. *More important*, she has devised a plan to restore confidence in local government.	

Transitions That Signal Spatial (Space) Order	near, nearby, far, alongside, next to, in front of, to the rear, above, below, over, across, under, around, beyond, beneath, on one side, to the left.

The high school is centrally located, and *directly behind* it is the football stadium.

Transitions That Signal Cause and Effect	so, therefore, since, if ... then, thus, as a result, because, hence, consequently

Only five hundred students bought tickets to the spring concert. *As a result*, the concert had to be canceled.

Transitions That Signal Contrast (Differences)	but, yet, still, however, in contrast, on the other hand, nevertheless

Nigel sprained his knee in practice; *however*, he plans to be in shape for Saturday's game.

Transitions That Signal Comparison (Similarities)	similarly, likewise, in the same way, in like manner

Most of today's movies are unsuitable for young viewers. *Similarly*, many television shows are not appropriate for children.

Transitions That Signal Purpose	for this reason, for this purpose, in order to

Theresa hopes to make the women's basketball team. *For this reason*, she is training very hard.

Transitions That Signal Chronological (Time) Order	now, then, later, after, before, soon, suddenly, next, afterward, earlier, at the same time, meanwhile, often, suddenly

Before buying a used car, a person should have it checked over by a reliable mechanic.

Transitions That Signal Emphasis	indeed, in fact, truly, certainly, to be sure, surely, without a doubt, undoubtedly

Our basketball team has the best record in our division. *Undoubtedly*, we will win a spot in a postseason tournament.

Transitions That Signal Summary or Clarification	in conclusion, in summary, to sum up, in other words, in brief, that is, all in all

I cannot support a candidate who is opposed to women's rights. *In other words*, I will not vote for Nathaniel Q. Wisherwaite.

| Transitions That Signal Admitting a Point | although, even though, while it is true, granted |

Although the temperature is rising quickly, I am still going skiing this weekend.

A second way to achieve transition is to repeat a key word or idea. Here is an example with a key word repeated:

The doctor put Dov on a special diet. This diet required him to restrict his intake of fats and proteins.

The second sentence repeats the word diet, which appears in the first sentence. This repetition helps the reader understand the relationship of the ideas in the two sentences, and it helps the first sentence flow smoothly into the second.

Now here is an example with a key idea repeated:

The senior class raised five thousand dollars for the homeless. Such an effort should not go unnoticed.

In this example, the second sentence opens with Such an effort. These words repeat the key idea of the first sentence: that the class raised five thousand dollars for the homeless. Repeating the key idea shows how the ideas in the two sentences relate to each other; it also helps the first sentence flow smoothly into the second.

PRACTICE 14.33

1. Read "Able-bodied but Addle-brained" on p. 71. Cite two transitions that signal chronological (time) order.

2. Read "One Step Forward and Two Steps Back" on p. 163. Cite one transition that signals illustration, one that signals cause and effect, and one that signals emphasis. Also, cite an example of repetition of a key word to achieve transition.

_____

_____

3. Read "Let's Hear It for Tradition" on p. 114. Cite one transition that signals chronological (time) order, one that signals admitting a point, and one that signals contrast. Also cite an example of repetition of a key idea.

_____

_____

_____

_____

PRACTICE 14.34

Fill in the blanks with a transitional word or phrase from the chart beginning on p. 235. The first one is done as an example.

1. Douglas is the biggest practical joker I know. ***For example,*** _____
   last week he glued Dana's shoes together.

2. I refuse to speak to Alonzo unless he learns to control his temper.

   _____ I refuse to be in the same room with him.

3. Diana was not expecting to be transferred to Houston.

   _____ she needs some time to adjust to the idea.

4. The novelty shop in the mall rarely advertises.

   _____ not many people realize what unusual items are
   sold there.

5. Television shapes our thinking more than we realize.

   _____ it can influence our emotions.

6. First I will make myself the most valuable employee I can be.

   _____ I will ask my boss for a raise.

PRACTICE 14.35

Fill in the blanks with suitable transitions. Use the words and phrases from the chart beginning on p. 235 and repetition of key words and ideas.

The idea that the number 13 is unlucky is a superstition. _____, it is probably the most widely held superstition there is. In one way or another, it is observed all over the world. _____ hotels everywhere do not have a 13th floor. _____, their rooms are not numbered with 13. Many people will not have 13 guests at the dinner table.

Strangely, there is no single explanation for the superstition. _____ has many different stories behind it. _____, some experts say that 13 was unpopular from the time when people learned to count. By using their ten fingers and two feet as a unit, people came upwith the number 12. _____ 13 became unlucky because it was unknown and frightening—beyond 12. In religious circles, the 13 superstition is traced to the Last Supper. In attendance were Jesus and the twelve Disciples—13 in all. Others trace the superstition to the story of the Valhalla banquet in Greek mythology, to which twelve gods were invited. _____, Loki, the Spiritof Strife and Mischief, intruded to make 13. _____ Balder, the favorite of the gods, was killed. _____ 13 is generally regarded as unlucky, the number was considered lucky by the ancient Chinese and Egyptians.

Thinking, Learning, and Writing in College

Improving Reading Comprehension

To better understand better understand what you read in all your classes, pay attention to the transitions, coordinating conjunctions, conjunctive adverbs, subordinating conjunctions, and transitions you learned in this chapter. They will indicate how ideas connect to each other by pointing out relationships like addition, similarity, contrast, cause, and effect. Take note of those relationships to improve your reading comprehension and help you learn.

Chapter 15

Avoiding Sentence Fragments

To be a **sentence**, a word group must have a subject, a verb, and enough information to create a sense of completeness. If any one of these elements is missing, the word group cannot be a sentence. A **sentence fragment** is a word group being passed off as a sentence because it has a capital letter and a period. However, a fragment cannot really stand as a sentence because it lacks a subject, a complete verb, or enough information for completeness.

The italicized words in the following examples are fragments.

fragment (subject missing):
The gale force wind toppled power lines. *And interrupted radio communications.*

fragment (complete verb missing):
The mother wondering what the children could be up to. She quietly peeked into the bedroom.

fragment (lacks completeness):
When the band played its last song. The audience cheered wildly.

If you have a tendency to write fragments, this chapter will help you. You will learn:

1. what a fragment is

2. how to identify fragments in your own writing

3. how to eliminate fragments from your writing

◆   ◆   ◆

PRETEST

Write *S* on the blank if the pair of word groups includes only sentences, and write *F* if the pair includes a fragment. Do not guess. If you are unsure, do not write anything. When you are done, check your answers in Appendix III.

1. _____ I enjoy one activity more than any other. Eating Mexican food.

2. _____ Rico's dog likes playing hide-and-seek. And playing with balls too.

3. _____ Although many people do not appreciate Sondra's sense of humor. I think she is very funny.

4. _____ After I took a study skills course, I learned to take better notes. Now my grades are improving steadily.

5. _____ One thing will convince Marion to study. The threat of flunking out of school.

6. _____ Pilar having spoken too soon. Regretted her action.

7. _____ Apologizing for the misunderstanding. Jeffrey asked for another chance.

8. _____ Before you go on a job interview, you should learn something about the company offering the job. This information will enable you to ask intelligent questions.

9. _____ Bitten by the acting bug. My sister went to New York to try for a career on the stage.

10. _____ Some people refuse to believe the earth's resources are dwindling. Even though the evidence is all around them.

FRAGMENTS THAT RESULT FROM MISSING SUBJECTS

To be a sentence, a word group must have its own subject. Without a subject, a word group is a fragment.

> The salesclerk told us she would be with us in a minute. *But spent ten minutes with another customer.*

The italicized words are a fragment because they contain no subject for the verb *spent.* The subject in the preceding sentence (*salesclerk*) cannot operate outside its own sentence. (If you need help finding subjects and verbs, study the material beginning on p. 177.)

Here is another example:

> Dr. Fine passed out the exam papers. *Then announced we would have one hour to complete the questions.*

The italicized words are a fragment because they contain no subject for the verb *announced.* The subject in the preceding sentence (*Dr. Fine*) cannot operate outside its own sentence.

To correct fragments that result from missing subjects, you have two options.

Method 1

Join the fragment to the sentence preceding it.

fragment: The salesclerk told us she would be with us in a minute. *But spent ten minutes with another customer.*

sentence: The salesclerk told us she would be with us in a minute but spent ten minutes with another customer.

Now the verb *spent* has a subject: *salesclerk.*

Method 2

Add a subject so the fragment becomes a sentence.

fragment: Dr. Fine passed out the exam papers. *Then announced we would have one hour to complete the questions.*

sentence: Dr. Fine passed out the exam papers. Then he announced we would have one hour to complete the questions.

Now the verb *announced* has a subject: *he.*

PRACTICE 15.1

Each pair of word groups has one sentence and one fragment. Underline the fragment. Then rewrite to eliminate the fragment, using the correction method given in parentheses. Method 1 is joining the fragment to the preceding sentence; method 2 is adding the missing subject. The first one is done as an example.

1. (method 1) Alexander enrolled in a CPR course. And learned valuable lifesaving techniques.

   Alexander enrolled in a CPR course and learned valuable

   lifesaving techniques.

2. (method 1) I quit smoking for three months. But started again when I changed jobs.

_____

_____

3. (method 1) During the depression, my grandmother raised four daughters alone. And sold insurance to keep food on the table.

_____

_____

4. (method 2) Dr. Juarez described the requirements for the research project. Then answered questions from the class.

_____

_____

5. (method 2) The movers gently positioned the antique sofa against the wall. However, dropped the oil lamp that has been in my family for generations.

_____

_____

6. (method 1) The cruel children made fun of their new classmate. And caused her to feel like an outcast.

_____

_____

7. (method 2) The comedy special earned the highest ratings for a program in that time slot. Still, offended many people because of the profanity used by three of the comedians.

_____

_____

PRACTICE 15.2

Revise to correct the four fragments created by missing subjects. If you have trouble finding the fragments, try reading the paragraph slowly, from last sentence to first sentence.

One modern convenience we tend to take for granted is the shopping cart. This device was invented by Sylvan Goldman, who lived in Oklahoma City. And ran a grocery store there. Goldman felt sorry for customers. He watched them struggling as they shopped and tried to hold onto their purchases. He hit upon an idea to help them. And built the first crude shopping cart. First, he fastened two folding chairs together. Then put wheels on the legs and baskets on the seats. The contraption looked weird. But worked. From that point on, shopping became easier. The next time you push a shopping cart, think of Sylvan Goldman.

FRAGMENTS THAT RESULT FROM INCOMPLETE VERBS

A fragment will result if you do not include a helping verb that belongs with an action verb. (See p. 179 on action and helping verbs.)

fragment: Jane going to the store.

sentence: Jane is (or was) going to the store. [The helping verb
              is (or *was*) is added.]

In general, *-ing* verb forms and past participle verb forms (see p. 312 and p. 317 for an explanation of past participles) must appear with a helping verb, or the result will be a fragment.

-ing fragment: The baby sleeping soundly in the crib.

sentence: The baby is (or was) sleeping soundly in
                             the crib.

past participle fragment: The police officer angered by the
                             driver's attitude.

sentence: The police officer was (or is) angered by
                             the driver's attitude.

To correct fragments that result from incomplete verbs, you have two options.

Method 1

Add the missing helping verb. Choose from *is, are, was, were, have, has,* or *had*—whichever is appropriate.

| fragment: | The sun setting in the west. |
| sentence formed by adding helping verb: | The sun is setting in the west. |

Method 2

Change the *-ing* or past participle form to the simple present or past tense, whichever is appropriate.

fragment:	The baby sleeping soundly in the crib.
sentence with simple present tense verb:	The baby sleeps soundly in the crib.
fragment:	The police officer angered by the driver's attitude.
sentence with simple past tense verb:	The driver's attitude angered the police officer.

PRACTICE 15.3

Change each fragment to a sentence using the method of correction given in parentheses. Method 1 is adding the missing helping verb; method 2 is changing the verb to the simple present or past tense form. The first two are done as examples.

1. (method 1) The university's faculty promotions committee considering the promotion requests of fifty instructors.

   The university's faculty promotions committee is considering the

   promotion requests of fifty instructors.

2. (method 2) The adolescent boys devouring everything in the refrigerator.

   The adolescent boys devoured everything in

   the refrigerator.

3. (method 2) Before the second half began, the coach reminding the front line to avoid off-sides penalties.

   _____

   _____

4. (method 2) The president's speech was enthusiastically received. Both Democrats and Republicans vowing to help pass the legislation requested.

_____

_____

5. (method 1) The hijackers want to call attention to their political agenda. Therefore, they taken a hardline stand during the negotiations.

_____

_____

6. (method 1) Many people believe that we are not the only life forms in the universe. They noting frequent UFO sightings and other unexplained events as proof.

_____

_____

7. (method 2) A female named Hatshepsut being an ancient Egyptian Pharoah.

_____

_____

8. (method 1) The hawk riding the air currents and soaring majestically.

_____

_____

PRACTICE 15.4

Revise to correct the four fragments that result from incomplete verbs. If you have trouble finding the fragments, try reading the paragraph slowly from last sentence to first.

When Allesandra makes up her mind, it is permanent. Nothing proves that point more than the following story about her broken engagement. Allesandra broken off her engagement with Roberto. Roberto hoping to win her back, so he sent her 1,480 roses. This amounted to one rose for each day of the more than four years they were engaged. One day after the arrival of the roses, Allesandra dining in a restaurant with her family. Roberto arrived on horseback to deliver the last rose in person. He made an empassioned plea to the woman to resume the engagement. Allesandra, however, not interested. She said, "no thanks," and continued eating her meal.

FRAGMENTS THAT RESULT FROM MISSING SUBJECTS AND VERBS

Some fragments are word groups that lack both a subject and a complete verb. In the examples that follow, the fragments are italicized.

Gloomy weather always depresses me. *Also snowy weather.*

All the Smiths are very considerate. *Particularly in times of trouble.*

Unable to assemble Leo's bike. Dad was frustrated.

I walked across campus. *Reading my biology notes.*

To correct fragments that result from missing subjects and verbs, you have two options.

Method 1

Some fragments can be corrected by joining them to preceding or following sentences.

fragment:	*Unable to assemble Leo's bike.* Dad was frustrated.
sentence:	Unable to assemble Leo's bike, Dad was frustrated.
fragment:	I walked across campus. *Reading my biology notes.*
sentence:	I walked across campus reading my biology notes.

Method 2

Some fragments can be corrected by adding the missing subject and verb.

fragment:	Gloomy weather always depresses me. *Also snowy weather.*
sentence:	Gloomy weather always depresses me. Also I am depressed by snowy weather.
fragment:	All the Smiths are very considerate. *Particularly in times of trouble.*

sentence: All the Smiths are very considerate. They are particularly considerate in times of trouble.

PRACTICE 15.5

Each set of word groups contains one fragment and one sentence. First underline the fragment. Then rewrite to eliminate the fragment, using either method 1 (joining the fragment to the sentence) or method 2 (adding the missing subject and verb). The first one is done as an example.

1. <u>Fearing she would not get a satisfactory grade in physics.</u> Joanie hired a tutor.

   Fearing she would not get a satisfactory grade in physics,

   Joanie hired a tutor.

2. Hoping to confuse the opposition. The coach switched defensive strategies.

   _____

   _____

3. Because of his high cholesterol level, Rudy began a lowfat, high carbohydrate diet. At the advice of his physician and at the urging of his wife.

   _____

   _____

4. To score high on the Law School Admissions Test. A person must have strong verbal skills.

   _____

   _____

5. All the starting players are sophomores. Except Morrison, who is a graduating senior.

   _____

   _____

6. Caffeine is found in many everyday foods. Including candy, soft drinks, and coffee.

_____

_____

7. A wide range of idea-generation techniques is available to writers. Facing writer's block and searching for ideas to write about.

_____

_____

8. Before beginning any exercise program. You should have a complete physical. With a blood pressure screening.

_____

_____

9. Surprisingly, some fruits are a prime cause of tooth decay. Raisins, for example, with their high sugar content.

_____

_____

PRACTICE 15.6

Revise to correct the five fragments that result from missing subjects and verbs. If you have trouble finding the fragments, read the paragraph slowly from last sentence to first.

There are fundamental differences between the alligator and the crocodile. The head of the alligator is shaped like a spade. The crocodile has a pointy nose. With protruding teeth. Living in swampy areas of the southeastern United States. The alligator is particularly numerous in Louisiana and parts of Florida. The crocodile, however, likes salt water, and in the United States is found only in south Florida. The alligator is dark brown. Also yellow markings. The crocodile is olive green and black. While there are differences, both animals benefit the ecology. Offering refuge to many species during floods. Their nests are important. Also, their droppings add vital nutrients to the water. Thus, these animals, which offer little threat to humans, should be protected. To preserve the balance of nature.

FRAGMENTS THAT RESULT FROM LACK OF COMPLETENESS

To be a sentence, a word group must have a subject and a complete verb. However, it must also have a sense of completeness. The following has both a subject and a complete verb. It is not a sentence, however, because it lacks a sense of completeness.

s.   v.

When Jorge was a child.

When you read this word group, you do not have a sense of completeness. You need to know what happened when Jorge was a child. Now read the following word group and notice that there *is* a sense of completeness. For this reason, the word group can stand as a sentence.

When Jorge was a child, he had several health problems.

The following fragments are caused by lack of completeness. Read them aloud to hear that something is missing.

After the meeting was over.

Before we can leave on our vacation.

Although Jessie admitted he made a mistake.

Since I have begun taking college courses.

Word groups with subjects and complete verbs but insufficient completeness to be sentences are called **subordinate clauses**. (See p. 192 for more on subordinate clauses.) Subordinate clauses begin with **subordinating conjunctions**, one of the words or short phrases in the list that follows. When you check your work for fragments, pay special attention to word groups that begin with one of these words or short phrases. Be sure the necessary completeness is there.

after	before	when
although	even though	whenever
as	if	where
as if	in order to	wherever
as long as	since	whether
as soon as	so that	while

as though   unless

because   until

Some subordinate clause fragments begin with *who, where, which,* or *that,* so watch for word groups that begin with one of these words.

fragment:	Who lives next door to my parents.
fragment:	Where the Allegheny River meets the Monongahela.
fragment:	That I told you about.

To correct fragments that result from lack of completeness, you can often join the fragment to a sentence that appears before or after it.

fragment:	*After the meeting was over.* We all went out for coffee.
sentence:	After the meeting was over, we all went out for coffee.
fragment:	My self-esteem has improved. *Since I have begun taking college courses.*
sentence:	My self-esteem has improved since I have begun taking college courses.
fragment:	This is the Italian restaurant. *That I told you about.*
sentence:	This is the Italian restaurant that I told you about.

PRACTICE 15.7

Each pair of word groups includes one fragment that results from lack of completeness and one sentence. Underline the fragment and correct it by joining it to the sentence. The first one is done as an example.

1. Because Miro's grades are so good. He is an excellent candidate for the humanities scholarship.

   Because Miro's grades are so good, he is an excellent

   candidate for the humanities scholarship.

2. If it snows another two inches. We will be able to go skiing in the morning.

   _____

   _____

3. Gail is an interesting person. Who understands how to relate to people.

_____

_____

4. Voter turnout is expected to reach an all-time high. Because the Senate race is so hotly contested.

_____

_____

5. By the time the box office opened at 6:00. A line had already formed halfway around the block.

_____

_____

6. If schoolchildren do not eat a nutritious lunch. Their schoolwork in the afternoon will suffer.

_____

_____

7. Professor Weinblatt is a talented teacher. Whose lectures hold everyone's attention.

_____

_____

8. If I were you. I would reconsider dropping out of school.

_____

_____

PRACTICE 15.8

Revise to eliminate the six fragments that result from lack of completeness. If you have trouble finding the fragments, try reading the paragraph slowly from last sentence to first.

Motown, the most successful black-owned American record company, was founded in 1960 in Detroit by Berry Gordy Jr. Who began as a songwriter in the mid-1950s. Led by the writing talents of Smokey Robinson, who also sang with the Miracles. Motown artists were an important presence on the record charts in the 1960s and 1970s. A reference to "Motor Town" (Detroit), Motown came to signify a particular performance style. A Motown song often featured elaborate structures, heavy rhythms, and background orchestras. Because the company kept a tight rein on the image of its performers. It often prescribed their manners and style of grooming. Live performances required carefully controlled choreography and elaborate costumes. Which added up to the Motown-style package. Clearly, the formula was a success. Because it made stars of many performers, including Diana Ross and the Supremes, Stevie Wonder, Marvin Gaye, the Jackson Five, and Lionel Richie. At its best, Motown represented the best of mass-produced, black-derived pop music. Although its later productions were more obviously the products of a musical assembly line. Motown was largely responsible for introducing the sounds of contemporary black music to a white audience.

 ## *Tips for Finding Sentence Fragments*

1. Read your essay backwards, from last sentence to first. You may notice fragments easier this way because you will be less likely to join them mentally to other sentences.

2. Isolate each word group you are calling a sentence by placing one finger of one hand at the beginning capital letter and a finger of the other hand at the period. Now study the words between your fingers to be sure they generate the sense of completeness needed for sentence status.

3. Pay special attention to word groups with *-ing* and *-ed* verb forms. Be sure the verb is complete.

4. Be sure each word group beginning with one of the subordinating conjunctions on page 250 has a sense of completeness.

5. Be sure word groups beginning with *who, which, where,* or *that* have the sense of completeness needed to be a sentence.

Thinking, Learning, and Writing in College   **Notetaking**

When you take notes in your classes, speed is important, so go ahead and use all the fragments you want to. Then as a study aid, read your notes several times after class, look away, and rewrite them in complete sentences. Compare your rewritten version to the original to determine whether you omitted anything.

POST TEST

Revise the paragraphs to eliminate the fragments.

A. All families should plan and practice how to escape from their homes in the event of a fire. Especially at night. Because every minute spent in a burning house means extra danger. Escape routes should be planned and practiced periodically. Family members should practice crawling through the house in the event rooms are filled with smoke. Also learning how to move through the house in darkness. In addition, family members should plan where to meet outdoors. And what to do when they get there. If families plan and practice their escape, a house fire does not have to mean complete tragedy. To learn more about fire safety in the event of a house fire. Contact your local fire department.

B. The California condor looks very strange. When perched in a tree. It has a bald head and a wrinkled neck. And a large black, feathered body. Near the ground, the bird is hilariously awkward. It lumbers on takeoffs, and it crashes on landings. In the air, however, the bird is a breathtaking sight. Its wings spreading out nine feet. It can soar at an amazing 80 miles an hour.

   At one time, one wild condor was left in California. Scientists managed to capture it when it swooped down to feed on a dead goat. The scientists took it to the San Diego Zoo. Where it lived with thirteen other condors. These condors, along with fourteen in the Los Angeles Zoo, the only remaining California condors in the world. Scientists captured these birds. To protect them from being shot or poisoned.

Chapter 16

Avoiding Run-On Sentences and Comma Splices

A single sentence can be made up of two main clauses (word groups that can be sentences) *only if* the main clauses are correctly separated. If the main clauses are not separated at all, the result is a problem called **run-on sentence**. If they are separated by just a comma, the result is a problem called **comma splice**.

Here are two main clauses (word groups that can be sentences):

Randy could not wait to tell everyone his good news.

He got the job he wanted so badly.

If you fail to separate these word groups, the result is a **run-on sentence**:

run-on:
Randy could not wait to tell everyone the good news he got the job he wanted so badly.

If you separate these word groups with just a comma, the result is a **comma splice**:

comma splice:
Randy could not wait to tell everyone the good news, he got the job he wanted so badly.

NOTE: Main clauses are discussed in more detail on p. 192.

If you write run-on sentences or comma splices, this chapter will help you. You will learn:

1. how to identify run-ons and comma splices
2. how to eliminate run-ons and comma splices from your writing

◆   ◆   ◆

PRETEST

If the word group is a run-on, write *RO* in the blank; if it is a comma splice, write *CS* in the blank; if it is correct, write *C* in the blank. You can check your answers in Appendix III.

1. _____ I heard a siren, I pulled my car to the edge of the road.

2. _____ The sudden spring rains caused flash flooding the townspeople moved to higher ground.

3. _____ Roberto's singing career is going very well he has signed a contract with an important talent agent.

4. _____ If I had the opportunity, I would travel to Europe.

5. _____ The last day of the month is the best time to buy a car at that time dealers are anxious to reduce their inventory.

6. _____ People are changing their eating habits, more of us are restricting fat and cholesterol.

7. _____ Because I spilled bleach on it, the shirt is ruined.

8. _____ I do all my grocery shopping on Sunday to avoid the crowds.

9. _____ Martha subscribes to ten magazines she doesn't know where to put them all.

10. _____ To be sure that your car runs well, change the oil regularly.

CORRECTING RUN-ONS AND COMMA SPLICES WITH A PERIOD AND CAPITAL LETTER

One way to eliminate a run-on sentence or comma splice is to use a period and capital letter to make each main clause (word group that can stand as a sentence) a separate sentence.

run-on:	I left the party at 11:00 then I went to a movie.
sentence:	I left the party at 11:00. Then I went to a movie.
comma splice:	Darla is the perfect person for the job, she is reliable, intelligent, and efficient.
sentence:	Darla is the perfect person for the job. She is reliable, intelligent, and efficient.

PRACTICE 16.1

Eliminate each run-on or comma splice by adding a period and capital letter. Two sentences are correct.

1. You have probably heard the expression "pan out," it is used when things work out satisfactorily.

2. When a plan goes well, you can say that "everything panned out."

3. When a plan does not go well, you can say the opposite, you can say that "things did not pan out."

4. "Pan out" is a gold mining term one method of finding gold is to take a handful of sand and place it in a little pan.

5. By sloshing the water back and forth in the pan, the lighter sand, dirt, and pebbles slide over the edge.

6. The heavier gold stays in the pan thus it "pans out."

7. We do not often pause to think about common expressions their origins can be very interesting, however.

PRACTICE 16.2

Eliminate the three run-on sentences and comma splices by using periods and capital letters. If you need help finding the run-ons and comma splices, study each word group with a period and capital letter. Determine how many main clauses there are. If there are more than one, be sure they are correctly separated.

Bill Haley was the first real rock and roll star, his recording of "Crazy Man Crazy" was the first rock and roll record to make Billboard's pop music charts. Although he started out as a country singer, Haley decided to make a bid for teen appeal in the mid-1950s. When his "Rock Around the Clock" became the theme song for the movie The Blackboard Jungle in 1955, Haley scored big with teen audiences he was at this point a genuine rock and roll star. For the next two years he had a dozen top-40 hits, these included "See You Later Alligator" and "Burn That Candle." When Haley died in 1981, he was 55, and he had sold 60 million records.

CORRECTING RUN-ONS AND COMMA SPLICES WITH A SEMICOLON

A second way to eliminate a run-on or comma splice is to use a semicolon to separate the main clauses (word groups that can stand as sentences).

run-on:	None of us wanted to go out we were all too tired.
sentence:	None of us wanted to go out; we were all too tired.

comma splice: Jim and Clarice bought a house that is a hundred years old, they will have to work hard to fix it up.

sentence: Jim and Clarice bought a house that is a hundred years old; they will have to work hard to fix it up.

A run-on or comma splice can also be corrected with one of the following (see also p. 201):

| ; however, | ; furthermore, | ; consequently, |
| ; nevertheless, | ; therefore, | ; moreover, |

run-on: The examination was harder than I expected I believe I passed it.

sentence: The examination was harder than I expected; however, I believe I passed it.

comma splice: On April Fools' Day my son put a rubber snake in my bed, he poured salt in my coffee.

sentence: On April Fools' Day my son put a rubber snake in my bed; furthermore, he poured salt in my coffee.

CAUTION: When you use a semicolon, to avoid a run-on sentence or comma splice, be sure you have a main clause on *both sides* of the semicolon.

Incorrect: Carol decorated the Christmas tree; before Philippe got home from work. (There is no main clause after the semicolon.)

Correct: Carol decorated the Christmas tree before Philippe got home from work.

PRACTICE 16.3

Eliminate the run-ons and comma splices by inserting semicolons. Three sentences are correct.

1. Some laws currently on the books are wacky it is hard to understand why.

2. For example, stores in Providence, Rhode Island, are not allowed to sell toothbrushes on Sunday, however, they can still sell toothpaste.

3. In Paraguay, dueling is illegal if both parties are blood donors.

4. In Atwoodville, Connecticut, people cannot play Scrabble while waiting for a politician to speak, now that is an odd ordinance.

5. According to the Recruitment Code of the U.S. Navy, anyone "bearing an obscene and indecent" tattoo will be rejected.

6. The U.S. patent laws prohibit granting patents on useless inventions, that law is not always enforced.

7. Items in the catalogs mailed to me prove that many useless items are patented.

PRACTICE 16.4

Insert semicolons to eliminate the three run-on sentences and comma splices. If you have trouble finding the run-ons and comma splices, study every word group with a period and capital letter and decide how many main clauses there are. If there is more than one main clause, be sure the clauses are correctly separated.

An increasing number of employers are providing day-care centers at their places of business they have learned that employees are more productive when they do not have to worry about baby-sitting arrangements for their children. In addition, when child-care is on company premises, employees do not have to call off work when the baby-sitter fails to show up. Many companies are learning that on-site day-care is a valuable fringe benefit. Employees are less likely to change their places of employment when day-care is available this means companies do not have to worry about rapid employee turnover. Undoubtedly, more and more companies will be providing day-care facilities, they are a benefit to both employer and employee.

CORRECTING RUN-ONS AND COMMA SPLICES WITH A COMMA AND COORDINATING CONJUNCTION

The words in the following list are **coordinating conjunctions**. These words are explained on p. 195, and now is a good time to review that explanation.

and	or	so
but	for	yet

You can eliminate a run-on sentence or comma splice by separating the main clauses (word groups that can stand as sentences) with a comma and coordinating conjunction.

run-on:	The hamburger was not completely cooked I asked the waiter to take it back to the kitchen.
sentence:	The hamburger was not completely cooked, so I asked the waiter to take it back to the kitchen.
comma splice:	The compact disc player costs more than a tape player, it is worth the added expense.
sentence:	The compact disc player costs more than a tape player, but [yet] it is worth the added expense.

PRACTICE 16.5

Eliminate the run-ons and comma splices by inserting commas and coordinating conjunctions. One sentence is correct. In some cases, more than one coordinating conjunction is correct.

1. Many dictionaries bear the name "Webster," Noah Webster does not have anything to do with these books.
2. Webster published the first major dictionary in the United States in the early 1800s his name is practically synonymous with "dictionary."
3. His rights to dictionaries ran out many years ago, the word "Webster's" entered the public domain.
4. Anyone can now use Webster's name in connection with a dictionary, regardless of the author or publisher.
5. Any company can call its dictionary "Webster's," many companies do.
6. We will most likely think of Noah Webster whenever we check a word in a dictionary he is the one whose name means "dictionary."

PRACTICE 16.6

Use commas and coordinating conjunctions to eliminate the four run-ons and comma splices. If you have trouble finding the run-ons and comma splices, study every word group with a period and capital letter. Decide how many main clauses there are. If there are more than one, be sure they are properly separated.

Exercise does not have to be unpleasant. If you follow some simple guidelines, you can enjoy the road to fitness. First pick a form of exercise you like, walking, swimming, running, bicycling, or whatever. You should set goals for yourself, you should make those goals a little harder as you move along. You should swim a bit further you should run a little longer each day. It is important to go slowly at first, you might sustain an injury. To avoid injuries, you should also do warm-up and cool-down stretching exercises. Finally, exercise with a friend you can encourage each other and enjoy the companionship.

WARNING WORDS

Pay special attention to the following words and phrases, for they often begin main clauses. When you edit and come across one of these words or phrases, check the number of main clauses in the sentence. If there are more than one, be sure the clauses are correctly separated.

however	then	moreover	nevertheless
therefore	thus	furthermore	similarly
hence	finally	consequently	next
as a result	in addition	on the contrary	for example

PRACTICE 16.7

Each word group includes a run-on and comma splice warning word or phrase. However, not all the word groups are run-ons or comma splices. If the word group is a run-on, write *RO* on the blank; if it is a comma splice, write *CS;* if it is a correct sentence, write *S.*

1. _____ Henri completed the committee report for his fraternity, then he took it to the chapter president.

2. _____ Carla's cavity was so deep she had to have two shots of novocaine consequently she could not feel the right side of her face for three hours.

3. _____ We waited most of the morning for Jeff to arrive; finally, we just left without him.

4. _____ Not everyone understands Dad's sarcastic sense of humor; as a result, some people feel insulted when he teases them.

5. _____ In addition to losing my keys last week, I misplaced my good leather gloves.

6. _____ First you should choose an advisor in your major field of study, next you should select an advisor in your minor field of study.

7. _____ Dr. Schultz is sick with the flu therefore our midterm has been postponed until next week.

8. _____ The football team lost three games in a row as a result of errors by the defensive squad.

 Tips for Finding Run-On Sentences and Comma Splices

1. Study every word group with a capital letter and a period, and determine the number of main clauses. If there are two or more, be sure these clauses are correctly separated with a semicolon or with a comma and coordinating conjunction.

2. Study every word group that contains a comma. If there is a main clause on both sides of the comma, be sure to include a coordinating conjunction with the comma.

3. Pay special attention to word groups with words or phrases of warning. If these words or phrases are separating main clauses, be sure a semicolon is used before the warning word or phrase.

4. Do not assume a long sentence is a run-on or comma splice. The only true test is whether main clauses are correctly separated—length is not a factor.

POST TEST

Revise to eliminate the run-on sentences and comma splices. You may use any or all of the correction methods discussed in this chapter.

A. Margaret Chase Smith was the first woman elected to both the United States House of Representatives and the United States Senate. Her husband, a Republican congressman from Maine, died in 1940, Mrs. Smith replaced him in the House of Representatives. She served in the House for eight years. She was elected to the Senate in 1948 she was reelected in 1954 and 1960. In 1950 she was one of the first senators to oppose Senator Joseph McCarthy. In 1965 she campaigned for the Republican presidential nomination, she was the first woman to do so. Smith was an influential legislator during her years in Congress, moreover, she was not put off by the fact that at the time, politics was largely the domain of males. In fact, Smith helped pave the way for other women to enter the political arena at the national level.

B. Many schools have alcohol-awareness programs to steer children away from drinking, however, parents need to be involved as well. Parents can do a number of things, for example, they can discuss drinking scenes in programs and movies they watch with their children. Parents should ask questions such as "Why do you think grown-ups drink?" and "Can grown-ups have fun without drinking?" Because children may become confused seeing adults drink when they have been told to say no, parents should explain the health risks associated with alcohol and the fact that the legal drinking age is 21. It is also a good idea to emphasize positive reasons for saying no: Children need to keep their heads clear for school, they also need to keep their bodies healthy for athletics. Parents can also role-play with their children. Give them a glass of water and have them practice saying "No thanks." Parents must be actively involved, they cannot leave the full responsibility to the schools.

Thinking, Learning, and Writing in College

Seeing Relationships between Ideas

When writers separate main clauses with a comma and coordinating conjunction, the conjunction indicates how the clauses relate to each other. For example, in the following sentence, the conjunction *but* indicates that the second clause is a contrast to the first:

> The government phased out lead in gasoline and paint, but the substance still exists in many other products.

However, when you read main clauses separated by a semicolon alone, you must determine on your own how the clauses relate to each other. Thus, you may need to reflect for a moment to assess the relationship between ideas. For example, what is the relationship between the main clauses in this sentence?

> Americans are weary of the preferential treatment given groups that contribute huge sums to political campaigns; Congress will have to consider campaign finance reform soon.

Visit the Clouse Website!

For additional exercises, quizzes, and Internet activities, visit our Website at:

http://www.ablongman.com/clouse

For even more activities, visit the Longman English pages at:

http://www.ablongman.com/englishpages

Chapter 17

Choosing Words Carefully

To communicate clearly and create a positive impression, choose words carefully. In this chapter, you will learn principles of effective word choice, including

1. using specific words

2. building your vocabulary

3. using idioms

4. distinguishing between frequently confused words

5. avoiding slang

6. avoiding clichés

7. eliminating wordiness

8. avoiding double negatives

9. improving your spelling

SPECIFIC WORD CHOICE

Specific words communicate your ideas as clearly and exactly as possible. Study the following chart to understand the difference between specific and general words:

General	Specific
car	red Camaro
book	*Gone with the Wind*
shoe	loafer
aunt	Aunt Millie
math course	Algebra II

sweater	yellow cardigan
walk	swagger
eat	gobble

Specific words give a more exact idea than the general ones do because they provide more specific information. Here are two sentences to consider. The first one includes general words, and the second includes specific ones. Which sentence communicates more precisely?

The girl sat on the chair feeling bad.

Susan slumped into the chair, worried about losing her job.

The second sentence communicates more exactly because the words are more specific; they provide more detailed information.

Chapter 2 discusses specific word choice in more detail. Now is the time to review that material, which begins on p. 56. In addition, Chapter 2 includes several *Practice* exercises to help you learn to use specific words. If you have not already done so, complete these exercises.

Some people think that the bigger and fancier their words are, the better their writing is, but this is not true at all. In fact, if you consistently choose fancy, twenty-dollar words, your writing will seem unnatural.

The truth is, effective writing is clear writing. To be clear, you probably know most of the words you need. Your job is to choose the right, specific words to convey your meaning as simply and exactly as possible. Consider, for a moment, this sentence taken from "Wear a Helmet" on p. 137:

For example, many times I have seen the flash of a helmet before I have seen the motorcycle itself.

This sentence is effective, in part because it communicates with clear, specific, *simple* language. Any reader will appreciate the natural style that comes from the simple, specific word choice.

Now consider how you react to this revision of the sentence, a revision that relies on overblown, fancy words:

By way of illustrative clarification, allow me to interject that on numerous occasions I have visually detected the sudden display of light from a helmet prior to visually acknowledging the two-wheeled, engine-propelled vehicle itself.

Like most readers, you probably find this sentence wordy and unclear. It shows, further, that you should not reach for high-sounding words to get your message across. Instead, be specific and be simple.

> ### ✳ *Tip for Specific Word Choice*
>
> Do not worry too much about specific word choice when you are writing a first draft. Instead, when you revise the draft, underline every general noun, verb, and modifier. Then substitute more specific words for some or all of what you underlined.

PRACTICE 17.1

1. Read "Wear a Helmet" on p. 137. Copy a sentence with specific yet simple word choice. Underline the simple, specific word(s).
2. Read "The Plant" on p. 79. Copy three sentences with specific, simple word choice. Underline the simple, specific words.
3. Read "Let's Hear It for Tradition" on p. 114. Copy two sentences with specific, simple word choice. Underline the specific, simple words.

REVIEW PRACTICE 17.2

Circle any seven general words and write more specific, simple alternatives above them. Feel free to add details and alter wording as you wish. The first sentence is done for you as an example.

watched in horror as
Cal's Diner   Tuesday   a man and woman

got When I was in (a restaurant) (recently), I (saw) (two people) get into an argument. At first, they were talking to each other loudly, but soon their voices became louder and louder until they were yelling at each other. Suddenly, the man stood up, took his plate and threw it at the wall, making a terrible noise. Food was all over the wall and some of the people sitting nearby. Fortunately, a police officer was in the restaurant. He immediately got out of his seat and took the man outside to calm down. Needless to say, I got out of there quickly.

VOCABULARY BUILDING

If you often say, "I know what I want to say, but I don't know how to say it," you probably need to increase your vocabulary. To be an effective writer, you must know enough words to express yourself with precision.

Furthermore, studies show that successful people are likely to have rich, varied vocabularies. If you need to add to your storehouse of words, *now* is the time to begin. Become interested in words, study words each day, and review the words you learn often. You will become a more effective writer, speaker, listener, and reader.

Finding Words to Learn

Vocabulary lists for study are available in any vocabulary-building book in your campus bookstore, study skills center, or library. However, more learning will occur if *you* decide on the words to learn.

To develop your own list, write down unfamiliar words you hear or read that you want to learn. Pay particular attention to unfamiliar words in your textbooks and class lectures. Note words you see in the newspaper and magazines and words you hear on television and radio. Also, write down unfamiliar words you hear friends and family use. In addition, write the sentence you saw or heard the word used in.

Learning New Words

1. Keep a small notebook with you. Each time you hear or read an unfamiliar word you wish to learn, write the word in the notebook with the sentence in which the word was used. If you do not want to interrupt your reading to write words in your notebook, underline the unfamiliar words and record them in your notebook after you have finished reading.

2. *Each day* transfer each new word in your notebook to its own index card. On the front of the card write the word, correctly spelled, and the sentence the word was used in. If you do not know how to pronounce the word, copy the dictionary pronunciation on the front of the card. Check a dictionary, and on the back of the card write the meaning of the word. If there is more than one meaning, record the one that fits the use of the word in the sentence on the front of the card. Then write a sentence of your own on the back of the card that uses the word correctly.

3. Study your cards *every day*. Learn each new word and review several from previous days.

4. When possible, learn meanings through association. For example, to learn that *ostracize* means "to banish or expel," you may associate it with an ostrich, which banishes itself by poking its head in the sand.

5. Learn clusters of words. For example, once you have learned what *luminous* means, learn *luminance, illuminate, luminary,* and *luminosity*. To discover word clusters, look for related words around each word you check in the dictionary.

6. Use the words you learn as you speak, write, and think, so they become a natural part of your vocabulary.

7. Work with a friend or classmate. Quiz each other, trade words, try to stump each other, use your new words in conversation with each other, and study your cards together. With a partner, the learning is more fun.

8. Buy two good dictionaries: a fat paperback and a hardbound collegiate dictionary. Carry the paperback with you to check words as they come up. Keep the hardbound dictionary where you study or read so it will be convenient to check words.

9. Many words share common **prefixes** (beginnings) and **suffixes** (endings). Study the meanings of prefixes and suffixes as an aid to learning meanings. To do this, consult a vocabulary book in the library or study skills center.

PRACTICE 17.3

1. For a day, record in a small notebook any words you see or hear that you do not know. At the end of the day, make index cards for the words according to the directions given in the previous discussion.

2. Find a vocabulary-building partner. Arrange a specific time and place to meet during the week to work on vocabulary according to the suggestions in the previous discussion.

3. Buy a copy of *Time* or *Newsweek* and read three articles. Underline every word that is not familiar to you. Add some of these words to your index cards. Read at least one article in the magazine each day and add unfamiliar words to your cards. When you are through with the magazine, buy another and begin again.

Thinking, Learning, and Writing in College   Learning Specialized Vocabulary

Each subject has its own specialized vocabulary to learn, use, and spell correctly. As you encounter this vocabulary in your classes, study it carefully and review it often. Be sure to learn the correct spelling of each word in all its forms.

1. Make note of vocabulary your instructor mentions or writes on the board. Listen for your instructor to shift tone of voice, slow down, or repeat a term to emphasize important vocabulary. Write out the meaning, and ask questions if you do not understand that meaning.

2. Make note of words in your textbooks that are italicized, boldfaced, or written in a second color. If a word is not defined where it appears, check for a glossary at the back of the book, or query your instructor.

3. When you decide on a major, consider purchasing a dictionary of specialized vocabulary in that discipline, a dictionary like *A Dictionary of Anthropology, A Dictionary of Economics,* or *The New Grove Dictionary of Music and Musicians.*

Idioms

An **idiom** is an expression whose meaning cannot be determined from the meaning of its individual words. Consider, for example, the idiom "drop someone a line." The four individual words in that expression do not add up to its rightful meaning, which is to write a letter or correspond in writing: As soon as I move into my new apartment, I will *drop you a line* with my address.

You are probably familiar with many idioms already. Others, however, may be new to you, particularly if you speak English as a second language. As you work to build your vocabulary, pay particular attention to idioms. When you look up a word in your dictionary, idioms associated with the word will be noted for easy reference. To become familiar with ten frequently occurring idioms, review the following list.

make allowance for—excuse; allow for

I can *make allowances for* Carla's bad behavior because she is very tense right now.

call the shots—be in charge

Joel is not happy unless he is *calling the shots*.

[out] in the cold—ignored

After I missed three committee meetings, all the members left me *out in the cold*, so I did not know what was happening.

to land on one's feet—to recover from a dangerous or difficult situation

Although Jacob lost his job last year, he *landed on his feet* and found a better job.

go to any lengths—do anything to reach a goal

Lizette wants a graduate assistantship so badly that she will *go to any lengths* to get it.

make one's mark—achieve success

As the most honored coach in the school's history, Rich Morales has *made his mark* in our community.

to play by ear—to go ahead without a plan

I am not sure what I will tell Katrina. I will have *to play it by ear*.

on the ropes—close to failure

I am really *on the ropes*. This project is due in two days, and I have no ideas.

strike a blow for—further the cause of

Forcing the dictator to leave the country *struck a blow* for democracy.

carry weight—have importance

Because of her reputation in scientific circles, Dr. Wang's opinion *carries considerable weight.*

PRACTICE 17.4

From the following list, pick five idioms that you are unsure of. Look up their meanings in your dictionary by checking under the italicized key word in the idiom. Then, on a separate sheet, write the meaning of each idiom and use each one in a sentence that you compose. If you are unfamiliar with more than five idioms, learn two or three each day until you know them all.

chew the fat	*rub* off on
chew the scenery	*rub* out
kick the bucket	*put* one's best foot forward
stay put	*put* something over on
steer clear of	*put* oneself out
still and all	in *store*
grasp at straws	set *store* by
goof off	*get* out of line
talk back to	*draw* the line at
take it upon oneself	*tough* it out
take five	keep *track* (lose *track*)
take responsibility	off the *track*
clear the air	over a *barrel*
up in the *air*	off *base*
do or die	touch *base*
in the *cards*	make *ends* meet
lay (put) one's *cards* on the table	give up the *ghost*
free and easy	*give* and take
be in someone's *shoes*	keep one's *head*
fix up	lose one's *head*
try one's hand at	be of one *mind*
keep a *hand* in	

FREQUENTLY CONFUSED WORDS

The words given here sometimes present problems for writers.

A/An

1. *A* is used before a consonant sound. (See p. 298 on vowels and consonants.)

   a tree, *a* friendly face, *a* unicycle (despite the opening vowel, this word begins with a consonant *sound*)

2. *An* is used before a vowel sound.

   an apple, *an* ice cream cone, *an* hour (despite the opening consonant, this word begins with a vowel *sound*)

PRACTICE 17.5

1. Fill in the blanks with *a* or *an*.

   A. _____ friendly stranger gave us directions.

   B. Ivan gave _____ interesting interpretation of the short story.

   C. _____ uncle of mine is _____ sheriff in _____ county west of here.

   D. Laughter is _____ universal language.

   E. _____ sink full of dirty dishes awaited me when I returned from

      _____ meeting of the Art Guild.

   F. _____ unicorn is _____ mythical beast.

2. On a separate sheet, write two sentences using *a* and two using *an*.

Accept/Except

1. *Accept* means "to receive."
   I *accept* your offer of help with thanks.
2. *Except* means "leaving out" or "excluding."
   All the votes *except* those from Precinct Z have been counted.

TIP: Think of the *ex* in *except* and *excluding.*

PRACTICE 17.6

1. Fill in the blanks with *accept* or *except.*

    A. I cannot _____ your explanation.

    B. It is not easy to _____ defeat with dignity.

    C. Everyone _____ Joanie found the movie dull.

    D. No teacher will _____ a paper as sloppy as this.

    E. _____ for the first number, the concert was very good.

    F. The examination was easy _____ for the last essay question.

2. On a separate sheet, write two sentences using *accept* and two using *except.*

Advice/Advise

1. *Advice* is a noun meaning a suggestion or opinion.

    In her column, Ann Landers gives *advice.*

2. *Advise* is a verb meaning to give advice.

    The doctor *advised* Harriet to quit smoking.

> TIP: If you have a vice, you need *advice.*

PRACTICE 17.7

1. Fill in the blanks with *advice* or *advise.*

    A. You should follow my _____ and go back to school.

    B. Why should I _____ you if you won't do as I say?

    C. If you reject my _____, I will offer no more help.

    D. Anton's _____ is always sound because he thinks problems through so carefully.

    E. I cannot _____ you without more information.

    F. No one can _____ you on matters of the heart.

2. On a separate sheet, write two sentences with *advice* and two with *advise.*

Affect/Effect

1. *Affect* is a verb meaning to influence.

    The steelworkers' strike has begun to *affect* the local economy.

2. *Effect* is usually a noun meaning result.

    The *effects* of the plant layoffs will be serious.

3. *Effect* is sometimes a verb meaning to bring about.

    Councilman Page will try to *effect* a change in the city charter.

PRACTICE 17.8

1. Fill in the blanks with *affect* or *effect.*

    A. The _____ of the drought will be felt in the marketplace early this fall.

    B. I hope my decision to resign from the committee will not have a

        negative _____ on the committee's work.

    C. The store owners petitioned the mall management to _____ a change in Christmas shopping hours.

    D. What people eat for breakfast can _____ how they perform all morning.

    E. An _____ of an oil shortage is higher gasoline prices.

    F. Childhood traumas _____ us as adults.

2. On a separate sheet, write two sentences using *affect* and two using *effect.*

All ready/Already

1. *All ready* means "all set," or "prepared."

    The crew was *all ready* to set sail.

2. *Already* means "by this time."

    Do not apply for the job because the position has *already* been filled.

> TIP: All ready and all set are both two words.

PRACTICE 17.9

1. Fill in the blanks with *all ready* or *already.*

A. The party was _____ over, and the guest of honor had not arrived.

B. I just cleaned this closet, and _____ it is cluttered.

C. The water skier waved his hand to the driver to signal he was

_____ .

D. Harry and Pilar were _____ to go, but I still had to make a phone call.

E. _____ Hank is whining, and we just got here.

F. As soon as Lateefa completes her last economics course, she will be

_____ to graduate.

2. On a separate sheet, write two sentences using *all ready* and two using *already.*

All right/Alright

In formal usage, *all right* is considered the acceptable form. *Alright* is not acceptable in college papers.

Among/Between

1. Use *between* for two people or things.

There are many differences *between* working in a fast food restaurant and working in a fancy restaurant.

2. Use *among* for more than two people or things.

The argument *among* the students lasted most of the class period.

PRACTICE 17.10

1. Fill in the blanks with *among* or *between.*

A. _____ the students in the class, only Mario earned an A on the final exam.

B. It is difficult for me to choose _____ teaching and research for my career.

C. The competition _____ the three teams is friendly.

D. My antique necklace is _____ my most prized possessions.

E. Ten-year-old Anna could not decide _____ the red bicycle and the green one.

F. Just _____ you and me, I do not trust Lee.

2. On a separate sheet, write two sentences using *among* and two using *between*.

Been/Being

1. *Been* is the past participle of *be*. It is usually used after *have, has,* or *had.*

   It has *been* years since I have seen Joel.

2. *Being* is the *-ing* (present participle) form of *be*. It is usually used after *am, is, are, was,* or *were.*

   Wanda is *being* careless when she leaves her purse there.

TIP: Do not use *been* without *have, has,* or *had.*

Incorrect:	I been working hard.
Correct:	I have been working hard.

PRACTICE 17.11

1. Fill in the blanks with *being* or *been*.

   A. Although I have _____ absent, I studied the assignments.

   B. The child does not understand that she is _____ rude.

   C. The Chens had _____ gone a week before they remembered they forgot to stop their mail.

D. I am _____ inducted into the honor society tonight.

E. Ned has _____ more than patient.

F. Six families are _____ relocated to make way for the new road.

2. On a separate sheet, write two sentences with *been* and two with *being*.

Beside/Besides

1. *Beside* means "alongside of."

   Park the car *beside* the garage.

2. *Besides* means "in addition to."

   Besides being too small, the house was poorly located.

PRACTICE 17.12

1. Fill in the blanks with *beside* or *besides*.

   A. _____ the shed, the dog buried its bones.

   B. _____ the creek, the collie lay sleeping peacefully.

   C. Mother hid the children's Christmas presents in the chest

      _____ the bed.

   D. Few people _____ you and me realize that Randy is insecure.

   E. _____ having a headache, I feel sick to my stomach.

   F. What is the restaurant's specialty, _____ pasta?

2. On a separate sheet, write two sentences using *beside* and two using *besides*.

Can/Could

1. *Can* is used for the present tense to mean "am/is/are able to."

   If I get an income tax refund, I *can* buy a stereo.

2. *Could* is used for the past tense to mean "was/were able to."

   I thought I *could* finish by noon, but I was wrong.

PRACTICE 17.13

1. Fill in the blanks with *can* or *could.* To determine if you need present or past tense, check the tense of the other verb in the sentence, or look for clues such as *yesterday* or *now.*

   A. Before I ＿＿＿＿＿＿ walk, I was reading.

   B. When I was sixteen, I ＿＿＿＿＿＿ stay up all night and feel

      great the next day; now I ＿＿＿＿＿＿ sleep for eight hours and still be tired.

   C. The photographer was certain he ＿＿＿＿＿＿ restore the old family picture I found in Grandma's steamer trunk.

   D. I ＿＿＿＿＿＿ never be sure if Sam is telling the truth or lying.

   E. Jenny is sure she ＿＿＿＿＿＿ help us draft a newsletter.

   F. Last year I ＿＿＿＿＿＿ not afford a vacation, but this year I

      ＿＿＿＿＿＿ manage a week at the ocean.

2. On a separate sheet, write two sentences using *can* and two using *could.*

Fewer/Less

1. Use *fewer* for things that can be counted.
   Fewer than half the class passed the midterm.
2. Use *less* for something considered as a unit, and for something that cannot be counted.
   There is *less* concern for the homeless than there should be.

TIP: Think of the word *countless.* It contains *count* and *less.* Then remember that *less* is used for things that are not counted.

PRACTICE 17.14

1. Fill in the blanks with *fewer* or *less.*

A. The older I get, the _____ I worry about minor matters.

B. If you take vitamin C, you may get _____ colds.

C. _____ accidents occurred on Fifth Avenue this year than last year.

D. The movie had _____ violent scenes than I expected.

E. If more people would exercise, there would be _____ depression in the world.

F. With _____ sex discrimination in the workplace, more women are executives.

2. On a separate sheet, write two sentences using *fewer* and two using *less.*

Good/Well

1. *Good* is an adjective, so it only describes nouns and pronouns.
   Lester is a *good* drummer. (*Good* describes the noun, *drummer.*)
2. *Well* is an adverb, so it describes verbs.
   Bonnie sings *well.* (*Well* describes the verb, *sings.*)
3. *Well* also refers to health.
   Tanya does not feel *well* enough to join us.

PRACTICE 17.15

1. Fill in the blanks with *good* or *well.*

A. This is a _____ time to plant a garden.

B. I hope I do as _____ as you did in the time trials.

C. I did not do very _____ on my chemistry exam because I did

   not understand covalent bonding _____ enough.

D. The movie was not as _____ as I expected it to be.

E. Isabella played a _____ tennis match today; I wish I had played

   as _____ .

F. The _____ behavior of the children earned them a treat.

G. After eating five cookies, I do not feel _____ .

2. On a separate sheet, write two sentences with *good* and two with *well.*

It's/Its

1. *It's* is the contraction form and means "it is" or "it has."

   It's time to head for home.

   It's been a pleasure serving you.

2. *Its* is the possessive form, so it shows ownership.

   The rubber tree plant is dropping *its* leaves.

TIP: Do not use *it's* unless you can substitute *it is* or *it has.*

PRACTICE 17.16

1. Fill in the blanks with *it's* or *its.*

   A. _____ a sure bet that the store will close if _____ merchandising policies don't improve.
   B. The head librarian announced that the library has increased

      _____ holdings by 30 percent.

   C. _____ hard to believe, but _____ been three years since we met.

   D. If _____ work you want, you have come to the right place.

   E. _____ a shame, but Cinema Sixty has changed _____ policy of showing only first-run features.

   F. The company decided to reduce _____ costs by switching from television to direct-mail advertising.

2. On a separate sheet, write two sentences using *it's* and two using *its.*

Of/Have

   Do not substitute *of* for *have. Have* is a helping verb (see p. 180), and *of* is a preposition (see p. 185).

Incorrect	Correct
could of	could have or could've
will of	will have
would of	would have or would've
should of	should have or should've
may of	may have
must of	must have
might of	might have or might've

Passed/Past

1. *Past* refers to a previous time. It can also mean "by."

   It is not possible to change the *past.*

   Past experiences affect us in the present.

   I drove *past* your house yesterday.

2. *Passed* is the past tense of the verb *to pass,* and means "went by" or "handed."

   As Rico *passed* Cathy's desk, he gave her a rose.

   The teacher *passed* the specimen around so all could see it.

TIP: Think of the letters *p* and *t,* as in *past* and *previous time.*

PRACTICE 17.17

1. Fill in the blanks with *past* or *passed.*

   A. When the police officer _____ the warehouse, she saw the flames.

   B. The _____ too often intrudes on the present.

   C. As the marching band _____ the reviewing stand, thunderous applause erupted.

   D. We should forgive Kurt for his _____ mistakes.

   E. The relay runner _____ the baton to his teammate, who

      quickly _____ the runner in first place.

   F. In times _____ it was safe to walk at night.

2. On a separate sheet, write two sentences with *past* and two with *passed*.

Quiet/Quit/Quite

1. *Quiet* means "silence/silent" or "calm."

   Some people can work with a radio on, but I need *quiet*.

2. *Quit* means "stop" or "give up."

   Even if I wanted to *quit* school, my parents would not let me.

3. *Quite* means "very" or "exactly."

   I am *quite* sure no one lives here.

   That is not *quite* the point I am making.

PRACTICE 17.18

1. Fill in the blanks with *quiet, quit,* or *quite*.

   A. If you are _____ certain you can remain _____ for an hour, I can get my work done.

   B. If you do not _____ smoking soon, you will _____ likely have health problems.

   C. The _____ in this room is almost eerie.

   D. Martha returned the paint because it was not _____ the color she wanted.

   E. If you are not _____ certain that you can finish this project,

      you should probably _____ .

   F. Alonzo _____ his fraternity because the parties were too

      _____ .

2. On a separate sheet, write two sentences using *quiet,* two using *quit,* and two using *quite*.

Suppose/Supposed

1. *Suppose* means "assume" or "guess."

   I *suppose* I can be done by six if I hurry.

2. *Supposed* means "ought" or "should." In this case, it is preceded by a form of *be* and is always followed by *to*. *Supposed* is also the past tense form of *suppose*.

We are *supposed* to clear the cafeteria tables when we are through eating. (should)

The mayor *supposed* he would win the election by a large margin. (past tense of *suppose*, meaning *assume*)

> TIP: Always use *supposed* (with the *-ed*) to mean "ought" or "should." *I am suppose to go* is an incorrect form written when the *t* in *to* is allowed to function as the *d* in *supposed*.

PRACTICE 17.19

1. Fill in the blanks with *suppose* or *supposed*.

   A. Franz is _____ to drive everyone to the party, but where

   do you _____ he will get a car?

   B. We all _____ Matthew would go on to graduate school.

   C. What do you _____ will happen if the research council

   does not get the grant it is _____ to?

   D. Cathy was _____ to meet me here an hour ago.

   E. Lorenzo is _____ to bring the chips to the party, but I

   _____ he will forget.

   F. Do you _____ it is possible to finish the cleaning before
   our guests arrive?

2. On a separate sheet, write two sentences using *suppose* and two using *supposed*.

Then/Than

1. *Then* refers to a certain time.

I asked Sylvia what she meant; *then* she yelled at me.

2. *Than* is used to compare.

The chicken is tastier *than* the veal.

TIP: *Then* and *time* have an *e; than* and *compare* have an *a.*

PRACTICE 17.20

1. Fill in the blanks with *then* or *than.*

A. My new apartment is less noisy _____ my previous one.

B. If you arrive _____, you will be able to meet my sister.

C. _____ she said that she would rather arrive late _____ not at all.

D. You asked for my advice and _____ refused to take it.

E. Diana would rather quit school _____ sell her stamp collection for tuition money.

F. Getting a campus job is easier _____ people realize.

2. On a separate sheet, write two sentences using *then* and two using *than.*

There/Their/They're

1. *There* shows direction. It can also come before *are, was, were, is,* or *will be.*

Put the boxes down over *there.*

There are twelve of us helping out at the senior citizens' center.

2. *Their* is a possessive form; it shows ownership.

The students opened *their* test booklets and began to work.

3. *They're* is the contraction form of *they are.*

If *they're* leaving now, I should go with them.

TIP: Use *they're* only when you can substitute *they are.*

---

1. Fill in the blanks with *there, their,* or *they're.*

   A. According to the evening paper _____ will be a serious wheat shortage next year.

   B Henri and Tom said _____ not going unless they can bring

   _____ boom boxes with them.

   C. If you put the couch over _____ then _____ will be

   enough room for _____ record collection.

   D. The police officers are concerned because the referendum that

   would grant _____ pay raises may not get on the November ballot.

   E. _____ asking five hundred dollars for _____ used piano.

   F. I looked _____ but I couldn't find _____ coats.

2. On a separate sheet, write two sentences using *there,* two using *their,* and two using *they're.*

Through/Though/Threw

1. *Through* means "in one side and out the other." It also means "finished."

   It was hard for Grandma to pass the thread *through* the needle.

   I will be *through* proofreading my essay in an hour.

2. *Though* means "although"; *as though* means "as if."

   Though Alan has never taken lessons, he plays the piano well.

   Maria acts *as though* she is mad at the world.

3. *Threw* is the past tense of *throw.*

   The quarterback *threw* an incomplete pass.

1. Fill in the blanks with *through, though,* or *threw.*

A. When she was _____ studying, Eleni rested for an hour.

B. _____ Hank pretends he does not care, anyone can see

_____ his act.

C. Cal won a stuffed rabbit when he _____ the baseball at the milk bottles on the midway.

D. _____ Tony made a basket, the shot did not count because

he _____ the ball after the buzzer.

E. Diane strolled _____ the park as _____ she did not have any worries.

F. If we elect Smith, we will have a better chance to work

_____ the police labor dispute.

2. On a separate sheet, write two sentences using *through,* two using *though,* and two using *threw.*

To/Too/Two

1. *To* means "toward." It can also be part of a verb, as in *to run.*

I was going *to* class when I saw Rhonda.

I wanted *to* ask you a favor.

2. *Too* means "excessively" or "also."

The movie was *too* violent for me.

I would like a piece of that cake *too.*

3. *Two* is the number.

Only *two* candidates for the school board have experience.

PRACTICE 17.23

1. Fill in the blanks with *to, too,* or *two.*

A. Before beginning _____ exercise, stretch for ten minutes.

B. _____ much smoking and _____ little exercise make Dan

a prime candidate _____ get a heart attack.

C. The car needed _____ new tires and a water pump _____ .

D. _____ tell you the truth, I was not _____ pleased

_____ be headed _____ the mall _____ days before Christmas.

E. The highlight of the trip was going _____ Disney World for

_____ days.

F. A week is _____ long for me _____ be gone.

2. On a separate sheet, write two sentences using *to,* two using *too,* and two using *two.*

Use/Used

1. *Use* is a noun that means "purpose." It is also a verb that means "make use of."

    What possible *use* could this have?

    How do you *use* this gadget?

2. *Used* is the past tense and past participle form of the verb *to use.* It also means "adjusted" or "accustomed"; in this case, it is followed by *to.*

    The child *used* the towel and threw it on the floor.

    I have *used* this product successfully before.

    I am not *used* to this kind of treatment.

TIP: *I am use to* is an incorrect form written when the *t* in *to* is allowed to function as the *d* in *used.* The correct form is *I am used to.*

PRACTICE 17.24

1. Fill in the blanks with *use* or *used.*

    A. I am not _____ to the idea that I am now an adult.

B. I _____ that shampoo, but I did not like the results.

C. This school does not make sufficient _____ of computers.

D. A person _____ to feel safe walking alone at night.

5. We have _____ that textbook in our English class.

6. I _____ to wear braces on my teeth.

2. On a separate sheet, write two sentences using *use* and two using *used.*

Where/Were/We're

1. *Where* refers to location.

   Home is *where* a person should feel safe.

2. *Were* is the past tense form of *are.*

   The Raiders *were* ahead until the third quarter.

3. *We're* is the contraction form of *we are.*

   We're certain that Mom will do well in school.

PRACTICE 17.25

1. Fill in the blanks with *where, were,* or *we're.*

   A. If you ask me, we do not know _____ we are going.

   B. The plans _____ changed because _____ uncertain about
   how long it will take us to drive to Cleveland.

   C. The new federal building will be built _____ the old court-
   house now stands.

   D. _____ all uncertain about what the future holds and _____
   we will be this time next year.

   E. Debbie and Lenny _____ the best-behaved children at the
   party.

   F. _____ going, but _____ not happy about it.

2. On a separate sheet, write two sentences using *were,* two using *where,*
   and two using *we're.*

Will/Would

1. *Will* looks to the future from the present tense.

   Dr. Schwartz believes [present tense] he *will* [at a later date] get his book published.

2. *Would* looks to the future from the past tense.

   Dr. Schwartz believed [past tense] he *would* [at a later date] get his book published.

3. *Would* is sometimes used to mean "will."

   Would you help me with this?

PRACTICE 17.26

1. Fill in the blanks with *will* or *would.*

   A. Councilwoman Drucker promised that she _____ not vote to raise city taxes.

   B. The regional basketball tournament _____ be played on our campus this spring.

   C. If you do not stop snapping at people, no one _____ want to be around you.

   D. The fans wondered who _____ pitch the last inning.

   E. The Academic Council plans to announce that graduation require-

   ments _____ change in the near future.

   F. The child _____ not leave unless he could take his toy.

2. On a separate sheet, write two sentences using *will* and two using *would.*

Whose/Who's

1. *Whose* indicates possession.

   The person *whose* car is double-parked got a ticket.

2. *Who's* is the contraction form of *who is* or *who has.*

   Who's on the telephone?

   Who's been watching the game?

TIP: Use *who's* only when you can substitute *who is* or *who has.*

PRACTICE 17.27

1. Fill in the blanks with *whose* or *who's.*

    A. _____ umbrella was left on the desk?

    B. Dr. Berringer is a teacher _____ lectures are always stimulating.

    C. It is impossible to know _____ been here in the last hour.

    D. They are the couple _____ children broke our window.

    E. _____ the instructor for this course?

    F. I cannot be sure _____ coming to Luis's surprise party.

2. On a separate sheet, write two sentences using *whose* and two using *who's.*

Your/You're

1. *Your* is a possessive form and therefore shows ownership.
    Remember to bring *your* ticket when you come.
2. *You're* is the contraction form of *you are.*
    You're the only person I can trust with this secret.

TIP: Use *you're* only when you can substitute *you are.*

PRACTICE 17.28

1. Fill in the blanks with *your* or *you're.*

    A. If you really don't want _____ bicycle anymore, Jane will buy it from you.

    B. _____ never really certain what _____ future holds.

    C. _____ best bet is to give Luigi a gift certificate because

    _____ never going to find something he doesn't already have.

D. The key to _____ success will be hard work, not _____ parents' money.

E. _____ my best friend, so I know you will help me.

F. I felt _____ prose was a bit too wordy, so I took the liberty of

revising some of _____ phrasing.

2. On a separate sheet, write two sentences with *your* and two with *you're*.

> ### REVIEW PRACTICE 17.29: FREQUENTLY CONFUSED WORDS

Eliminate the nine errors with frequently confused words in the following paragraph.

Sadly, more and more young children are developing negative body images and starting to diet as a result. However, young children are not suppose to diet. Instead, it's much better if their encouraged to develop healthy attitudes toward food, exercise, and body types. If overweight children could develop good eating habits and maintain there weight during their formative years, than they will have a good chance of slimming down once they hit the growth spurts of puberty. Its true that the habits children learn at a young age will stay with them long passed childhood and into adulthood. There would be far less eating disorders if children were taught proper nutrition and self-acceptance. As a country, were so concerned with being skinny that we teach children—unconsciously or otherwise—to have unrealistic and unhealthy expectations for desirable weight.

SLANG

Slang expressions are very informal usages unsuitable for most formal writing. Slang can originate with one group of people, say musicians or artists, and spread to the larger population. Slang often originates with young people and makes for colorful, vital speech. However, until a slang expression works its way into the language of the general population (if it ever does), avoid it in your college writing, unless you need it to create a special effect.

Here are examples of slang expressions. Because slang changes quickly, many of them may not be current slang by the time you read them.

pass the bone (share knowledge)   no stress (don't worry)

go postal (get violent)   jam (to leave)

whacked (crazy)   da bomb (great)

wired (nervous)   chill out (relax)

PRACTICE 17.30: WORKING TOGETHER

With some classmates, make a list of as many slang expressions as you can think of. Limit your list to the slang that you and your friends currently use. Your instructor may want to share some of the slang that was current when he or she was in college. Next, with your group members, pick two of the slang expressions and use each of them in a separate sentence. Then rewrite the sentences, eliminating the slang and substituting language more appropriate to formal writing.

CLICHÉS

Clichés are overworked expressions. At one time they were fresh and interesting, but years of overuse have made them tired and dull. An experienced reader will find clichés annoying.

Here is a partial list of clichés. Studying it will help you become sensitive to the kinds of expressions to avoid.

over the hill	sadder but wiser	crack of dawn
free as a bird	last but not least	busy as a beaver
cold as ice	fresh as a daisy	light as a feather
spring chicken	love conquers all	green with envy
hour of need	shadow of a doubt	slowly but surely
white as snow	high as a kite	sharp as a tack

PRACTICE 17.31

Write three clichés not on the list.

1. _____

2. _____

3. _____

PRACTICE 17.32

Rewrite the sentences, substituting fresh phrasings for the underlined clichés. The first one is done as an example.

1. I dread going shopping with Dotty because she is <u>like a bull in a china shop</u>.

   I dread going shopping with Dotty because she is so clumsy she is always bumping into displays and breaking things.

2. If I were you, I would not <u>bet the rent</u> that Julian will keep his promise.

   _____

   _____

3. The comedian is not very funny because his jokes are <u>as old as the hills</u>.

   _____

   _____

4. Trying to find my contact lens in the dark was like <u>looking for a needle in a haystack</u>.

   _____

   _____

5. It is a <u>crying shame</u> that more is not being done to help the homeless.

   _____

   _____

6. Nina and Jacob were <u>busy as beavers</u> completing their wedding plans.

   _____

   _____

WORDINESS

Because unnecessary words weaken your style, when you revise, prune away words that add no meaning or that repeat meaning. Words that add no meaning are **deadwood** and should be eliminated.

Sentences with Deadwood	Revisions
Two different kinds of cake were offered	Two different cakes were offered. (Kinds of adds no meaning.) or Two kinds of cake were offered.
Diane's new Corvette is brown in color.	Diane's new Corvette is brown. (Can brown be anything but a color?)
We rushed quickly to see what was wrong	We rushed to see what was wrong. (Rushing has to be done quickly.)

Another form of annoying wordiness is purposeless **repetition**. Consider this sentence:

To relax before my exam, I watched and viewed a movie.

Viewed repeats the idea included in *watched,* so *viewed* is needless repetition. Here is the sentence revised to eliminate the repetition:

To relax before my exam, I watched a movie.

Here are more examples to study:

Sentences with Repetition	Revisions
Carol finally came to the realization and understanding that she had to help herself.	Carol finally came to the realization that she had to help herself or Carol finally came to the understanding that she had to help herself. (*Realization* and *understanding* mean the same.)
Some people think and believe that drug abuse is our nation's most serious problem.	Some people think that drug abuse is our nation's most serious problem. or Some people believe that drug abuse is our nation's most serious problem. (*Think* and *believe* mean the same.)

PRACTICE 17.33

Revise the following sentences to eliminate wordiness.

1. In the year of 1912, Theodore Roosevelt was campaigning in the city of Milwaukee.

_____

_____

2. A would-be assassin who wanted to kill Roosevelt shot him on the right side part of his chest.

_____

_____

3. Much of the force of the bullet was absorbed by the President's eyeglasses case and by the 50-page speech he was carrying double-folded in two in his breast pocket.

_____

_____

4. The end result was that the bullet lodged just short of his lung, and, dripping blood, the President pulled and tugged himself up to the podium.

_____

_____

5. In our modern world today, Secret Service agents would have whisked and rushed the President away, but Roosevelt was the type of person who carried on no matter what.

_____

_____

6. He announced and said he planned to deliver the speech as long as he still had life in his body.

_____

_____

7. He spoke for 90 minutes of time, but was unable to refer to or check his text.

_____

_____

8. There was a gaping, wide hole in the pages where the bullet had torn through them.

_____

_____

PRACTICE 17.34

Cross out deadwood and unnecessary repetition to eliminate wordiness.

The first metal coins were minted in about approximately 800 B.C. Before that time in history, all trade had been done by barter. For example, a tool-maker craftsman might barter and trade tools in exchange for meat or clothing to wear. As civilization developed, trade became more intricately complex, and barter became too clumsily awkward. A trader needed easily carried tokens that were small in size, but the tokens had to be valuable. So the first coins were made of metal, in particular gold and silver metal. This simple invention of money made trade much simpler.

DOUBLE NEGATIVES

These words are negatives (they communicate the idea of *no*):

no	none	hardly
not	nowhere	scarcely
no one	nobody	
never	nothing	

any contraction form with *not* (*can't, don't, won't,* etc.)

In English, only one negative is used to express a single negative idea.

Incorrect (two negatives):	I *can't* see *no* reason to go.
Correct (one negative):	I can see *no* reason to go.

Correct (one negative):	I *can't* see any reason to go.
Incorrect (two negatives):	Dee would *never* tell *no one.*
Correct (one negative):	Dee would *never* tell anyone.
Correct (one negative):	Dee would tell *no one.*
Incorrect (two negatives):	The boys could *not hardly* eat.
Correct (one negative):	The boys could *hardly* eat.
Correct (one negative):	The boys could *not* eat.

If you study the preceding examples, you will notice that eliminating one negative may mean changing *no one* to *anyone, nowhere* to *anywhere, never* to *ever,* and *no* or *none* to *any.*

PRACTICE 17.35

The following sentences contain double negatives. First underline each negative. Then revise each sentence by eliminating one negative. The first one is done as an example.

1. The board member came under attack because he is <u>not never</u> at the meetings.

   The board member came under attack because he is never at

   the meetings.

2. Paul didn't do nothing to start the fight.

   _____

   _____

3. I gave the cashier $20.00, but I didn't get no change.

   _____

   _____

4. Mom couldn't find nowhere to hide the Christmas presents.

   _____

   _____

5. Some people won't ask nobody for nothing.

_____

_____

6. The street department hardly never swept the streets this fall.

_____

_____

SPELLING

Spelling errors distract readers, and they can be annoying. If spelling is a serious problem for you, the tips and rules that follow will help.

 Tips for Improving Your Spelling

1. Study your draft word by word, very slowly. Each time you encounter a word that might be misspelled, underline it. Then check every underlined word in a dictionary. Never overlook a word even if your suspicion is very slight.

2. Keep a list of words you misspell, and study your list daily. Ask someone to quiz you on the words once a week, and study even harder any words you miss on the quiz. You may find it helpful to underline the troublesome parts of words like this:

for<u>ei</u>gn

3. Learn the correct pronunciation of words. You may misspell *disastrous* if you pronounce it incorrectly as "*disasterous.*"

4. Break words into parts when you spell, like this:

with*hold	class*room	under*standing
under*statement	break*fast	table*cloth
room*mate	shoe*lace	beach*front

5. Some words may be easier to handle if you spell them syllable by syllable. For example, *organization* may be easier to spell if you say each syllable as you go: "or*gan*i*za*tion."

6. Be aware of **prefixes** (word beginnings) like *un, inter, mis,* and *dis.* When they are added to words, the spelling of the base word is not likely to change.

dis*satisfaction	inter*related	mis*spell

un*noticed   dis*engage   un*nerve

7. Use tricks to help you remember correct spellings. For example, *instrument* contains the word *strum*, and you strum a guitar, which is an instrument; *tragedy* contains the word *rage*.

8. Study the frequently confused words beginning on p. 271 and learn the spellings and meanings given.

9. Learn the spelling rules that follow.

Spelling Rules

To apply many of the spelling rules, you must know the difference between vowels and consonants.

Vowels: *a, e, i, o, u*

Consonants: *b, c, d, f, g, h, j, k, l, m, n, p, q, r, s, t, v, w, x, z*

NOTE: *Y* can be a vowel or a consonant, depending on how it sounds.

y as a vowel: *funny, shy*

y as a consonant: *yellow, yesterday*

Rule 1:   *I* before *e* except after *c*, or when sounding like long *a* as in *neighbor* and *weigh*.

The *i* comes before the *e*:
niece, field, grief, believe, friend, relieve, belief

The *e* comes before the *i* because the letters are after *c*:
conceive, ceiling, deceive, receipt, conceit, receive

The *e* comes before the *i* because of the long *a* sound:
neighbor, weight, weigh, sleigh

Words with a *shin* sound are spelled *ie* after *c*:
ancient, conscience, efficient, sufficient

Some exceptions to the rule:
either, neither, seize, weird, height, foreign, society

TIP: The following nonsense sentence contains five of the most common exceptions to the ie/ei rule: Either foreigner seized weird leisure.

Rule 2:   Before adding an ending other than *ing*, change *y* to *i* if there is a consonant before the y.

Change *y* to *i* because there is a consonant before the *y:*

study + ed = studied	plenty + ful = plentiful
happy + ness = happiness	cry + ed = cried
pretty + est = prettiest	lovely + er = lovelier

Keep the *y* because there is a vowel before it:

enjoy + ment = enjoyment	stay + ed = stayed
play + s = plays	toy + s = toys
employ + ed = employed	destroy + er = destroyer

Keep the *y* because the ending is *ing:*

hurry + ing = hurrying	study + ing = studying
employ + ing = employing	cry + ing = crying
fly + ing = flying	imply + ing = implying

Some exceptions to the rule:

dry + ly = drily	say + ed = said
day + ly = daily	lay + ed = laid
pay + ed = paid	sly + ness = slyness
shy + ly = shyly	gay + ly = gaily

Rule 3:   When you add an ending to a word that ends with a silent *e*, drop the *e* if the ending begins with a vowel, but keep the *e* if the ending begins with a consonant.

Drop the *e* because the ending begins with a vowel:

hope + ing = hoping	dine + ing = dining
pleasure + able = pleasurable	write + er = writer
dine + er = diner	dense + ity = density
praise + ing = praising	rhyme + ed = rhymed
time + ed = timed	

Keep the *e* because the ending begins with a consonant:

hope + ful = hopeful	complete + ly = completely
loose + ly = loosely	state + ment = statement
hate + ful = hateful	home + less = homeless

time + less = timeless   move   + ment = movement

rude + ness = rudeness

Some exceptions to the rule:

acknowledge + ment = acknowledgment

judge   + ment = judgment

mile   + age = mileage

notice   + able = noticeable

argue   + ment = argument

nine   + th   = ninth

acre   + age = acreage

awe   + ful = awful

true   + ly   = truly

courage   + ous = courageous

Rule 4:   When adding an ending that begins with a vowel to a one-syllable word, double the final consonant if the last three letters of the word
are consonant-vowel-consonant (c-v-c).

Double the final consonant because the one-syllable word ends c-v-c:

swim + ing = swimming   fat + est = fattest

thin + er = thinner   skip + ing = skipping

drop + ed = dropped   run + er = runner

Do not double the final consonant because the one-syllable word does not
end c-v-c:

eat + ing = eating   burn + er = burner   boil + ed = boiled

Rule 5:   When adding an ending that begins with a vowel to a word of
more than one syllable, double the final consonant if the last three letters
of the word are consonant-vowel-consonant (c-v-c) *and* if the stress is on
the last syllable.

Double the final consonant because the word ends c-v-c, and the stress is
on the last syllable:

begin + er = beginner   regret + ed = regretted

admit + ing = admitting

Do not double the final consonant because the stress is not on the last syllable:

pardon + ed = pardoned   ripen + ing = ripening

labor   + er = laborer

Do not double the final consonant because the word does not end c-v-c:

evict   + ing= evicting   pretend + er = pretender

ordain + ed = ordained

Do not double the consonant if the stress shifts from the last syllable when the ending is added.

prefer (stress on last syllable)

confer (stress on last syllable)

         but

preference (stress shifts to first syllable)

conference (stress shifts to first syllable)

Rule 6: Most nouns form the plural by adding *s*. However, if the noun ends in *ch, sh, s, x, z,* or *o,* add *es* to form the plural.

genius + es = geniuses   mix   + es = mixes

potato + es = potatoes   church + es = churches

Some exceptions to the rule:

memos   radios   solos

Rule 7: When you change the final *y* to *i,* add *es* to form the plural (see pp. 298–299).

candy + es = candies   party + es = parties   fly + es = flies

                       but

key   + s = keys   boy   + s = boys   toy + s   = toys

PRACTICE 17.36

1. To check your understanding of spelling rule 1, fill in the blanks with either *ie* or *ei*. If you are unsure, check a dictionary.

a. ch __ __ f   g. perc __ __ ve

b. br __ __ f   h. sh __ __ ld

c. fr __ __ ght   i. r __ __ gn

d. ach __ __ ve   j. v __ __ n

e. w __ __ gh   k. th __ __ r

f. c __ __ ling

2. To check your understanding of spelling rules 2–5, add the given endings to the words below. If you are unsure, consult the rule given in parentheses or look up the word in a dictionary.

a. sorry + er _____ (rule 2)

b. bat + er _____ (rule 4)

c. make + s _____ (rule 3)

d. hammer + ing _____ (rule 5)

e. hop + ed _____ (rule 4)

f. enjoy + able _____ (rule 2)

g. advertise + ment _____ (rule 3)

h. ask + ing _____ (rule 4)

i. sense + ible _____ (rule 3)

j. slip + ed _____ (rule 4)

k. gossip + ed _____ (rule 5)

l. omit + ing _____ (rule 5)

m. wealthy + er _____ (rule 2)

n. rake + ing _____ (rule 3)

o. ship + ment _____ (rule 4)

p. permit + ed _____ (rule 5)

q. bite + ing _____ (rule 3)

r. marry + ed _____ (rule 2)

s. big + er _____ (rule 4)

t. lazy + ness _____ (rule 2)

3. To check your understanding of rules 6 and 7, write the plural of each noun. If you are unsure, check a dictionary.

a. toy _____

b. brush _____

c. jelly _____

d. mosquito _____

e. television _____

f. veto _____

g. tax _____

h. girl _____

i. enemy _____

j. match _____

Frequently Misspelled Words

The following seventy-five words are often misspelled. Learn to spell every word on the list by making flash cards to study. Have someone quiz you until you can spell all of these words with ease

1. absence
2. across
3. actually
4. a lot
5. analyze

6. appreciate
7. argument
8. athlete
9. awkward
10. beginning

11. belief
12. business
13. coming
14. committee
15. criticism

16. definitely	36. laboratory	56. prejudice
17. dependent	37. leisure	57. privilege
18. develop	38. length	58. pursue
19. discuss	39. library	59. receipt
20. eighth	40. marriage	60. receive
21. embarrass	41. mathematics	61. religious
22. especially	42. meant	62. rhythm
23. existence	43. medicine	63. sacrifice
24. February	44. necessary	64. safety
25. foreign	45. neither	65. scene
26. government	46. ninety	66. schedule
27. grammar	47. ninth	67. separate
28. guarantee	48. occasionally	68. severely
29. guidance	49. opinion	69. success
30. height	50. parallel	70. surprise
31. hoping	51. persuade	71. thoroughly
32. immediately	52. physical	72. through
33. independent	53. planned	73. until
34. intelligence	54. pleasant	74. weight
35. knowledge	55. preferred	75. written

The Hyphen

Hyphens are most often used to form compound words and to show that a word continues from the end of one line to the beginning of the next. For some word-processing programs, use one horizontal line for the hyphen (-) and two lines for the dash (—).

1. Use a hyphen between words that form a single adjective before a noun.

state-of-the-art stereo	well-known speaker
comparison-contrast essay	run-of-the-mill Sunday
strong-willed child	so-called advice

   Do not use a hyphen when the compound comes after the noun:

   Fran is a success because she is strong willed.

   Do not use a hyphen with an *-ly* word:

The slowly moving traffic made me an hour late.

2. Use hyphens between compound numbers from twenty-one through ninety-nine.

thirty-six   seventy-seven

forty-two   fifty-eight

3. Use a hyphen between the numerator and denominator in written fractions.

one-fourth   two-thirds

4. Use a hyphen after the prefixes *self-*, *all-*, *ex-* (meaning *former*), and before the suffix -*elect*.

self-assured   ex-governor

all-inclusive   mayor-elect

5. Use a hyphen with a prefix before a word that begins with a capital letter.

un-American   pro-Cuban   mid-January

6. Use a hyphen to divide a word at the end of a line, but remember these cautions:

a.   Do not divide one-syllable words.

b.   You should not leave a single letter at the end of the line, so do not divide a word such as *a-void*.

PRACTICE 17.37

Add hyphens where they are needed in the following paragraph.

My mother in law is a first rate artist who will show her paintings at a gallery on the twenty first of the month. Her show will last until mid May. In addition to being a highly acclaimed artist, my mother in law is the ex chair of the United Way campaign in our city and an energetic fund raiser for anti drug campaigns. At sixty seven, she is a remarkable, self possessed, high powered woman whom I admire greatly.

Chapter 18

Using Verbs Correctly

I n this chapter you will learn important information about using verbs correctly, including how to:

1. use correct verb forms

2. make subjects and verbs agree

3. avoid tense shifts

◆ ◆ ◆

VERB FORMS

The following pages will help you use verb forms correctly. If your instructor marks verb errors on your compositions, pay careful attention to this material.

PRETEST

If the underlined verb is correct, write *C* on the blank. If it is incorrect, write *I* on the blank. If you are unsure, do not guess; leave the space blank. Check your answers in Appendix III.

1. _____ Six weeks ago Leo <u>decide</u> to move out of the dorm.

2. _____ The sun <u>shone</u> so brightly I couldn't see to drive.

3. _____ Maria <u>be</u> the one to ask about that.

4. _____ I <u>don't</u> understand a thing Alfie says.

5. _____ We <u>had driven</u> two hundred miles when the fuel pump broke.

6. _____ Larry explained, "A man <u>do</u> what he has to do."

7. _____ I <u>hopes</u> I can get a part-time job this summer.

8. _____ We <u>have did</u> everything you asked.

9. _____ Mother <u>has worn</u> that old coat for ten years.

10. _____ The teachers <u>began</u> their strike the day after Christmas.

11. _____ They <u>has told</u> me they do not plan to go with us.

12. _____ My sister Hannah <u>decided</u> to join the navy.

13. _____ The movie was so sad that Hank <u>starts</u> to cry.

14. _____ Olga <u>brang</u> her botany notes for me to copy.

15. _____ I <u>sings</u> when I'm working hard.

Regular Verb Forms

Most English verbs are **regular verbs**. Regular verbs form the past tense by adding *d* or *ed*. Here are some examples of regular verbs:

Present Tense	Past Tense
walk	walked
yell	yelled
study	studied
love	loved
smell	smelled

To use regular verbs correctly, use the verb endings correctly. Study the charts on the pages that follow to learn how endings are used with regular verbs.

REGULAR VERB FORMS: PRESENT TENSE

Use these forms when you want to write or speak of events occurring in the present time.

I play.	We play.
You play.	They play.
He plays.	The children (or *more than*
She plays.	*one* person or thing) play.
It plays.	

He plays. / She plays. / It plays. } Watch for the *s* or *es* ending here.

The child (or any *one* person or thing) plays. }   Watch for the *s* or *es* ending here.

CAUTION: A common error is forgetting the *s* or *es* ending for a regular, present tense verb used with *he, she, it,* or any singular noun subject.

Incorrect:	Mary *like* chocolate pudding.
Correct:	Mary *likes* chocolate pudding.

PRACTICE 18.1

Rewrite the paragraph, changing the past tense verbs to present tense forms. Be careful to use the *s* or *es* ending when needed. The first sentence is done as an example.

                               support
African grasslands ~~supported~~ large numbers of insect-eating and seed-eating birds. The ostrich, one of these birds, survived on fruit, seeds, and small animals. The Kori, the world's heaviest bird, also lived on the grasslands. This bird weighed 110 pounds. Oxpeckers, another grassland bird, perched on the backs of grazing animals and chewed ticks and other parasites they discovered there. Still other grassland birds included bulbuls, shrikes, storks, cranes, and ground hornbills. One of the most interesting birds, the weaverbird, designed elaborate hanging nests in trees. Unfortunately, large flocks of these birds caused extensive damage to African trees. Birds of prey on the grasslands included the vulture and the lanner falcon. Indeed, birdwatchers often traveled to this part of the world to observe the rare and wonderful birds.

PRACTICE 18.2

Complete each of the sentences by using a present tense form of a regular verb from the list and any other words you want. Do not use the same verb in more than one sentence, and be sure to use *s* or *es* endings where needed. The first one is done as an example.

play	laugh	organize
smile	move	follow
study	practice	learn
worry	joke	collect

1. The excited children *play happily in the school yard*

   during recess.

2. My best friend _____

   _____

3. Professor Bauer _____

   _____

4. We _____

   _____

5. The planning committee _____

   _____

6. You _____

   _____

7. I _____

   _____

8. He _____

   _____

9. My younger sister _____

_____

PRACTICE 18.3

Fill in the blanks with the correct present tense form of the verb in parentheses. The first blank is filled in as an example.

Because of my cold, my nose no longer (to function)

functions as part of my respiratory system. I (to inhale)

_____ deeply, but no air (to penetrate) _____ the

blocked passages. I (to race) _____ to the bathroom

and (to grab) _____ a tissue before I (to sneeze)

_____ myself to the floor. Pulling myself up, I (to head)

_____ for the kitchen. My throat (to rust) _____

out, and my mouth (to enter) _____ the drought sea-

son. Switching on the light, I (to tug) _____ at the

refrigerator door, which (to seem) _____ like wrench-

ing a two-ton vault. Struggling for strength, I (to open)

_____ the door, (to grab) _____ the orange juice,

and (to pour) _____ the liquid. The juice (to burn)

_____ my aching throat. I (to reach) _____ for a

cold tablet and (to pop) _____ it in. To clear my nose,

I (to reach) _____ for the nasal spray. I (to squirt)

_____ twice in each nostril and (to tilt) _____ my

head back. I (to head) _____ back to bed, but I (to

toss) _____ and (to turn) _____ for hours until

exhausted I (to drift) _____ off to sleep, hoping not to

awaken until the cold (to burn) _____ itself out.

REGULAR VERB FORMS: PAST TENSE

Use these forms when you want to write or speak of events that occurred in the past.

I played.	We played.
You played.	They played.
He played.	The children (or *more than one* person or thing) played.
She played.	
It played.	

The child (or any *one* person or thing) played.

CAUTION: A common error is forgetting the *d* or *ed* ending for a regular, past tense verb.

Incorrect:	Yesterday I *walk* to work.
Correct:	Yesterday I *walked* to work.

PRACTICE 18.4

On a separate sheet, write a sentence using the regular verb in parentheses in its past tense form. Circle the past tense ending, and use a different subject for each sentence. The first one is done as an example.

1. (start) *The referee started the sudden death overtime play.*
2. (look)
3. (want)
4. (talk)
5. (expect)
6. (discover)

PRACTICE 18.5

On a separate sheet, rewrite *Practice 18.3*. This time fill in the blanks with past tense forms of the verbs given.

REGULAR VERB FORMS: PAST PARTICIPLE

The **past participle** is the verb form that can be used with the helping verbs *has, have,* and *had.* The past participle of regular verbs is formed in the same way the past tense of regular verbs is formed: by adding *d* or *ed.*

I have played.	We have played.
I had played.	We had played.
You have played.	They have played.
You had played.	They had played.
He has played.	The children (or *more than one* person
He had played.	or thing) have played.
She has played.	The children (or *more than one* person
She had played	or thing) had played.
It has played.	
It had played.	

The child (or any *one* person or thing) has played.

The child (or any *one* person or thing) had played.

NOTE: As you tell from the preceding examples, the past participle form does not change even though the form of the helping verb changes.

CAUTION: A common error is forgetting the *d* or *ed* ending for the past participle form of a regular verb.

Incorrect:	The union *has decide* to accept the wage offer.
Correct:	The union *has decided* to accept the wage offer.

PRACTICE 18.6

Find and correct the errors with the past participle and accompanying helping verbs. If you need help, consult the previous chart. The first one is done as an example.

planned

Donna and Rico have ~~plan~~ their wedding for August 16, but suddenly Rico have decided that he wants to elope. At one time, he had agreed that a big wedding would be desirable, but lately he have wonder if a big, splashy affair is too much trouble and expense. Donna, surprisingly, has agree to think about eloping, even though she have wanted a big wedding all her life. Fortunately, the caterer has agreed to return the couple's deposit if they cancel the reception.

PRACTICE 18.7

On a separate sheet, write a sentence using the helping verb and past participle form of the regular verb in parentheses. The first one is done as an example.

1. (has + walk) *For the past year, Jill has walked three miles a day.*
2. (had + jump)
3. (has + change)
4. (had + open)
5. (has + work)
6. (had + apply)

Irregular Verb Forms

A **regular verb** forms the past and past participle by adding *d* or *ed.* (see p. 308.) An **irregular verb** does not add *d* or *ed* to form the past and past participle forms. Instead, irregular verbs form the past and past participle a variety of ways.

A list of some irregular verbs with their past and past participle forms follows. Study the list and place a star next to the forms you do not already know. Then learn these forms.

Present	Past	Past Participle
be (am/ is/ are)	was/ were	been
become(s)	became	become
begin(s)	began	begun
bend(s)	bent	bent
bite(s)	bit	bitten
blow(s)	blew	blown
break(s)	broke	broken
bring(s)	brought	brought
buy(s)	bought	bought
catch(es)	caught	caught
choose(es)	chose	chosen
come(s)	came	come
cost(s)	cost	cost
draw(s)	drew	drawn
drink(s)	drank	drunk
drive(s)	drove	driven
eat(s)	ate	eaten
fall(s)	fell	fallen
feed(s)	fed	fed

Present	Past	Past Participle
feel(s)	felt	felt
fight(s)	fought	fought
find(s)	found	found
fly(flies)	flew	flown
forget(s)	forgot	forgotten
forgive(s)	forgave	forgiven
freeze(s)	froze	frozen
get(s)	got	got *or* gotten
give(s)	gave	given
go(goes)	went	gone
grow(s)	grew	grown
hang(s)—a picture	hung	hung
hang(s)—a person	hanged	hanged
hear(s)	heard	heard
hide(s)	hid	hidden
hold(s)	held	held
hurt(s)	hurt	hurt
keep(s)	kept	kept
know(s)	knew	known
lay(s)—to place	laid	laid
lead(s)	led	led
leave(s)	left	left
lend(s)	lent	lent
lie(s)—to rest	lay	lain
light(s)	lit	lit
lose(s)	lost	lost
make(s)	made	made
meet(s)	met	met
pay(s)	paid	paid
read(s)	read	read
ride(s)	rode	ridden
ring(s)	rang	rung
rise(s)	rose	risen
run(s)	ran	run
say(s)	said	said
see(s)	saw	seen
sell(s)	sold	sold

Present	Past	Past Participle
send(s)	sent	sent
set(s)	set	set
shake(s)	shook	shaken
shine(s)—to give light	shone	shone
shine(s)—to polish	shined	shined
shrink(s)	shrank	shrunk
sing(s)	sang	sung
sit(s)	sat	sat
sleep(s)	slept	slept
speak(s)	spoke	spoken
spend(s)	spent	spent
stand(s)	stood	stood
steal(s)	stole	stolen
sting(s)	stung	stung
strike(s)	struck	struck
swim(s)	swam	swum
take(s)	took	taken
teach(es)	taught	taught
tear(s)	tore	torn
tell(s)	told	told
think(s)	thought	thought
throw(s)	threw	thrown
wake(s)	woke *or* waked	woken *or* waked
wear(s)	wore	worn
win(s)	won	won
write(s)	wrote	written

To understand how irregular verb forms are used, study the charts.

IRREGULAR VERB FORMS:

Present Tense

Use the present tense form in the first column of the chart beginning on p. 314 when you want to write or speak of events occurring in the present time.

I drink.	We drink.
You drink.	They drink.

He drinks. ⎫
She drinks. ⎬ Watch for the *s* or *es* ending here.
It drinks. ⎭

The dogs (or *more than one* person or thing) drink.

The dog (or any *one* person or thing) drinks. } Watch for the *s* or *es* ending here.

CAUTION: A common error is forgetting the *s* or *es* ending for an irregular present tense verb used with *he, she, it,* or any singular noun subject.

Incorrect: Helga *sing* beautifully.

Correct: Helga *sings* beautifully.

Past Tense

Use the past tense form in the second column of the chart beginning on p. 314 when you are speaking or writing of events that occurred in the past.

I drank.   We drank.

You drank.   They drank.

He drank.   The dogs (or *more than one* person or thing) drank.

She drank.

It drank.

The dog (or any *one* person or thing) drank.

CAUTION: A common error is using the past participle form (in the third column) for the simple past tense. Remember, the past participle appears with a helping verb (see p. 180).

Incorrect: Jim *done* the work. (past participle without helping verb)

Correct: Jim *has done* the work. (helping verb with past participle)

Correct: Jim *did* the work. (past tense form)

Past Participle

The **past participle** is the verb form used with the helping verbs *has, have,* and *had.* The past participle of irregular verbs is the form in the third column of the chart beginning on p. 314.

I have drunk.   We have drunk.

I had drunk.   We had drunk.

You have drunk.   They have drunk.

You had drunk.   They had drunk.

continued

He has drunk.

He had drunk.

She has drunk.

She had drunk.

It has drunk.

It had drunk.

The dog (or any *one* person or thing) has drunk.

The dog (or any *one* person or thing) had drunk.

The dogs (or *more than one* person or thing) have drunk.

The dogs (or more than one person or thing) had drunk.

NOTE: As you can tell from the preceding examples, the past participle form does not change even though the form of the helping verb changes.

CAUTION: The past participle form must be used with a helping verb; it is not used alone.

Incorrect:	I *seen* Nancy. (past participle without helping verb)
Correct:	I *have seen* Nancy. (past participle and helping verb)
Correct:	I *had seen* Nancy. (past participle and helping verb)
Incorrect:	I *seen* her yesterday. (past participle without helping verb)
Correct:	I *saw* her yesterday. (past tense form)

PRACTICE 18.8

Rewrite the sentences, changing the underlined past tense verbs to present tense forms. Be careful to use the *s* or *es* ending when needed. If you are unsure of the correct form, check the chart beginning on p. 314. The first one is done as an example.

1. The golden sun <u>rose</u> over the Atlantic Ocean.

   The golden sun rises over the Atlantic Ocean.

   _____

2. Matteo always <u>forgot</u> to meet me at the library after class.

   _____

   _____

3. The thoughtful dinner guest <u>brought</u> the hostess a bottle of wine.

_____

_____

4. For a moment the center fielder <u>lost</u> the ball in the sun, but he <u>caught</u> it anyway.

_____

_____

5. I <u>knew</u> you <u>drove</u> because I <u>saw</u> your car.

_____

_____

6. Jannine <u>left</u> her car keys in the ignition.

_____

_____

7. When the church bells <u>rang</u>, the congregation <u>rose</u> and <u>sang</u> a hymn.

_____

_____

8. The Jefferson Tigers <u>won</u> most of their games because their star forward <u>made</u> most of his shots.

_____

_____

PRACTICE 18.9

Complete each sentence with a present tense form of an irregular verb from the list beginning on p. 314 and any other words. Use *s* or *es* endings where needed. The first one is done as an example.

1. The scouts and their leader *take a group of senior citizens* _____

   shopping every week. _____

2. She _____

   _____

3. During the meeting, Boris and I _____

   _____

4. Before leaving for work, Luis _____

   _____

5. They _____

   _____

6. The customer _____

   _____

PRACTICE 18.10

Fill in the blank with the past tense form of the irregular verb in parentheses. If you are unsure of the form, check the chart beginning on p. 314. The first one is done as an example.

1. (hold) As Grandma ____*held*____ the quilt I made for her, she smiled gratefully.

2. (forget) Michael was embarrassed because he _____ his sister's birthday.

3. (hear) When Eleni _____ about the earthquake in California, she raced home to call her relatives in San Diego.

4. (lend) José is sorry he _____ Lenny $50 because Lenny never repaid the loan.

5. (begin) Once everyone was seated, the orchestra _____ the overture.

6. (steal) As Aaron Cohen released the pitch, Brett Butler _____ second base.

7. (wake) The alarm on the clock radio sounded at 6:45, and I

_____ with a start.

8. (teach) Yesterday Professor Morales _____ us several techniques for successful revising.

9. (buy) The angora sweater I _____ for Nuha is one size
too large.

PRACTICE 18.11

Pick five irregular verbs that you do not already know the parts of (use
the chart beginning on p. 314). Then, on a separate sheet, use the past
tense form of each of these verbs in a sentence.

PRACTICE 18.12

Fill in the blank with the past participle form of the irregular verb in
parentheses.

1. (bring) Fortunately, Gina has _____ a first-aid kit.

2. (blow) The strong winds have _____ since early this morning.

3. (choose) Lars has _____ to attend St. Bonaventure.

4. (go) The stray dogs had _____ by the time the dog warden
arrived.

5. (lie) Doreen has _____ down for awhile to try to get rid of her
headache.

6. (ride) After Peter and Sondra had _____ the merry-go-round
for the fifth time, they wanted some cotton candy.

7. (write) Thousands of angry consumers have _____ the Better
Business Bureau to complain about the faulty appliance.

PRACTICE 18.13

Write a sentence using the helping verb and past participle form of the
irregular verb in parentheses. If you are unsure, check the chart beginning
on p. 314. The first one is done as an example.

1. (has + teach) *Dr. Yurak has taught both English and history for*

   twenty years.

2. (had + wake) _____

   _____

3. (has + go) _____

   _____

4. (had + sting) _____

   _____

5. (has + stand) _____

   _____

6. (had + see) _____

   _____

7. (has + meet) _____

   _____

REVIEW PRACTICE 18.14: IRREGULAR VERBS

Rewrite each sentence twice, first using the past tense form of the underlined irregular verb, then using the past participle form. The first one is done as an example.

1. The family <u>eats</u> a vegetarian supper of corn chowder and wheat rolls.

   A. *The family ate a vegetarian supper of corn chowder and*

      wheat rolls.

   B. *The family has eaten a vegetarian supper of corn chowder*

      and wheat rolls.

2. Mom and Dad <u>hide</u> the eggs for the annual Easter egg hunt.

A. _____

_____

B. _____

_____

3. Few people <u>understand</u> the significance of the governor's decision.

A. _____

_____

B. _____

_____

4. The honor guard <u>stands</u> at attention for an hour.

A. _____

_____

B. _____

_____

5. Jan <u>swims</u> five miles before breakfast.

A. _____

B. _____

Verb Forms for *Be, Have,* and *Do*

The charts that follow will help you learn the forms for the three common irregular verbs, *be, have,* and *do:*

BE	
Present Tense Forms	
I am.	We are.
You are.	They are.

continued

He is.

She is.

It is.

The toys (or *more than one* person or thing) are.

The toy (or any *one* person or thing) is.

Past Tense Forms

I was.

You were.

He was.

She was.

It was.

We were.

They were.

The toys (or *more than one* person or thing) were.

The toy (or any *one* person or thing) was.

Past Participle Forms

I have been.

I had been.

You have been.

You had been.

He has been.

He had been.

She has been.

She had been.

It has been.

It had been.

We have been.

We had been.

They have been.

They had been.

The toys (or *more than one* person or thing) have been.

The toys (or *more than one* person or thing) had been.

The toy (or any *one* person or thing) has been.

The toy (or any *one* person or thing) had been.

CAUTION: The past participle form must be used with another helping verb; do not use the past participle form alone for the past tense.

Incorrect: I *been* alone too long. (past participle without helping verb)

Correct: I *have been* alone too long. (helping verb and past participle)

Correct: I *had been* alone too long. (helping verb and past participle)

Correct: I *was* alone too long. (past tense form)

HAVE

Present Tense Forms

I have.	We have.
You have.	They have.
He has.	The children (or *more than one*
She has.	person or thing) have.
It has.	

The child (or any *one* person or thing) has.

Past Tense Forms

I had.	We had.
You had.	They had.
He had.	The children (or *more than one*
She had.	person or thing) had.
It had.	

The child (or any *one* person or thing) had.

Past Participle Forms

I have had.	We have had.
I had had.	We had had.
You have had.	They have had.
You had had.	They had had.
He has had.	The children (or *more than one*
He had had.	person or thing) have had.
She has had.	The children (or *more than one*
She had had.	person or thing) had had.
It has had.	
It had had.	

The child (or any *one* person or thing) has had.

The child (or any *one* person or thing) had had.

DO

Present Tense Forms

I do.	We do.
You do.	They do.

continued

He does.

She does.

It does.

The child (or any *one* person or thing) does.

The children (or *more than one* person or thing) do.

CAUTION: Use the contraction forms *don't* and *doesn't* carefully. A common mistake is to use *don't (do not)* when *doesn't (does not)* is needed.

Incorrect:	The toy *don't* work anymore.
Correct:	The toy *doesn't* work anymore.
Incorrect:	He *don't* want to work outside.
Correct:	He *doesn't* want to work outside.

Past Tense Forms

I did.

You did.

He did.

She did.

It did.

The child (or any *one* person or thing) did.

We did.

They did.

The children (or *more than one* person or thing) did.

Past Participle Forms

I have done.

I had done.

You have done.

You had done.

He has done.

He had done.

She has done.

She had done.

It has done.

It had done.

The child (or any *one* person or thing) has done.

The child (or any *one* person or thing) had done.

We have done.

We had done.

They have done.

They had done.

The children (or *more than one* person or thing) have done.

The children (or *more than one* person or thing) had done.

CAUTION: *Done* must appear with a helping verb. Do not use it alone as a past tense form.

Incorrect:	I *done* the dishes. (past participle without a helping verb)
Correct:	I *have done* the dishes. (helping verb and past participle)

Correct: I *had done* the dishes. (helping verb
                       and past participle)

Correct: I *did* the dishes. (past tense form)

PRACTICE 18.15

Change the underlined past tense verb forms to present tense forms.
The first one is done as an example.

1. Teenage unemployment <u>was</u> a major problem in this state.

   Teenage unemployment is a major problem in this state.

   _____

2. High school dances <u>were</u> always a disappointment for me.

   _____

   _____

3. Many parents <u>didn't</u> understand their teenage children.

   _____

   _____

4. I <u>had</u> the information you asked for.

   _____

   _____

5. The books I <u>had</u> for you <u>were</u> on the coffee table.

   _____

   _____

6. Sheila <u>didn't</u> understand today's psychology lecture, but I <u>did</u>.

   _____

   _____

7. I was sure he was here.

_____

_____

8. You were wrong to accuse Jake of lying.

_____

_____

9. Samir and I had the dean's approval to take extra courses.

_____

_____

10. You did well, but I did not because I had exam anxiety.

_____

_____

PRACTICE 18.16

Fill in the blank with the correct past tense form of the verb in parentheses.

1. (have) The house _____ a security system.

2. (do) The children _____ exactly what they have always done.

3. (have) We _____ heard that you _____ the flu.

4. (be) The doctor _____ certain that rest and a better diet

_____ all you needed.

5. (do) Jamal _____ the best he could, but I _____ not always recognize that fact.

6. (be) I _____ here if you needed help, and your parents

_____ too.

PRACTICE 18.17

On a separate sheet, write sentences with the following past participle forms.

1. have + been
2. had + been
3. have + done
4. had + done
5. has + done
6. has + been
7. have + had
8. has + had

POST TEST

1. Find and correct the verb form errors in the following paragraph.

Henry Louis Aaron, known as "Hank," be American baseball's all-time champion home-run hitter. He entered the record books on April 8, 1974, when he breaked Babe Ruth's record of 714 home runs. Aaron then went on to hit a total of 755 homers before he complete his 23-year major-league career. Aaron begun playing professionally for all-black teams in Mobile and Indianapolis, but he signed with the National League's Milwaukee Braves when he be 18. He had reach the major leagues when he was only 20 and quickly become one of the game's finest players. He played for the Braves almost exclusively, first in Milwaukee and then in Atlanta. Along with a lifetime batting average of .305, Aaron had 2,297 runs batted in. He was the National League's most valuable player in 1957 and lead the league in home runs and runs batted in. A favorite with fans, Aaron done much to generate enthusiasm for the game he loved to play.

2. On a separate sheet, write a sentence for each of the following verb forms.

A. the present tense of *smile*

B. the past tense of *escape*

C. the past participle of *go*

D. the past tense of *be*

E. the past participle of *talk*

F. the present tense of *be*

G. the past participle of *take*

H. the past tense of *do*

I. the present tense of *move*

J. the past tense of *think*

SUBJECT-VERB AGREEMENT

Subject-verb agreement means a singular subject must be paired with a singular verb, and a plural subject must be paired with a plural verb.

PRETEST

Fill in the blank with the correct present tense form in parentheses. If you are unsure, do not fill in the blank. When you are done, check your answers in Appendix III.

1. (means/mean) My collection of shells from Ocean City _____ a great deal to me.

2. (visits/visit) Either Mother or Aunt Harriet _____ Grandma in the nursing home every day.

3. (plans/plan) Both Hans and his best friend _____ to attend Ohio State University.

4. (likes/like) Everyone _____ a good mystery.

5. (practices/practice) The football team _____ twice a day in August.

6. (decides/decide) The personnel committee _____ whom to hire for the teaching positions.

7. (is/are) Here _____ the papers you lost.

8. (wants/want) Each of the children _____ to take karate lessons.

9. (works/work) Stavros is one of those people who _____ harder than necessary.

10. (sleeps/sleep) The cat, along with her kittens, _____ in the garage.

Making Subjects and Verbs Agree

A word that refers to one person or thing is **singular**; a word that refers to more than one person or thing is **plural**.

Singular (refers to one person or thing)		Plural (refers to more than one person or thing)	
dog	month	dogs	months
desk	I	desks	we
box	he	boxes	they
cup	she	cups	they

To achieve subject-verb agreement, use a singular verb with a singular subject and a plural verb with a plural subject. Subject-verb agreement is only an issue with present tense verb forms and the past tense forms *was* (singular) and *were* (plural).

Look back at the verb form charts on p. 309 and p. 316. Notice that present tense verb forms add *s* or *es* when used with *he, she, it,* or a singular noun. Now look at the chart on p. 324. Notice that *was* is used with singular nouns and *I, he, she,* and *it.* This is much of what you have to remember to achieve subject-verb agreement. The following charts summarize this subject-verb agreement rule.

PRESENT TENSE—MOST VERBS

Singular Subject/ Singular Verb	**Plural Subject/ Plural Verb**
I move slowly.	We move slowly.
You move slowly.	You move slowly.
He moves slowly.	They move slowly
She moves slowly.	The dogs (or any plural noun) move slowly.
It moves slowly.	
The dog (or any singular noun) moves slowly.	

NOTE: Add *s* or *es* to the verb only when the subject is *he, she, it,* or a singular noun.

PAST TENSE: WAS/WERE

Singular Subject/	**Plural Subject/**
Singular Verb	**Plural Verb**
I was here.	We were here.
You were here.	They were here.
He was here.	The dogs (or any plural noun) were here.
She was here.	
It was here.	
The dog (or any singular noun) was here.	

NOTE: Use *was* only when the subject is *I, he, she, it,* or a singular noun.

PRACTICE 18.18

1. Fill in each blank with the correct present tense form of the verb in parentheses.

From time to time, you probably (to wake up) _____ with dark circles under your eyes. These circles (to indicate) _____ that you (to need) _____ more sleep. Blood vessels under the eyes (to drain) _____ blood from your head. However, blood circulation (to slow) _____ when you are tired. This slow-down (to cause) _____ the blood vessels to swell. Under the eyes, the skin (to thin) _____. When blood vessels (to swell) _____, you (to see) _____ right through the skin. The darkness you (to notice) _____ is actually blood.

2. Fill in the blanks with either *was* (singular) or *were* (plural).

   A. We _____ certain that Jamal _____ not here yet.

   B. You _____ the best person for the job because Joyce _____ not available.

   C. This class _____ difficult, but they _____ able to handle it.

   D. Jane _____ new in town, but she _____ making friends easily.

E. It _____ too early to leave, but we _____ too tired to stay.

F. The spring rains _____ over, but the summer heat _____ not here yet.

Find and eliminate the errors in subject-verb agreement in the following paragraph.

> Lighthouses guide sailors to safe anchorages. They also warns them of danger. The most famous ancient lighthouse was the Pharos of Alexandria, built in Egypt about 300 B.C. Early lighthouses was just wooden towers with metal baskets of burning wood or coal hung from poles on the top. Today, the most powerful lighthouse shine from the Creac'h d'Ouessant lighthouse. It warn of treacherous rocks of northwest France. Most lighthouses have sirens that blare out coded fog warnings. However, some lighthouses emits radio signals to guide ships with radio direction finders. Without lighthouses, the sea would be even more treacherous than it already is.

Compound Subjects

A **compound subject** is a two-part subject with the parts connected by *and, or, either . . . or, neither . . . nor,* or *not only . . . but [also]*.

1. If the subjects are joined by *and,* the verb will usually be plural. Here is an example:

   My best friend and I *spend* spring break in Florida.

2. When the subjects are considered one unit, like *ham and eggs* and *rock and roll,* use a singular verb:

   Rock and roll *is* here to stay.

3. If the subjects are joined by *or, either . . . or, neither . . . nor,* or *not only . . . but [also],* the verb agrees with the closer subject. Here are two examples:

   Either my brothers or my sister *is* going. (singular verb to agree with the singular *sister*)

   Neither my hat nor my gloves *are* where I left them. (plural verb to agree with the plural *gloves*)

NOTE: If you do not like the sound of "Either my brothers or my sister is going," reverse the order to place the plural subject second, so you can use a plural verb:

Either my sister or my brothers *are* going.

PRACTICE 18.20

Follow each compound subject with the correct present tense form of the verb in parentheses. Then finish the sentence with any other words you care to add. The first one is done as an example.

1. (taste) The meat and the potatoes *taste overcooked and bland.*

2. (know) Neither the club president nor the treasurer _____

   _____

3. (grow) Cotton and tobacco _____

   _____

4. (sing) The choir or the choir master _____

   _____

5. (visit) The children and their teacher _____

   _____

6. (taste) Neither the meat nor the potatoes _____

   _____

7. (plan) Not only Sue but also Helen _____.

   _____

8. (volunteer) Either Mr. Chen or his wife _____

   _____

Collective Nouns

Collective nouns refer to groups. They are words like these:

congregation	committee	band	faculty
group	team	jury	flock
herd	audience	family	class

1. If the collective noun is thought of as one group acting as a whole, a singular verb is used. Here is an example:

At noon, the band *boards* the bus for the trip to the Rose Parade. (The singular verb is used because *band* is acting as a whole.)

2. If the members of the group are acting individually, the collective noun takes a plural verb. Here is an example:

The faculty *have* debated that issue for years. (The plural verb is used because the individual members of the faculty are acting individually.)

PRACTICE 18.21

On a separate sheet, write sentences using the given collective nouns as subjects and the correct present tense forms of the verbs in parentheses. Be prepared to explain why you used the verb form that you did. The first one is done as an example.

1. flock (migrate) *The flock migrates to a warmer climate for the* _____

   winter. _____

2. army (attack)

3. family (eat)

4. jury (argue)

5. committee (decide)

6. team (practice)

Indefinite Pronouns

Indefinite pronouns refer to a group without specifying the specific members.

1. These indefinite pronouns always take a singular verb:

anyone	anybody	anything	each
everyone	everybody	everything	one
no one	nobody	nothing	none
someone	somebody	something	

Anyone *is* welcome to attend the open house.

Everything *works* out eventually.

Each student *writes* a term paper during the senior year.

Somebody *helps* Grandma clean her house every week.

2. These indefinite pronouns always take a plural verb:

both	many	few	several

Many *believe* that Congress will defeat the budget proposal.

3. These indefinite pronouns take either a singular or plural verb, depending on whether the sense of the subject is singular or plural:

all   more   some
any   most

Some of my homework *is* missing. (The verb is singular because the sense of the subject is that one unit is missing.)

Some of the puzzle pieces *are* missing. (The verb is plural because the sense is that more than one unit is missing.)

PRACTICE 18.22

Circle the indefinite pronoun subjects and fill in the blanks with the correct present tense form of the verb in parentheses. The first one is done as an example.

1. (be) (All) of the lost money ____*is*____ in the back of the drawer.

2. (believe) Each of us _____ the tax increase will improve the economy.

3. (find) Many of the band members _____ the new director enthusiastic and creative.

4. (be) Everyone _____ invited to the tailgate party before the homecoming game.

5. (be) All of the hem _____ torn from the skirt.

6. (seem) None of the proposals _____ adequate to solve the problem.

7. (be) Some of the desserts _____ low in fat and sugar.

8. (go) Everything _____ wrong when you are in a hurry.

9. (taste) All of the items _____ underseasoned to me.

10. (expect) Nobody _____ you to be perfect.

Phrases Between the Subject and Verb

Phrases, particularly prepositional phrases (see p. 185), often come between the subject and verb. Do not be fooled by these phrases, for they do not affect subject-verb agreement.

The theme of the stories *is* middle-class greed. (A singular verb is used to agree with the singular subject *theme.* The phrase *of the stories* does not affect agreement.)

PRACTICE 18.23

After each subject and phrase, write a present tense verb and any other words you want to add. (Use forms of the verb *to be* no more than twice.) Underline the subject once and the verb twice; draw a line through the phrase between the subject and verb. The first one is done as an example.

1. The <u>carton</u> ~~of records~~ *is blocking the entrance to the room.*

2. The people on the bus _____

3. Many paintings by that artist _____

4. The students from Sri Lanka_____

5. The scouts, along with their scoutmaster, _____

6. The group of children_____

7. The mistakes on the last page of the essay_____

8. The seats in the tenth row _____

9. The ragweed in the fields_____

10. One of the kittens _____

_____

Inverted Order

When a sentence has **inverted order**, the subject comes *after* the verb. (See p. 186 for more on inverted order.) Inverted order often occurs when a sentence begins with *here* or *there*. The following sentences have inverted order. The subjects are underlined once, and the verbs are underlined twice.

Here are the items for the charity garage sale.

There is only one movie suitable for children.

Even if a sentence has inverted order, the subject and verb must agree. If you have trouble finding the subject and verb, find the word or words that change form to show tense—that's the verb. Then ask "who or what?" before the verb—your answer will be the subject. (See p. 178 and p. 184 on this procedure.)

PRACTICE 18.24

Complete the following sentences, being sure your subjects and verbs agree. The first one is done as an example.

1. Here is *an unusual painting.* _____

_____

2. Here are _____

_____

3. There is _____

_____

4. There are _____

_____

5. There were_____

_____

6. There was_____

_____

Who, Which, That

Who, which, and *that* are **relative pronouns** that refer to nouns. (See p. 212.) Use a singular verb when *who, which,* or *that* refers to a singular noun; use a plural verb when *who, which,* or *that* refers to a plural noun. Study these two examples:

Peter is one of those students who *study* constantly. (The plural verb is used because *who* refers to the plural noun *students.*)

This is the book that *has* the surprise ending. (The singular verb is used because *that* refers to the singular noun *book.*)

PRACTICE 18.25

Draw an arrow from *who, which,* or *that* to the noun referred to. Then fill in the blank with the correct present tense form of the verb in parentheses. The first one is done as an example.

1. (follow) Vashti is a person who ___*follows*___ every rule to the letter.

2. (do) A person who _____ not understand trigonometry will have trouble with physics.

3. (support) The beams which _____ this section of roof are beginning to rot.

4. (believe) Dr. Perni is one of those instructors who _____ her students can succeed.

5. (divide) This is the lake that _____ the property in half.

6. (scare) This is the kind of movie that always _____ me.

REVIEW PRACTICE 18.26: SUBJECT-VERB AGREEMENT

Find and eliminate the subject-verb agreement problems in the following passage, drawing on what you have learned about compound, indefinite pronoun, and collective noun subjects, phrases between the subject and verb, inverted order, and relative clauses.

Beluga whales live in groups called pods, which are social units that may consists of two to 25 whales. Both males and females makes up a pod, although mothers with calves often form separate pods during calving season. A pod of belugas hunt and migrate together as one group.

The behavior of belugas are interesting to observe. One of their most common behaviors are vocalizing. Also, during calving season, adult belugas at sea have been observed carrying objects such as planks, nets, and even caribou skeletons on their heads and backs. Females in zoological habitats have also been seen carrying floats or buoys on their backs after losing a newborn. Experts thus theorize that this carrying is surrogate behavior. Belugas, which exhibits a great deal of curiosity toward humans, often swim up to boats. They seem as interested in us as we are in them.

POST TEST

1. Drawing on everything you have learned about subject-verb agreement, fill in the blanks with the correct verb in parentheses.

   A. (was/were) There _____ three accidents at the corner of Broadway and Elm Street last month.

   B. (needs/need) The rose bush in the middle of the petunias

   _____ more sun.

   C. (stands/stand) A bookcase and a record cabinet _____ against the wall opposite the fireplace.

   D. (has/have) Some of the mess _____ been straightened up.

   E. (belongs/belong) Every six-year-old _____ in school.

   F. (makes/make) Either magazines or a mystery novel _____ a suitable gift to someone in the hospital.

   G. (is/are) Some of my family members _____ not able to attend this year's annual Thanksgiving reunion.

   H. (has/have) The decision of the three judges _____ been disputed by the skater and her coach.

I. (was/were) There _____ no question about the wisdom of electing Lynne president of student council.

J. (makes/make) Maureen is one of those people who _____ friends wherever she goes.

K. (is/are) Here _____ the supplies you need to complete the project.

L. (dislikes/dislike) The Beast, a roller coaster at King's Island, is not for people who _____ speed and heights.

M. (speaks/speak) The chief of police and two police officers

_____ about drug abuse at local schools.

N. (decides/decide) A panel of writing instructors _____ who wins the senior essay award.

O. (drives/drive) Either Jesse or Carlos _____ me to school every morning.

2. On a separate sheet, rewrite the following paragraphs, changing the underlined past tense verbs to present tense verbs. Pay careful attention to subject-verb agreement.

A. After the noon rush hour, Leo's Pizzeria was a mess. The once clean, stainless steel table where pizzas were made was splattered with sauce and flooded with oil. On the table, crusty dough and hardening strands of mozzarella contributed to the mess, which included crumbled plastic dough bags dripping with oil. A mountain of dirty dishes sat in wait, threatening to topple if someone did not come soon to wash them. A collection of torn pizza boxes, strewn across the counter, hid spatulas, used and abandoned. Blackened pizzas, burned and forgotten during the rush, filled the air with the scent of charcoal. Added to this smell were the watering onions near the ovens. The flour used to make the crusts covered everything in the room with a fine dust. Anyone who entered the kitchen would surely think twice before eating at Leo's.

B. Everything seemed to be shrinking, even the size of the incisions doctors made for certain kinds of back surgery. For some kinds of herniated spinal disks, for example, doctors used "microdiskectomy." This was one of those procedures that allowed surgeons to use a a very thin tool that cut and removed the damaged part of the disk. A possible drawback of such procedures was that surgeons didn't have as wide a view of what they were operating on. To balance this problem was the fact that patients went home sooner and got back to work earlier than people who had traditional surgery. Either microdiskectomy or traditional surgery was recommended in many cases. Thus, there were good reasons to consult with your physician before deciding what to do. The medical community believed that the final decision rested with you, the patient.

TENSE SHIFTS

A writer must use the tense (present, past, or future) that correctly shows the time of an event and avoid moving from one tense to another without a good reason. Moving unnecessarily from one tense to another creates a problem called **tense shift**.

PRETEST

If there is a tense shift, write *TS* on the blank; if the sentence is correct, write *C* on the blank. If you are unsure, do not write anything. You can check your answers in Appendix III.

1. _____ After I took my algebra midterm examination, I walk to the student union to relax for a while.

2. _____ Chuck is a man with a dream, and he planned to make it come true.

3. _____ When I finished the novel, I was moved by what I had read.

4. _____ Dr. Juarez explains difficult points in detail and was always glad to answer student questions patiently.

5. _____ I was struggling to get the top up on my convertible when the storm hits and the downpour starts.

6. _____ The doctor explained that the child's tonsils were badly infected and that they had to be surgically removed when the infection was gone.

7. _____ All of us are prepared for an emergency. We have first-aid kits, flashlights, waterproof clothing, and extra food.

8. _____ When the nature guide turned over the leaf, the scouts see the monarch butterfly egg.

9. _____ The killer whale feeds on seals, fish, and other whales. It did not attack human beings.

10. _____ The blue whale can grow to be 100 feet long, although it eats only microscopic animals.

Avoiding Inappropriate Tense Shifts

A writer uses a **present tense** verb form to show that an event is occurring now, a **past tense** verb form to show that an event occurred before the present, and a **future tense** verb form to show that an event will occur after the present. For more information on verb tenses, see p. 178. Writers should use the same verb tense throughout the composition unless they want to show a change in time. A writer who changes verb tense without a valid reason creates a problem called **tense shift**. Here is an example:

tense shift: When I *left* the house this morning, I *go* to school.

explanation: The first verb (*left*) is in the past tense to show that an event occurred before the present. However, the second verb (*go*) shifts to the present tense for no reason.

correction: When I *left* the house this morning, I *went* to school.

explanation: Both verbs are now in the past tense, so the shift in tense is eliminated.

Some tense shifts are not a problem because a change of time is called for. Consider the following example:

appropriate tense shift: "Frankfurters" *are* named for the city where they *were* first made: Frankfurt, Germany.

explanation: The present tense *are* is used because frankfurters are named *in the present*. The past tense *were* is used because frankfurters were first made *in the past*.

PRACTICE 18.27

Underline the verbs and then eliminate each inappropriate tense shift by crossing out the problem verb and writing the correct form above it. The first one is done as an example.

1. After I completed my research paper for sociology class, I ~~treat~~ *treated* myself to dinner and a movie.

2. My high school teachers always asked for an outline whenever I submit my final essay.

3. As I drive into my old neighborhood, I saw that the house I grew up in was no longer standing.

4. Painting the walls in my bedroom went quickly, but painting the ceiling takes most of the day.

5. The eager science students collect specimens in the park. Then they mounted them on slides and view them under the microscope.

6. Before leaving the house, I make sure the stove is turned off, and then I checked the security locks.

PRACTICE 18.28

On a separate sheet, rewrite the paragraphs eliminating inappropriate tense shifts by changing verb tenses where necessary. Remember not all tense changes are a problem. Eliminate only the inappropriate shifts.

1. The smallest deer in the world live on islands off the southern tip of Florida. They are called key deer, and each one is only the size of a Great Dane dog. The key deer thrived for thousands of years, and then Columbus stops at the islands on one of his trips to the New World. Soon explorers are coming and discovering the deer. Eventually, settlers move on the island, and the deer were hunted. By the 1940s, only several dozen of these small creatures were left. The deer remained unprotected until the late 1950s, when Congress passes a law establishing a refuge for the key deer. Now the number of these endangered animals is 350, up from fewer than 30 in 1948.

2. In 1937, pilot Amelia Earhart and Fred Noonan, her navigator, were attempting an around-the-world flight. They planned to land and refuel on Howland Island. However, Earhart's plane is lost over the Pacific Ocean, although she gave compass readings over the plane's radio, hoping to be guided to a safe landing. "We're on the line of 157–337. . . . We are running north and south," the pilot says. These were the last words the outside world heard Earhart speak. The ground crew on Howland listens in vain for the twin-engine plane, but Earhart and Noonan are never heard from again. Still, Earhart lives in the memory of millions of Americans who admire her as a pioneer who, as the first woman to fly the Atlantic Ocean alone, is not afraid of adventure.

Thinking, Learning, and Writing in College   **Notetaking**

Successful students can identify what they should take notes on during lectures. They often use these strategies:

- Read assigned material beforehand and identify the key points. Make note of those key points if they are mentioned in the lecture.
- Listen for a change in voice tone that signals emphasis.
- Note points written on the board.
- Note points that are repeated.
- Note anything the instructor says is important.
- Notice nonverbal cues that signal emphasis, things like hand gestures and walking toward the class.

POST TEST

On a separate sheet, rewrite the following paragraph, eliminating inappropriate tense shifts by changing verb forms where necessary.

Scientists raise fleas in laboratories to learn more about how these pests caused disease in humans and to learn more about effective ways to control the insects. The fleas are kept in special jars that contain sieves. The fleas lay eggs in the jars, and these eggs drop through the sieves. The scientists collected the eggs so they can raise more fleas from them. The jars also have tubes that carry warm water to heat blood that is contained underneath a skinlike sheath. The fleas bit through this sheath to drink the blood, which served as their food. Interestingly, these laboratory breeding grounds for fleas are called fake pups.

Visit the Clouse Website!

For additional exercises, quizzes, and Internet activities, visit our Website at:

http://www.ablongman.com/clouse

For even more activities, visit the Longman English pages at:

http://www.ablongman.com/englishpages

Chapter 19

Using Pronouns Correctly

A **pronoun** takes the place of a noun or refers to a noun (a noun names a person, place, idea, emotion, or thing).

The noun the pronoun stands for or refers to is the **antecedent**. In the following examples an arrow is drawn from the pronoun to the noun antecedent:

Some consumers do not understand their legal rights.

Michelle understood that if she did not find a suitable baby-sitter, she would not be able to return to college.

The oak tree must be diseased, for it is dropping its leaves.

In this chapter you will learn much about pronouns, including

1. how to ensure that pronouns agree with their antecedents
2. how to avoid unclear reference to antecedents
3. how to avoid distant reference to antecedents
4. how to avoid reference to unstated antecedents
5. when to use subject pronouns and when to use object pronouns
6. how to avoid problems with person shift

◆　◆　◆

PRETEST

Fill in the blanks with the correct pronoun form in parentheses, and then check your answers in Appendix III. Do not guess; if you are unsure, do not put anything in the blank.

1. (I, me) My sister and _____ are attending the same college.

2. (they, them) Each morning I jog farther than _____.

3. (I, me) Because there was a fly in the soup, the manager gave my date

   and _____ a free dinner.

4. (her, their) Each of the mothers complained that _____ children watched too much television.

5. (his or her, their) All of the students were instructed to bring

   _____ books and notes to the examination.

6. (its, their) The book of old photographs fell off _____ shelf.

7. (its, their) The committee felt _____ authority should be extended to making and enforcing rules.

8. (who, whom) That is the person _____ I told you about.

9. (I, me) The police officer told the other driver and _____ that it was impossible to determine who caused the accident.

10. (its, their) One of the dresses has lost _____ shape.

PRONOUN-ANTECEDENT AGREEMENT

A pronoun must be singular if the word it refers to (the antecedent) is singular. The pronoun must be plural if the antecedent is plural. Matching singular pronouns with singular antecedents and plural pronouns with plural antecedents creates **pronoun-antecedent agreement**.

singular pronoun/singular antecedent: The child cried because
                                        she broke her favorite toy.

plural pronoun/plural antecedent: The basketball players
                                        cheered when they won
                                        the game in double over-
                                        time.

Here is a chart of singular and plural pronouns.

Singular Pronouns	**Plural Pronouns**
I, me, my, mine	we, us, our, ours
he, she, it, him, her	they, their, theirs
his, hers, its	them

Pronouns That Are Both Singular and Plural
you, your, yours

PRACTICE 19.1

Fill in each blank with a pronoun from the above chart. Then draw an arrow from the pronoun to its antecedent. The first one is done as an example.

At 4:00 a.m., Gregory was awakened by the blare of

_____*his*_____ his smoke detector. _____ was dazed at

first, but quickly _____ realized that the house was on

fire. Gregory's roommates downstairs had also been awak-

ened, and _____ were shouting to Greg to get out of

the house. However, Greg realized that Mike and his sister

Darla were still asleep in the attic, so _____ ran

upstairs to get _____. Greg pounded on _____

door to wake _____ up. Then, the three of them began

descending the stairs to the front door. Before they reached

_____, Darla was overcome by smoke and Mike had to

carry _____ part of the way. The three of them

escaped just in time, for as they exited there was an explo-

sion upstairs and fire shot through the windows. Firefight-

ers blame the fire on a space heater. _____ was placed

too close to some rags and ignited _____. _____

said the boys are fortunate that _____ detector was

working. Everyone is safe, but Darla suffered from smoke

inhalation, so _____ had to be hospitalized.

Compound Subject Antecedents

A **compound subject** is a two-part subject with the parts connected by *and, or, either . . . or,* or *neither . . . nor.* Follow these rules when a pronoun refers to all or part of a compound subject.

1. When the noun antecedents are joined by *and,* the pronoun will usually be plural.

   My father and mother sold their house and moved into an apartment. (Their is plural because it refers to two people, father and mother.)

2. If the noun antecedents are joined by *or, either . . . or,* or *neither . . . nor,* the pronoun agrees with the closer antecedent.

   Ivan or Ralph will lend me his car to use while mine is in the shop. (The singular his is used to agree with Ralph, the closer antecedent.)

   Neither the president nor his advisors believe they can get the disarmament bill through Congress. (The plural they is used to agree with advisors, the closer antecedent.)

   Either Jeff or his brothers will bring their extension ladder over so I can clean the gutters around the house. (The plural their is used to agree with brothers, the closer antecedent.)

NOTE: To avoid an awkward-sounding (but grammatically correct) pronoun usage, place the plural part of a compound subject last.

Correct but awkward:	Either the scouts or the scout leader will bring *his* leaf identification manual.
Correct and natural sounding:	Either the scout leader or the scouts will bring *their* leaf identification manual.

PRACTICE 19.2

Fill in the blank with the correct pronoun.

1. The students and their teacher decorated _____ classroom for the Martin Luther King memorial celebration.

2. Joyce and Burt handed in _____ research papers early.

3. Either my mother or my grandmother will make _____ chocolate chip cookie recipe for the family reunion.

4. Neither the teachers nor the school board members changed

   _____ positions after hours of negotiating.

5. I thought Rico or Elliot would offer to bring _____ Coleman stove on the camping trip.

6. The Hummel figurine and the Royal Copenhagen plate were knocked

   from _____ shelves during the brief earth tremor.

Collective Noun Antecedents

A **collective noun** refers to a group. These words are examples of collective nouns:

band	committee	jury
group	family	team
herd	audience	faculty

1. If the sense of the collective noun is that the group is acting as one unit, the pronoun that refers to the collective noun will be singular:

   The <u>committee</u> was unsure of <u>its</u> assignment.

NOTE: If you find it awkward to use the singular *its,* add "members of" before the collective noun and use a plural verb and pronoun:

The members of the committee were unsure of their assignment.

---

2. If the members of the group are acting individually, the pronoun that refers to the collective noun will be plural:

   The <u>committee</u> argued about <u>their</u> differing opinions.

PRACTICE 19.3

Circle the collective noun antecedent. Then fill in the blank with the singular *its* or the plural *their*.

1. The women's softball team scored _____ third upset of the season against the top-ranked team in the league.

2. The jury debated all night in order to resolve _____ differences of opinion.

3. The audience shouted _____ approval by calling for an encore.

4. After the curtain fell on the third act, the cast came out and took

   _____ bow.

5. The coach reminded the team to bring _____ playbooks to every practice.

6. The orchestra lifted _____ instruments, signaling that the concert was about to begin.

7. At the general membership meeting, the committee reported

   _____ findings.

Indefinite Pronoun Antecedents

An **indefinite pronoun** refers to a part of a group without mentioning the specific members. An indefinite pronoun can be an antecedent for another pronoun.

1. These indefinite pronouns are always singular, so any pronoun that refers to one of them will also be singular:

anyone	everybody	nothing
everyone	nobody	something
no one	somebody	each
someone	anything	one
anybody	everything	none

Everyone should bring his or her notebook to the lecture.

Each of the priests is volunteering his time to help at the battered persons' shelter.

None of the mothers brought her children to the meeting.

> NOTE: As the last two examples illustrate, a prepositional phrase that comes after the indefinite pronoun does not affect pronoun-antecedent agreement. (See also "Phrases After the Antecedent" on p. 355.)

---

2. These indefinite pronouns are always plural, so any pronoun that refers to them should also be plural:

both   many   few   several

Few understand all their rights under the law.

Many believe their educational backgrounds are not adequate.

3. These indefinite pronouns are either singular or plural. Any pronoun that refers to one of them will be singular if the meaning of the indefinite pronoun is singular, and plural if the meaning of the indefinite pronoun is plural.

all	more	some
any	most	

All of the class finished their research papers. (The plural pronoun is used because the antecedent all has a plural sense.)

All of the report fell out of its folder. (The singular pronoun is used because the antecedent all has a singular sense.)

PRACTICE 19.4

Fill in the blanks with the correct pronoun; choose *his, her, its, they,* or *their:*

1. All of the contestants hoped _____ entries would be judged the best of the show.

2. None of the girl scouts had trouble finding _____ way out of the woods during the survival training exercise.

3. Most of the curtain has slipped off _____ rod.

4. Many of the protesters shouted that _____ civil rights had been violated.

5. To pass inspection, you must be sure that everything is in_____ place.

6. Each of the boys on the varsity basketball team is expected to keep

   _____ grades up to a B average.

7. The salesclerk was alarmed because one of the expensive designer

   dresses was missing from _____ hanger.

8. Very few of the contestants believed _____ had much of a chance to win.

Nonsexist Usage

In the past, writers would use the masculine forms *he, his, him,* and *himself* to refer to nouns and indefinite pronouns that included both males and females. Thus, sentences like the following were frequently written and spoken:

Each student is expected to bring <u>his</u> book to class.

Every person has <u>his</u> own opinion.

Everybody described <u>his</u> career goals.

Today more writers and speakers understand that this use of the masculine pronoun is grammatically correct, but it excludes women. To avoid using a masculine pronoun to refer to groups that include both men and women, you have three options.

1. Use *he or she, him or her, his or hers, himself or herself.*

   Everybody described his or her career goals. (*Instead of:* Everybody described his career goals.)

   Using pairs of pronouns works in many situations. However, when this solution becomes awkward, it is better to use one of the two solutions that follow.

2. Use plural forms.

All students are expected to bring their books to class. (*Instead of*: Each student is expected to bring his book to class.)

3. Reshape the sentence to avoid the masculine reference.

Every person has an opinion. (*Instead of*: Every person has his own opinion.)

Thinking, Learning, and Writing in College   Assessing Popular Usage

In their efforts to avoid sexist usage, more and more people are using plural pronouns to refer to singular antecedents, like this: Everybody should bring their textbook to class. Strictly speaking, the lack of pronoun-antecedent agreement makes this usage incorrect. However, its acceptance is becoming increasingly widespread. Nonetheless, before using a plural pronoun to refer to a singular antecedent that includes both males and females, carefully assess your teacher or other reader's opinion of this usage.

PRACTICE 19.5

Rewrite each sentence so it has nonsexist pronoun usage. Refer to the three preceding suggestions for how to do this, and try to use each suggestion twice. The first one is done as an example.

1. None of the people who entered the writing contest had his manuscript returned.

The people who entered the writing contest did not have their

manuscripts returned.

2. Anyone who cannot reach his goal is sure to feel frustrated.

_____

_____

3. Everyone who entered the poetry contest is convinced that his poem will win the $500 prize.

_____

_____

4. Anyone who puts his money in a money market fund now will earn an average of 4 percent interest.

_____

_____

5. None of the audience felt the play was worth the price he paid.

_____

_____

6. Each of the investment brokers advised his clients to avoid the risks of penny stocks.

_____

_____

7. Someone has left his chemistry book and notes on the desk.

_____

_____

Phrases After the Antecedent

Sometimes a prepositional phrase comes after the antecedent (see p. 185 for an explanation of prepositional phrases). When this happens, the phrase will not affect pronoun-antecedent agreement.

The can of sardines fell off its shelf in the cupboard. (The prepositional phrase of sardines does not affect agreement. The singular its is used to agree with the singular can.)

Each of the windows had slipped off its track. (The prepositional phrase of the windows does not affect agreement. The singular its is used to agree with the singular each.)

The students in the class asked if their test would be given on Wednesday. (The prepositional phrase in the class does not affect agreement. The singular their is used to agree with the singular students.)

PRACTICE 19.6

Draw a line through each prepositional phrase. Then fill in the blanks with the correct pronoun (choose *its* or *their*).

1. Each of the birds spread _____ wings and flew from the nest.

2. The last two cars in the caravan lost _____ way after taking a wrong turn north of Cincinnati.

3. Each of the items for the experiment is in _____ proper place on the counter.

4. The baby birds in the nest opened _____ mouths to be fed.

5. The box of Christmas presents fell from _____ hiding place on the shelf in the back of the closet.

6. Two of the women sold _____ stereo systems to buy a one-way ticket to Toronto.

REVIEW PRACTICE 19.7: PRONOUN-ANTECEDENT AGREEMENT

Fill in the blanks with the correct pronoun.

Because hypertension (high blood pressure) is the cause of 1.5 million heart attacks a year, everyone should learn if _____ has it. It is also important to understand that in most people, there are no symptoms of hypertension, which is why it is called the "silent killer." For example, neither my uncle nor my father discovered _____ high blood pressure until it was almost too late—after having a major heart attack. As a result, our family has _____ blood pressure checked regularly. In a few cases, people do experience one or more symptoms. One of my family members, for example, discovered _____ hypertension after experiencing vision changes.

Other people discover _____ high blood pressure when they investigate chest pains, shortness of breath, heart palpitations, nose bleeds, or swelling of the ankles. Whether or not you have a family history of heart disease, you should be aware of the "silent killer" and have regular blood pressure screenings.

 Tips for Solving Pronoun-Antecedent Agreement Problems

1. When you edit, compare each pronoun and antecedent to be sure they are both singular or they are both plural.
2. Memorize the group of indefinite pronouns that is singular, the group that is plural, and the group that can be either singular or plural, so you can use pronouns correctly with them.
3. Edit one extra time, just looking for pronoun-antecedent agreement errors.
4. Find a pattern to your errors. For example, maybe you usually make mistakes with collective noun antecedents. If this is the case, you can pay special attention to your use of pronouns with collective nouns.

POST TEST

Cross out each incorrect pronoun and write the correct one above it.

A person who lives in constant fear of becoming a victim of crime can solve their problem easily—by turning off their television. Several years ago, a set of studies was done. They showed that when people watch a great deal of television, they suffer an exaggerated sense of fear. Apparently, all the murder and mayhem on the small screen make frequent TV-viewers feel at risk. Thus, someone who spends most of their time in front of the set will worry far more about being victimized by crime than someone who watches little or no television. Women and children may find his or her fears even greater. This is because women on television are most often shown as the victims of violent crime, and young children do not recognize the unrealistic nature of much programming. Thus, women and children feel more threatened than adult male viewers. Obviously, the studies show that parents of a young child should limit his or her child's viewing time.

PRONOUN REFERENCE

In general, two kinds of pronoun reference problems are common:

1. unclear reference
2. unstated reference

The next pages will explain these pronoun reference problems.

Unclear Reference

When the reader cannot tell which antecedent a pronoun refers to, the problem is **unclear reference**. Here is a sentence that has unclear reference because the pronoun could refer to two nouns:

Kathy was having lunch with Sasha when she heard the news.

Because the pronoun reference is unclear, the reader cannot tell whether Kathy or Sasha heard the news. Here is another example:

After I put the cereal and orange juice on the table, my dog jumped up and spilled it.

What was spilled, the cereal or the orange juice? Because the pronoun reference is unclear, the reader cannot tell for sure.

To solve a problem with unclear reference, you may have to use a noun instead of a pronoun:

Kathy was having lunch with Sasha when Sasha heard the news.

After I put the cereal and orange juice on the table, my dog jumped up and spilled the juice.

PRACTICE 19.8

Rewrite the following sentences to solve problems with unclear pronoun reference. The first one is done as an example.

1. Lenny told Jake that he would have to return the book by Friday.

   Lenny told Jake that Jake would have to return the book

   by Friday.

2. I put the chicken in the oven and the broccoli in the microwave. An hour later it burned.

   _____

   _____

3. Tatiana carefully removed the vase from the coffee table before dusting it.

   _____

   _____

4. My mother explained to my sister that she had to leave for school in an hour.

   _____

   _____

5. Before Jack could give Marvin his class notes, he fell asleep.

   _____

   _____

6. As I was placing the ceramic bowl on the glass table, it broke.

   _____

   _____

Unstated Reference

Unstated reference occurs when a pronoun refers to an unstated antecedent. To solve the problem, add the unstated form.

unstated reference:	Anika is known as a patient tutor. It is a trait the other tutors admire. [It is meant to refer to *patience*, but that word does not appear—patient does.]
correction:	Anika is known as a patient tutor. Her patience is a trait the other tutors admire.
unstated reference:	Because Joel is so insecure, he has very few friends. It causes him to seek constant approval. [It is meant to refer to insecurity, but that word does not appear—insecure does.]
correction:	Because Joel is so insecure, he has very few friends. His insecurity causes him to seek constant approval.

Unstated reference also occurs when *this, that, which, it,* or *they* has no stated antecedent. To solve the problem, add the missing word or words.

unstated reference:	During my last physical examination, the doctor urged me to lower my salt intake. This means my food tastes bland. [This has no stated antecedent.]
correction:	During my last physical examination, the doctor urged me to lower my salt intake. This change means my food tastes bland.
unstated reference:	The auto workers and GM negotiated all night, but it failed to produce a contract. [It has no stated antecedent.]
correction:	The auto workers and GM negotiated all night, but the session failed to produce a contract.

Unstated reference will occur when *they* or *you* has no stated antecedent. To solve the problem, add the missing word or words.

unstated reference:	I called the billing office to complain about my bill, but they said it was correct. [They has no stated antecedent.]
correction:	I called the billing office to complain about my bill, but the clerk said it was correct.

unstated reference: Worker dissatisfaction occurs when you do not let employees participate in decision-making. [You has no stated antecedent.]

correction: Worker dissatisfaction occurs when <u>employers</u> do not let employees participate in decision-making.

NOTE: *You* and *your* address the reader directly. Avoid these pronouns unless you mean to address the reader; do not use them for general statements that apply to more people than the reader.

no: At election time, <u>you</u> always see politicians promising things they can't deliver.

yes: At election time, politicians are always promising things they can't deliver.

Unstated reference occurs when a pronoun refers to a possessive form (a form that designates ownership). To solve the problem, rewrite to eliminate the possessive form.

unstated reference: The speaker's words were inspirational because he was so emotional. [The antecedent of <u>he</u> is <u>speaker</u>, not <u>speaker's</u>, but <u>speaker</u> does not appear.]

correction: The speaker's words were so inspirational because the speaker was so emotional. [<u>Speaker</u> is substituted for <u>speaker's</u>.]

unstated reference: Janet's library books are three months overdue. She will have to pay a stiff fine. [<u>She</u> cannot refer to <u>Janet's</u>.]

correction: Janet's library books are three months overdue. Janet will have to pay a stiff fine. [<u>Janet</u> is substituted for <u>she</u>.]

 Tips for Solving Problems with Pronoun Reference

1. Find the specific antecedent for each pronoun. If you cannot find a stated antecedent, you have a problem with unstated reference, which you can correct by supplying the missing antecedent.

2. Check to be sure the pronoun does not have two possible antecedents. If it does, use a noun instead of a pronoun.

3. Check your use of *you, it,* and *they.* Be sure these pronouns have stated antecedents. If they do not, supply the missing antecedents.

PRACTICE 19.9

Revise the sentences to eliminate the unstated reference problems. The first one is done as an example.

1. Because he had a tension headache, Nick was irritable. It made him very difficult to be around.

   Because he had a tension headache, Nick was irritable.

   His irritability made him very difficult to be around.

2. The comedian told several ethnic jokes. It annoyed most of the audience.

   _____

   _____

3. The movie was excessively violent and too long. This caused most of the critics to review it badly.

   _____

   _____

4. The paint had a few blisters in it near the ceiling, but for the most part, they did an excellent job.

   _____

   _____

5. My mechanic explained that my car's starter and shock absorbers must be replaced, so I am thinking of trading it in.

   _____

   _____

6. I went to see my advisor, but they said that he was sick.

   _____

   _____

7. Ivan felt nervous about the upcoming examination. It made sleep difficult for him.

_____

_____

8. Betty's problem will not be easy to solve. She will probably have to get professional help.

_____

_____

9. During finals week, you always know that students are working hard.

_____

_____

10. The police officer explained to the suspects that they had a right to an attorney, which is guaranteed by law.

_____

_____

11. Corrine is a very talented artist. It helped her earn a scholarship to the state art institute.

_____

_____

SUBJECT, OBJECT, AND POSSESSIVE PRONOUNS

Subject Pronoun   A pronoun can be the *subject* of a sentence. That is, it can be the word that shows who or what the sentence is about (see p. 184 for more on identifying subjects). In the following sentences, the italicized pronouns act as subjects:

He slammed the car door on John's finger.

During summer school, *she* took a word processing course.

They ate quickly and left.

In the spring and summer, *I* walk five miles a day.

Object Pronoun   A pronoun can also be the **object of a verb**. That is, it can be the word that receives the action the verb expresses.

Daniela carried *it* upstairs.

In this example, the verb is *carried. It* receives the action of the verb *carried* and is, therefore, the object of the verb.

To find the object of a verb, ask "whom or what?" *after* the verb. Here are some examples:

Pat ate *it.* (Ask "ate whom or what?" and the answer is *it,* so *it* is the object of the verb.)

Ida always understands *him.* (Ask "understands whom or what?" and the answer is *him,* so *him* is the object of the verb.)

The ending of the book surprised *me.* (Ask "surprised whom or what?" and the answer is *me,* so *me* is the object of the verb.)

You may remember from an earlier chapter that asking "who or what?" is a good way to find the subject of a sentence. Just keep in mind that to find the subject you ask "who or what?" *before* the verb, and to find the object you ask "whom or what?" *after* the verb.

I invited them to the party.

In this sample sentence, the verb is *invited.* (If you are unsure about how to find the verb in a sentence, see p. 178.) Ask "who or what invited?" and you get the answer *I,* so *I* is the subject. Ask "invited whom or what?" and you get the answer *them,* so *them* is the object of the verb.

In addition to being the subject of a sentence or the object of a verb, a pronoun can be the *object of a preposition.* That is, pronouns can come after prepositions—words like *to, in, at, near, around.* (See page 185 on prepositions.) In the sentences that follow, the italicized pronouns function as objects of prepositions:

Janine put the chair next to *us.* (The preposition is *to.*)

The annoyed pitcher threw the ball at *me.* (The preposition is *at.*)

Raul always wants to be near *her.* (The preposition is *near.*)

Sometimes the preposition is not stated. Instead it is understood to be *to* or *for.* This often happens after the verbs *give, tell, buy, bring,* and *send.*

The instructor gave *him* the answer. (The instructor gave the answer *to him*.)

Mother sent *me* a rose for my birthday. (Mother sent a rose *to me* for my birthday.)

I bought *him* the book. (I bought the book *for him*.)

The particular pronoun used depends on whether the pronoun is functioning as a subject or object (either the object of a verb or the object of a preposition).

Possessive Pronoun   A pronoun can also be possessive; that is, it can show ownership, as in these sentences:

Diane lets *her* cat sleep in bed with *his* cat toys.

Wise investors never put all of *their* money in one stock.

The chart that follows shows you subject pronouns, object pronouns, and possessive pronouns.

	Subject Pronouns:	Object Pronouns:	Possessive Pronouns:
first person singular	I	me	my/mine
first person plural	we	us	our/ours
second person singular	you	you	your/yours
second person plural	you	you	your/yours
third person singular	he	him	his
	she	her	her/hers
	it	it	its
third person plural	they	them	their/theirs

USING *WHO* AND *WHOM* CORRECTLY

Deciding whether to use *who* or *whom* can be tricky. Just remember that *who* is a subject pronoun and *whom* is an object pronoun. Thus, use *who* for a subject of a sentence or clause and *whom* for the object of a verb or preposition.

subject of sentence: Who wants to eat dinner now?

subject of clause: Josef is the one who can help you.

object of verb: The person whom you need works in this office.

object of preposition: To whom should I mail the form?

PRACTICE 19.10

Above each underlined pronoun, write *S* if it is a subject pronoun, *O* if it is an object pronoun, or *P* if it is a possessive pronoun.

Danny is someone whom I could never trust. I lent him my car because his was in the shop, but little did I know that I would never see it again. Danny drove my little Cavalier to the gas station, but when he went inside to pay, he foolishly left the keys in the ignition and the door unlocked. As he was inside, a thief jumped in and drove off. Unfortunately, the guy was more than a car thief, for he used my car in an armed robbery an hour later. The police caught up with him, but a high-speed chase ensued, followed by a crash. My car ended up down a ravine. It has been two years since the incident, and the car still has not been returned to me. My father and I have tried to get it back, but the police told us that they need it for the upcoming trial. We can try again when the trial is over. The wheels of justice may turn slowly, but the wheels of my car are not turning at all.

PRACTICE 19.11

Fill in the blanks with a correct subject, object, or possessive pronoun. Write *S* if you have used a subject pronoun, *O* if you have used an object pronoun, or *P* if you have used a possessive pronoun. In the first and last sentences, choose *who* or *whom*.

Roy was a high school quarterback for _____ the future looked bright. As a sophomore, _____ broke the school passing records, and as a junior _____ led _____ team to a conference championship. Many college scouts were watching _____, and _____ were ready to offer _____ rather impressive scholarships. Unfortunately, an incident occurred in Roy's senior year. Two hefty players on an opposing team sacked Roy at the line of scrimmage. _____ tackled _____ so hard that _____ was knocked unconscious and rushed to the hospital. He had a concussion, but _____ came out of it just fine. However, when I went to see Roy in the hospital, he told _____ that he had no desire to play football again. When Roy got out of the hospital, _____ friends and coaches tried to change his mind, but _____ were unable to persuade _____ to go back to the game. Roy was just too afraid of getting hurt again. Roy went to college, but _____ had to give up his athletic scholarship. He does not seem to have any regrets, though. In fact, when I last spoke to _____, he told _____ he was sure he had done the right thing. _____ would have thought Roy could be happy without football?

Choosing Subject and Object Pronouns in Compounds

And or *or* can link a pronoun to a noun to form a **compound**.

Bob and *me*	the children and *us*
the boy and *I*	Gloria and *he*

Sometimes writers are unsure whether to use subject or object pronouns in compounds. They wonder whether to use "Bob and *me*" or "Bob and *I*," "Gloria and *he*" or "Gloria and *him*," and so forth.

If the pronoun is part of a compound that acts as a subject, use a subject pronoun. If the pronoun is part of a compound that acts as the object of a verb or the object of a preposition, use an object pronoun.

Bob and I bought season tickets to the Steelers' games. (The italicized compound is the subject of the sentence, so the subject pronoun is used.)

The car almost hit *Bob and me*. (The italicized compound is the object of the verb, so the object pronoun is used.)

The coach was angry with *Bob and me*. (The italicized compound is the object of the preposition *with*, so the object pronoun is used.)

Tip For Selecting Pronouns in Compounds

To decide if a subject or object pronoun is needed in a compound, you can cross out everything in the compound except the pronoun. Then decide if the remaining pronoun is a subject or an object.

~~The children and~~ I went to the movie.

~~The children and~~ me went to the movie.

When everything but the pronoun is crossed out in each compound, it is clear that the pronoun is part of the subject. Thus, the subject form *I* is needed:

The children and I went to the movies.

Here is another example:

Professor Hernandez explained to ~~Colleen, Louise, and~~ I that our project was well researched and informative.

Professor Hernandez explained to ~~Colleen, Louise, and~~ me that our project was well researched and informative.

With everything in the compound except the pronoun crossed out, it is easier to see that the pronoun is part of the object of the preposition *to*. Therefore an object pronoun is needed:

Professor Hernandez explained to Colleen, Louise, and me that our project was well researched and informative.

NOTE: When a noun and pronoun form a compound, place the pronoun at the end of the compound.

Avoid:	I and the teacher disagreed about the correct answer.
Use:	The teacher and I disagreed about the correct answer.
Avoid:	The boat belongs to me and Joyce.
Use:	The boat belongs to Joyce and me.

PRACTICE 19.12

Fill in each blank with the correct subject or object pronoun in parentheses. If you have trouble choosing, cross out everything in the compound except the pronoun and decide whether a subject or object pronoun is needed.

1. (I, me) The salesclerk gave Jim and _____ the wrong packages.

2. (we, us) The band was too loud for Dikla and _____ so we left.

3. (I, me) Sora and _____ searched the piles of sweaters for my size.

4. (we, us) The movers or _____ will pack the dishes in the kitchen.

5. (they, them) I gave you and _____ the directions to the farm that sells fresh produce.

6. (he, him) Dr. Amin wants Julia and _____ as lab assistants.

7. (she, her) To make money for college, Wanda and _____ worked all summer as table servers.

8. (I, me) Give the library books to Hans or _____ to return for you.

Choosing Subject and Object Pronouns Paired with Nouns

When a pronoun is paired with its noun antecedent, you can decide whether a subject or object pronoun is needed by crossing out the noun and deciding whether the remaining pronoun is a subject or object. For example, crossing out the nouns in the following sentences will help you choose the correct pronoun:

> We ~~nonsmokers~~ favor banning smoking in public places.

> Us ~~nonsmokers~~ favor banning smoking in public places.

With the nouns crossed out, it is easier to see that the pronoun acts as a subject, so the subject pronoun *we* is needed. This makes the first example the correct sentence. Now look at these sentences:

> Smokers are sometimes inconsiderate of we ~~nonsmokers~~.

> Smokers are sometimes inconsiderate of us ~~nonsmokers~~.

With the nouns crossed out, we can see that the pronoun is the object of the preposition *of,* so the second sentence is correct because it uses the object pronoun *us.*

PRACTICE 19.13

For each pair of sentences, cross out the paired noun and decide if a subject or object pronoun is needed. Then place a check mark next to the correct sentence. The first one is done as an example.

1. __✓__ We ~~students~~ believed that the tuition hike was unfortunate but necessary in light of increasing costs.

   _____ Us ~~students~~ believed that the tuition hike was unfortunate but necessary in light of increasing costs.

2. _____ Some of we golfers were unhappy with the condition of the course.

   _____ Some of us golfers were unhappy with the condition of the course.

3. _____ None of the legislators considered the impact of the tax increase on we, the middle-class property owners.

   _____ None of the legislators considered the impact of the tax increase on us, the middle-class property owners.

4. _____ Dr. Wren asked I, the only one who did not understand the problem, to put my answer on the board.

   _____ Dr. Wren asked me, the only one who did not understand the problem, to put my answer on the board.

5. _____ We new pledges must stick together if we are going to make it through the fraternity initiation.

   _____ Us new pledges must stick together if we are going to make it through the fraternity initiation.

6. _____ The club charter prevents we new members from holding office for a year.

   _____ The club charter prevents us new members from holding office for a year.

Choosing Subject and Object Pronouns in Comparisons

The words *than* and *as* can be used to show comparisons.

Marta is friendlier *than* Lorraine. (Marta's friendliness is being compared with Lorraine's friendliness.)

Larry is not as good at math *as* John. (Larry's math ability is being compared with John's math ability.)

Notice that when *than* or *as* is used to show comparison, words that could finish the comparison go unstated.

Marta is friendlier than Lorraine.

> *could be*

Marta is friendlier than Lorraine *is*.

Larry is not as good at math as John.

> *could be*

Larry is not as good at math as John *is*.

When a pronoun follows *than* or *as* in a comparison, decide whether to use a subject or object pronoun by adding the unstated words. Which sentence uses the correct pronoun?

Marcus is a better basketball player than *I*.

Marcus is a better basketball player than *me*.

To decide which pronoun is correct, add the unstated word or words:

Marcus is a better basketball player than I am.

Marcus is a better basketball player than me am.

With the unstated *am* added, you can see that the pronoun functions as the subject of the verb *am*. Since *I* is a subject pronoun, the first example is correct. Here is another example:

The news report disturbed Harriet as much as *I*.

The news report disturbed Harriet as much as *me*.

To decide on the correct pronoun, add the unstated words:

The news report disturbed Harriet as much as it disturbed *I*.

The news report disturbed Harriet as much as it disturbed *me*.

With the unstated words *it disturbed* added, you can see that the pronoun functions as the object of the verb *disturbed*. Since *me* is an object pronoun, the second example is correct.

Correct pronoun choice in comparisons is important because the pronoun can affect meaning. Here is an example:

Carol always liked Julio more than I.

Carol always liked Julio more than me.

The first sentence means that Carol liked Julio more than I liked Julio. The second sentence means that Carol liked Julio more than she liked me.

> **PRACTICE 19.14**
>
> Fill in the blank with the correct pronoun in parentheses. If you are unsure, mentally rewrite each sentence, supplying the unstated words.
>
> 1. (we, us) Carol and I were annoyed to discover that Ted and Janet had
>
>   better seats for the concert than _____.
>
> 2. (I, me) Making friends has always been easier for Eleni than _____.
>
> 3. (he, him) Studying together helps you as much as _____
>
> 4. (she, her) I believe in the power of positive thinking more than _____.
>
> 5. (we, us) On opening night, Francis was less nervous than _____.
>
> 6. (I, me) Since you do not care for classical music as much as _____, you should meet me after the concert for dinner.

PERSON SHIFT

When you write or speak about yourself, you use these pronouns: *I, we, my, mine, our, ours, me,* and *us.* They are called **first person pronouns**.

> *I* hated to leave, but *I* had to get *my* car home by 10:00. (The pronouns *I* and *my* are first person pronouns; they allow the writer or speaker to refer to himself or herself.)

When you write or speak directly to a person, you use these pronouns: *you, your,* and *yours.* They allow you to address directly the person you are writing or speaking to. These pronouns are **second person pronouns**.

> *You* should bring *your* dictionary to class on Thursday. (The pronouns *you* and *your* are second person pronouns; they allow the speaker or writer to refer to the person spoken to or written to.)

To write about people or things that do not include yourself or a person you are addressing, you use *he, she, it, they, his, hers, its, their, theirs, him, her,* and *them.* These are **third person pronouns**.

> *She* told *him* to pick *her* up at 7:00. (The pronouns *she, him,* and *her* are third person pronouns; they allow writers or speakers to refer to someone or something other than themselves or the person addressed.)

Here is a chart of first, second, and third person pronouns.

First Person Pronouns   (The speaker or the writer refers to himself or herself.)

I, we, me, us, my, mine, our, ours

Second Person Pronouns   (The speaker or writer refers to the person spoken to or written to.)

you, your, yours

Third Person Pronouns   (The speaker or writer refers to someone or something other than the speaker or writer or person addressed.)

he, she, it, they, his, her, hers, its, their, theirs, him, them

If you move unnecessarily from one person to another person within a sentence or longer passage, you create a problem called **person shift**:

I attend aerobics classes three times a week. The exercise helps *you* relax. (shift from the first person *I* to the second person *you*)

Here is the example rewritten to eliminate the person shift:

I attend aerobics classes three times a week. The exercise helps *me* relax. (Both *I* and *me* are first person pronouns.)

To avoid person shifts, remember that nouns are always third person, so pronouns that refer to nouns should also be third person.

person shift:	*Salesclerks* have a difficult job. *You* are on *your* feet all day dealing with the public. (shift from the third person *salesclerks* to the second person *you* and *your*)
shift eliminated:	*Salesclerks* have a difficult job. *They* are on *their* feet all day dealing with the public. (The third person pronouns *they* and *their* refer to the third person *salesclerks.*)

NOTE: The most frequent problems with person shift occur when writers shift from the first person or third person to the second person *you*. For this reason, be sure when using *you* that you are really addressing the reader and not shifting from a first or third person form.

PRACTICE 19.15

Rewrite the sentences to eliminate troublesome person shifts. The first one is done as an example.

1. Chemistry was not as hard as I thought it would be. You just had to keep up with the reading and ask questions when you did not understand.

   Chemistry was not as hard as I thought it would be. I just had to keep up with the reading and ask questions when I did not understand.

2. It was a mistake for me to try to teach my son to drive because you lose patience quickly when working with your own children.

   _____

   _____

3. Learning to use a computer was not difficult for me. You just had to study the user's manual and practice a bit.

   _____

   _____

4. I realize too much sun is not good for your skin, but every summer I neglect to use sunscreen.

   _____

   _____

5. Before high school seniors select a college, you should visit several campuses and speak to the admissions counselors.

   _____

   _____

6. Many doctors believe women should take calcium supplements. Doing this can help you guard against osteoporosis.

   _____

   _____

PRACTICE 19.16

Cross out pronouns that create troublesome person shifts and write the correction above the line.

Some people are saying that men are less willing to mentor women in the workplace because they fear charges of sexual harassment. However, male employees can still coach and support women to help them advance their careers. First, companies should have formal mentor programs. You should assign experienced employees to show newer employees the ropes. That way, no one will suspect that the mentoring is anything other than a professional work arrangement. Second, employers should draw up rules for people in the mentoring program. Then, you do not have to wonder if your behavior will be seen as inappropriate. You just follow the rules for mentoring and you will know that your behavior is acceptable. Finally, new employees should have more than one mentor when possible to avoid the suspicion that people are pairing up. If these guidelines were introduced into the workplace, both employees and employers would be comfortable with mentoring. You would not have to worry that charges of sexual harassment would be leveled.

Thinking, Learning, and Writing in College

Using Writing as a Study Aid

In all your courses, writing can help you study. Here is one strategy to try. After reading a chapter in a textbook, go back to the first heading, look away from the book, and write out everything you know that is relevant to that heading. Then reread the material, check for important points you omitted, and add them to your writing in a contrasting color. Now move on to the next heading and repeat this procedure. Do this for every heading. This procedure will help you learn and provide you with an excellent study sheet.

POST TEST

1. Fill in the blanks with the correct pronoun in parentheses.

A. (its, their) After days of discussion, the jury felt confident

_____ verdict was the correct one.

B. (his or her, their) The instructor told everyone to bring _____ dictionary to class each day for the next two weeks.

C. (her, their) Several of the mothers agreed that _____ preschool children would benefit from a play group.

D. (its, their) Some of the essay strays from _____ topic.

E. (its, their) When he was through playing, Tommy put his bag of mar-

bles on _____ shelf.

F. (her, their) Each of the kindergarten girls brought _____ favorite toy for sharing day.

G. (I, me) Between you and _____, I am sure that Janet is plan-ning to break up with Phil.

H. (he, him) Carla and _____ are sure to take first prize in the sci-ence fair, just as they did last year and the year before that.

I. (I, me) Even though Eduardo is stronger than _____ , he rarely pins me in a wrestling match.

J. (we, us) Some of _____ fans felt the official's call was incorrect.

K. (we, us) _____ students should insist that the administration explain why tuition was raised 20 percent.

L. (we, you) Last weekend I went camping with three of my friends.

However, it was not very relaxing because _____ had to work too hard setting up and maintaining the camp.

M. (who, whom) For _____ did Antonio buy the book?

N. (who, whom) I cannot recall _____ is bringing the extra chairs for the party.

2. Cross out each incorrect pronoun, and write in the correction.

Most volunteer youth coaches find it a rewarding experience because you can make an important contribution to the lives of young people. To make coaching a positive experience, coaches must remember several points. First, successful coaches' priorities should be fun and learning—they should not emphasize winning above all. You should remember that the players are kids first and athletes second. Coaches should know the players and respect their limits. For example, ten-year-olds should not be asked to lift weights. This could harm young bodies. They say that successful coaches allow for a wide range of abilities and resist the temptation to field only the best players. Most important of all, however, is making sure that the kids feel they are a valued part of a team.

Visit the Clouse Website!

For additional exercises, quizzes, and Internet activities, visit our Website at:

http://www.ablongman.com/clouse

For even more activities, visit the Longman English pages at:

http://www.ablongman.com/englishpages

Chapter 20

Modifiers

A word or word group that describes another word or word group is a **modifier**. In the following sentences, the modifiers are italicized. An arrow is drawn from the modifier to the word it describes.

The *cloudy* sky threatened rain.

The pitcher threw a *sinker* ball.

The *marathon* runner was breathing *heavily*.

In this chapter, you will learn a great deal about modifiers, including:

1. when to use adjectives and when to use adverbs
2. when to use *good* and when to use *well*
3. how to use comparative and superlative forms
4. how to avoid dangling modifiers
5. how to avoid misplaced modifiers

PRETEST

If the underlined modifier is used correctly, write *yes* on the blank. If the underlined modifier is not used correctly, write *no* on the blank. Do not guess; if you are unsure, do not write anything. You can check your answers in Appendix III.

1. _____ Whistling <u>soft</u>, Chuyen worked in the kitchen.
2. _____ Professor Smith <u>quickly</u> explained the directions before he passed out the exam questions.

3. _____ The splinter in Fluffy's paw caused her to limp <u>bad</u>.

4. _____ The <u>frustrated</u> toddler pounded her fists against the floor and screamed in rage.

5. _____ Les is <u>more happier</u> now that he has changed his major to physical therapy.

6. _____ Diana plays the cello <u>good</u>.

7. _____ Ivan felt his history midterm was the <u>easiest</u> test he had taken this semester.

8. _____ <u>Whistling as he walked down the street</u>, Tom's mood could not have been better.

9. _____ <u>Wondering which route to take</u>, Katrina pulled to the side of the road and studied the map.

10. _____ The second day I had the flu, I felt <u>worser</u> than I did the day before.

ADJECTIVES AND ADVERBS

Words or word groups that describe nouns and pronouns are **adjectives**. In the following sentences, the adjectives are italicized and an arrow is drawn from the adjective to the word it describes:

Janet spilled *hot* coffee.   (*Hot* describes the noun *coffee*.)

Michael is *shy*.   (*Shy* describes the noun *Michael*.)

She seems *angry*.   (*Angry* describes the pronoun *she*.)

Adverbs are words or word groups that describe verbs, adjectives, or other adverbs. Adverbs often tell *how, when,* or *where*. Here are some examples:

The lecturer spoke *briefly*. (*Briefly* describes the verb *spoke;* it tells *how* the lecturer spoke.)

The lecturer spoke *very* briefly. (*Very* describes the adverb *briefly;* it tells *how* briefly.)

I just finished an *extremely* difficult job. (*Extremely* describes the adjective *difficult;* it tells *how* difficult.)

I just finished an extremely difficult job *yesterday*. (*Yesterday* describes the verb *finished;* it tells *when* the job was finished.)

The car stalled *in my driveway*. (*In my driveway* describes the verb *stalled;* it tells *where* the car stalled.)

PRACTICE 20.1

Draw an arrow from each bracketed modifier to the word described. Above each bracketed modifier, write *adj* if the modifier is an adjective (if it describes a noun or pronoun) or *adv* if the modifier is an adverb (if it describes a verb, adjective, or adverb). The first one is done as an example.

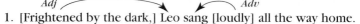

1. [Frightened by the dark,] Leo sang [loudly] all the way home.

2. The [experimental] therapy relieved Jan's [painful] symptoms [in twenty-four hours.]

3. [Briefly] the waiter explained the specials [of the day], and then he turned and walked away [quickly].

4. The [silver] tinsel sparkled [brightly] in the [colorful] lights of the Christmas tree.

5. The [elderly] man spoke [fondly] of his [childhood] days on a farm [in Indiana].

6. The [high] [academic] standards of the university are [well] known throughout the country.

-ly Adverbs

Many adjectives can be made into adverbs by adding an *-ly* ending. Here are some examples:

Adjective	Adverb
glad	gladly
painful	painfully
quick	quickly
loud	loudly
quiet	quietly

The *painful* tooth kept me awake all night. (*Painful* is an adjective describing the noun *tooth*.)

The dog limped *painfully* into the garage. (*Painfully* is an adverb describing the verb *limped*.)

NOTE: Be careful to use the adverb form when the modifier describes a verb, adjective, or adverb.

No: Marvin ran quick into the house.

Yes: Marvin ran *quickly* into the house. (The adverb form
is needed because the modifier is describing a verb.)

PRACTICE 20.2

Circle the correct form in each set of parentheses. Then draw an arrow
to the word described.

Egyptian tombs were not always as grand as the pyramids. The first Egyptians were buried (shallow/shallowly) under a pile of rocks in desert pits. The bodies were wrapped (tight/tightly) in goatskin or reed mats, and the desert's hot sand preserved them rather (adequate/adequately). Personal goods were placed (close/closely) around the body. Then around 3000 B.C., kings and officials began to build large, flat-topped tombs made of sunbaked mud and bricks, which provided protection against the (harmful/harmfully) effects of nature. Each of these tombs had a (vast/vastly) burial chamber and (large/largely) rooms filled with goods. Around 2700 B.C. came the invention of stone architecture and the first pyramid, called the Step Pyramid. The tomb of King Djoser lies buried under the structure. Like later pyramids it had two purposes. It was both a royal tomb and a temple for worshipping the dead king. The pyramids of Egypt are a (massive/massively) reminder of the pharaohs' power and a creative ancient civilization.

PRACTICE 20.3

On a separate sheet, use each adjective and adverb in its own sentence.
Draw an arrow from the adjective or adverb to the word it describes.

1. easy

2. easily

3. comfortable

4. comfortably

5. fearful

6. fearfully

Good/Well

Good and *well* sometimes give people trouble. Just remember that *good* is an adjective, so it describes nouns and pronouns. *Well*—except when it means "healthy"—is an adverb, so it describes verbs, adjectives, and other adverbs.

It saddens me that Felipe is moving because he is a *good* friend. (*Good* is an adjective describing the noun *friend.*)

Two weeks after my surgery, I felt *well* again. (Here, *well* means "healthy" and is an adjective describing the pronoun *I.*)

For a beginner, you skate very *well*. (*Well* is an adverb describing the verb *skate.*)

Be careful not to use *good* as an adverb.

Incorrect:	Marla did good on her test.
Correct:	Marla did well on her test. (*Well* is an adverb describing the verb *did.*)

> NOTE: *Good* is used as an adjective after verbs like *feel* and *taste:*
>
> I feel good today. (Here, *good* suggests "in good spirits" and describes the pronoun *I.*)
>
> The food tastes good. (*Good* describes the noun *food;* no action is being described.)
>
> The cool breeze feels good. (Again, no action is described; *good* describes *breeze.*)

PRACTICE 20.4

Fill in each blank with *good* or *well*, whichever is correct.

1. The children's production of Hansel and Gretel was _____ staged,

   and the sets were particularly _____.

2. The horse I bet on ran _____ until the home stretch, and then

   she did not do very _____ .

3. Although I have been taking my allergy medicine, I still do not feel

   _____ .

4. Nao plays the clarinet _____ enough to have his first recital, even
   though he has had only a dozen lessons.

5. With her red hair, Marsha looks _____ in green.

Comparative and Superlative Forms

Adjectives and adverbs can be used to show how two or more things compare to each other. Here are some examples:

Katherine is *thinner* than Mario. (The adjective *thinner* compares how thin Katherine and Mario are.)

The audience is cheering *more loudly* now. (The adverb *more loudly* compares how loudly the audience is cheering now with how loudly it cheered at some point in the past.)

Lee is the *tallest* member of the basketball team. (The adjective *tallest* compares Lee's height with the height of the other team members.)

The **comparative** form of an adjective or adverb compares two things. The **superlative** compares more than two things. The comparative form of adjectives and adverbs is usually made by adding *-er* or using the word *more* before the modifier. The superlative form is usually made by adding *-est* or using the word *most* before the modifier.

Modifier	Comparative (compares two things)	Superlative (compares more than two things)
loud	louder	loudest
heavy	heavier	heaviest
young	younger	youngest
annoyed	more annoyed	most annoyed
beautiful	more beautiful	most beautiful
intelligent	more intelligent	most intelligent

continued

modifier:	Joy and Ned bought a *large* house. (no comparison here)
comparative:	Joy and Ned bought a *larger* house than Kay and Tom. (two houses are compared)
superlative:	Joy and Ned bought the *largest* of the three houses they looked at. (more than two houses are compared)
modifier:	Etty told a *ridiculous* story. (no comparison here)
comparative:	Etty told a *more ridiculous* story than Carl did. (two stories are compared)
superlative:	Etty told the *most ridiculous* story I have ever heard. (more than two stories are compared)

Keep the following guidelines in mind when you form the comparative and superlative forms of modifiers:

1. With one-syllable modifiers, *-er* and *-est* are usually used.

sad	sadder	saddest
loud	louder	loudest
near	nearer	nearest

2. With three-syllable words, use *more* and *most*.

usual	more usual	most usual
rapidly	more rapidly	most rapidly
important	more important	most important

3. With adverbs of two or more syllables, use *more* and *most*.

quickly	more quickly	most quickly
clearly	more clearly	most clearly
freely	more freely	most freely

4. With two-syllable adjectives ending in *-y*, change the *y* to *i* and add *-er* and *-est*.

happy	happier	happiest
angry	angrier	angriest
easy	easier	easiest

5. Some two-syllable adjectives that do not end in *-y* use *-er* and *-est*, and some use *more* and *most*. Many of these you know; the others you will learn with experience.

foolish	more foolish	most foolish
careful	more careful	most careful
quiet	quieter	quietest

6. The following comparative and superlative forms are irregular. Memorize them or check this chart each time you use them.

good	better	best
well	better	best
bad	worse	worst
badly	worse	worst
many	more	most
much	more	most
some	more	most
little	less	least

7. Never use an *-er* form with *more* or an *-est* form with *most*.

Incorrect:	Maria is *more happier* now that she quit her job.
Correct:	Maria is *happier* now that she quit her job.
Incorrect:	Lionel is the *most foolhardiest* child I know.
Correct:	Lionel is the *most foolhardy* child I know.

Thinking, Learning, and Writing in College — **Studying Graphs, Charts and Tables**

You may be tempted to ignore graphs, charts, and tables in your textbooks, but don't. By offering a visual depiction of important points, they can help you learn if you

- Note how data is organized.
- Check the headings on columns.
- Check designations for horizontal and vertical areas of graphs.
- Consider the relationships among facts and look for trends and patterns.

In addition, charts, tables, and graphs—like comparative and superlative forms of modifiers—can show comparisons, such as the fact that more women than men have undiagnosed heart ailments.

PRACTICE 20.5

The base form of a modifier appears in parentheses. Fill in the blank with the correct comparative or superlative form of the modifier (whichever is called for).

1. (young) My sister is two years _____ than I.

2. (loud) When I banged on the wall to request quiet, the person in the

   next apartment turned the radio up _____.

3. (quickly) Of all the runners in the race, Dana is expected to run the

   _____.

4. (talented) Of the two actors auditioning for the role, Stavros is the

   _____.

5. (easy) John drew Henry a map showing an _____ way to get to the lake than taking Route 11.

6. (bad) Christmas is the _____ holiday for those who have no friends or family.

PRACTICE 20.6

The base form of a modifier appears in parentheses. Fill in the blank with the correct comparative or superlative form. If you are unsure of the correct form, check the list of irregular forms on p. 385.

1. (good) I like studying in the library _____ than studying in my room.

2. (bad) Of all the movies playing in town this week, you selected the

   _____ one to see.

3. (well) Since I began to exercise regularly, I feel _____ than I ever did before.

4. (some) _____ of us are going to our twenty-year reunion than went to the ten-year reunion.

5. (good) The score Jamie got on his third algebra quiz was

   the _____ one he has earned this term.

6. (bad) Lying to a friend is bad; refusing to admit the lie is _____.

Dangling Modifiers

If you use a modifier without providing a word for it to describe, you have written a **dangling modifier**. Dangling modifiers are a problem because they create silly or confusing sentences like this:

Standing at the street corner, a car splashed mud all over my new coat. (There is no word for *standing at the street corner* to describe. Therefore, it seems that the *car* was standing at the street corner.)

Standing at the street corner is a dangling modifier because it has no stated word to describe. Here is another example:

Tired after a hard day of classes, sleep was needed. (With no word for *tired after a hard day* to describe, it seems that *sleep* was tired.)

Dangling modifiers can be eliminated two ways. First, you can supply a word for the modifier to describe just after the modifier.

dangling modifier:	Feeling depressed, an evening with friends was needed. (Was the evening depressed?)
correction:	Feeling depressed, Colleen needed an evening with friends. (Now *feeling depressed* has a word to describe—*Colleen.*)
dangling modifier:	Unsure of which choice to make, an academic advisor was needed. (Was the advisor unsure of which choice to make?)
correction:	Unsure of which choice to make, I needed an academic advisor. (Now *unsure of which choice to make* has a word to describe—*I.*)

A second way to eliminate a dangling modifier is to change the modifier to a subordinate clause. (Subordinate clauses are discussed on p. 192.)

dangling modifier:	Walking across the street, a truck turned the corner and narrowly missed me. (Was the truck walking across the street?)
correction:	While I was walking across the street, a truck turned the corner and narrowly missed me. (The opening modifier is rewritten as a subordinate clause.)
dangling modifier:	When entering the bar, an ID must be shown. (Does the ID enter the bar?)

| correction: | When a person enters the bar, an ID must be shown. (The opening modifier is rewritten as a subordinate clause.) |

Tip For Finding Dangling Modifiers

When you edit, check sentences opening with an *-ing* or *-ed* form. Be sure these forms are closely followed by words they can logically describe.

PRACTICE 20.7

On a separate sheet, rewrite each sentence to eliminate the dangling modifier.

1. Tired after a full day of yard work, a nap was what I needed.
2. Feeling the chill in the air, a roaring fire in the fireplace sounded perfect.
3. Before beginning to make the Mississippi mud cake, all the ingredients were assembled on the kitchen counter.
4. Frightened by the menacing dog, my knees began to shake.
5. Unsure of the best course of action, the decision was difficult.
6. Making no errors in the field and batting the best they have all season, the game was easily won by the Meadville Tigers.

Misplaced Modifiers

A modifier placed too far away from the word it describes is a **misplaced modifier**. Misplaced modifiers are a problem because they create confusing or silly sentences.

| misplaced modifier: | Andrea bought a silk dress at a thrift shop with a broken zipper. (Did the thrift shop have a broken zipper? It seems so because *with a broken zipper* is too far from *dress*, the word the modifier is meant to describe.) |
| misplaced modifier: | The litterbug threw a plastic wrapper out of the car window driving down Route 11. (Was the car window driving down Route 11? It seems so because *driving down Route 11* is too far from *litterbug*, the word the modifier is meant to describe.) |

To eliminate a misplaced modifier, move the modifier as close as possible to the word it describes:

Andrea bought a silk dress with a broken zipper at a thrift shop. (*With a broken zipper* is now next to *dress,* the word the modifier describes.)

Driving down Route 11, the litterbug threw a plastic wrapper out of the car window. (*Driving down Route 11* is now next to *litterbug,* the word the modifier describes.)

PRACTICE 20.8

Rewrite the sentences to eliminate the misplaced modifiers.

1. The children stuck in the hospital for Halloween got candy from the visiting clown that was chocolate.

_____

_____

2. Carlo asked Henry to help him fix his flat tire in the restaurant.

_____

_____

3. At a garage sale, I bought a lovely end table for my apartment with drawers.

_____

_____

4. Gregory gave an electronic keyboard to his brother with a memory and playback functions.

_____

_____

5. For the New Year's Eve celebration, Jorge borrowed noise makers from his roommate with colored streamers.

_____

_____

POST TEST

Eliminate the errors with modifiers by crossing out and writing above the line.

Johnny Heisman, for whom the Heisman Trophy is named, was one of football's inventivest coaches. One of his most odd inventions was the hidden-ball trick. Once a player asked him if it was illegal to hide a ball during a play in 1895. Heisman knew it was not against the rules, and he wondered how it could be done. Thinking the ball could be hidden under a running back's jersey, a play was devised by Heisman and two of his players. As the ball was snapped to "Tick" Tichenor, the rest of the team would drop back and form a circle around him. Then Tichenor would drop to one knee and slip the ball quick under his jersey. The team would run to the right, and the defenders would follow them. Then Tichenor would get up quick and run the other way. Trying the trick against Vanderbilt, a touchdown was scored. More tighter uniforms and more faster play have made the hidden-ball trick more hard to perform. The bizarre play is rarely used today.

Visit the Clouse Website!
For additional exercises, quizzes, and Internet activities, visit our Website at:
http://www.ablongman.com/clouse
For even more activities, visit the Longman English pages at:
http://www.ablongman.com/englishpages

Chapter 21

Capitalization and Punctuation

Until you have mastered them, check these pages to be sure you are applying the rules for

1. capital letters
2. periods, question marks, and exclamation points
3. commas
4. semicolons
5. colons
6. parentheses
7. dashes
8. apostrophes
9. quotation marks

◆ ◆ ◆

CAPITALIZATION

Most often, capital letters are used to identify something specific. The capital letters in *Fifth Avenue* signal that Fifth Avenue is a specific street; the capital letters in *General Motors* signal that General Motors is a specific car manufacturer.

PRETEST

If all the necessary capital letters appear, write *yes* on the blank; if one or more capitals are missing, write *no*. Do not guess; if you are unsure, do not write anything. Check your answers in Appendix III.

1. _____ My dog, Laddie, ran away last week, but he was seen near lake jewel.

2. _____ My favorite holiday is memorial day because it signals the start of summer.

3. _____ This semester my favorite class is psychology, although I am also enjoying Western Civilization 303.

4. _____ Ever since I was a child, I have eaten Kellogg's Rice Krispies for breakfast along with Minute Maid orange juice.

5. _____ Last summer, I was sure the Cleveland indians would be in the pennant race.

6. _____ After Brian graduated with his degree in spanish, he went to Central America to work with the poor.

7. _____ I asked dad to lend me five hundred dollars so I could take the trip to Lake Michigan.

8. _____ Thomas Jefferson died fifty years after the signing of the declaration of independence.

9. _____ Sophia bought her Pontiac after her Buick was stolen near the South Avenue interchange.

10. _____ At the student gallery, there is a new exhibition of african art that will be on display until January.

Using Capital Letters

1. Capitalize the first word of a sentence.

> The door slammed shut on Henry's finger.

2. Capitalize the first word of a direct quotation.

> Doreen explained, "You must get an advisor's signature before you can register for this course."

> *but*

> "You must get an advisor's signature," Doreen explained, "before you can register for this course." (Do not capitalize *before* because it does not begin a sentence that is a direct quotation.)

3. Capitalize the names of people and animals.

Lucy	Fido	Madonna
Douglas	Rover	Bill Clinton

> *but*

Do not capitalize words such as *man, boy, girl, woman, cat, rock star, collie,* and *child.*

> Mohan bought a sheepdog he named Hairy.

4. Always capitalize I.

> Curt and I felt I had a good chance of winning the competition.

5. Capitalize titles before people's names.

Mayor Morales	Judge Fulks	Senator Glenn
Reverend Jones	Rabbi Mendel	Captain McKenna

Professor O'Brien	Uncle Raymond	President Clinton

but

Do not capitalize titles used without the names.

a mayor	the judge	a senator
a reverend	a rabbi	the captain
a professor	my uncle	a president

The instructor, Professor Chang, introduced the guest lecturer, Councilman Luntz, who used to be a senator.

6. Capitalize months, days of the week, and holidays.

January	Tuesday	Easter
May	Saturday	Labor Day

The first Monday in September is Labor Day.

7. Capitalize specific geographic locations, including specific cities, states, countries, bodies of water, roads, and mountains.

Georgia	Columbus, Ohio	Lake Erie
Route 86	Stark County	Atlantic Ocean
Mt. Rushmore	Grand Canyon	France
Colorado River	Northwest Territory	Pike's Peak

but

Do not capitalize general geographic locations.

state	city	the country
a lake	the mountain	north of town
the ocean	a river	my county

We left the city at ten and headed west; by late afternoon, we had arrived in St. Louis to see the Mississippi River.

8. Capitalize the names of nationalities, religions, languages, and the adjective forms of these words.

English	Judaism	Spanish
Catholic	Thai food	Chinese
African dance	French restaurant	Latin American music

This town has excellent Japanese restaurants and art galleries with extensive European collections.

9. Capitalize names of organizations, companies, colleges, and buildings.

Fraternal Order of Police	General Foods
Democratic Party	Yale University
Empire State Building	American Cancer Society

but

organization   university

political party   building

When I was in New York for the Modern Language Association conference, I stayed near the World Trade Center.

10. Capitalize historic events and documents.

Gettysburg Address	the Roaring '20s
the Reformation	Battle of the Bulge
the Declaration of Independence	the Korean War
World War I	the Constitution

The television show *MASH* was set in the Korean War, but it was first shown during the Vietnam War.

11. Capitalize the names of sacred books, and words referring to God. Also capitalize pronouns that refer to God.

the Lord	the Talmud	the Scriptures
the Trinity	the Koran	Jehovah
the Old Testament	the Torah	the Bible

The man prayed to the Almighty for His help.

12. Capitalize the names of specific course titles, but not the general names of courses unless they are languages.

History 101	French	Survey of English Literature
Chemistry 709	Italian	Business Management II

but

sociology	accounting	mathematics

My geography course was not as difficult as I expected it to be, but Child Psychology 303 and German were very hard.

13. Capitalize the brand names of products but not the general names of product types.

Aim toothpaste	Jell-O	Tretorn sneakers
Marlboro	Chevrolet	London Fog

but

toothpaste	gelatin	tennis shoes
cigarettes	car	raincoat

At the grocery store, I remembered to get the Roman Meal bread, but I forgot the ice cream and Hershey's syrup.

14. Always capitalize the first and last word of a title. In between, capitalize everything except articles (*a*, *an*, and *the*), conjunctions (words like *and*,

but, or, for, so, if, as), and prepositions (words like *of, at, in, near, by*). If the title has a colon, capitalize the first word after the colon.

> *Gone with the Wind*   *Star Trek II: The Wrath of Khan*
>
> "A Modest Proposal"   *Around the World in Eighty Days*
>
> *A Farewell to Arms*   "Politics and the English Language"
>
> In English class we read *Tender Is the Night.*

15. Capitalize words that show family relationships if names can be substituted for these words.

> Ask Mother what she wants for her birthday. (We can say, *Ask Lucille what she wants for her birthday.*)
>
> During World War II, Grandpa was a medic. (We can say, *During World War II, Charles was a medic.*)
>
> but
>
> Ask my mother what she wants for her birthday. (We do not say *Ask my Lucille what she wants for her birthday.*)
>
> During World War II, my grandpa was a medic. (We do not say *During World War II, my Charles was a medic.*)

PRACTICE 21.1

Fill in the blanks according to the directions given in parentheses. The first one is done as an example.

1. (Use a street.) For most of my life, I lived on _____ *Elm Avenue* _____ .

2. (Use the title of a television show or movie; underline the title to indicate italics.) If you are interested in good entertainment, be sure

   to see _____ .

3. (Use the title of a book; underline the title.)

   In literature class, I read _____ .

4. (Use the specific title of a course.)

   Besides composition, this term I am taking_____ .

5. (Use the general name of a course other than a language.)

   So far in college, my favorite course has been _____ .

6. (Use a holiday.)

   The holiday that I enjoy the least is _____ .

7. (Use a date.)

My birthday is_____.

8. (Use the brand names of three specific products and use the general name of one other product.)

At the grocery store, I spent twenty dollars on _____

_____.

9. (Use a specific geographic location.)

This summer, I would very much like to see _____

_____.

10. (Use a specific historic period or event.)

In history, I enjoyed studying about_____.

11. (Use a congressperson's title and last name.)
When I learned that the legislature was considering raising the

speed limit, I wrote a letter of protest to_____.

12. (Use mother or father as a substitute for a name.)

As I was growing up, _____ taught me to take responsibility for my actions.

13. (Use mother or father.)

As I was growing up, my _____ taught me to take responsibility for my actions.

PUNCTUATION

By signaling complete stops, pauses, possession, conversation, and such, punctuation helps writers express meaning. In the next pages, you will learn rules for using a number of punctuation marks.

Ending Sentences

To end a sentence, writers can use a period (.), question mark (?), or exclamation point (!). These marks signal a full stop at the end of one sentence to let the reader know there is a complete break between ideas in that sentence and the ideas in the following sentence.

PRETEST

Add a period, question mark, or exclamation point, whichever is most appropriate. Check your answers in Appendix III.

1. My advisor asked me when I planned to graduate

2. The hysterical child screamed, "My dog has been hit by a car " (Put the punctuation inside the quotation mark.)

3. I wondered why Janie never introduced me to her family

4. How many eggs do you add to the cake batter

5. My parents wanted to know when I would get a part-time job to help with college expenses

6. Close the door before the cat gets out

7. Is there any way I can help you finish your project on time

8. Call 911; the kitchen is on fire

9. If you ask me, Paolo should major in psychology because he understands people so well

10. Which of your cousins will be at the reunion

The Period, Question Mark, and Exclamation Point

The period (.), question mark (?), and exclamation point (!) are all used to end sentences.

Period   Use a period to end a sentence that makes a statement, makes a request, or issues an order.

> Because of the heavy rains, the lowlands are flooded. (a statement)
>
> Bring me the evening paper, please. (a request)
>
> Leave me alone so I can study. (an order)

Question Mark   Use a question mark to end a sentence that asks a direct question.

> Will you lend me your history notes?
>
> Is this seat taken?
> How can I help you if you refuse my advice?

NOTE: Use a period—not a question mark—to end a sentence with an indirect question. An **indirect question** is a statement, even though it notes that someone asked a question.

indirect question:	I wonder where I will be in ten years.
direct question:	Where will I be in ten years?
indirect question:	The waiter asked whether we wanted dessert.
direct question:	The waiter asked, "Do you want dessert?"

continued

> indirect question: Kevin wanted to know whether he could borrow my car.
>
> direct question: May I borrow your car?

Exclamation Point   Use an exclamation point after a statement or command that shows strong feeling or surprise.

Get out of the car before the engine catches on fire! (a command with strong feeling)

I will get even with you if it is the last thing I do! (a statement with strong feeling)

I couldn't believe I earned the highest grade ever scored on the exam! (a statement with surprise)

NOTES: 1. Be careful not to overuse exclamation points. If you must use them often, your words are not conveying the message.

2. Do not use an exclamation point with a period or question mark.

no:	Are you sure you want to go?!
yes:	Are you sure you want to go?
no:	I am amazed at her nerve.!
yes:	I am amazed at her nerve.
yes:	I am amazed at her nerve!

3. Do not use more than one exclamation point at a time.

no:	I hate you!!
yes:	I hate you!

PRACTICE 21.2

On a separate sheet, write sentences according to the directions given, ending each sentence with a period, question mark, or exclamation point—whichever is appropriate.

1. Write a sentence you might hear spoken on campus; be sure the sentence makes a statement.

2. Write a direct question you might ask a waiter in a restaurant.

3. Write a sentence that asks an indirect question. Begin the sentence with "Shelly asked whether."

4. Write a sentence that expresses great anger or fear.

5. Write a sentence that expresses a request a parent might make of a child.

6. Write a sentence that expresses a command a fire chief might give to firefighters; the command should express strong emotion.

Using Commas

Some writers place commas wherever they would pause or draw a breath in speech. However, this is not a reliable way to determine when commas are needed. If you are not sure how to use commas, promise yourself to learn the rules now.

PRETEST

If commas are used correctly, write *yes* in the blank; if they are used incorrectly, write *no*. Do not guess, if you are unsure, do not write anything. Check your answers in Appendix III.

1. _____ After storming onto the floor and arguing with the referee Coach Bennett was given a technical foul.

2. _____ The withered, ivy plant could not be saved, so I tossed it in the trash.

3. _____ I left for Nashville, Tennessee, on August 22, 1983.

4. _____ Uncertain yet eager, Josh began his first day as a camp counselor.

5. _____ When we have children of our own we come to understand how our own parents worried, sacrificed, and planned to ensure our own futures.

6. _____ Without telling the children where they were going, we picked them up at school, put them in the car, and headed for Virginia Beach Virginia.

7. _____ Rosa was well prepared for the test and feeling confident, so she was sure she did well.

8. _____ Suddenly, and unexpectedly, the string snapped, and the kite was carried off.

9. _____ George in my opinion is trustworthy, and he is certainly a hard worker.

10. _____ Because the spring was unusually dry the crop yield was low, and produce prices rose.

11. _____ Dikla, I need you to help me unload the car.

12. _____ In the heat of the afternoon, Louise fell asleep in the sun, and got a bad burn.

Commas with Dates

With dates, use a comma to separate the day and the year.

I expect to graduate June 14, 2004.

On June 14, 2004, I will graduate.

You may use either form, but be consistent; do not mix the two forms.

> NOTE: One form of writing dates does not use commas. Do not use commas if the day precedes the month and year.
>
> I expect to graduate 14 June 2002.

If no day is given, there is no comma between the month and the year.

Julia began working for the United Parcel Service in January 1998.

Do not use a comma between the month and the day.

no:	My birthday is May, 4, 1949.
yes:	My birthday is May 4, 1949.

Commas with Places and Addresses

Use commas to separate the names of cities and states.

When they retired, my parents moved to Naples, Florida.

or

My parents moved to Naples, Florida, when they retired.

Place a comma between the street address and the city. There is no comma before the zip code.

Garth's Flower Shop is located at 311 West Palm Lane, Warren, Ohio 44484.

PRACTICE 21.3

On a separate sheet, write sentences as directed.

1. Write a sentence that begins with *I live at*. Include your complete street address, city, state, and zip code.

2. Write a sentence that gives the city and state of a place you want to visit. Begin the sentence with *I would like to visit*.

3. Write a sentence that gives the month and year you began college. Begin the sentence with *I began college*.

4. Write a sentence that gives your complete date of birth. Begin the sentence with *I was born*.

Commas with Words, Phrases, and Clauses in a Series   A **series** is three or more words, phrases, or clauses. (See p. 185 and p. 225 on phrases; see

p. 191 on clauses.) All but the last item in a series should be followed by a comma.

> When I arrived at my hotel, I realized I had forgotten my *shampoo, brush, and pajamas.* (words in a series)

> Since beginning my exercise program, I have *lost weight, toned my muscles, and increased my flexibility.* (phrases in series)

> If you want to help me, *you can take these books back to the library, you can pick up my dry cleaning, and you can wash the car.* (clauses in a series)

NOTE: When all the items in a series are separated by *and* or *or,* no comma is used.

> The dessert cart held fancy *pies and cakes and tortes.*

> Place the plant *in the kitchen window or on the television or on the coffee table.*

PRACTICE 21.4

Use each series or pair in a sentence, being careful to use commas correctly. The first one is done as an example.

1. the spaghetti   the veal   and the broiled chicken

   The waiter explained that the specials of the day were the

   spaghetti, the veal, and the broiled chicken.

2. the hardback   or the paperback

   _____

   _____

3. the noise   the pollution   and the crowds

   _____

   _____

4. a fever   a sore throat   a stuffy nose   and body aches

   _____

   _____

5. the food was overpriced   the service was slow   and the seating was uncomfortable

_____

_____

6. a relaxing bath   or an invigorating shower

_____

_____

7. swept the downstairs   and washed the clothes   and cleaned the garage

_____

_____

8. on the shelf   in the car   or in my room

_____

_____

Commas with Coordination   **Coordination** means that two word groups that can stand alone as sentences (**main clauses**) are joined by *and, but, or, for, so,* or *yet* (**coordinating conjunctions**). Coordination is explained more fully on p. 194.

Place a comma before a coordinating conjunction (*and, but, or, for, so,* or *yet*) that joins two main clauses.

I would ask you to join me, but I know that you are busy.

Jillian gently picked up the baby chick, and she stroked it lovingly.

Our current basketball coach will probably be fired, for he has won only a fourth of his games the past two years.

The corporate offices of Raphael Industries will move to our town, so we can expect a decrease in our unemployment rate.

Do not place a comma every time you use a coordinating conjunction. Many times these conjunctions do not connect main clauses. When they do not, no comma is used.

The Corvette raced down the street and sped around the corner. (No comma is used because *and* does not join two main clauses, only two verb phrases.)

Remember that main clauses cannot be joined by a comma alone—the comma must be used with the coordinating conjunction, or you will have written a comma splice. (See p. 255.)

(See p. 255.)

PRACTICE 21.5

Circle every coordinating conjunction. When the conjunction joins main clauses, add a comma before it.

You will never find the pot of gold at the end of the rainbow for rainbows do not end. They are actually circles and the arc of color you see is just a small part of the rainbow. In order for a rainbow to form, sunshine and air loaded with water are needed. The sunlight looks white but white light really is made up of all colors. The water in the air bends the light and separates it into the colors so you see a rainbow. How much of the rainbow you see depends on where the sun is in the sky. When the sun is high, most of the rainbow is below the horizon yet when the sun is lower, more of the rainbow is visible. When the sun is near the horizon, an observer on a high mountain or in an airplane may be lucky enough to see the whole rainbow circle. Occasionally, the light of the moon forms a rainbow. However, the moon's light is faint so the lunar rainbow's colors are faint and difficult to see.

Commas with Introductory Words, Phrases, and Clauses.

Use a comma after introductory words (words that come before the subject of the sentence).

Carefully, the child placed the precious china doll on the shelf.

Whistling, Kobina sanded the cupboard doors.

Exhausted and discouraged, I could not finish the marathon.

Disappointed but hopeful, Sue vowed to do better next time.

Use a comma after an introductory phrase (a phrase that comes before the subject of the sentence).

Playing both offense and defense, Mario was the most valuable member of the football team.

In the middle of the night, the smoke alarm went off and roused all of us from our beds.

After borrowing ten thousand dollars from private investors, Alma opened her own children's clothing store.

> NOTE: You may omit the comma after a short introductory phrase of two words.
>
> By morning I was not angry with Joe any longer.

Use a comma after an introductory subordinate clause (a subordinate clause that comes before the subject of the sentence). (Subordinate clauses are discussed on p. 192.)

When the steel mills closed, over a thousand people were out of work.

Before you leave, please say good-bye to Grandpa.

If the union does not get a pay raise, its members will take a strike vote.

PRACTICE 21.6

Add commas after introductory elements in the following paragraph and cross out any incorrect commas.

In Babylon some 4,000 years ago the first paved roads appeared. As people, began living in town and trading with their neighbors they needed better means of transport. A cart could not cross wild country because it could break an axle or sink into mud or sand. Thus paved roads were developed in response to a need. Undoubtedly, the greatest road-builders were the ancient Romans. Built by army engineers Roman roads were made of stones and gravel and ran straight from town to town. The roads were sloped so that rain would drain away to the sides. A marvel of engineering these roads were used by Roman armies to march across the empire and keep the peace.

Commas with Interrupters   An **interrupter** is a word or phrase that interrupts the flow or main idea of a sentence. Some common interrupters are:

I believe	it seems to me
incidentally	as a matter of fact
in fact	to tell the truth
believe it or not	I am sure

by all means	if you ask me
by the way	without a doubt

Interrupters are set off from the rest of the sentence with commas.

The physical education requirement, *if you ask me*, should be abolished. (The interrupter comes in the middle of the sentence, so there is a comma *before and after* it.)

By the way, Kwame has decided to run for a seat on the student council. (The interrupter comes at the beginning of the sentence, so a comma is placed *after* it.)

Mayor Juarez has no choice but to lay off some city workers, *it seems to me*. (The interrupter comes at the end of the sentence, so a comma is placed *before* it.)

Transitions are often considered interrupters and are set off from the rest of the sentence with commas. (Transitions are explained on p. 235.)

As a result, Donofrio won the election by a fifty percent margin. (The transition comes at the beginning of the sentence, so a comma is placed *after* it.)

Dr. Wright, *however*, disagrees with my view. (The transition comes in the middle of the sentence, so a comma is placed *before and after* it.)

Nonessential elements are set off from the rest of the sentence with commas. A **nonessential element** is a word, phrase, or clause that is not essential for identifying the person or thing referred to. Here are some examples of sentences with nonessential elements:

Asa, *my oldest brother*, joined the Air Force. (My *oldest brother* is nonessential because it is not needed to identify who joined the Air Force: *Asa* does that.)

The woman next door, *determined to strike out on her own*, quit her job and moved to Tennessee. (*Determined to strike out on her own* is nonessential because it is not needed to identify who quit her job and moved to Tennessee; *the woman next door* does that.)

Xenia, Ohio, *which was once devastated by a tornado*, is now back on its feet. (*Which was once devastated by a tornado* is nonessential because it is not needed to identify what is now back on its feet; *Xenia, Ohio* does that.)

The same word group can be nonessential in one sentence and essential in another. Here is an example:

Alexis Ellington, *who won three major poetry contests*, will read some of her poems on campus this Friday night. (*Who won three major poetry contests* is nonessential for identifying who will read her poems, so commas are used.)

A woman *who won three major poetry contests* will read some of her poems on campus this Friday night. (*Who won three major poetry contests* is now essential for identifying who will read her poems; therefore, no commas are used.)

PRACTICE 21.7

Insert commas where they are needed to set off interrupters.

To my way of thinking Mississippi has a number of interesting places to visit. In northeastern Mississippi for example there is the site of the Chickasaw fort that was attacked by the French in 1736. Jackson, Mississippi which is the state capital offers many reminders of the state's rich history. The Old Capital now the State Historical Museum was built chiefly by slave labor. It was here that Mississippi voted to secede from the Union. It is also the place where Jefferson Davis who was president of the Confederacy made his last speech. A traveler who has the time may want to visit Delta and Pine Land Company Plantation which is one of the largest cotton plantations in the world. It covers 38,000 acres near Scott. For those who enjoy nature, Mississippi has 16 state parks and six national forests. If you find yourself in Mississippi, you will discover much to keep you occupied I am sure.

Commas with Coordinate Modifiers   Use a comma to separate coordinate modifiers not already separated by *and*. **Coordinate modifiers** describe the same word equally.

Be careful on the *wet, slippery* floor. (*Wet* and *slippery* are coordinate modifiers because they both describe *floor,* so a comma is placed between them.)

To test if modifiers are coordinate, try placing *and* between them. If the result sounds natural, the modifiers are coordinate.

Davey could not part with his *old, faded* shorts because he wore them in the state basketball championships. (*Old and faded shorts* sounds natural, so the modifiers are coordinate, and a comma is used.)

I asked the waiter for *fresh apple* pie for dessert. (*Fresh and apple pie* does not sound natural, so the modifiers are not coordinate, and no comma is used.)

Another way to test if modifiers are coordinate is to reverse their order. If the result sounds natural, the modifiers are coordinate. In the preceding examples, *old, faded shorts* can be changed to *faded, old shorts,* so the modifiers are coordinate. However, *fresh apple pie* cannot be changed to *apple fresh pie,* so the modifiers are not coordinate.

NOTE: Do not use a comma between coordinate modifiers separated by *and.*

| no: | The speaker was given a warm, and enthusiastic welcome. |
| yes: | The speaker was given a warm and enthusiastic welcome. |

PRACTICE 21.8

Use each pair of modifiers and the noun in a sentence of your own. If the modifiers are coordinate and *not* already separated by *and,* place a comma between them.

1. hot blinding sun

_____

_____

2. cut bleeding knee

_____

_____

3. elegant silk scarf

_____

_____

4. steaming chicken soup

_____

_____

5. sensitive and caring nurse

_____

_____

6. warm gentle breeze

_____

_____

Commas with Direct Address   In **direct address**, you use the name of the person or animal you are speaking to. Names used in direct address are set off with commas.

> *Marvin,* I need to borrow your class notes.
>
> If you ask me, *Harriet,* we should leave now.
>
> Stop rolling in the clean laundry, *you silly cat.*

Do not set off the name of a person or animal spoken *about;* set off only the names of persons or animals spoken *to.*

direct address:	Carla, let me use your car for an hour. (Carla is spoken *to.*)
no direct address:	Carla will let me use her car for an hour. (Carla is spoken *about.*)

PRACTICE 21.9

On a separate sheet, write six sentences of your own. Two sentences should have direct address at the beginning, two should have direct address in the middle, and two should have direct address at the end. Remember, a comma is used *after* direct address at the beginning, *before* direct address at the end, and *before and after* direct address in the middle.

Commas with Direct Quotations   In *direct quotations,* commas are used to separate the words that identify the speaker from the words that are spoken.

> Dr. Herndon explained, "High blood pressure is serious, but it can be treated."
>
> "High blood pressure is serious, but it can be treated," Dr. Herndon explained.
>
> "High blood pressure is serious," Dr. Herndon explained, "but it can be treated."

For more on punctuating quotations, see p. 422.

POST TEST

Place commas where they are needed in the following paragraphs.

1. When I woke up I knew it was going to be "one of those days." First I heard my roommate cry, "Ryan come quickly." I sprinted to the living room and saw the cause of Ralph's scream: We had been robbed. Amazed I scanned the room. The stereo was gone the television was gone and the VCR was gone. The couch was gone and the coffee table was gone. In fact the only thing that was not taken was the laundry basket which stood alone in the middle of the room. Ralph and I just looked at each other in disbelief. Not knowing what else to do we started to laugh for we both realized at the same moment that this was the day we were going to put new locks on the doors. Timing I guess is everything.

2. Paul Revere was born on January 1 1735 in Boston Massachusetts. He was the third child of a silversmith Apollos De Revoire. Appollos a French Huguenot had come to Boston as a boy. When he was older he changed his name to the simpler Revere. Young Paul became an excellent craftsman in fine metals. In 1757 he married Sarah Orne. When she died in 1773 Revere married Rachel Walker. He had eight children by each wife but five of them died in infancy. Revere was an early member of the Sons of Liberty and he was one of the leaders of the Boston Tea Party in 1773. On the night of April 15 1775 Paul Revere rode to warn American patriots northwest of Boston that the British intended to raid Lexington and Concord. As a result of Revere's warnings the Lexington minutemen were ready for the British and for the important historic battle that launched the American Revolution. During the war Revere engraved the printing plates for the first currency for Massachusetts set up a powder mill and served in the local militia. In 1792 he opened a foundry to cast canon and bells. At 65 he learned how to roll sheet copper and became the first man in the United States to do this. His copper sheets in fact were used on the famous ship "Old Ironsides." Revere died in Boston on May 10 1818.

Using Semicolons

A **semicolon** (;) can separate **main clauses** (word groups that can stand alone as sentences). The semicolon can also separate items in a series when the series already contains commas.

PRETEST

If the semicolon is used correctly, write *yes* in the blank; if it is not used correctly, write *no.* Do not guess; if you are unsure, do not write anything. Check your answers in Appendix III.

1. _____ I told you not to go; it's too bad you didn't listen to me.

2. _____ People who do not vote; do not understand how a democracy functions.

3. _____ My mother was born in Alexandria, Virginia; my father was born in Denver, Colorado; my sister was born in Tucson, Arizona; and I was born in Detroit, Michigan.

4. _____ The wedding was a disaster; by the end of the evening, the bride and groom were not speaking to each other.

5. _____ When the lifeguard put up the gale warning flags; everyone left the beach.

6. _____ The honored guests included Marie Sanchez, president of Willit Industries; Paul Romeo, director of the local mental health center; and Lee Myers, mayor of the city.

Semicolons to Separate Main Clauses Semicolons can separate **main clauses** (word groups that can stand alone as sentences). For a discussion of main clauses, see p. 192.

The table has been in my family for four generations; it was given to me by my mother.

The fund-raising drive was a success; we collected enough pledges to keep the soup kitchen open another year.

When you use a semicolon, be sure you have main clauses on *both* sides. A semicolon cannot separate a main clause from a word group that is not a main clause.

no: Because Hank was having trouble with math; he decided to hire a tutor. (The word group before the semicolon is not a main clause that can stand alone as a sentence.)

Semicolons can also be used with conjunctive adverbs to join main clauses. This rule is discussed in detail on p. 201.

Some people agreed with the speaker's remarks; however, most seemed to disagree.

State aid to public schools has been cut drastically; therefore, it will be necessary to pass a school levy.

PRACTICE 21.10

Place semicolons where they are needed in the following sentences:

1. The December snowfall set a record however, it was never necessary to close the schools.
2. A person who runs for public office must endure considerable scrutiny every facet of a politician's life is subject to examination.
3. Louisa was finally realizing her dream she was about to open her own toy and hobby shop.
4. I took my complaint to three company officials nonetheless, no one was sure how to help me.
5. The driver failed to see the stop sign partially hidden by the bushes as a result, he narrowly missed hitting an oncoming van.
6. My son studied ecology in his fourth-grade science class he then convinced me to recycle aluminum and paper.

Semicolons with Items in a Series   A semicolon can separate items in a series when the series already has commas in it.

> The menu featured omelets, pancakes, and sausage for breakfast; hero sandwiches, soup, and burgers for lunch; and pasta, steak, and fish for dinner.

PRACTICE 21.11

Place semicolons where they are needed in the following sentences. In some cases, you will replace commas with semicolons.

1. The team's infield is strong: Jakes, a senior, plays first base Juarez, a sophomore, plays second Wallace, a junior, plays third and Sniderman, a freshman, plays shortstop.
2. Tony looked for his Christmas presents in the linen closet, where they were hidden last year, in the attic, where years of castoffs were stored and in the garage, where Dad has his workroom.
3. At the flea market I bought an old chair, which should fit in my living room a weathered porch swing, which I plan to refinish and a broken record player, which I have no use for at all.
4. On the cruise, my parents met a couple from Juneau, Alaska, a woman from Nashville, Tennessee, and a family from Great Neck, New York.

POST TEST

In the following paragraph, add semicolons where they are needed and strike out semicolons that are incorrectly used.

Every summer I go to the beach, and usually there is some mishap. I have cut myself on shells, which is always a danger because I walk barefoot, received a severe sunburn, which made me very sick, and gotten sand in my eye, which caused a nasty abrasion on my cornea. Last summer for the first time, I was stung by a jellyfish. I was standing in shallow water; when I felt the painful sting. Fortunately, I had just read an article about how to deal with jellyfish stings; so I knew just what to do. Quickly, I scooped up some sand, then rubbed it on the sting underwater. This helped wash away any remaining jellyfish nettles. Next, I went to my room and applied alcohol this neutralized the majority of the toxins. (I could have also used vinegar or meat tenderizer.) Finally, I washed the area with soap and fresh water. In the case of a severe jellyfish sting, especially if there are allergic reactions, I would have consulted a physician or gone to an emergency ward; additional help may have been necessary. For the next 24 hours, I felt a bit nauseous, somewhat headachy, and a little feverish however, after that, I was fine.

Using Colons, Parentheses, and Dashes

The **colon** (:) introduces a long list, a quotation, or an explanation. **Parentheses** [( )] enclose material that is downplayed. **Dashes** (—) signal long pauses for emphasis or dramatic effect.

PRETEST

If the colon, parentheses, or dash is used correctly, write *yes* in the blank. If the mark is used incorrectly, write *no.* If you are unsure, do not write anything. Check your answers in Appendix III.

1. _____ We went to the restaurant at eight o'clock, but it was closed. (I'm not really sure why.)

2. _____ Joey was voted the most valuable player of the game—he scored 26 points, he had 19 rebounds, and he made 10 assists.

3. _____ The topic of my research paper is: why eating disorders are more common among females than males.

4. _____ Franklin Roosevelt said this: "We have nothing to fear except fear itself."

5. _____ My earliest memory of my father—and it is indeed a pleasant one—is of him putting me on his shoulders and parading around the house.

6. _____ Drexel (what an unusual name) has a sister named Drexine (good grief!).

7. _____ I told you not to go: but you would not listen to me.

8. _____ The audience was growing restless—they had already waited two hours for the show to start—and they began stomping their feet and chanting.

The Colon Use a colon to introduce a list:

> The doctor told me to avoid the following: salt, chocolate, caffeine, and artificial preservatives.

> I got a job for these reasons: bills, bills, and more bills.

Use a colon to introduce material that explains something in the main clause.

> The evening ended on a bad note: a prankster pulled the fire alarm, and the building had to be evacuated.

Use a colon to introduce an example of something in the main clause.

> Jake has become a compulsive buyer: just yesterday he spent a hundred dollars on a silk shirt and fifty dollars on a leather belt.

Use a colon to introduce a quotation.

> Herman Melville wrote one of the most famous opening sentences in literature: "Call me Ishmael."

NOTE: Do not use a colon after a linking verb (see p. 179), after a preposition (see p. 185), or between a verb and its object (see p. 364).

no: Michael is: bright, motivated, and talented. (The colon appears after a linking verb.)

yes: Michael is bright, motivated, and talented.

no: I looked for my lost wallet in: the house, the car, and the office. (The colon appears after a preposition.)

continued

---

yes:	I looked for my lost wallet in the house, the car, and the office.
no:	At the outlet mall, Karen bought: pottery, baskets, and shoes. (The colon comes between the verb and its object.)
yes:	At the outlet mall, Karen bought pottery, baskets, and shoes.

Parentheses Use parentheses to enclose material that you want to downplay or deemphasize because it is not essential to the main idea of the sentence. Often material in parentheses is a side comment.

My physics teacher (Dr. Garner) has agreed to give me extra help before the final exam.

Translators (the unsung heroes of the literary world) must preserve the meaning and intent of the original work.

Before beginning assembly, check to be sure you have all the parts (twelve in all).

The Dash Use a dash to signal a long pause for emphasis or dramatic effect.

My flight was canceled because of bad weather—what an annoyance that proved to be.

Eight of us—all wearing heavy winter coats—squeezed into the car.

Carla—an extremely talented violinist—was asked to be the youngest member of the symphony orchestra.

NOTE: If you want to downplay material, parentheses can sometimes be used in place of a colon. If you want to emphasize the material, dashes can sometimes be used.

colon:	Harvey cares about just one person: himself.
parentheses to downplay:	Harvey cares about just one person (himself).
dash to emphasize:	Harvey cares about just one person—himself.

PRACTICE 21.12

Add colons, parentheses, and dashes to the following passage, and be prepared to explain your reason for each addition. (The passage can be punctuated correctly in several different ways.)

The elevator is the product of centuries of development, beginning with the ancient Greeks. The Greeks knew how to lift objects using pulleys grooved wheels that ropes can slide over and winches machines that have broad drums with ropes fastened to them. By turning the drum with a crank, the rope can be wound up on the drum or let out; running the rope over a pulley allows a load to be raised or lowered.

In the 17th century came the "flying chair," which was designed to carry people to the top floors of a building by means of a system of weights and pulleys. Because it operated outside the building, the flying chair never became popular a fact that does not surprise most people.

During the last half of the 19th century, elevators were in existence, but they were mostly used for freight. Steam power was used to turn the hoisting drums of these elevators. People did not use these elevators much for one reason they were afraid the rope holding the elevator might snap, and the elevator would go crashing down. Then Elisha Otis invented a safety device that prevented this from happening, and elevators became popular. Also, at this time, hydraulic power fluid under pressure began to be used to raise and lower elevators. Finally, the electric elevator, which is what is used today, was developed by the German engineer, Werner von Siemens.

POST TEST

On a separate sheet, write two sentences that use the colon correctly, two sentences that use parentheses correctly, and two sentences that use the dash correctly. Be prepared to explain why you have used each punctuation mark.

Using Apostrophes

Apostrophes serve two main purposes: they signal ownership, and they signal that letters or numbers have been omitted in contractions and other forms.

PRETEST

If apostrophes are used correctly, write *yes* in the blank; if they are used incorrectly, write *no*. If you are unsure, do not write anything. Check your answers in Appendix III.

1. _____ The hat I found belongs to one of the boy's.

2. _____ I can't understand why Carmen is so angry at Ralph.

3. _____ Its' been quite some time since I've had a vacation.

4. _____ In the '50s life was simpler.

5. _____ Both senators' bills died in committee.

6. _____ Someone's car is double-parked and sure to be ticketed.

7. _____ My boss's top priority right now is increasing efficiency in all departments.

8. _____ My father-in-law's condominium in Florida is for rent.

9. _____ All of her *e*'s look like *i*'s to me.

10. _____ The childrens' Christmas play was canceled because the roads were snow-covered and slippery.

Apostrophes for Possession   **Possession** means ownership. One way to show possession is with a phrase beginning with *of*, and the other way is with an apostrophe.

> The brightness *of the sun* makes it difficult to drive. (The brightness belongs to the sun.)

> The *sun's* brightness makes it difficult to drive. (The brightness belongs to the sun.)

> The office *of the vice president* is on the second floor. (The office belongs to the vice president.)

> The *vice president's* office is on the second floor. (The office belongs to the vice president.)

> The paw *of the dog* is badly cut. (The paw belongs to the dog.)

> The *dog's* paw is badly cut. (The paw belongs to the dog.)

A number of rules govern how to use the apostrophe to show possession. These are given for you in the following pages.

1. Add an apostrophe and an *s* to all singular nouns and to plural nouns that *do not* end in *s*.

Noun Is Singular or Does Not End in s	Add 's	Possessive Form
Bill	Bill's	Bill's coat
car	car's	car's driveshaft
children	children's	children's toys
teacher	teacher's	teacher's desk
men	men's	men's clothing
Doris	Doris's	Doris's job

2. Add an apostrophe to plural nouns ending in *s*.

Plural Noun Ending in *s*	Add an Apostrophe	Possessive Form
brothers	brothers'	brothers' room
shoes	shoes'	shoes' laces
babies	babies'	babies' diapers

3. When a word is hyphenated, add the apostrophe after the last part of the word.

> This is my mother-in-law's car.

> All of my editor-in-chief's decisions were carefully made.

4. With two or more nouns, use the apostrophe after the last noun to show joint possession. Use the apostrophe after each noun to show individual possession.

> Carol and Dan's son will go to Italy this summer as part of the Children's International Summer Village program. (The son belongs to both Carol and Dan; this is joint ownership.)

> Carol's and Dan's businesses are enjoying excellent growth. (Carol and Dan each have a business; this is individual ownership.)

5. Use an apostrophe and *s* to make indefinite pronouns possessive. **Indefinite pronouns** refer to members of a group without specifying the particular members. (Indefinite pronouns are explained more fully on p. 335.)

> *Someone's* car is parked so closely to mine that I cannot get in on the driver's side.

> *Everyone's* responsibility is to help the poor.

6. Do not use apostrophes with possessive pronouns. These words already show ownership, so no apostrophe is needed. Here is a list of possessive pronouns:

hers	mine	theirs
his	my	yours
its	ours	

> yes: The winning number is his.
>
> no: The winning number is his'.

> NOTE: *Its* is a possessive pronoun, so no apostrophe is needed to show ownership. *It's* is a contraction form of "it is" or "it has." There is no form *its'*.
>
> yes: The dog keeps licking *its* paw as if something is wrong. (*Its* is the possessive form; the paw belongs to the dog.)
>
> yes: *It's* difficult to predict who will win the Democratic presidential nomination. (*It's* is the contraction form meaning "it is.")

PRACTICE 21.13

Fill in the blank with the correct possessive form; use the information in parentheses as a guide. The first one is done as an example.

1. (The dog belongs to Mona.) ___*Mona's*___ dog will weigh over a hundred pounds when it is grown.

2. (The questions belong to the students.) The instructor was careful to answer all the _____ questions.

3. (The mattress belongs to the bed.) I have trouble sleeping in the dorm because my _____ mattress is too soft.

4. (The blades belong to the knives.) All of the steak _____ blades are too dull to cut easily.

5. (The paycheck belongs to Phyllis.) A mistake was made in _____ paycheck, and she was shorted twenty dollars.

6. (The laces belong to the shoes.) Both of the _____ laces broke when I tried to tie them.

7. (The ring belongs to my sister-in-law.) My _____ square-cut emerald ring is a family heirloom worth much money.

8. (The help belongs to everyone.) _____ help is needed if the fundraiser is to be a success.

9. (Rhonda and Helen made different mistakes.) _____ and _____ mistakes are easy to correct.

10. (Rhonda and Helen have the same expectations.) _____ and

_____ expectations are too high.

11. (The van belongs to Morris.) _____ van has 100,000 miles on it, but he has no plans to trade it in.

12. (The fillings belong to the teeth.) Most of my _____ fillings are loose.

13. (The natural resources belong to the country.) The _____ natural resources must be protected.

14. (The leg belongs to the table.) The _____ leg is marred because the cat uses it as a scratching post.

15. (The gloves belong to several boys.) The _____ gloves were left in a pile to dry by the radiator.

Apostrophes for Contractions   A **contraction** is formed when two words are joined to make one. When the words are joined, at least one letter is omitted. An apostrophe stands for the missing letter or letters. Here are some common contractions:

Two Words	Contraction	Missing Letter(s)
are not	aren't	o
is not	isn't	o
does not	doesn't	o
have not	haven't	o
can not	can't	no
could not	couldn't	o
they will	they'll	wi
she will	she'll	wi
he will	he'll	wi
who is	who's	i
who has	who's	ha
will not	won't	irregular: ill/o
would not	wouldn't	o
we are	we're	a
they are	they're	a
she had	she'd	ha
he would	he'd	woul

> NOTE: Although they are acceptable in semiformal and informal writing, avoid contractions in formal writing.

PRACTICE 21.14

Fill in the blank with the contraction form of the words in parentheses.

1. (I am) _____ changing my major to computer technology because the job opportunities are excellent in that field.

2. (we are) Although Higgins is a longshot candidate, _____ still planning to campaign for him.

3. (do not; you are) _____ look now, but the person

   _____ talking about just walked in the room.

4. (do not; I am) If I _____ get at least a *C* in my circuits class,

   _____ going to change my major to computer science.

5. (would not) Juanita turned down the job offer because she knew she

   _____ like the hours.

6. (he has; does not) Now that _____ had a year of physical ther-

   apy, Lee _____ have trouble with his back.

7. (it is) _____ possible to be happy living anywhere as long as you have good friends.

8. (she will) Pilar called to say _____ be an hour late.

9. (I will) _____ help you in any way I can as long as you coop-erate with me.

10. (who is) Jamison is the attorney _____ likely to be appointed a municipal judge.

11. (who has) _____ been borrowing my tapes without my per-mission?

Other Uses for the Apostrophe

1. The apostrophe can stand for missing numbers.

I graduated with the class of '71. (The apostrophe stands for the missing *19.*)

2. The apostrophe can stand for missing letters in words that are not contractions. This is often the case in quotations that include informal speech or dialect.

> Grandpa always said, "Feelin' sorry fer yourself is a waste of time."

> "Bring 'em with ya," Mike shouted.

3. The apostrophe is used with an *s* to form the plural of letters. No apostrophe is used to form the plural of numbers, symbols, abbreviations, and words used as terms.

> How many *s*'s are in *embarrass?*

> Be more careful about how you make your 4s.

> All your *there*s are used incorrectly.

> Write out the word *number* instead of using #s.

> There are three M.D.s here tonight.

PRACTICE 21.15

Place apostrophes where needed. Some sentences are correct.

1. In the 90s, a computer revolution occurred.
2. The second grader was having trouble learning how to make *rs.*
3. Gary announced, "The best things in life are eatin, sleepin, and partyin."
4. The English department hired three new Ph.D's to teach full time.
5. Marta was having trouble with her *thens* and *thans.*

POST TEST

Place apostrophes where they are needed in the following sentences. One sentence requires an apostrophe and an *s.*

1. The quarterbacks spectacular pass sparked the offenses scoring drive.
2. Once youve owned a car with a CD player, youll never buy a car without one again.
3. Chris short story was accepted for publication by one of this countrys leading magazines.
4. The *Cs* that Dana earned kept her off of the Deans list.
5. Johns and Marthas problems arent going to be solved overnight; it will take years of counseling before theyre able to understand and alter their behavior.

6. Three companies employees were honored with Chamber of Commerce awards of excellence.

7. My sister-in-laws business, which she started in the late 70s, is now grossing over two hundred thousand dollars a year.

8. Angelo snapped, "Were comin; dont be so impatient."

9. The teams locker room was jammed with reporters, following their upset victory over the Division I champs.

10. The cab drivers strike is a problem for those visiting the city.

11. The Reading Labs speed-reading class is designed for students whose reading rate is very low.

12. The three doctors opinions were the same: my tonsillectomy cant be postponed.

Using Quotation Marks

Quotation marks are most frequently used to enclose someone's spoken or written words or the titles of short published writings.

PRETEST

If quotation marks are used correctly, write *yes* in the blank; if they are used incorrectly, write *no*. If you are unsure, do not write anything. Check your answers in Appendix III.

1. _____ "Dad said, If you decide to go to graduate school, I will pay half of your tuition."

2. _____ One of the best novels I have read is Barbara Kingsolver's "The Poisonwood Bible."

3. _____ "Before writing your research paper," Dr. Jones explained, "examine at least three books and ten articles on your topic."

4. _____ The salesperson in the pet store said that "the goldfish we bought will not live very long unless we buy a filter for the water."

5. _____ I remember thinking to myself, "If I get out of this mess, I will never take an unnecessary risk again."

6. _____ "Ma'am, you were traveling 50 miles per hour in a school zone," the police officer snapped.

7. _____ "They Also Wait Who Stand and Serve Themselves" is a delightful essay written by Andrew Ward.

8. _____ "Slow down the pace," the coach shouted from the sidelines.

Quotation Marks with Exact Spoken or Written Words   When you reproduce the exact words someone spoke or wrote, enclose the words in quotation marks. A sentence with someone's exact words usually has two parts: a statement of who spoke or wrote the words and the words themselves. The sentence is punctuated according to where in the sentence the exact words appear, as the following examples show.

1. Exact words after the statement of who spoke or wrote the words:

    > Judy warned me, "Be sure to study hard for the chemistry exam because it's a real killer."

    > *A Tale of Two Cities* begins, "It was the best of times. It was the worst of times."

    > I asked Mario, "Will you join me for lunch tomorrow?"

    A. A comma separates the statement of who spoke from the exact words.

    B. The first word of the exact words is capitalized.

    C. The period or question mark appears inside the final quotation marks.

2. Exact words before the statement of who spoke or wrote the words:

    > "There is a reason for everything," Eleni always said.

    > "Take me to your leader," the alien ordered.

    > "Will I ever be promoted?" the weary office worker wondered.

    A. If the exact words do not ask a question, a comma appears before the final quotation marks.

    B. If the exact words ask a question, a question mark appears before the final quotation marks.

    C. The first word after the exact words is not capitalized unless it is a person's name.

3. Exact words before and after the statement of who spoke or wrote the words:

    > "Before we begin today's lecture," said Dr. Sanchez, "let's review yesterday's material."

    > "I think we can go now," I said. "The rain has stopped."

    > "Are you sure," I asked, "that we can come along?"

    A. A comma appears after the first group of exact words, inside the quotation marks.

    B. If the first group of exact words does not form a sentence, a comma appears after the statement of who spoke or wrote the words. The second group of exact words does not begin with a capital letter.

    C. If the first group of exact words forms a sentence, a period appears after the statement of who spoke or wrote the words. The second group of exact words begins with a capital letter.

D. A period or question mark appears inside the final quotation marks.

4. A person's thoughts are punctuated like exact words:

> I asked myself, "How did I get into this mess?"

> "I know I can do it," I thought.

5. Before using quotation marks, be sure you really have someone's exact words.

use quotation marks:	Jane said, "I hate snow."
do not use quotation marks:	Jane said that she hates snow. (No one's exact words are repeated here.)
use quotation marks:	The lawyer said, "The case will be settled out of court."
do not use quotation marks:	The lawyer said that the case will be settled out of court. (No one's exact words are repeated here.)

PRACTICE 21.16

On a separate sheet, write sentences according to the directions given.

1. Write a sentence that you recently heard spoken on campus. Place the exact words after the statement of who spoke.

2. Write a sentence you recently spoke to a friend. Place the exact words after the statement of who spoke.

3. Write a sentence that includes a question a teacher has asked you. Place the exact words before the statement of who spoke.

4. Write a sentence that includes words a waiter might say. Place the exact words before the statement of who spoke.

5. Write two sentences that you might speak to a classmate before an exam. Place the exact words before and after the statement of who spoke.

6. Write a sentence a grandparent might speak. Use the words *When I was young* to begin the exact words. Place the exact words before and after the statement of who spoke.

7. Write a sentence that includes a question you might ask your doctor. Place the exact words after the statement of who spoke.

8. Write a sentence that includes words you would think to yourself after waiting for fifteen minutes in a traffic jam.

Quotation Marks with Short Published Titles   Quotation marks enclose the titles of short published works: the titles of magazine and newspaper articles, essays, short stories, short poems, songs, and book chapters.

Titles of longer works, such as books, magazines, newspapers, record albums, television shows, plays, and movies are underlined, or placed in italics (slanted type).

Use Quotation Marks	Underline
"Araby" (a short story)	Gone with the Wind (a novel/film)
"That Lean and Hungry Look" (an essay)	Arsenic and Old Lace (a play)
"Art at Its Best" (newspaper article)	Wall Street Journal (a newspaper)
"Ode to the West Wind" (a short poem)	Twentieth Century American Poets (a book)
"Rootbeer Rag" (a song)	Streetlife Serenade (an album)

Thinking, Learning, and Writing in College   Seeing Connections

Just as punctuation shows how various sentence elements relate to each other, learning involves seeing the connections among facts and ideas. You should think about how the information in each class relates to what you have learned in other classes or other aspects of your life. Seeing how points connect and apply outside any particular class will "set" the learning and make it more useful and interesting. For example, in a psychology class, you may learn that positive reinforcement is most likely to affect behavior. Perhaps you can apply this information to what you learn about motivating students in an education class or to how you interact with your children. If you learn about the Puritans in a history class, you can apply that information to your reading in an early American literature class.

POST TEST

On a separate sheet, write the sentences, punctuating and capitalizing the quoted material correctly. One sentence is already correct.

1. The magician raised his arms and said there is nothing up my sleeves.
2. I couldn't possibly have been at the scene of the crime the defendant told the attorney because I was in the dentist's office.
3. I asked myself do I really want to go to graduate school?
4. Congressman Howard explained that because population has decreased significantly in our state, one congressional district might be eliminated.
5. The professional writer who visited our classroom said keep a journal and you will never be at a loss for ideas to write about.
6. The ozone layer must be protected, or planet Earth will be in big trouble the environmentalist explained.

7. If I were you Louise cautioned I would not be so quick to judge others.

8. In poetry class we are reading Robert Browning's My Last Duchess.

9. My favorite short story is Young Goodman Brown, but I also enjoy Flannery O'Connor's story Good Country People.

10. Kevin wondered out loud is all this effort going to pay off?

POST TEST: CAPITALIZATION AND PUNCTUATION

Drawing on everything you have learned in this chapter, add the missing capitalization and punctuation in the following passage.

Although she died in the early 60s, Marilyn Monroe continues to fascinate the american public. The actress combined glamour with wholesomeness and sex appeal with innocence to create a legend summed up in a single word Marilyn. As Carl Sandburg explained, she wasnt the usual movie idol.

Born as Norma Jean Mortenson on June 1 1926 in Los Angeles California the actress first called herself Norma Jean Baker and then Marilyn Monroe. Her film debut was in Scudda-Hoo! in 1948 and her career blossomed with small parts in all about eve in 1950 and the asphalt jungle in the same year. Her gift for comedy became apparent in Gentlemen prefer blondes 1953 and How to Marry a millionaire 1953. Part of her humor lay in the idea that her gorgeous blonde character didnt seem to understand why people thought she was beautiful or funny.

Monroes life was scrutinized by the press her marriages to baseball great Joe DiMaggio and playwright Arthur Miller were widely publicized. She was always troubled by her lack of privacy. To convince the world that she was more than a blonde bombshell Monroe took acting lessons and starred in complex films like Bus Stop 1956 and The Misfits 1961.

Monroes career was cut short when she died in Los Angeles from an overdose of sleeping pills on August 5 1962. However her sudden death seemed only to enhance the mystique of the actress.

Chapter 22

Sentence Skills Workshop

Each of the eleven practice exercises in this chapter requires you to edit paragraphs to correct more than one kind of error. Working through these exercises will give you the experience you need to edit your own papers more effectively.

◆ ◆ ◆

PRACTICE 22.1: TRANSITIONS, COORDINATION, SUBORDINATION, AND PARALLELISM

The following paragraph is choppy, it lacks transitions, and it has an error with parallelism. On a separate sheet, rewrite the paragraph so that it includes transitions, coordination, subordination, and appropriate parallelism.

A catcher-outfielder named Michael Joseph "King" Kelly was one of the most popular baseball players of the 1880s. Kelly played for Cincinnati, Chicago, New York, and he also played for Boston. He was a good hitter and a great baserunner. Kelly was an alert ballplayer. He was always looking for a way to get an advantage over the other team. He was sitting on the bench one day. An opposing batter hit a high foul ball. None of Kelly's teammates would be able to catch the ball. Kelly leaped off the bench. He went after the ball. He was shouting to the umpire at the same time, "Kelly now catching!" Kelly caught the ball. The umpire refused to allow the catch. Kelly insisted the catch was not against the rules. The rules allowed substitutions at any time. The umpire still would not call the batter out.

Kelly was right. A new rule was written into the rule book that winter. The new rule said that a player could not enter the game while the ball is in play.

PRACTICE 22.2: SENTENCE FRAGMENTS, RUN-ON SENTENCES, AND COMMA SPLICES

The following paragraph has five sentence fragments, one run-on sentence, and three comma splices. Edit the paragraph to eliminate these errors.

Although most colleges and universities are on a semester system. Many schools favor an academic year divided into quarters. And with good reason. The quarter system offers students more flexibility. They have an opportunity to take more classes they change their schedules three times a year, four with summer school. Therefore, students can sample a greater variety of courses and instructors. Students who have trouble deciding on a major appreciate this variety, it provides them exposure to more courses. Thus helping them make up their minds. Also, students who find themselves in courses they do not like need only sweat out a ten or eleven week quarter, not a fifteen or sixteen week semester. Another advantage of quarters being that they often do not begin until after Labor Day. This means students have a more traditional summer break. One criticism of the quarter system is that it goes too fast, thus, students cannot take the time they need to learn many subjects. Quarters do progress quickly, but students adjust to the pace and learn efficient study habits. Nonetheless, the semester system is likely to remain the dominant pattern. It is cheaper to administer, there are only three registrations a year, rather than the four registrations that occur with the quarter system. Colleges always looking for ways to save money.

PRACTICE 22.3: SUBJECT-VERB AGREEMENT, TENSE SHIFTS, AND VERB FORMS

The following paragraph has six subject-verb agreement errors, four tense shifts, and one incorrect verb form. Cross out the incorrect verbs and write the correct ones above the line.

Either elaborate rituals or simple copulation mark the courtship of spiders. Some crab spiders, for example, showed almost no courtship behaviors other than actual copulation. Others wrap the female in silk threads. The threads does not immobilize the female but communicate the intentions of the male. Then there is wolf spiders. When a female wolf spider passes a male, the male begins a series of exhausting courtship behaviors. These included crouching, foreleg extension and waving, drumming, and abdominal vibrations. Similarly, jumping male spiders used visual signals to communicate with females. Although some lifts a leg or two, others perform a complex dance to attract the female. If one of the females are receptive, she assumes a crouching posture. The male then extends his forelegs, touches the female, and climbs on her back to begin copulation. Because the webs of a spider is used for prey capture, it is essential that males who are courting web spinners vibrate the female's web in a way that is distinct from the vibrations of a trapped insect. One group of male spiders only approaches the female after she has eaten and thus unlikely to gobble up a suitor. Despite their best efforts, however, the male spider often be in big trouble. In certain species, the females, which are commonly larger than the males, kill and eat the male after mating. Although this is not always what happened, most males live only long enough to mate once or twice before they die.

PRACTICE 22.4: SUBJECT-VERB AGREEMENT AND PRONOUN-ANTECEDENT AGREEMENT

The following paragraph has eight errors with subject-verb agreement and six errors with pronoun-antecedent agreement. Cross out the incorrect verbs and pronouns and write the correct forms above the line.

Computer technology is making life more convenient for students. Any student who can take advantage of e-mail, the Internet, and word processing programs will find that their productivity is increased and that their time is used efficiently. For example, instead of spending hours in the library looking for books and articles, students is using the Internet for research. At some schools, a class of students receive questions via the Internet and debate the answers with students at other schools. At other schools, a cluster of courses are offered online, and students can take these courses with his or her peers from other institutions, even ones out of the country. Another one of the electronic conveniences are e-mail, which makes it possible for a student to communicate with their instructor, friends, and family quickly, easily, and cheaply. Anyone who want to check their grades, ask a professor a question, register, or find out what is happening on campus can do so with e-mail. Both students and professors benefits from this technology. Finally, word processing allows every student to turn their paper into a professional-looking piece in record time. It also allow for easy editing, saving of manuscript, and collaboration. Yes, technology is not without its problems, but on college campuses, it sure makes life easier.

PRACTICE 22.5: TENSE SHIFT AND PERSON SHIFT

The following paragraph has four inappropriate tense shifts and four person shifts. Cross out the incorrect verbs and pronouns and write the corrections above the line.

The productivity of the land of medieval Europe was limited by inadequate technology. The farmers of this land were so poorly equipped that you cannot efficiently cultivate and harvest your crops. Almost all agricultural tools were made of wood, a weak and impractical material for use on the thick European soil. These tools were so limiting that much work is invariably accomplished with bare hands, a technique that caused the soil to lose fertility. As a result, you have to rest large portions of land for entire growing seasons, which decreased the output of your farm. The lack of technology and equipment allowed the unpredictable weather to wreak havoc on farm productivity. Without advanced drainage systems, fields are flooded during an excessively wet season. Similarly, without irrigation technology, fields were dried up by droughts. Because of the lack of advanced technology, medieval Europe often suffered severe food shortages.

PRACTICE 22.6: FORMS OF ADJECTIVES AND ADVERBS AND DANGLING MODIFIERS

The following paragraph contains seven errors with forms of adjectives and adverbs, and two dangling modifiers. Cross out the errors and make corrections above the line.

Some people are just natural funny. They manage to find humor in even the most commonest situations. My friend Peggy, for example, is one of the most funniest people I know. In fact, she has been funny for as long as I have known her good. I remember all the way back to junior high school when Peggy got up to sharpen her pencil. Wearing her pencil down in math class, the pencil sharpener located in the closet on the wall was needed. Peggy walked to the closet, and some perverse impulse must have taken over because she entered the closet, closed the door behind her, and stayed there for the rest of class. Wondering if she was missed, the door was cracked from time to time and she peeked out. No one, apparently, noticed but me. It was all I could do to keep from falling on the floor laughing hysterical. When the bell sounded, Peggy just walked out of the closet casual and headed for her next class, sharpened pencil in hand. Of all of the stunts Peggy has pulled, that is one of the memorablest.

PRACTICE 22.7: COMMAS AND CAPITAL LETTERS

The following paragraph has 17 comma errors as a result of missing commas or misplaced commas. It also has 8 errors with capitalization as a result of missing capitals or incorrect capitals. Make the necessary corrections directly on the page.

The Toll House cookie an american favorite has an interesting origin. In 1930 Ruth Wakefield and her husband bought the Toll House inn which was located in whiteman Massachusetts. While she was making a batch of brown sugar dough for her butter cookies Ruth cut a chocolate bar into chunks mixed the chunks in and hoped the chunks would melt during baking to create chocolate cookies. That did not happen. Instead the chocolate did soften slightly and history was made—the chocolate chip cookie was born. When she served these surprise creations the response was to say the least enthusiastic. Pleased with her success Ruth named the cookies after her Inn. Subsequently the nestle company bought the toll house name, and developed the little chocolate chip. If nothing else this story reminds us that sometimes, the best discoveries are the result of happy accidents.

PRACTICE 22.8: ALL PUNCTUATION

Using everything you have learned about commas, semicolons, dashes, parentheses, colons, apostrophes, and quotation marks, add missing punctuation and strike incorrect punctuation in the following paragraph.

You probably know that Benjamin Franklin was a statesman publisher and public servant. Did you know that as an inventor and scientist Franklin had few equals. First Franklin and his kite showed the world that lightning is actually electricity then he invented the lightning rod which saved many buildings from fires caused by lightning. His Franklin stove gave more heat than other stoves and used much less fuel. Also Franklins bifocal lenses were invented for both reading and distance use. One of Franklins discoveries was of particular importance the discovery that disease flourishes in poorly ventilated rooms. In addition Franklin showed Americans how to improve acid soil by using lime something vitally important to a society dependent upon farming. Interestingly Franklin refused to patent any of his inventions, or use them for profit he preferred to have them used freely for the benefit of society. As a result of his' discoveries and generosity Franklin was elected to membership in the Royal Society of London a rare honor for someone living in the colonies. The great English statesman William Pitt said, "Franklin is an honor to the English nation and to human nature."

PRACTICE 22.9: RANGE OF ERRORS

The following paragraph contains

1 incorrect verb form	1 run-on sentence
2 errors with subject-verb agreement	1 comma splice
1 error with pronoun-antecedent agreement	4 comma errors
1 sentence fragment	1 dangling modifier
2 errors with parallelism	2 errors with capital letters

Edit directly on the page to correct the errors. In some cases, more than one correction is possible

Thunderstorms be most likely to happen in the spring and summer months and during the afternoon and evening hours, however, they can occur year-round and at all hours. Along the gulf coast and across the southeastern and western United States, most thunderstorms occurring during the afternoon. In the Plains states, thunderstorms frequently occurs in the late afternoon and at night. Occasionally thunder and lightning accompanies snow or freezing rain. For example lightning resulted in power outages near Washington D.C. during the blizzard of 1993. A person should never take a thunderstorm lightly, for they are at risk from lightning, flooding, and tornadoes can pose a threat. People who are outdoors, in or on water, and people on or near hilltops are at risk from lightning associated with thunderstorms. During heavy thunderstorms, people in cars are at risk from flash flooding also people in mobile homes are at risk from tornadoes. When learning of an approaching thunderstorm, reasonable caution should be exercised.

PRACTICE 22.10: RANGE OF ERRORS

The passage below has

1 semicolon error	1 confused word
3 errors with sets of quotation marks	4 spelling errors
6 errors with capitals	3 apostrophe errors
2 comma errors	1 comma splice
1 error with end punctuation	1 sentence fragment
2 errors with subject-verb agreement	1 incorrect verb form

Editing directly on the page, correct the errors. In some cases, more than one correction is possible.

When someone sneezes; do you say god bless you. You probably do but may not no why. One explanation relates to superstition. It is said that early people beliefed that a persons spirit was in the form of breath contained in the head, thus a sneeze might acidentally expel it. Saying god bless you was an appeal to god not to let the spirit escape.

On the other hand, there is some experts who claim the custom isnt based on superstition. They beleive it started during a great plague that took place in anceint athens. A sneeze being the first sign that a person had became ill. Saying god bless you was asking for gods blessing for someone who were going to die.

PRACTICE 22.11: RANGE OF ERRORS

The following passage has

1 spelling error	1 unstated antecedent
1 semicolon error	1 confused word
4 comma errors	1 sentence fragment
3 errors with apostrophes	1 incorrect modifier form
2 tense shifts	1 comma splice
1 incorrect noun form	4 errors with capital letters

Editing directly on the page, correct the errors. In some cases, more than one correction is possible.

Susan B. Anthony who was born in 1820 and died in 1906 was an american pioneer of womens rights. The daughter of a quaker abolitionist she became a teacher after being educated in New York. Disatisfaction with it caused her to except the position of assistant manager of the family farm in upstate New York. Here she being exposed to the strong held views of such men as William Lloyd Garrison and Frederick Douglass. As a result, she becomes an advocate of reform. Her early efforts in this area failed, she was not taken seriously because she was a women. Eventually, she teamed up with Elizabeth Cady Stanton and together they found the American equal rights association to work for womens' suffrage. For the remainder of her life; she was devoted to this cause. As a result of her tireless work and ceaseless travel, womens' suffrage became a recognized cause in both America and Europe.

Thinking, Learning, and Writing in College

Editing Across the Curriculum

Editing is important in all of your course work, not just in your writing class. Although professors in other classes may not specifically mention editing, they likely will expect you to find and correct your errors. In fact, they may be less tolerant of errors than your writing teacher, who understands that mistakes are part of learning to write.

Visit the Clouse Website!

For additional exercises, quizzes, and Internet activities, visit our Website at:

http://www.ablongman.com/clouse

For even more activities, visit the Longman English pages at:

http://www.ablongman.com/englishpages

Chapter 23

Writing in Response to Reading

A s a college student, you read a great deal: studying textbooks, preparing research assignments, and reading required books calls upon you to read frequently and thoughtfully. What you may not realize is that reading can help you improve your writing skills. If you read often, paying attention to the characteristics of what you read and how other writers handle their tasks, you will learn about writing, and you can bring what you learn to your own writing tasks.

The focus of this chapter is on reading because reading is an important part of college life and because reading can help you improve your writing. Also, because much of your writing in college will be written responses to reading material, this chapter takes up writing in response to reading. You will learn

1. how to interact with a text through active reading

2. what to look for when you read

3. how to write a summary of what you have read

4. how to write essay examination answers

◆ ◆ ◆

ACTIVE READING

When you read for your own enjoyment, all that matters is that you have a good time. If you skip a paragraph or fail to understand a word or read with the television on, it does not matter—as long as you are enjoying yourself. However, when you read for your college classes, more is expected of you. You must read attentively for full comprehension. To do this, you must follow a different reading procedure than you follow when you read for pleasure alone; you must follow a process called **active reading.**

Active reading gets you involved. It helps you understand what is read, and it helps you form judgments about what is read. As an active reader, do not consider your job done until you have answered the questions in the following box.

QUESTIONS AN ACTIVE READER ASKS

1. What is the author's main idea (thesis)?
2. What main points support the thesis?
3. Is the support for the thesis adequate and convincing?
4. Is the author expressing facts, opinions, or both?
5. What is the author's tone or attitude (serious, sarcastic, preachy, humorous, angry, insulting, etc.)?
6. What is the author's purpose (to share, inform, entertain, and/or persuade)?
7. Who is the author's intended audience?
8. What is the source of the author's detail (observation, personal experience, research, and/or reasoning)?

To be an active reader, you must do more than let the words sound in your ears. You must become actively involved by focusing on what you are reading. The steps described in the following pages—*surveying, uninterrupted reading, studied reading,* and *testing yourself*—will show you how to do this. Keep in mind, however, that the key to your success will be *reading the material more than once.*

Step 1—Surveying

Survey your reading material to get an idea of what to expect. First check the title. What does it suggest the reading will be about? Who is the author? Have you read anything by this person before? If so, what might you expect based on your past experience? Has your instructor said anything about this material? If so, what can you expect based on these comments?

Now look through the material. Are there headings, boldface type, italics, lists, or pictures with captions? If so, what do these suggest you can expect from the reading?

Now read the opening and closing paragraphs quickly. What clues do these provide to content and the writer's purpose? Read the first sentence of each paragraph. What clues to content do these provide?

Once you have surveyed the material, you will have a sense of what to expect when you read. You will probably know what the writer's general subject is and whether the author is expressing feelings, explaining something, or trying to convince you of something. Just as important, you will form some questions about the reading. When you are through surveying and move on to reading, you should look for the answers to your survey questions.

Step 2—Uninterrupted Reading

Read the material quickly but attentively, without stopping. If you encounter a word you do not understand, circle it to check later; if there is a passage you do not understand, place a question mark next to it. The important thing is to keep going, getting as much as you can without laboring over anything. As you read, try to determine the writer's main point (thesis).

After this reading, write the answers to as many of the active-reader questions as you can. Then look up every word you circled, and write the meanings in the margin near the circled word. Now take a break if you feel the need.

Step 3—Studied Reading

Pick up your pen and read again. This time underline the author's thesis (if it is stated) and the main points to support the thesis (often found in topic sentences). Do not underline too much—just go for the thesis and main points. As you read, use your pen to write your reactions in the margins. Record your observations (even personal ones like "This makes me think of Chris"); note strong agreement or disagreement ("how true" or "absolutely not"); indicate where more detail is needed ("This isn't proven."). In addition, put stars next to passages you particularly like and question marks next to parts you do not understand. (See p. 443 for an example of how to mark an essay.) After this reading, return to the active-reading questions and answer the ones that remain.

If the material is long or difficult, take a break and then read it one more time, again using your pen to record your observations and underline main points. If you are unable after this reading to answer all the questions an active reader asks, or if there is anything you do not understand, write your questions down and ask your teacher.

Step 4—Testing Yourself

Close the book after your studied reading and write a brief summary of the material. Or recite a summary to yourself or to another person. This testing helps lock the main points in your memory.

NOTE: Do not confuse active reading with speed-reading. Speed is not the issue here. Rather, your goal is to understand the form and content of what you read and to make judgments about its truth and effectiveness.

A Sample Active Reading

The following essay has been marked the way an active reader might mark it. After the essay are the answers to the questions an active reader asks. Studying this material will help you appreciate how an active reader interacts with a text.

Students in Shock

John Kellmayer

If you feel overwhelmed by your college experiences, you are not alone–many of today's college students are suffering from a form of shock. Going to college has always had its ups and downs, but today the "downs" of the college experience are more numerous and difficult, a fact that the schools are responding to with increased support services.

1

thesis

Lisa is a good example of a student in shock. She is an attractive, intelligent twenty-year-old college junior at a state university. Having been a straight-A student in high school and a member of the basketball and softball teams there, she remembers her high school days with fondness. Lisa was popular then and had a steady boyfriend for the last two years of school.

2

Now, only three years later, Lisa is miserable. She has changed her major four times already and is forced to hold down two part-time jobs in order to pay her tuition. She suffers from sleeping and eating disorders and believes she has no close friends. Sometimes she bursts out crying for no apparent reason. On more than one occasion, she has considered taking her life.

3

good, realistic examples

Dan, too, suffers from student shock. He is nineteen and a freshman at a local community college. He began college as an accounting major but hated that field. So he switched to computer programming because he heard the job prospects were excellent in that area. Unfortunately, he discovered that he had little aptitude for programming and changed majors again, this time to psychology. He likes psychology but has heard horror stories about the difficulty of finding a job in that field without a graduate degree. Now he's considering switching majors again. To help pay for school, Dan works nights and weekends as a sales clerk at Kmart. He doesn't get along with his boss, but since he needs the money, Dan feels he has no choice except to stay on the job. A few months ago, his girlfriend of a year and a half broke up with him.

4

Howie is like Dan.

Not surprisingly, Dan has started to suffer from depression and migraine headaches. He believes that in spite of all his hard work, he just

5

Source: Reprinted with permission of Townsend Press.

443

Common reaction to idea of counseling

A frightening statistic. How was it learned?

call for

an eating disorder involving starvation

an eating disorder involving binge eating followed by forced vomiting

caused by one's self

Why blame families for problems schools create?

permanence

I know several people who had to drop out because of lack of money.

This school does a terrible job of advising on majors and careers.

isn't getting anywhere. He can't remember ever being this unhappy. A few times he considered talking to somebody in the college psychological counseling center. He rejected that idea, though, because he doesn't want people to think there's something wrong with him.

6   What is happening to Lisa and Dan happens to millions of college students each year. As a result, roughly one-quarter of the student population at any time will suffer from symptoms of depression. Of that group, almost half will experience depression intense enough to warrant professional help. At schools across the country, psychological counselors are booked up months in advance. Stress-related problems such as anxiety, migraine headaches, insomnia, anorexia, and bulimia are epidemic on college campuses.

7   Suicide rates and self-inflicted injuries among college students are higher now than at any other time in history. The suicide rate among college youth is fifty percent higher than among nonstudents of the same age. It is estimated that each year more than five hundred college students take their own lives.

8   College health officials believe that these reported problems represent only the tip of the iceberg. They fear that most students, like Lisa and Dan, suffer in silence.

9   There are three reasons today's college students are suffering more than in earlier generations. First is a weakening support structure. The transition from high school to college has been difficult, but in the past there was more family support to help get through it. Today, with divorce rates at a historical high and many parents experiencing their own psychological difficulties, the traditional family is not always available for guidance and support. And when students who do not find stability at home are bombarded with numerous new and stressful experiences, the results can be devastating.

10   Another problem college students face is financial pressure. In the last decade tuition costs have skyrocketed–up about sixty-six percent and ninety percent at private schools. For students living away from home, costs range from five thousand dollars to as much as twelve thousand a year and more. And at the same time that tuition costs have been rising dramatically, there has been a cutback in federal aid to students. College loans are now much harder to obtain and are available only at near-market interest rates. Consequently, most college students must work at least part-time. And for some students, the pressure to do well in school while holding down a job is too much to handle.

11   A final cause of student shock is the large selection of majors available. Because of the magnitude and difficulty of choosing a major, college can prove a time of great indecision. Many students switch majors, some a number of times. As a result, it is becoming commonplace

to take five or six years to get a degree. It can be depressing to students not only to have taken courses that don't count towards a degree but also to be faced with the added tuition costs. In some cases these costs become so high that they force students to drop out of college.

While there is no magic cure-all for student shock, colleges have begun to recognize the problem and are trying in a number of ways to help students cope with the pressures they face. First of all, many colleges are upgrading their psychological counseling centers to handle the greater demand for services Additional staff is being hired, and experts are doing research to learn more about the psychological problems of college students. Some schools even advertise these services in student newspapers and on campus radio stations. Also, upperclassmen are being trained as peer counselors. These peer counselors may be able to act as a first line of defence in the battle for students' well-being by spotting and helping to solve problems before they become too big for students to handle.   **12**

This school could use better RA's in the dorms.

In addition, stress-management workshops have become common on college campuses. At these workshops, instructors teach students various techniques for dealing with stress, including (biofeedback,) meditation, and exercise.   **13**

Technique for monitoring + controlling body functions.

Finally, many schools are improving their vocational counseling services. By giving students more relevant information about possible majors and career choices, colleges can lessen the anxiety and indecision often associated with choosing a major.   **14**

If you ever feel that you're in shock, remember that your experience is not unique. Try to put things in perspective. Certainly, the end of a romance or an exam is not an event to look forward to. But realize that rejection and failure happen to everyone sooner or later. And don't be reluctant to talk to somebody about your problems. The useful services available on campus won't help you if you don't take advantage of them.   **15**

What about unreasonable profs + difficult classes as causes of shock?

Answers to Active-Reader Questions for "Students in Shock"

1. What is the author's main idea (thesis)?
   "Going to college has always had its ups and downs, but today the 'downs' of the college experience are more numerous and difficult, a fact that the schools are responding to with increased support services."

2. What main points support the thesis?
   About a quarter of the student population will experience depression; half of that group will need professional help.

Stress-related problems are epidemic. Suicide and self-inflicted injuries are at an all-time high.
One cause of the student shock is decreased family support.
A second cause is financial pressure as a result of higher tuition and less financial aid.
A third cause is difficulty choosing a major.
Colleges are addressing the problem of shock by upgrading counseling services, offering stress-management workshops, and improving vocational counseling.

3. Is the support for the thesis adequate and convincing?
   The opening examples are well detailed and convince me that shock is a problem, but I think the reasons for the shock given are sketchy and incomplete.
   Other causes exist, such as difficult classes, unreasonable professors, and unprepared students. I'd also like to know where the author got his information. That would make the piece more convincing.

4. Is the author expressing facts, opinions, or both?
   both

5. What is the author's tone or attitude (serious, sarcastic, preachy, humorous, angry, insulting, etc.)?
   The author seems serious, concerned, and objective.

6. What is the author's purpose (to share, to inform, to entertain, and/or to persuade)?
   The author wants to inform the reader about the problem of student shock and explain how the problem is being addressed. He seems to do this to help students who suffer from shock.

7. Who is the author's intended audience?
   The __you__ in the last paragraph indicates that the author is addressing students.

8. What is the source of the author's detail (observation, personal experience, research, and/or reasoning)?
   Some research would be needed to learn about the extent of the problem and what colleges are doing. Otherwise, it's hard to know if any personal experience or observation was involved.

Thinking, Learning, and Writing in College   Questioning

To get the most out of class lectures, read all pertinent text material beforehand. As you do, make a list of any questions you have, and listen for answers to those questions during the lecture. If you do not get the answers, be sure to ask questions.

On Being 17, Bright, and Unable to Read

David Raymond

—— —— ——

*All of us have felt inadequate at some time, so we sympathize with the
pain the author felt because he could not read, and we rejoice in his victory when he confronts his learning disability and triumphs. As you
read, ask yourself what can be learned from the author's experience.*

*You will notice that the essay is a narration (it tells a story). Like
most narrations, it answers the questions who? what? when? where?
why? and how? Notice the answers to these questions and decide which
answers are emphasized the most.*

*You will also notice that the narration lacks a stated thesis and that
some supporting paragraphs lack topic sentences. Often narrations do
not have stated thesis sentences and topic sentences because the time
sequence provides an adequate organizational framework and topic
sentences are not required as an ordering device.*

Before reading the essay, review the following vocabulary:

dyslexia—a learning disability

*potter's wheel—a device with a rotating horizontal dish upon which
clay is molded*

*cross-country team—a track team that runs over fields and through
woods, etc., rather than on a track*

*Leonardo da Vinci—a brilliant Italian painter, sculptor, architect,
engineer, and scientist who lived from 1452 to 1519*

One day a substitute teacher picked me to read aloud from the textbook. When I told her "No, thank you," she came unhinged. She thought I
was acting smart, and told me so. I kept calm, and that got her madder and
madder. We must have spent 10 minutes trying to solve the problem, and
finally she got so red in the face I thought she'd blow up. She told me she'd
see me after class. 1

Maybe someone like me was a new thing for that teacher. But she was-
n't new to me. I've been through scenes like that all my life. You see, even 2

Source: The New York Times, April 25, 2000. Copyright © 2000 by The New York
Times Company. Reprinted by permission.

though I'm 17 and a junior in high school, I can't read because I have dyslexia. I'm told I read "at a fourth-grade level," but from where I sit, that's not reading. You can't know what that means unless you've been there. It's not easy to tell how it feels when you can't read your homework assignments or the newspaper or a menu in a restaurant or even notes from your own friends.

3   My family began to suspect I was having problems almost from the first day I started school. My father says my early years in school were the worst years of his life. They weren't so good for me, either. As I look back on it now, I can't find the words to express how bad it really was. I wanted to die. I'd come home from school screaming, "I'm dumb. I'm dumb—I wish I were dead!"

4   I guess I couldn't read anything at all then—not even my own name—and they tell me I didn't talk as good as other kids. But what I remember about those days is that I couldn't throw a ball where it was supposed to go, I couldn't learn to swim, and I wouldn't learn to ride a bike, because no matter what anyone told me, I knew I'd fail.

5   Sometimes my teachers would try to be encouraging. When I couldn't read the words on the board they'd say, "Come on, David, you know that word." Only I didn't. And it was embarrassing. I just felt dumb. And dumb was how the kids treated me. They'd make fun of me every chance they got, asking me to spell "cat" or something like that. Even if I knew how to spell it, I wouldn't; they'd only give me another word. Anyway, it was awful, because more than anything I wanted friends. On my birthday when I blew out the candles I didn't wish I could learn to read; what I wished for was that the kids would like me.

6   With the bad reports coming from school, and with me moaning about wanting to die and how everybody hated me, my parents began looking for help. That's when the testing started. The school tested me, the child-guidance center tested me, private psychiatrists tested me. Everybody knew something was wrong—especially me.

7   It didn't help much when they stuck a fancy name onto it. I couldn't pronounce it then—I was only in second grade—and I was ashamed to talk about it. Now it rolls off my tongue, because I've been living with it for a lot of years—dyslexia.

8   All through elementary school it wasn't easy. I was always having to do things that were "different," things the other kids didn't have to do. I had to go to a child psychiatrist, for instance.

9   One summer my family forced me to go to a camp for children with reading problems. I hated the idea, but the camp turned out pretty good, and I had a good time. I met a lot of kids who couldn't read and somehow that helped. The director of the camp said I had a higher I.Q. than 90 percent of the population. I didn't believe him.

10   About the worst thing I had to do in fifth and sixth grade was go to a special education class in another school in our town. A bus picked me up, and I didn't like that at all. The bus also picked up emotionally disturbed kids and retarded kids. It was like going to a school for the retarded. I

always worried that someone I knew would see me on that bus. It was a relief to go to the regular junior high school.

Life began to change a little for me then, because I began to feel better about myself. I found the teachers cared; they had meetings about me and I worked harder for them for a while. I began to work on the potter's wheel, making vases and pots that the teachers said were pretty good. Also, I got a letter for being on the track team. I could always run pretty fast. 11

At high school the teachers are good and everyone is trying to help me. I've gotten honors some marking periods, and I've won a letter on the cross-country team. Next quarter I think the school might hold a show of my pottery. I've got some friends. But there are still some embarrassing times. For instance, every time there is writing in the class, I get up and go to the special education room. Kids ask me where I go all the time. Sometimes I say, "to Mars." 12

Homework is a real problem. During free periods in school I go into the special ed room and staff members read assignments to me. When I get home my mother reads to me. Sometimes she reads an assignment into a tape recorder, and then I go into my room and listen to it. If we have a novel or something like that to read, she reads it out loud to me. Then I sit down with her, and we do the assignment. She'll write, while I talk my answers to her. Lately I've taken to dictating into a tape recorder, and then someone—my father, a private tutor or my mother—types up what I've dictated. Whatever homework I do takes someone else's time, too. That makes me feel bad. 13

We had a big meeting in school the other day—eight of us, four from the guidance department, my private tutor, my parents and me. The subject was me. I said I wanted to go to college, and they told me about colleges that have facilities and staff to handle people like me. That's nice to hear. 14

As for what happens after college, I don't know and I'm worried about that. How can I make a living if I can't read? Who will hire me? How will I fill out the application form? The only thing that gives me any courage is the fact that I've learned about well-known people who couldn't read or had other problems and still made it. Like Albert Einstein, who didn't talk until he was 4 and flunked math. Like Leonardo da Vinci, who everyone seems to think had dyslexia. 15

I've told this story because maybe some teacher will read it and go easy on a kid in the classroom who has what I've got. Or, maybe some parent will stop nagging his kid, and stop calling him lazy. Maybe he's not lazy or dumb. Maybe he just can't read and doesn't know what's wrong. Maybe he's scared, like I was. 16

STUDY QUESTIONS

1. "On Being 17, Bright, and Unable to Read" is a narration (it tells a story). Paragraph 1 tells a brief narration, but it is not the main story. Where does the main narration begin?

2. The essay does not have a sentence that states exactly what the essay is about (a thesis), but the thesis is implied in paragraph 2. Write a sentence that expresses the thesis idea.

3. In his last paragraph, Raymond explains his purpose for writing, and he mentions his intended audience. What is his purpose? Who is his intended audience?

4. Are all the who? what? when? where? why? how? questions answered? Which ones get the most emphasis?

5. Raymond's time sequence (his chronology) begins with his early years of school. What are the next three time periods discussed in the narration?

6. Is Raymond's detail adequate enough to fulfill his purpose? Explain.

7. Can "On Being 17, Bright, and Unable to Read" be viewed as a definition essay? Explain.

WRITING ASSIGNMENTS

1. Raymond's narration explains how his dyslexia affected him. In a narrative paragraph, tell about a time you were unable to do something. For example, tell about what happened one time when you could not sing, play a sport, speak in front of a group, dance, handle yourself well in a job interview, etc. (See p. 71 on writing a narrative paragraph.)

2. Raymond's opening paragraph tells a brief story (called an **anecdote**) about a time a teacher became angry with him. In a paragraph, narrate an account of time a teacher became angry or frustrated with you or someone you know. (See p. 71 on writing a narrative paragraph.)

3. Raymond was treated cruelly by his classmates. In a paragraph, explain why you think the other kids in school made fun of him. (See p. 118 on the cause-and-effect paragraph.)

4. Raymond's dyslexia has had a profound impact on his life. In an essay, use cause-and-effect analysis to explain the effects of one fact of your life (being tall or short, overweight or underweight, rich or poor, an only child or part of a large family, having allergies, etc.). (See p. 118 for the characteristics of cause-and-effect analysis.)

5. Raymond expresses concern for his future. Are you concerned about yours? In an essay, explain what you are concerned about and why.

6. Were your school years happy or unhappy ones? In an essay, write a narration that expresses your happiness or unhappiness. Like Raymond, begin with the early years and progress to the present, focusing on 3–4 periods in the time sequence (for example, first grade, eighth grade, and twelfth grade). (See p. 71 for the characteristics of narration.)

My Way!

Margo Kaufmann

Margo Kaufmann is an essayist whose work has appeared in the Baltimore City Paper, L.A. Weekly, *the* New York Times, Newsweek, *and the* Los Angeles Times Magazine. *"My Way!" is taken from her book* 1–800-Am-I-Nuts *(1993).*

You will quickly recognize that "My Way!" is a definition of the control freak, the person who has to be in charge of even the smallest detail. As you read, notice Kaufmann's use of examples. Notice, too, the change that comes over the author as the essay progresses.

Before reading, review the following vocabulary:

atrophy—waste away

compulsively—with an irresistible impulse

scoffs—scorns or mocks

compromised—affected unfavorably

hyperventilating—breathing rapidly, causing a decrease of carbon dioxide in the blood

laissez-faire—noninterference

1 Is it my imagination, or is this the age of the control freak? I'm standing in front of the triceps machine at my gym. I've just set the weights, and I'm about to begin my exercise when a lightly muscled bully in turquoise spandex interrupts her chest presses to bark at me. "I'm using that," she growls as she leaps up from her slant board, darts over to the triceps machine, and resets the weights.

2 I'm tempted to point out that, while she may have been planning to use the machine, she was, in fact, on the opposite side of the room. And that her muscles won't atrophy if she waits for me to finish. Instead, I go work on my biceps. Life's too short to fight over a Nautilus machine. Of course, *I'm* not a control freak.

3 Control freaks will fight over anything: a parking space, the room temperature, the last pair of marked-down Maude Frizon pumps, even whether

Source: From 1-800-AM-I-NUTS by Margo Kaufman. Copyright © 1993 by Margo Kaufman. Reprinted by permission of Random House, Inc.

you should barbecue with the top on or off the Weber kettle. Nothing is too insignificant. Everything has to be just so.

4   Just so they like it. "These people compulsively have to have their own way," says Los Angeles psychologist Gary Emery. "Their egos are based on being right," Emery says, "on proving they're the boss." (And it isn't enough for the control freak to win. Others have to lose.)

5   "Control freaks are overconcerned with the means, rather than the end," Emery says. "So it's more important that the string beans are the right kind than it is to just enjoy the meal."

6   "What do you mean just enjoy the meal?" scoffs my friend Marc. "There's a right way to do things and then there's everything else." It goes without saying that he, and only he, has access to that Big Right Way in the Sky. And that Marc lives alone.

7   "I really hate to be in any situation where my control over what I'm doing is compromised," he admits. "Like if somebody says, 'I'll handle the cooking and you can shuck the corn or slice the zucchini, I tell them to do it without me."

8   A control freak's kitchen can be his or her castle. "Let me show you the right way to make rice," said my husband the first time I made the mistake of fixing dinner. By the time Duke had sharpened the knives, rechopped the vegetables into two-inch squares, and chided me for using the wrong size pan, I had decided to surrender all control of the stove. (For the record, this wasn't a big sacrifice. I don't like to cook.)

9   "It's easier in a marriage when you both don't care about the same things," says Milton Wolpin, a psychology professor at the University of Southern California. "Otherwise, everything would be a battle."

10   And every automobile would be a battleground. There's nothing worse that having two control freaks in the same car. "I prefer to drive," my friend Claire says. "But no sooner do I pull out of the driveway than Fred starts telling me what to do. He thinks that I'm an idiot behind the wheel and that I make a lot of stupid mistakes."

11   She doesn't think he drives any better. "I think he goes really, really fast, and I'm sure that someday he's going to kill us both," she says. "And I complain about it constantly. But it's still a little easier for me to take a back seat. I'd rather get to pick him apart than get picked on."

12   My friend Katie would withstand the abuse. "I like to control everything," she says. "From where we're going to eat to what we're going to eat to what movie we're going to see, what time we're going to see it, where we're going to see it, where we're going to park. Everything!"

13   But you can't control everything. So much of life is beyond our control. And to me, that's what makes it interesting. But not to Katie. "I don't like having my fate in someone else's hands," she says firmly. "If I take charge, I know that whatever it is will get done and it will get done well."

14   I shuffle my feet guiltily. Not too long ago I invited Katie and a bunch of friends out to dinner to celebrate my birthday. It was a control freak's nightmare. Not only did I pick the restaurant and arrange to pick up the

check, but Duke also called in advance and ordered an elaborate Chinese banquet. I thought Katie was going to lose her mind.

"What did you order? I have to know," she cried, seizing a menu. "I'm a vegetarian. There are things I won't eat." Duke assured her that he had accounted for everybody's taste. Still, Katie didn't stop hyperventilating until the food arrived. "I was very pleasantly surprised," she confesses. "And I would trust Duke again." 15

"I'm sure there are areas where you're the control freak," says Professor Wolpin, "areas where you're more concerned about things than your husband." Me? The champion of laissez-faire? "You get very upset if you find something visible to the naked eye on the kitchen counter," Duke reminds me. "And you think you know much better than me what the right shirt for me to wear is." 16

But I'm just particular. I'm not a control freak. 17

"A control freak is just someone who cares about something more than you do," Wolpin says. 18

So what's wrong with being a control freak? 19

STUDY QUESTIONS

1. Although an essay's thesis (statement of what the essay is about) usually comes near the beginning, in "My Way!" the thesis is delayed until near the end. Which sentence is the thesis?

2. According to the essay, what are the chief characteristics of a control freak?

3. In paragraph 6, Kaufmann tells about the control freak named Marc. Why do you think he lives alone? Why did the author think that the control freak named Katie was going to lose her mind (paragraph 14)?

4. Which paragraphs include examples? What purpose do those examples serve?

5. Kaufmann quotes sources in paragraphs 4, 5, and 9. What purpose do these quotations serve?

6. By the end of the essay, the author has changed her view of the control freak. How does her view change? What causes the change?

WRITING ASSIGNMENTS

1. Are you a control freak? In a paragraph provide examples to show that you are—or are not—a control freak. (See p. 86 on writing an illustration paragraph.)

2. In a paragraph, narrate an account of an encounter you have had with a control freak. (See p. 71 on narrative paragraphs.)

3. In paragraphs 1 and 2, Kaufmann tells about an encounter she had with a control freak in the gym. In a paragraph, explain how you

would have reacted to this woman and why you would have reacted that way.

4. In an essay, write your own definition of control freak. Like Kaufmann, illustrate your definition with examples. (See p. 101 on the characteristics of definition.)

5. In an essay, write a defense of the control freak by arguing that control freaks contribute something important to society. As an alternative, write an attack on the control freak, arguing that the control freak creates problems. (See p. 137 on the characteristics of persuasion.)

6. Write a definition of some other personality type: the procrastinator, the sports nut, the exercise fanatic, the computer nerd, and so forth.

Money for Morality

Mary Arguelles

Mary Arguelles has written for several magazines, including New
Mother, Baby Talk, *and* Reader's Digest. *In "Money for Morality," which
first appeared in* Newsweek *in 1991, she uses examples to persuade the
reader that we have misplaced our most important virtues because we
seek incentives and rewards for doing the right thing. As you read, ask
yourself whether Arguelles makes a convincing case for her view.*

Before you read, review the following vocabulary:

good samaritan—a person who helps people in distress

presumption—assuming something is true

legacy—something handed down

ubiquitous—existing everywhere

catapulted—hurled

*kowtowing—touching the head to the floor while kneeling;
    worshiping*

I recently read a newspaper article about an 8-year-old boy who found   1
an envelope containing more than $600 and returned it to the bank whose
name appeared on the envelope. The bank traced the money to its rightful owner and returned it to him. God's in his heaven and all's right with
the world. Right? Wrong.

As a reward, the man who lost the money gave the boy $3. Not a lot,   2
but a token of his appreciation nonetheless and not mandatory. After all,
returning money should not be considered extraordinary. A simple "thank
you" is adequate. But some of the teachers at the boy's school felt a reward
was not only appropriate, but required. Outraged at the apparent stingi-
ness of the person who lost the cash, these teachers took up a collection
for the boy. About a week or so later, they presented the good Samaritan
with a $150 savings bond, explaining they felt his honesty should be rec-
ognized. Evidently the virtues of honesty and kindness have become com-
modities that, like everything else, have succumbed to inflation. I can't
help but wonder what dollar amount these teachers would have deemed
a sufficient reward. Certainly they didn't expect the individual who lost

Source: From *Newsweek*, October 29, 1991.

the money to give the child $150. Would $25 have been respectable? How about $10? Suppose that lost money had to cover mortgage, utilities, and food for the week. In light of that, perhaps $3 was generous. A reward is a gift; any gift should at least be met with the presumption of genuine gratitude on the part of the giver.

3   What does this episode say about our society? It seems the role models our children look up to these days—in this case, teachers—are more confused and misguided about values than their young charges. A young boy, obviously well guided by his parents, finds money that does not belong to him and he returns it. He did the right thing. Yet doing the right thing seems to be insufficient motivation for action in our materialistic world. The legacy of the '80s has left us with the ubiquitous question: what's in it for me? The promise of the golden rule—that someone might do a good turn for you—has become worthless collateral for the social interactions of the mercenary and fast-paced '90s. It is in fact this fast pace that is, in part, a source of the problem. Modern communication has catapulted us into an instant world. Television makes history of events before any of us has even had a chance to absorb them in the first place. An ad for major-league baseball entices viewers with the reassurance that "the memories are waiting," an event that has yet to occur has already been packaged as the past. With the world racing by us, we have no patience for a rain check on good deeds.

4   Misplaced virtues are running rampant through our culture. I don't know how many times my 13-year-old son has told me about classmates who received $10 for each A they receive on their report cards—hinting that I should do the same for him should he ever receive an A (or maybe he was working on $5 for a B). Whenever he approaches me on this subject, I give him the same reply: "Doing well is its own reward. The A just confirms that." In other words, forget it! This is not to say that I would never praise my son for doing well in school. But my praise is not meant to reward or elicit future achievements, but rather to express my genuine delight in the satisfaction he feels at having done his best. Throwing $10 at that sends out the message that the feeling alone isn't good enough.

5   ***Kowtowing to ice cream:*** As a society, we seem to be losing a grip on our internal control—the ethical thermostat that guides our actions and feelings toward ourselves, others, and the world around us. Instead, we rely on external "stuff" as a measure of our worth. We pass this message to our children. We offer them money for honesty and good grades. Pizza is given as a reward for reading. In fact, in one national reading program, a pizza party awaits the entire class if each child reads a certain amount of books within a four-month period. We call these things incentives, telling ourselves that if we can just reel them in and get them hooked, then the built-in rewards will follow. I recently saw a television program where unmarried teenaged mothers were featured as the participants in a parenting program that offers a $10 a week "incentive" if these young women don't get pregnant again. Isn't the daily struggle of being a sin-

gle, teenaged mother enough of a deterrent? No, it isn't, because we as a society won't allow it to be. Nothing is permitted to succeed or fail on its own merits anymore.

I remember when I was pregnant with my son I read countless child-care books that offered the same advice: don't bribe your child with ice cream to get him to eat spinach; it makes the spinach look bad. While some may say spinach doesn't need any help looking bad, I submit it's from years of kowtowing to ice cream. Similarly, our moral taste buds have been dulled by an endless onslaught of artificial sweeteners. A steady diet of candy bars and banana splits makes an ordinary apple or orange seem sour. So too does an endless parade of incentives make us incapable of feeling a genuine sense of inner peace (or inner turmoil). 6

The simple virtues of honesty, kindness and integrity suffer from an image problem and are in desperate need of a makeover. One way to do this is by example. If my son sees me feeling happy after I've helped out a friend, then he may do likewise. If my daughter sees me spending a rainy afternoon curled up with a book instead of spending money at the mall, she may get the message that there are some simple pleasures that don't require a purchase. I fear that in our so-called upwardly mobile world we are on a downward spiral toward moral bankruptcy. Like World War II Germany, where the basket holding the money was more valuable than the money itself, we too may render ourselves internally worthless while desperately clinging to a shell of appearances. 7

STUDY QUESTIONS

1. What is the purpose of the first three paragraphs of the essay?

2. What is the thesis of "Money for Morality"? Where is that thesis expressed?

3. What examples does Arguelles use? What is the purpose of those examples?

4. What is the topic sentence of paragraph 3? Of paragraph 4 ? Of paragraph 5?

5. Do you think the teachers should have taken up the collection? Explain.

6. What traits does Arguelles cite as positive values?

WRITING ASSIGNMENTS

1. Arguelles believes that "misplaced virtues are running rampant through our culture." In a paragraph, use examples to show that this statement is or is not true. (See p. 86 on writing an illustration paragraph.)

2. In a paragraph, write a definition of virtue. (See p. 101 on writing a definition paragraph.)

3. In a paragraph, tell a story that shows how the boy reacted to the three-dollar reward. (See p. 71 on writing a narrative paragraph.)

4. Should students be rewarded for good academic performance? Answer this question in an essay. (See p. 137 on writing persuasion.)

5. In an essay, agree or disagree with Arguelles's thesis. (See p. 137 on writing persuasion.)

6. Many of Arguelles's examples are related to school. Using examples from your own experience and observation, tell how good a job you think schools are doing teaching positive values. (See p. 86 on writing illustration.)

Green Frog Skin

John Lame Deer

*John Lame Deer, a tribal priest of the Sioux, has strong views about the
way whites feel about money and nature, and the way they treat the
land. He expresses these views in "Green Frog Skin." As you read, try to
decide why he expresses these views. Also, ask yourself how the process
analysis in the essay helps the author achieve his purpose.*

*Despite Lame Deer's serious purpose, "Green Frog Skin" is an enter-
taining piece, largely because of the relaxed, energetic language and the
interest-holding opening narration. Before you read, however, review the
following vocabulary:*

> *gally-hooting—racing*
>
> *gully—ditch*
>
> *buffalo chips—dried manure*
>
> *strychnine—a poison used to kill rodents*

THE GREEN FROG SKIN—that's what I call a dollar bill. In our attitude   1
toward it lies the biggest difference between Indians and whites. My grandparents grew up in an Indian world without money. Just before the Custer
battle the white soldiers had received their pay. Their pockets were full of
green paper and they had no place to spend it. What were their last
thoughts as an Indian bullet or arrow hit them? I guess they were thinking
of all that money going to waste, of not having had a chance to enjoy it, of
a bunch of dumb savages getting their paws on that hardearned pay. That
must have hurt them more than the arrow between their ribs.

The close hand-to-hand fighting, with a thousand horses gally-hoot-   2
ing all over the place, had covered the battlefield with an enormous cloud
of dust, and in it the green frog skins of the soldiers were whirling around
like snowflakes in a blizzard. Now, what did the Indians do with all that
money? They gave it to their children to play with, to fold those strange
bits of colored paper into all kinds of shapes, making them into toy buffalo and horses. Somebody was enjoying that money after all. The books
tell of one soldier who survived. He got away, but he went crazy and
some women watched him from a distance as he killed himself. The writ-

Source: Reprinted with permission of Simon & Schuster from *Lame Deer: Seeker
of Visions* by John Fine/Lame Deer and Richard Erdoes. Copyright © 1994 by
Pocket Books. Copyright © 1972 by John Fine/Lame Deer and Richard Erdoes.

ers always say he must have been afraid of being captured and tortured, but that's all wrong.

3   Can't you see it? There he is, bellied down in a gully, watching what is going on. He sees the kids playing with the money, tearing it up, the women using it to fire up some dried buffalo chips to cook on, the men lighting their pipes with green frog skins, but mostly all those beautiful dollar bills floating away with the dust and the wind. It's this sight that drove that poor soldier crazy. He's clutching his head, hollering, "Goddam, Jesus Christ Almighty, look at them dumb, stupid, red sons of bitches wasting all that dough!" He watches till he can't stand it any longer, and then he blows his brains out with a six-shooter. It would make a great scene in a movie, but it would take an Indian mind to get the point.

4   The green frog skin—that was what the fight was all about. The gold of the Black Hills, the gold in every clump of grass. Each day you can see ranch hands riding over this land. They have a bagful of grain from their saddle horns, and whenever they see a prairie-dog hole they toss a handful of oats in it, like a kind little old lady feeding the pigeons in one of your city parks. Only the oats for the prairie dogs are poisoned with strychnine. What happens to the prairie dog after he has eaten this grain is not a pleasant thing to watch. The prairie dogs are poisoned, because they eat grass. A thousand of them eat up as much grass in a year as a cow. So if the rancher can kill that many prairie dogs he can run one more head of cattle, make a little more money. When he looks at a prairie dog he sees only a green frog skin getting away from him.

5   For the white man each blade of grass or spring of water has a price tag on it. And that is the trouble, because look at what happens. The bobcats and coyotes which used to feed on prairie dogs now have to go after a stray lamb or a crippled calf. The rancher calls the pest-control officer to kill these animals. This man shoots some rabbits and puts them out as bait with a piece of wood stuck in them. That stick has an explosive charge which shoots some cyanide into the mouth of the coyote who tugs at it. The officer has been trained to be careful. He puts a printed warning on each stick reading, "Danger, Explosive, Poison!" The trouble is that our dogs can't read, and some of our children can't either.

6   And the prairie becomes a thing without life—no more prairie dogs, no more badgers, foxes, coyotes. The big birds of prey used to feed on prairie dogs, too. So you hardly see an eagle these days. The bald eagle is your symbol. You see him on your money, but your money is killing him. When a people start killing off their own symbols they are in a bad way.

7   The Sioux have a name for white men. They call them *wasicun*—fat-takers. It is a good name, because you have taken the fat of the land. But it does not seem to have agreed with you. Right now you don't look so healthy—overweight, yes, but not healthy. Americans are bred like stuffed geese—to be consumers, not human beings. The moment they stop consuming and buying, this frog-skin world has no more use for them. They have become frogs themselves. Some cruel child has stuffed a cigar into

their mouths and they have to keep puffing and puffing until they explode. Fat-taking is a bad thing, even for the taker. It is especially bad for Indians who are forced to live in this frog-skin world which they did not make and for which they have no use.

STUDY QUESTIONS

1. In paragraphs 1–3, Lame Deer tells a brief story about a battle between Native Americans and General Custer. What purpose does the narration serve? What does it contribute to the essay?

2. Which paragraphs include process analysis (an explanation of how something is made or done)? What purpose does this process analysis serve?

3. In your own words, write out the thesis of "Green Frog Skin."

4. For what purpose do you think the author wrote the essay?

5. Who do you think the author's intended audience is?

6. Lame Deer does not specifically explain what happens to a prairie dog after it eats strychnine. He simply says that its death is "not a pleasant thing to watch" (paragraph 4). Why do you think he omits the specific details?

7. Lame Deer uses informal language. For example, he refers to the Native Americans' hands as "their paws" (paragraph 1). Cite two other examples of informal language. What does this language contribute to the essay?

WRITING ASSIGNMENTS

1. In a paragraph, summarize John Lame Deer's opinion about whites and how they have affected Native Americans.

2. Lame Deer says that Americans are "consumers, not human beings" (paragraph 7). In a paragraph, agree or disagree with this statement, citing at least two examples to support your view.

3. In a paragraph, explain what Lame Deer means when he says, "When a people start killing off their own symbols they are in a bad way" (paragraph 6). What point is the author making?

4. In an essay, agree or disagree with Lame Deer's view that Americans are "fat-takers" (paragraph 7). Be sure to cite examples to support your view.

5. In an essay, agree or disagree with Lame Deer's view of whites. Be sure to cite examples to support your view.

6. Which would you choose if given the chance: a $100,000 a year job that involved harm to the environment or a $20,000 a year job that involved helping the environment? Be sure to explain the reasons for your choice.

The Company Man

Ellen Goodman

Ellen Goodman is a Pulitzer Prize–winning writer whose Boston Globe *column is carried by newspapers around the country. She has also been a* Newsweek *reporter and* Today *show commentator. "The Company Man" is from* Close to Home *(1979), which is a collection of her newspaper columns.*

In the essay, Goodman offers details not given in the obituary of Phil, a workaholic, dedicated company man who died on the job. However, you will notice that the piece says as much about the corporate scheme of things as it does about Phil. As you read, ask yourself what description of corporate America Goodman presents.

Before reading, review the following vocabulary:

obituary—death notice, often in a newspaper

coronary thrombosis—a clot that blocks an artery to the heart

workaholic—a person addicted to work

conceivably—possibly

stock options—shares of company stock available to employees, usually below market value

Type A—an intense, highly competitive person

discreetly—carefully, without being obvious

1   He worked himself to death, finally and precisely, at 3:00 A.M. Sunday morning.

2   The obituary didn't say that, of course. It said that he died of a coronary thrombosis—I think that was it—but everyone among his friends and acquaintances knew it instantly. He was a perfect Type A, a workaholic, a classic, they said to each other and shook their heads—and thought for five or ten minutes about the way they lived.

3   This man who worked himself to death finally and precisely at 3:00 A.M. Sunday morning—on his day off—was fifty-one years old and a vice-president. He was, however, one of six vice-presidents, and one of three

who might conceivably—if the president died or retired soon—have moved to the top spot. Phil knew that.

He worked six days a week, five of them until eight or nine at night, during a time when his own company had begun the four-day week for everyone but the executives. He worked like the Important People. He had no outside "extracurricular interests," unless, of course, you think about a monthly golf game that way. To Phil, it was work. He always ate egg salad sandwiches at his desk. He was, of course, overweight, by 20 or 25 pounds. He thought it was okay, though, because he didn't smoke.

On Saturdays, Phil wore a sports jacket to the office instead of a suit, because it was the weekend.

He had a lot of people working for him, maybe sixty, and most of them liked him most of the time. Three of them will be seriously considered for his job. The obituary didn't mention that.

But it did list his "survivors" quite accurately. He is survived by his wife, Helen, forty-eight years old, a good woman of no particular marketable skills, who worked in an office before marrying and mothering. She had, according to her daughter, given up trying to compete with his work years ago, when the children were small. A company friend said, "I know how much you will miss him." And she answered, "I already have."

"Missing him all these years," she must have given up part of herself which had cared too much for the man. She would be "well taken care of."

His "dearly beloved" eldest of the "dearly beloved" children is a hard-working executive in a manufacturing firm down South. In the day and a half before the funeral, he went around the neighborhood researching his father, asking the neighbors what he was like. They were embarrassed.

His second child is a girl, who is twenty-four and newly married. She lives near her mother and they are close, but whenever she was alone with her father, in a car driving somewhere, they had nothing to say to each other.

The youngest is twenty, a boy, a high-school graduate who has spent the last couple of years, like a lot of his friends, doing enough odd jobs to stay in grass and food. He was the one who tried to grab at his father, and tried to mean enough to him to keep the man at home. He was his father's favorite. Over the last two years, Phil stayed up nights worrying about the boy.

The boy once said, "My father and I only board here."

At the funeral, the sixty-year-old company president told the forty-eight-year-old widow that the fifty-one-year-old deceased had meant much to the company and would be missed and would be hard to replace. The widow didn't look him in the eye. She was afraid he would read her bitterness and, after all, she would need him to straighten out the finances—the stock options and all that.

Phil was overweight and nervous and worked too hard. If he wasn't at the office, he was worried about it. Phil was a Type A, a heart-attack natural. You could have picked him out in a minute from a lineup.

So when he finally worked himself to death, at precisely 3:00 A.M. Sunday morning, no one was really surprised.

16   By 5:00 P.M. the afternoon of the funeral, the company president had begun, discreetly of course, with care and taste, to make inquiries about his replacement. One of three men. He asked around: "Who's been working the hardest?"

STUDY QUESTIONS

1. Describe the relationship Phil had with his wife and his children.

2. Describe the view of corporate America presented in "The Company Man."

3. What does the last paragraph suggest is the lesson to be learned from "The Company Man"?

4. Twice at the beginning and once near the end of the essay, Goodman emphasizes the time of Phil's death. Why?

5. Why does Goodman mention the time the company president began looking for Phil's replacement (paragraph 16)?

WRITING ASSIGNMENTS

1. In a paragraph, define workaholic. (See p. 101 on writing a definition paragraph.)

2. Do you think Phil was a good employee? In a paragraph, explain why or why not.

3. If you have held a job, in a paragraph, describe yourself as an employee. If you have not held a job, describe the kind of employee you expect you will be in the future.

4. Phil was a workaholic rather than a family man. In an essay, define *family man*. (See p. 101 on the characteristics of definition.)

5. In an essay, explain what you think causes people to become workaholics. (See p. 118 on the characteristics of cause-and-effect analysis.)

6. If you had to choose between being a workaholic who made a great deal of money, or a person with a more balanced life who made just enough money to get by, which would you choose? Explain why.

Time to Look and Listen

Magdoline Asfahani

Magdoline Asfahani, the child of Arab immigrants, has experienced the prejudice born of stereotypical thinking about Arabs. In this 1995 Newsweek essay, she narrates the causes and effects of the shame she began to feel about her heritage because of the prejudice of others. She also tells how that shame was transformed into ethnic pride and draws an important conclusion about the role education plays in building understanding.

Before you read the essay, review the following vocabulary:

diverted—turned aside from a path

taunted—teased and ridiculed

alluding—hinting, suggesting

nuances—shades

1   I love my country as many who have been here for generations can-not. Perhaps that's because I'm the child of immigrants, raised with a con-scious respect for America that many people take for granted. My parents chose this country because it offered them a new life, freedom, and pos-sibilities. But I learned at a young age that the country we loved so much did not feel the same way about us.

2   Discrimination is not unique to America. It occurs in any country that allows immigration. Anyone who is unlike the majority is looked at a little suspiciously, dealt with a little differently. The fact that I wasn't part of the majority never occurred to me. I knew that I was an Arab and a Muslim. This meant nothing to me. At school I stood up to say the Pledge of Alle-giance every day. These things did not seem incompatible at all. Then everything changed for me, suddenly and permanently, in 1985. I was only in seventh grade, but that was the beginning of my political education.

3   That year a TWA plane originating in Athens was diverted to Beirut. Two years earlier the U.S. Marine barracks in Beirut had been bombed. That seemed to start a chain of events that would forever link Arabs with ter-rorism. After the hijacking, I faced classmates who taunted me with cruel names, attacking my heritage and my religion. I became an outcast and had to apologize for myself constantly.

4   After a while, I tried to forget my heritage. No matter what race, religion, or ethnicity, a child who is attacked often retreats. I was the only Arab I knew of in my class, so I had no one in my peer group as an ally. No matter what my parents tried to tell me about my proud cultural history, I would ignore it. My classmates told me I came from an uncivilized, brutal place, that Arabs were by nature anti-American, and I believed them. They did not know the hours my parents spent studying, working, trying to preserve part of their old lives while embracing, willingly, the new.

5   I tried to forget the Arabic I knew, because if I didn't I'd be forever linked to murderers. I stopped inviting friends over for dinner, because I thought the food we ate was "weird." I lied about where my parents had come from. Their accents (although they spoke English perfectly) humiliated me. Though Islam is a major monotheistic religion with many similarities to Judaism and Christianity, there were no holidays near Chanukah or Christmas, nothing to tie me to the "Judeo-Christian" tradition. I felt more excluded. I slowly began to turn into someone without a past.

6   Civil war was raging in Lebanon, and all that Americans saw of that country was destruction and violence. Every other movie seemed to feature Arab terrorists. The most common questions I was asked were if I had ever ridden a camel or if my family lived in tents. I felt burdened with responsibility. Why should an adolescent be asked questions like "Is it true you hate Jews and you want Israel destroyed?" I didn't hate anybody. My parents had never said anything even alluding to such sentiments. I was confused and hurt.

7   As I grew older and began to form my own opinions, my embarrassment lessened and my anger grew. The turning point came in high school. My grandmother had become very ill, and it was necessary for me to leave school a few days before Christmas vacation. My chemistry teacher was very sympathetic until I said I was going to the Middle East. "Don't come back in a body bag, " he said cheerfully. The class laughed. Suddenly, those years of watching movies that mocked me and listening to others who knew nothing about Arabs and Muslims except what they saw on television seemed like a bad dream. I knew then that I would never be silent again.

8   I've tried to reclaim those lost years. I realize now that I come from a culture that has a rich history. The Arab world is a medley of people of different religions; not every Arab is a Muslim, and vice versa. The Arabs brought tremendous advances in the sciences and mathematics, as well as creating a literary tradition that has never been surpassed. The language itself is flexible and beautiful, with nuances and shades of meaning unparalleled in any language. Though many find it hard to believe, Islam has made progress in women's rights. There is a specific provision in the Koran that permits women to own property and ensures that their inheritance is protected—although recent events have shown that interpretation of these laws can vary.

9   My youngest brother, who is 12, is now at the crossroads I faced. When initial reports of the Oklahoma City bombing pointed to "Arab-looking individuals" as the culprits, he came home from school crying. "Mom, why do Muslims kill people? Why are the Arabs so bad?" She was angry and bro-

kenhearted but tried to handle the situation in the best way possible: through education. She went to his class, armed with Arabic music, pictures, traditional dress, and cookies. She brought a chapter of the social-studies book to life, and the children asked intelligent, thoughtful questions, even after the class was over. Some even asked if she was coming back. When my brother came home, he was excited and proud instead of ashamed.

I only recently told my mother about my past experience. Maybe if I had   10 told her then, I would have been better equipped to deal with the thoughtless teasing. But, fortunately, the world is changing. Although discrimination and stereotyping still exist, many people are trying to lessen and end it. Teachers, schools, and the media are showing greater sensitivity to cultural issues. However, there is still much that needs to be done, not for the sake of any particular ethnic or cultural group but for the sake of our country.

The America that I love is one that values freedom and the differences   11 of its people. Education is the key to understanding. As Americans we need to take a little time to look and listen carefully to what is around us and not rush to judgment without knowing all the facts. And we must never be ashamed of our pasts. It is our collective differences that unite us and make us unique as a nation. It's what determines our present and our future.

STUDY QUESTIONS

1. In your own words, write out the thesis of "Time to Look and Listen."

2. Explain the meaning of the title. How is the title related to the rest of the essay?

3. Why did Asfahani try to forget her Arab heritage?

4. What does the author mean when she says that she loves the United States "as many who have been here for generations cannot" (paragraph 1)?

5. In narrations, transitions of time are important because they help readers follow the chronology (time-sequence). What transition of time opens paragraph 3? Paragraph 4? Paragraph 7? Paragraph 10?

6. Whole paragraphs can function as transitions when they link what comes before them with what comes after them. Explain how paragraph 7 functions as a transitional paragraph.

WRITING ASSIGNMENTS

1. Asfahani refers to the stereotype of the Arab. In a paragraph, describe the stereotype of some group that you belong to. You can use an ethnic group, national or religious group, or another group, such as student athletes, blondes, farmers, math majors, or body builders.

2. Asfahani says it is "our collective differences that unite us and make us unique as a nation" (paragraph 11). In a paragraph, use examples to show that this statement is true. (See p. 86 on writing an illustration paragraph.)

3. In a paragraph, define *prejudice*. (See p. 101 on writing a definition paragraph.)

4. Decide on one thing schools can do to promote the understanding of cultural differences, and in an essay argue for the adoption of your idea. Be sure to note whether you are referring to elementary schools, secondary schools, or colleges. (See p. 137 on the characteristics of persuasion.)

5. Narrate an account of a time you experienced, witnessed, or participated in an act of discrimination. (See p. 71 on narration.)

6. In an essay, tell about some aspect of your own cultural heritage and the effects of that aspect on you. (See p. 118 on cause-and-effect analysis.)

WRITING A SUMMARY

A **summary** is a restatement—*in your own words*—of an author's main ideas. When you summarize, you record an author's major points and major supporting details using your own wording and style.

You may be asked to summarize readings or chapters in textbooks so an instructor can check whether you understand reading assignments. In addition, when you write research papers, you may have to include summarized material.

The Characteristics of a Summary

To write a successful summary keep the following points in mind:

1. *Include only the author's main points and major supporting details.* Do not include minor details, examples, or explanation unless these are necessary to clarify a main point.

2. *Include only the author's ideas.* You may be tempted to comment on something the author has said, but you must resist because a summary may not contain anything not in the original.

3. *Keep the summary significantly shorter than the original.* Because you are including only the main ideas, your summary is bound to be shorter than the original.

4. *Preserve the author's meaning.* Do not alter the author's meaning in any way.

      original: Some states still have not enacted legislation mandating barrier-free structures.

unacceptable restatement:	No laws require barrier-free buildings in many states.
explanation:	*Many* in the restatement changes the meaning of the original because the author said *some*.
acceptable restatement:	No laws require barrier-free buildings in a number of states.
explanation:	Use of *a number of* does not alter the author's meaning.
original:	States that did not raise the drinking age to 21 lost their federal highway funds.
unacceptable restatement:	States were being pressured to make 21 the legal age to drink.
explanation:	The restatement alters meaning by omitting important information: the fact that states that did not raise the drinking age lost federal highway funds.
acceptable restatement:	States that did not make 21 the legal drinking age faced the loss of federal highway funds.
explanation:	All the important information is in the restatement.

5. *Use your own wording and sentence style.* You must preserve the author's meaning, but you should restate the author's ideas in your own way. Here is an example:

original:	The trouble with Little League is that the coaches have emphasized winning at the expense of skill acquisition and having fun.
restatement:	Little League coaches stress winning rather than enjoyment and learning, which creates problems.

When you summarize, do not merely substitute synonyms (words with similar meaning) for the original words. Substituting synonyms is *not* restating in your own style because sentence structure is not altered.

original:	The trouble with Little League is that the coaches have emphasized winning at the expense of skill acquisition and having fun.

unacceptable restatement:	The problem (synonym) with Little League is that the managers (synonym) have stressed (synonym) beating the opponent (synonym) at the cost of (synonym) acquiring skills (synonym) and having a good time (synonym).
explanation:	The preceding restatement is unacceptable because sentence structure has not been changed. Instead, synonyms have been substituted for words in the original.

6. *You may use the author's words when there is no acceptable substitute, or when you particularly like the author's phrasing.* In the Little League example, a restatement may use the words Little League because no other words will do. However, if you use original words that are not part of your normal vocabulary or that are part of the author's distinctive phrasing, use quotation marks around the words. Here is an example:

original:	The trouble with Little League is that the coaches have emphasized winning at the expense of skill acquisition and having fun.
restatement:	Little League coaches stress winning but do not stress "skill acquisition" and the enjoyment of the game.
explanation:	"Little League," "coaches," and "winning" are used without quotation marks because there is no substitute and the words are part of my vocabulary. "Skill acquisition" appears with quotation marks because the phrase is part of the author's distinctive phrasing.

Use quotations when necessary, but do not overuse them. Most of the summary should be in your own words.

7. *The opening sentence of a summary should include the author's name, the title of the material being summarized, and the author's focus, purpose, and/or thesis.* Here are sample openings for summaries of the essays beginning on pages 447, 451, 443, and 462.

A. In "On Being 17, Bright, and Unable to Read," David Raymond narrates an account of the difficulties he faced in school because of his dyslexia. (author's focus presented)

B. Margo Kaufmann's "My Way!" explains that anyone can be a *control freak*. To qualify, one need only care more than you do. (author's thesis presented)

C. In "Students in Shock," John Kellmayer warns students about the stress associated with college and advises them to cope with the stress by taking advantage of certain campus resources. (author's focus presented)

D. To point out the dangers of being a workaholic, Ellen Goodman describes the life and death of Phil in "The Company Man." (author's purpose and thesis presented)

Notice that in each example the verb that functions with the author's name or essay title is in the present tense. Even though the work was written in the past, use the present tense:

"My Way" *explains* ...

John Kellmayer *warns* ...

David Ramond *narrates* ...

Ellen Goodman *describes* ...

8. *To achieve transition, repeat the author's name with a present tense verb*. Use phrases like these:

Raymond also explains ...

Goodman continues by describing ...

Kaufmann goes on to show ...

A Sample Summary

The essay that follows, "If You Had to Kill Your Own Hog," was written by Dick Gregory. The main ideas and important supporting details have been underlined to mark them for inclusion in the summary that follows.

Read through the essay, paying particular attention to the underlined material. Then read the summary that follows the essay. Notes in the margin of the summary call your attention to important features.

If You Had to Kill Your Own Hog

Dick Gregory

1 My momma could never understand how white folks could twist the words of the Bible around to justify racial segregation. Yet she could read the Ten Commandments, which clearly say, "Thou shalt not kill," and still justify eating meat. Momma couldn't read the newspaper very well, but she sure could interpret the Word of God. "God meant you shouldn't kill people," she used to say. But I insisted, "Momma, He didn't say that. He said, 'Thou shalt not kill.' If you leave that statement alone, a whole lot of things would be safe from killing. But if you are going to twist the words about killing to mean what you want them to mean, then let white folks do the same thing with justifying racial segregation."

2 "You can't live without eating meat," Momma would persist. "You'd starve." I couldn't buy that either. You get milk from a cow without killing it. You do not have to kill an animal to get what you need from it. You get wool from the sheep without killing it. Two of the strongest animals in the jungle are vegetarians—the elephant and the gorilla. The first two years are the most important years of a man's life, and during that period he is not involved with eating meat. If you suddenly become very ill, there is a good chance you will be taken off a meat diet. So it is a myth that killing is necessary for survival. The day I decide that I must have a piece of steak to nourish my body, I will also give the cow the same right to nourish herself on human beings.

3 There is so little basic difference between animals and humans. The process of reproduction is the same for chickens, cattle, and humans. If suddenly the air stopped circulating on the earth, or the sun collided with the earth, animals and humans would die alike. A nuclear holocaust will wipe out all life. Life in the created order is basically the same and should be respected as such. It seems to me the Bible says it is wrong to kill—period.

4 If we can justify *any* kind of killing in the name of religion, the door is opened for all kinds of other justifications. The fact of killing animals is not as frightening as our human tendency to justify it—to kill and not even be aware that we are taking life. It is sobering to realize that when you misuse one of the least of Nature's creatures, like the chicken, you are sowing the seed for misusing the highest of Nature's creatures, man.

Source: From *The Shadow That Scares Me* by Dick Gregory. Copyright © 1968 by Dick Gregory. Used by permission of Doubleday, a division of Bantam Doubleday Dell Publishing Group, Inc.

Animals and humans suffer and die alike. If you had to kill your own   5
hog before you ate it, most likely you would not be able to do it. To hear
the hog scream, to see the blood spill, to see the baby being taken away
from its momma, and to see the look of death in the animal's eye would
turn your stomach. So you get the man at the packing house to do the
killing for you. In like manner, if the wealthy aristocrats who are perpe-
trating conditions in the ghetto actually heard the screams of ghetto suffering, or saw the slow death of hungry little kids, or witnessed the
strangulation of manhood and dignity, they could not continue the killing.
But the wealthy are protected from such horror. They have people to do
the killing for them. The wealthy profit from the daily murders of ghetto
life but they do not see them. Those who immerse themselves in the daily
life of the ghetto see the suffering—the social workers, the police, the local
merchants, and the bill collectors. But the people on top never really see.

By the time you see a piece of meat in the butcher shop window, all   6
the blood and suffering have been washed away. When you order a steak
in the restaurant, the misery has been forgotten and you see the finished
product. You see a steak with butter and parsley on it. It looks appetizing
and appealing and you are pleased enough to eat it. You never even consider the suffering which produced your meal or the other animals killed
that day in the slaughterhouse. In the same way, all the wealthy aristocrats
ever see of the black community is the finished product, the window dress-
ing, the steak on the platter—Ralph Bunche and Thurgood Marshall. The
United Nations or the Supreme Court bench is the restaurant and the
ghetto street corner is the slaughterhouse.

Life under ghetto conditions cuts short life expectancy. The Negro's   7
life expectancy is shorter than the white man's. The oppressor benefits
from continued oppression financially; he makes more money so that he
can eat a little better. I see no difference between a man killing a chicken
and a man killing a human being, by overwork and forcing ghetto conditions upon him, both so that he can eat a little better. If you can justify
killing to eat meat, you can justify the conditions of the ghetto. I cannot
justify either one.

Every time the white folks made my momma mad, she would grab the   8
Bible and find something bitter in it. She would come home from the rich
white folks' house, after they had just called her "nigger," or patted her on
the rump or caught her stealing some steaks, open her Bible and read
aloud, "It is easier for a camel to pass through the eye of a needle than for
a rich man to get into Heaven." When you get involved with distorting the
words of the Bible, you don't have to be bitter. The same tongue can be
used to bless and curse men.

Summary of "If You Had to Kill Your Own Hog"

[1]In "If You Had to Kill Your Own Hog," Dick Gregory
argues that the continued practice of eating meat is like
the continued practice of segregation. He makes this point

[1]Opening sentence includes
author, title, and thesis. Notice
the present tense of the verb
argues.

[2]Author's name repeated for transition. Note the present tense verb. Restatement of first main point.

[3]Quotation marks because phrase is the author's distinctive style.

[4-5]Author's name repeated for transition. Note the present tense verbs. Restatement of main points.

[6]No quotation marks around *respected* because not part of author's distinctive style.

[7]Quotation marks around exact words.

[8]Author's name repeated for transition. Verb in present tense. Restatement of main point.

[9]Restatement of main point.

[10]Author's name repeated for transition. Verb is in present tense. Restatement of main point.

[11]Exact words in quotation marks.

[12]Final point restated.

by showing a contradiction in the way his mother viewed the Bible. [2]Gregory says that his mother could not understand how whites could use the Bible [3]"to justify racial segregation," but she herself failed to see that the commandment "Thou shalt not kill" prohibits the killing of animals for food.

[4]Gregory explains that his mother believed that people needed meat to live. [5]Gregory counters this argument, however, by noting that it is untrue. Further, he contends that all life is to be [6]respected, and, thus, killing animals is wrong. In fact, taking animal life is [7]"sowing the seed for misusing the highest of Nature's creatures, man."

[8]Gregory believes that if people had to kill the animals they ate, they would not eat animals. [9]The fact that people do not watch the suffering allows it to continue—just as ghetto conditions persist because the wealthy do not witness the suffering there. [10]Gregory extends the comparison between the suffering of animals and the suffering of blacks in the ghetto when he says, [11]"If you can justify killing to eat meat, you can justify the conditions of the ghetto. . . ." [12]Gregory finds them both wrong.

How to Write a Summary

Step 1

Read the material as many times as necessary to understand everything the author says. Look up any words you do not understand.

Step 2

Underline the thesis, topic sentences, and main points. Underline *only* those supporting details necessary for clarifying main points. If a main point is clear enough, do not underline supporting details.

Step 3

On a separate sheet, write the underlined ideas in your own words. Keep a dictionary nearby to look up alternatives for words you are having trouble with. A good way to restate an underlined idea in your words is to read the idea until you are sure you understand it. Then look away from your book, imagine how you would explain that idea to a friend in your own words, and write the idea the same way you would explain it to your friend. If you cannot satisfactorily restate something in your own words, use the author's words in quotation marks. However, use the author's words sparingly.

Step 4

Write a first draft, opening with a sentence that includes the author, title, and the author's thesis, focus, or purpose. Use a present tense verb with the author's name. Then go to your list of restatements and write these in the same order the ideas appear in the original.

Step 5

Read your summary out loud. If you hear an awkward gap, add a transition and/or repeat the author's name with a present tense verb. If an idea is not clear, add a restatement of a clarifying detail.

Step 6

Review the summary to be sure you can answer yes to these questions:

Did you open with the author, title, and thesis, focus, or purpose?

Did you include only main points and major supporting details?

Did you alter the author's sentence structure and wording?

Did you preserve the author's meaning?

Have you used quotation marks around words that are part of the author's special phrasing?

Have you avoided adding meaning not in the original?

Is the summary significantly shorter than the original?

Did you avoid substituting synonyms?

Step 7

Edit your summary carefully for mistakes.

Thinking, Learning, and Writing in College

Summarizing as a Study Aid

Summarizing can be a powerful study aid, particularly with difficult material. Try summarizing parts of chapters in textbooks to be sure you understand the material. Then review your summaries frequently to help you learn the information.

Three Essays to Summarize

Summarizing the three essays that follow (or summarizing the ones your instructor assigns) will give you practice.

Language and Culture

Manuel G. Mendoza
and Vince Napoli

Have you ever wondered how you know what you know or why your view of reality is what it is? As the following selection explains, language is in large measure responsible for your particular perception of reality, a perception likely to differ somewhat from the views held by speakers of other languages. "Language and Culture," taken from a sociology textbook, may cause you to think about language a new way.

Before reading the essay, review the following vocabulary:

continuity—uninterrupted flow

conjugating—giving the various forms of a verb

cohesive—uniting

1   Perception refers to the awareness of aspects of the environment. Perception is always limited and selective. That is, your senses cannot possibly "take in" all that is going on out there in the external world at any given time. The most you can experience at any given time is only a fraction of what is actually happening. Your perception, therefore, is limited to what you select to be aware of. For example, right now you are sitting or standing somewhere reading this book. You are probably aware only of the idea you are presently concentrating on. If, however, we direct your attention to the weight of the book in your hands, you will temporarily lose the continuity of your thought. You will find that it is difficult, if not impossible, to concentrate at the same time on both the ideas contained in the book and the weight of the book itself. Certainly you will agree that the book always has had the quality of weight, but when you were concentrating on its ideas you were not consciously aware of the book's weight. And so it is with other aspects of your immediate environment. There are literally hundreds of events occurring around you right now that you are not perceiving. The perceptual process, then, is a selective process.

2   By sensitizing people to particular aspects of both the internal and the external world, language structures their perception. We can see this

Source: From Systems of Society: An Introduction to Social Science, Fifth Edition by Manuel G. Mendoza and Vince Napoli. Copyright © 1990 by D. C. Heath and Company. Used by permission of Houghton Mifflin Company.

clearly when we compare the grammars of different languages. The Hopi Indian language, for example, emphasizes *validity* in conjugating its verbs. In describing an action the Hopi must indicate whether he or she is reporting a direct experience, a belief or expectation, or a generalization about experience. The verb chosen to describe an action will communicate the nature of the evidence that is the basis for the report; but it will not specify when the action takes place. Conversely, the English language emphasizes *tense* in conjugating its verbs; the speaker always indicates whether the action is part of the past, present, or future. As you might guess, the Hopi is more conscious of validating sources of information than the English-speaking person, and the English-speaking person is more conscious of time than the Hopi.

In fact, time consciousness seems to be such a part of the English language that we treat words for time the same as we do words for material objects. This leads us to such concepts as "buying time," "saving time," or "time is money," which, in turn, lead us to emphasize speed and hurrying. In English, then, the clock *runs,* but in Spanish *el reloj anda,* "he walks." This simple difference has enormous implications. If clocks run, there isn't a minute to lose! If they walk, we can take our time. There is, of course, a great deal of evidence to suggest that people of different cultures conceive of time differently.   3

Our conceptions of other aspects of experience are also rooted in language. Anthropologist Edward T. Hall speaks of a learned "silent language" which structures our perceptions of space, play activities, and sexuality, as well as time. He points out, for instance, that a comfortable distance for interaction in Latin America is much less than it is in the United States.   4

> [Latin Americans] cannot talk comfortably with one another unless   5
> they are very close to the distance that evokes either sexual or hostile
> feelings in the North American. The result is that when they move
> close, we withdraw and back away. As a consequence, they think we
> are distant or cold, withdrawn and unfriendly. We, on the other hand,
> are constantly accusing them of breathing down our necks, crowding
> us, and spraying our faces.

The reason the Latin American and the North American react differently is because each has been taught a "silent language" that structures the perception of space differently from the other.   6

Language, then, shapes our experience. To a great extent it determines how and what we will think. In this fashion it serves as a guide to social reality. Although he may be overstating the case somewhat, Edward Sapir seems to be striking a chord of truth when he says that human beings "are very much at the mercy of the particular language which has become the medium of expression for their society. . . .No two languages are ever sufficiently similar to be considered as representing the same social reality.

The worlds in which different societies live are distinct worlds, not merely the same world with different labels attached."

7   Language is the vehicle through which we know our world. As we have seen, language structures our perception of reality and gives meaning to our experiences; through it, we identify objects and ideas, and we express our thoughts. It allows us to accumulate vast stores of knowledge, and to transmit culture from one generation to the next. Language is at the very core of culture. It is the foundation upon which the cooperation necessary for human survival is based. It is one of the cohesive bonds that unite people together, hold culture together, and coordinate the efforts of people in society. And, in Hayakawa's words, "this coordination of effort necessary for the functioning of society is *of necessity achieved by language or else it is not achieved at all.*"

America's Gambling Craze

James Popkin with Katia Hetter

Gambling, once universally regarded as a vice, has become a popular American pastime. But at what price? Popkin and Hetter examine the effect of gambling on the cities it is supposed to be helping.

Before reading the essay, review the following vocabulary:

sanctioned—approved

jai alai—a fast court game played with hand-shaped baskets and a ball

revenue—income

fickle—changeable, unstable

1   No one howled in protest last month when H&R Block set up makeshift tax-preparation offices in four Nevada casinos and offered gamblers same-day "refund-anticipation loans." And few people cared recently when a Florida inventor won a U.S. patent that could someday enable television audiences to legally bet on game shows, football games, and even beauty pageants from their homes,

2   What's the deal? Not that long ago, Americans held gambling in nearly the same esteem as heroin dealing and applauded when ax-wielding police paid a visit to the corner dice room. But moral outrage has become as outmoded as a penny slot machine. In 1955, for example, baseball commissioner Ford Frick considered wagering so corrupt he prohibited major leaguers from overnighting in Las Vegas. Last year, by contrast, Americans for the first time made more trips to casinos than they did to Major League ballparks—some 92 million trips, according to one study.

3   It took six decades for gambling to become America's Pastime, from the legalization of Nevada casinos in 1931 to April Fool's Day 1991, when Davenport, Iowa, launched the Diamond Lady, the nation's first legal riverboat casino. The gradual creation of 37 state lotteries broke down the public's mistrust, conveying a clear message that the government sanctioned gambling; indeed, is even coming to depend on it as a tax-revenue source. Corporate ownership of casinos helped in its own way, too, replacing shady operators with trusted brand names like Hilton and MGM. Casinos

Source: Copyright, March 14, 1994, *US News & World Report*. Visit our Website at www.usnews.com for additional information.

479

now operate or are authorized in 23 states, and 95 percent of all Americans are expected to live within a three- or four-hour drive of one by the year 2000.

4   Today, the Bible Belt might as well be renamed the Blackjack Belt, with floating and land-based casinos throughout Mississippi and Louisiana and plans for more in Florida, Texas, Alabama and Arkansas. Meanwhile, the Midwest is overrun with slot hogs, none of the porcine variety. Iowa, Illinois, Indiana and Missouri allow riverboat gambling, and a 50,000-square-foot land-based casino is scheduled to open in mid-May just outside Detroit, in Windsor, Ontario. Low-stakes casinos attract visitors to old mining towns in Colorado and South Dakota, and Indian tribes operate 225 casinos and high-stakes bingo halls nation-wide. Add church bingo, card rooms, sports wagering, dog and horse racing, and jai alai to the mix and it becomes clear why Americans legally wagered $330 billion in 1992—a 1,800 percent increase over 1976.

5   **Calling for new games.** Like the first bars that opened after Prohibition, modern gambling halls are enormously successful. "It will be impossible not to make a lot of money," one executive in New Orleans bragged before his casino had even opened. "It's like spitting and missing the floor." Such boasts—and the real possibility that the boom will create 500,000 jobs nationwide this decade—have not been lost on federal, state, and local lawmakers. In the first six weeks of this year alone they introduced more than 200 bills regarding gambling.

6   But casinos and lotteries may not guarantee the jackpots many politicians expect. When urban-planning professor Robert Goodman reviewed the economic-impact studies that 14 government agencies relied upon before deciding to embrace casino gambling, he found that most were written with a pro-industry spin and only four were balanced and factored in gambling's hidden costs. Goodman's two-year study, due out next week, concludes that newly opened casinos "suck money out of the local economy," away from existing movie theaters, car dealerships, clothing shops and sports arenas. In Atlantic City, for example, about 100 of 250 local restaurants have closed since the casinos debuted in 1978, says Goodman, who teaches at the University of Massachusetts at Amherst.

7   **"Slum by the sea."** States that get hooked on gambling revenues soon suffer withdrawal symptoms when local competition kicks in. Although pioneering casinos and lotteries typically are profitable, gambling grosses decline when lotteries or casinos open in neighboring states. In Biloxi, Miss., for example, slot revenues at first topped about $207 per machine per day. A year later when competitors moved in, however, the daily win-per-machine figure dipped to $109.

8   States frequently overestimate the financial impact of gambling revenues, too. "Legalized gambling is never large enough to solve any social

problems," says gambling-law professor and paid industry consultant I. Nelson Rose. In New Jersey, for example, horse racing alone accounted for about 10 percent of state revenue in the 1950s. Today, despite the addition of a lottery and 12 casinos, the state earns only 6 percent of its revenue through gambling. "Atlantic City used to be a slum by the sea," says Rose. "Now it's a slum by the sea with casinos."

America's love affair with dice and cards has always been a fickle romance, and some academics predict a breakup soon. Legalized gambling in America has been running on a 70-year boom-and-bust cycle since the colonists started the first lotteries. "We're now riding the third wave of legal gambling" that began with the Depression, says Rose, who has written extensively on the subject and teaches at Whittier Law School in Los Angeles. The trend self-destructs after a few decades, when the public simply gets fed up and embraces more conservative values. Rose believes a cheating or corruption scandal will trigger the next crash in about 35 years, an idea that most casino officials think is ludicrous.

9

The sky is not falling yet. Apart from a handful of academics and the odd politician, few Americans are seriously questioning the morality of an industry that is expected to help gamblers lose a record $35 billion in 1995 alone. Religious leaders have been oddly silent, perhaps because so many churches and synagogues rely on bingo revenues. "The biggest things we have to help people are churches and temples and the government," says Arnie Wexler, executive director of the Council on Compulsive Gambling of New Jersey. "And now they're all in the gambling business."

10

Getting hooked. The consequences can be damaging. Wexler says he got a phone call late last week from a man in his 70s who ran up $150,000 in debt just by buying lottery tickets. Although most gambling experts believe that only 1 percent to 3 percent of Americans have a serious gambling problem at any given time, a July 1993 Gallup Poll funded by Wexler's group suggests that the figure may be closer to 5 percent. Regardless, now that casinos are no longer located just in Atlantic City and Nevada it's reasonable to assume that the total number of problem gamblers will soar. "If you put a guy who wouldn't cheat on his wife in a room with a gorgeous nude woman, some guys would fall by the wayside," Wexler says. "When you make gambling legal and socially acceptable, people will try it and some of them will get hooked."

11

But try telling that to a gambler happily feeding a slot machine and waiting for a multimillion-dollar payoff. Fifty-one percent of American adults now find casino gambling "acceptable for anyone," and 35 percent describe it as "acceptable for others but not for me," according to a recent Yankelovich Inc. survey paid for by Harrah's Casinos. The attraction is simple. "The action for them is the thrill of what's going to happen in the next pull of that slot-machine handle," explains Harrah's president, Phil Satre.

12

Black Men and Public Space

Brent Staples

Brent Staples has been a reporter for the Chicago Sun-Times *and an editor with the* New York Times Book Review *and the* Times *Metropolitan section. In addition, he has written a number of magazine articles. In "Black Men and Public Space," Staples describes a problem he often faces: because people perceive him as dangerous, he, himself, is at risk.*

Before you read, review the following vocabulary:

affluent—wealthy

impoverished—poor

discreet—cautious

menacingly—threateningly

quarry—hunted animal

foyer—entrance way

errant—wrong

taut—tense

warrenlike—crowded

bandolier—belt that holds bullets, worn across the chest

perpetrators—people who cause something

lethality—deadliness

bravado—pretended courage

perilous—dangerous

ad hoc—formed for a specific purpose

labyrinthine—like a maze

constitutionals—walks

1   My first victim was a woman—white, well dressed, probably in her early twenties. I came upon her late one evening on a deserted street in Hyde Park, a relatively affluent neighborhood in an otherwise mean, impoverished section of Chicago. As I swung onto the avenue behind her, there seemed to be a discreet, uninflammatory distance between us. Not so. She cast back a worried glance. To her, the youngish black man—a broad six feet two inches with a beard and billowing hair, both hands shoved into the pockets of a bulky military jacket—seemed menacingly close. After a few more quick glimpses, she picked up her pace and was soon running in earnest. Within seconds she disappeared into a cross street.

2   That was more than a decade ago. I was twenty-two years old, a graduate student newly arrived at the University of Chicago. It was in the echo of that terrified woman's footfalls that I first began to know the unwieldy

Source: Reprinted by permission, *Harpers,* December 1986.

inheritance I'd come into—the ability to alter public space in ugly ways. It was clear that she thought herself the quarry of a mugger, a rapist, or worse. Suffering a bout of insomnia, however, I was stalking sleep, not defenseless wayfarers. As a softy who is scarcely able to take a knife to a raw chicken—let alone hold one to a person's throat—I was surprised, embarrassed, and dismayed all at once. Her flight made me feel like an accomplice in tyranny. It also made it clear that I was indistinguishable from the muggers who occasionally seeped into the area from the surrounding ghetto. That first encounter, and those that followed, signified that a vast, unnerving gulf lay between nighttime pedestrians—particularly women—and me. And I soon gathered that being perceived as dangerous is a hazard in itself. I only needed to turn a corner into a dicey situation, or crowd some frightened, armed person in a foyer somewhere, or make an errant move after being pulled over by a policeman. Where fear and weapons meet—and they often do in urban America—there is always the possibility of death.

In that first year, my first away from my hometown, I was to become 3 thoroughly familiar with the language of fear. At dark, shadowy intersections, I could cross in front of a car stopped at a traffic light and elicit the *thunk, thunk, thunk, thunk* of the driver—black, white, male, or female—hammering down the door locks. On less traveled streets after dark, I grew accustomed to but never comfortable with people crossing to the other side of the street rather than pass me. Then there were the standard unpleasantries with policemen, doormen, bouncers, cab drivers, and others whose business it is to screen out troublesome individuals *before* there is any nastiness.

I moved to New York nearly two years ago and I have remained an avid 4 night walker. In central Manhattan, the near-constant crowd cover minimizes tense one-on-one street encounters. Elsewhere—in SoHo, for example, where sidewalks are narrow and tightly spaced buildings shut out the sky—things can get very taut indeed.

After dark, on the warrenlike streets of Brooklyn where I live, I often 5 see women who fear the worst from me. They seem to have set their faces on neutral, and with their purse straps strung across their chests bandolier-style, they forge ahead as though bracing themselves against being tackled. I understand, of course, that the danger they perceive is not a hallucination. Women are particularly vulnerable to street violence, and young black males are drastically overrepresented among the perpetrators of that violence. Yet these truths are no solace against the kind of alienation that comes of being ever the suspect, a fearsome entity with whom pedestrians avoid making eye contact.

It is not altogether clear to me how I reached the ripe old age 6 of twenty-two without being conscious of the lethality nighttime pedestrians attributed to me. Perhaps it was because in Chester, Pennsylvania, the small, angry industrial town where I came of age in the 1960s, I was scarcely noticeable against a backdrop of gang warfare, street knifings, and murders. I grew up one of the good boys, had perhaps a half-dozen fistfights. In retrospect, my shyness of combat has clear sources.

7   As a boy, I saw countless tough guys locked away; I have since buried several, too. They were babies, really—a teenage cousin, a brother of twenty-two, a childhood friend in his mid-twenties—all gone down in episodes of bravado played out in the streets. I came to doubt the virtues of intimidation early on. I chose, perhaps unconsciously, to remain a shadow—timid, but a survivor.

8   The fearsomeness mistakenly attributed to me in public places often has a perilous flavor. The most frightening of these confusions occurred in the late 1970s and early 1980s, when I worked as a journalist in Chicago. One day, rushing into the office of a magazine I was writing for with a dead-line story in hand, I was mistaken for a burglar. The office manager called security and, with an ad hoc posse, pursued me through the labyrinthine halls, nearly to my editor's door. I had no way of proving who I was. I could only move briskly toward the company of someone who knew me.

9   Another time I was on assignment for a local paper and killing time before an interview. I entered a jewelry store on the city's affluent Near North Side. The proprietor excused herself and returned with an enormous red Dober-man pinscher straining at the end of a leash. She stood, the dog extended toward me, silent to my questions, her eyes bulging nearly out of her head. I took a cursory look around, nodded, and bade her good night.

10   Relatively speaking, however, I never fared as badly as another black male journalist. He went to nearby Waukegan, Illinois, a couple of sum-mers ago to work on a story about a murderer who was born there. Mis-taking the reporter for the killer, police officers hauled him from his car at gunpoint and but for his press credentials would probably have tried to book him. Such episodes are not uncommon. Black men trade tales like this all the time.

11   Over the years, I learned to smother the rage I felt at so often being taken for a criminal. Not to do so would surely have led to madness. I now take precautions to make myself less threatening. I move about with care, particularly late in the evening. I give a wide berth to nervous people on subway platforms during the wee hours, particularly when I have exchanged business clothes for jeans. If I happen to be entering a building behind some people who appear skittish, I may walk by, letting them clear the lobby before I return, so as not to seem to be following them. I have been calm and extremely congenial on those rare occasions when I've been pulled over by the police.

12   And on late-evening constitutionals I employ what has proved to be an excellent tension-reducing measure: I whistle melodies from Beethoven and Vivaldi and the more popular classical composers. Even merely New Yorkers hunching toward nighttime destinations seem to relax, and occa-sionally they even join in the tune. Virtually everybody seems to sense that a mugger wouldn't be warbling bright, sunny selections from Vivaldi's *Four Seasons*. It is my equivalent of the cowbell that hikers wear when they know they are in bear country.

WRITING ESSAY EXAMINATION ANSWERS

Essay examinations require you to respond to questions with answers that are paragraph length or longer. Because these examinations are an important part of a college student's life, you should learn to deal with them effectively.

How to Take an Essay Examination

Remembering information is not enough when you are taking an essay examination. You must also present that information in a clear, well-written answer. The following steps can help you.

Step 1

Read the directions before doing anything. The directions may tell you how many questions to answer and how long your answers should be, like this:

> Answer three of the five questions. Each of your answers should be at least a page.

Step 2

Read all the questions before you begin. Part of your brain can work on question 2 while you are answering question 1 and so forth. Also, you may find clues to answers for later questions while you are working through the exam.

Step 3

Decide how to budget your time. If you must answer four questions in 60 minutes, then you know you can devote 15 minutes to each answer. However, pay attention to how many points each question is worth. If you must answer three questions in 60 minutes and one question is worth 50 points and the other two are worth 25 points, you should spend 30 minutes on the 50-point question and 15 minutes on each 25-point question.

Step 4

Check the question for direction words. Words like these will direct the form your answer should take:

analyze—Break something down into its parts and discuss each part.

> Analyze the doctrine of manifest destiny.

classify—Group things according to their characteristics.

> Classify the most frequently occurring defense mechanisms.

compare—Technically, this means "show the similarities," but often-*compare* is used to mean "show the similarities *and* differences."

Compare the symbolism in the poetry of Maxine Kumin and Margaret Atwood.

contrast—Show the differences.

Contrast the foreign policies of Presidents George Bush and Bill Clinton.

define—Give the meaning of a term and include some information (often examples) to show you understand it.

Define anomie.

describe—Give the significant features or tell how something works.

Describe how plants convert carbon dioxide into oxygen.

discuss—Mention all the important points about a topic.

Discuss the influences that led to the failure of the League of Nations.

evaluate—Give your view about the worth of something, being sure to support your opinions with detail.

Evaluate competency testing as a way to ensure that students learn basic skills.

explain—Give the reasons for an occurrence.

Explain the main causes of the Great Depression.

illustrate—Provide examples.

Illustrate the use of intermittent positive reinforcement to control behavior.

show—Explain or demonstrate something.

Show how hypnosis can improve the quality of daily life.

summarize—Briefly give the major points.

Summarize Jefferson's reasons for opposing the World Bank.

support—Give reasons in favor of something.

Support the plan to institute 12-month school years in grades kindergarten through twelve.

Step 5

Plan your answer. Jot down the points you will cover (on the back of or in the margin of your test sheet), and then number the points in the order you will write them. This planning will help you write a well-organized answer. Also, if you list your points, you need not worry about forgetting something in the heat of the moment. Organize simply—do not write introductions or conclusions; just give the information needed in the answer.

Step 6

Begin your answer with a sentence that reflects the question. For example, if the question is "Contrast the psychoanalytic views of Freud and Jung," you could begin with something like this: "The psychoanalytic views of Freud and Jung differ in several important ways."

Step 7

After writing your answer, revise and edit quickly. Pay special attention to clarity and completeness, but also look for serious mistakes in grammar and usage. Make changes directly on the original—you do not have time to recopy.

 Test-Taking Tips

1. *If you do not understand the directions or a question, ask the instructor.* You may not get help, but there is no harm in trying.

2. *Wear a watch* so you can keep track of the time and know when to move on to the next question.

3. *Leave generous margins and write on every other line* so you have space in case you must add something when you revise.

4. *Skip the questions you are unsure of and return to them after answering the ones you are more confident about.* In the course of answering other questions, you may think of the answers to a question you skipped.

5. *If you do not know, guess.* You may get partial credit.

6. *If you start to run out of time, list the points you would include if you had more time.* Although the answer is not in essay form, you may get partial credit.

7. *Do not write more than you are asked for.* You will not get extra credit, and you are taking time away from answers that will give you credit.

8. *Never pad your answers with unrelated information to hide that you do not know the information requested.* Your instructor will recognize the stall.

Two Answers to Study

To understand the traits of an effective essay examination answer, study the two answers that follow. They were written in response to this question about "Language and Culture" (p. 476).

Explain and illustrate the way language affects perception.

The first answer is acceptable, but the second is not. Study the marginal notes that call your attention to the traits of each answer.

Acceptable Answer

The answer opens with words that reflect the question. Every sentence contributes accurate information to the answer. There is no padding and no unrelated information. Transitions help the answer flow well. There is no introduction or conclusion.

Language affects perception because it determines what we know about the world; in fact, it affects both what we know and how we think. By emphasizing certain aspects of reality, language calls them to our attention; by deemphasizing other aspects, it causes us not to notice them. Thus, language structures our perception. For example, the Hopi Indians focus on the validity of information more than when actions occur, but we are more interested in time than validity. This distinction is partly a result of the fact that Hopi verb conjugations indicate whether information is being reported directly, whether it is a belief, or whether it is a generalization. English verb conjugations, however, communicate when an event occurs. "Silent language" also affects our perception of reality. For example, Latin Americans, through silent language, learn to stand very close to people when they communicate, but people in the United States learn to stand farther apart. As a result, Latin Americans view us as cold, while we often feel that Latin Americans are crowding us. Thus, our perceptions of people are affected.

Unacceptable Answer

The first two sentences stall. They contribute nothing, and they do not reflect the question. The third and fourth sentences begin to acknowledge the question, but they are wordy. Sentence 5 addresses the question directly, but it is the only one that does, so the answer is incomplete. Sentences 6 and 7 relate to the question, but they are unclear. The next sentence is repetitious, and the last two are padding.

No one will deny that language is very important in many areas. Language is so important that linguistics is a vital area of scholarship. One thing that we know is that language is very important to perception. In fact, it affects perception dramatically in many ways. Most important is the fact that language affects our view of reality. This can be seen by the way Hopi Indians conjugate verbs to show that validity is important. For us, tense is important because our reality is related to time. Everyone should understand that the perception of reality is based upon language. We should, therefore, appreciate language far more than we do. I know that I plan to take as many linguistics courses as I can, which should also help me learn more about reality.

PRACTICE

Answering the following essay questions will give you valuable practice and help you become more skilled. In parentheses after each question is the essay the question is taken from.

1. What is Dick Gregory's view of eating meat? Explain why he believes as he does, and explain the connection between eating meat and segregation. ("If You Had to Kill Your Own Hog," p. 472)

2. Explain why Margo Kaufmann thinks participation in sports is good for females. Then go on to agree or disagree with her point of view, citing your own experience and observation for support. ("My Way!" p. 451)

3. Summarize the causes of shock among college students and what schools are doing to help students deal with that shock. Mention at least one other action schools can take to help students deal with shock. ("Students in Shock," p. 443)

4. Describe the corporate mentality presented in the essay by Ellen Goodman, and how that mentality affects families. Offer a suggestion for what can be done to make companies more "family-friendly." ("The Company Man," p. 462)

Thinking, Learning, and Writing in College   Preparing for Exams

One way to prepare for an exam is to form a study group with some classmates. Each of you can develop 2 or 3 essay questions, and you can take turns answering each other's questions.

Visit the Clouse Website!

For additional exercises, quizzes, and Internet activities, visit our Website at:

http://www.ablongman.com/clouse

For even more activities, visit the Longman English pages at:

http://www.ablongman.com/englishpages

Appendix I

A Problem-Solving Guide

The following suggestions will not solve every writing problem, but when you are stuck, consult this guide. You may get the help you need.

Problem	Possible Solutions
1. "I don't know what to write."	A. Try listing, brainstorming, journal writing, clustering, or freewriting. If you have already tried one of these, try another.
	B. Go about your normal routine for a day, keeping your writing task in mind. Ideas may occur to you, and if they do, write them down so you do not forget them.
	C. Talk to people about your writing task. Their ideas will stimulate your thinking.
2. "I have some ideas, but I can't seem to get started."	A. Write your draft like a letter to a friend. You may feel more relaxed and able to write this way.
	B. Write your draft as if you were speaking to a friend. This may relax you enough to get started.
	C. Remind yourself that the first draft is supposed to be rough. You may be expecting too much too soon.
	D. Begin in the middle. If openings are hard, start with any idea you feel you can write; then go back to the beginning.

E. Write your draft for yourself, not for another reader, so you are not blocked by thinking of a reader's criticisms.

F. Do some additional brainstorming, clustering, listing, journal writing, or freewriting. You may not yet have enough ideas to begin.

3. "I don't like my draft."

A. Put the draft aside for a day. After some time away, you may feel better about it.

B. Remember, a first draft is supposed to be rough, so do not look for polished material. Be accepting and look for raw material you can shape.

C. Try to identify parts that can be salvaged. Ask someone else to read the draft and help identify what can be saved.

D. If you decide to start over, do not despair. Many times a writer figures out what *not* to do before figuring what *to* do.

4. "I'm not sure what revisions to make."

A. Leave your draft for a day. When you return, you will be better able to decide what changes to make.

B. Read your draft aloud to hear problems, or read your draft into a tape recorder and play back the tape.

C. See p. 27 on using reader response to identify necessary changes.

D. Study your draft in stages by checking separately each item in the list of revision concerns on p. 26.

5. "I know what changes to make, but I'm having trouble making them."

A. Make the easier changes first and then go on to the harder ones. You will build momentum this way.

B. See p. 27 on using reader response. Ask your reader for ways to make revisions.

	C. Take a break for a day to relax and then try again.
	D. Ask your instructor for advice.
6. "I need more detail."	A. Add examples for support.
	B. Tell a story to support a point.
	C. Try some additional idea generation.
	D. Check to see if your thesis or topic sentence is too narrow.
7. "My writing seems boring."	A. Circle general words and substitute specific ones to make your writing more lively.
	B. See p. 217 on sentence variety.
	C. Add specific examples and stories for vividness.
	D. Add description for vividness.
	E. Check to be sure you are not stating the obvious.
	F. Revise clichés.
8. "My ideas do not seem related to each other."	A. Use transitions to show relationships between ideas.
	B. Use subordination and coordination to show how ideas relate to each other.
	C. Outline your draft after you have written it to be sure all ideas are logically placed.
	D. Check all your ideas against your thesis and topic sentences to be sure you do not have a relevance problem.
9. "I have trouble finding and correcting my errors."	A. Read your work aloud to listen for errors, or read your work into a tape recorder. Play back the tape, listening for mistakes.
	B. Become sensitive to the kinds of mistakes you make by using the Personal Editing Profile on the

inside cover. Check the profile before you edit to remind yourself of your usual errors.

C. Edit a separate time for each kind of error you have a tendency to make.

D. Place a ruler under each line so you are not distracted by other words on the page.

E. Edit *very slowly*. If you go quickly, you will overlook errors.

F. Check the editing concerns on p. 30. Edit in stages, checking one or two of these concerns in each stage.

G. Learn the rules to be a confident editor.

H. When in doubt, check the rules in this book. If you are still in doubt, ask your teacher.

I. Trust your feelings. If you sense a problem, the chances are good that there is a problem.

Appendix II

Ten Tips for ESL Students

1. Be sure that all your sentences have both a subject and a complete verb.

   no: Is happy to help you find an apartment. [missing subject]

   yes: *Dimitri* is happy to help you find an apartment.

   no: The wind blowing at hurricane force. [part of the verb is missing]

   yes: The wind *is blowing* at hurricane force.

   no: Monica been in this country for three years. [part of the verb is missing]

   yes: Monica *has been* in this country for three years.

   Exception: Sentences that give a command or make a request do not always have stated subjects. Instead, the subject of such sentences is the unstated *you*.

   command: Leave that dog alone. [*You* leave that dog alone.]

   request: Please bring me that book. [*You* please bring me that book.]

2. Remember the *s* in third person singular verbs in the present tense.

   no: In the evenings, Juan *play* guitar in a band.

   yes: In the evenings, Juan *plays* guitar in a band.

   no: Ice *cover* all the major highways east of town.

   yes: Ice *covers* all the major highways east of town.

3. When a verb is made up of two words, do not add *s* or *es* to the second verb.

   no: My mother can *helps* me pay my tuition bill.

   yes: My mother can *help* me pay my tuition bill.

4. Use correct word order.

   A. Most often, the subject comes before the verb.

V   S

no: *Have been married* 25 years *my parents.*

S   V

yes: *My parents have been married* 25 years.

Exception: When you ask a question, the main verb comes before the subject.

V   S

Was the *chili* too spicy?

When a question has a helping verb and a main verb, place the subject after the helping verb:

HV S MV

Why *did you eat* your ice cream before your sandwich?

Exception: When sentences begin with *here is, here are, here was, here were, there is, there are, there was, there were,* the subject comes after the helping verb:

HV   S   MV

There *were five tornadoes sighted* in the area.

B. Refer to the following chart when you have questions about word order.

BASIC WORD ORDER

1. articles/demonstratives/possessives
2. adjectives of number
3. adjectives of judgment
4. adjectives of size or shape
5. adjectives of color
6. nouns used as modifiers
7. nouns/pronouns
8. helping verbs
9. main verbs
10. indirect object
11. direct object
12. adverbs of direction and place
13. adverbs of manner or means
14. adverbs of frequency
15. time expressions

Examples

The two large brown English terriers sleep near the window in the afternoon.

(labels: article, adj. of number, adj. of size, adj. of color, noun as modifier, noun, main verb, adv. (prepositional phrase) of place, time expression)

Sam's unusual play may be produced by the local theater group for three weekends in May.

(labels: possessive, adj. of judgment, noun, helping verb, helping verb, main verb, adv. of means (prepositional phrase), adv. of frequency (prepositional phrase))

My aunt gave me this old bronze picture frame five years ago.

(labels: possessive, noun, main verb, indirect object, direct object, time expression)

5. Use *a* or *an* with a singular count noun whose identity has not been made known.

> Note: A **count noun** refers to a person, place, thing, idea, or emotion that can be counted; count nouns are words like these: city, muscle, sister, baseball.

> **no:** Maria is knitting *a* sweaters for her brothers.

> **yes:** Maria is knitting sweaters for her brothers. (*Sweaters* is plural.)

> **no:** Boris borrowed *a* luggage for his trip.

> **yes:** Boris borrowed luggage for his trip. (*Luggage* is not a count noun.)

> Note: Do not use *a* or *an* with plural nouns.

> **no:** The store is having a sale on *a* computers.

> **yes:** The store is having a sale on computers.

6. Use *the* with a singular count noun whose identity is known.
> Corrine's Ford is in the repair shop. *The* car needs a new fan belt. (The identity of the car has been established.)

7. Use *in, on,* and *at* correctly to show time and place.

A. For seasons, months, and years without a specific date, use *in*.

In 1999, Stavros will graduate with two degrees.

I usually take my vacation *in* the winter.

B. Use *on* for a specific day or date.

On the first of March, Joseph begins his new job.

This office will close *on* Friday.

C. Use *in* for a period of the day.

My exercise class meets *in* the early evening.

Note: Sometimes *at* is used for a period of the day. Experience will show you when to use *in* and when to use *at*.

At midnight, Cinderella had to leave the ball.

D. Use *at* for a specific location and *in* for a location surrounded by something else.

The dentist you should see is located *at* 3150 Fifth Avenue.

Gregory lived *in* Salzburg for a semester.

8. Use modals correctly. The following chart can help you with many of the modals.

MODAL	INDICATES	EXAMPLE
can	ability	Henri *can* speak three languages.
	informal request	*Can* you drive me to work?
could	request	*Could* I have a piece of your candy?
	possibility	We *could* leave later if you like.
may	request or grant permission	*May* I have an apple? You *may* leave now.
might	possibility	It *might* rain tonight.
must	probability	Olin *must* be at school, for he is not here.
	need	You *must* submit an application by noon.
ought to	advisability	I *ought to* major in physical therapy.
	expectation	The play *ought to* begin at 8:00.

MODAL	INDICATES	EXAMPLE
should	advisability	I *should* major in physical therapy.
	expectation	The play *should* begin at 8:00.
will	intention	I *will* begin eating more protein.
would	request	*Would* you answer the phone for me?
	preference	I *would* rather eat at home tonight.
be able to	ability	I *am able to* leave at noon.

Note: The following modals show past time.

could	ability	Charles *could* work harder than anyone.
could have	possibility	We *could have* gone if we wanted to.
might have	possibility	The team *might have* a chance at a championship.
must have	probability	The teacher *must have* been very angry at the class.
would	habitual	The team *would* always practice on Saturday morning.

9. Do not separate main clauses with a comma.

   In some languages, two main clauses can correctly be separated with a comma. However, this is not the case in English, where main clauses must be separated with a period and capital letter or with a semicolon.

   no: The wind is getting stronger, I believe a storm is coming.

   yes: The wind is getting stronger. I believe a storm is coming.

   yes: The wind is getting stronger; I believe a storm is coming.

10. Do not use a pronoun to refer to a noun when that noun is already referred to by *who, whom, which,* or *that.*

    no: I gave the sales clerk my credit card, which I then forgot to get it back.

    yes: I gave the sales clerk my credit card, which I then forgot to get back.

Appendix III

Answers to Pretests

P. 177—FINDING SUBJECTS AND VERBS

Subjects	*Verbs*
1. mother	packed
2. Tuition	is
3. Marcos	has eaten
4. Mother	returned, studied
5. people	do know
6. Joan, her brothers	bought
7. carton	is
8. Jacques	has been studying
9. keys	are
10. excuse	will be
11. (you)	answer
12. holidays; all of us	are; can relax, recover
13. students	are making
14. accidents	can be
15. my parents, I	will move, buy

P. 241—FRAGMENTS

1. F	5. F	9. F
2. F	6. F	10. F
3. F	7. F	
4. S	8. S	

P. 256—RUN-ONS AND COMMA SPLICES

1. CS	5. RO	9. RO
2. RO	6. CS	10. C
3. RO	7. C	
4. C	8. C	

P. 307—VERB FORMS

1. I	6. I	11. I
2. C	7. I	12. C
3. I	8. I	13. I
4. C	9. C	14. I
5. C	10. C	15. I

P. 330—SUBJECT-VERB AGREEMENT

1. means	5. practices	9. work
2. visits	6. decides	10. sleeps
3. plan	7. are	
4. likes	8. wants	

P. 342—TENSE SHIFTS

1. TS	5. TS	9. TS
2. TS	6. C	10. C
3. C	7. C	
4. TS	8. TS	

P. 347—PRONOUNS

1. I	5. their	9. me
2. they	6. its	10. its
3. me	7. its	
4. her	8. whom	

P. 378—MODIFIERS

1. no	5. no	9. yes
2. yes	6. no	10. no
3. no	7. yes	
4. yes	8. no	

P. 391—CAPITALIZATION

1. no	5. no	9. yes
2. no	6. no	10. no
3. yes	7. no	
4. yes	8. no	

P. 396—ENDING SENTENCES

1. .	5. .	9. .
2. !	6. . or !	10. ?
3. .	7. ?	
4. ?	8. !	

P. 399—USING COMMAS

1. no	5. no	9. no
2. no	6. no	10. no
3. yes	7. yes	11. yes
4. yes	8. no	12. no

P. 410—USING SEMICOLONS

1. yes	3. yes	5. no
2. no	4. yes	6. yes

P. 412—USING COLONS, PARENTHESES, AND DASHES

1. yes	4. yes	7. no
2. yes	5. yes	8. yes
3. no	6. yes	

P. 415—APOSTROPHES

1. no	5. yes	9. yes
2. yes	6. yes	10. no
3. no	7. yes	
4. yes	8. yes	

P. 422—USING QUOTATION MARKS

1. no	4. no	7. yes
2. no	5. yes	8. yes
3. yes	6. yes	

Index